The Circle of Our Vision

The Circle of Our Vision

Dante's Presence in English Romantic Poetry

RALPH PITE

CLARENDON PRESS · OXFORD
1994

Oxford University Press, Walton Street, Oxford OX2 6DP
Oxford New York Toronto
Delhi Bombay Calcutta Madras Karachi
Kuala Lumpur Singapore Hong Kong Tokyo
Nairobi Dar es Salaam Cape Town
Melbourne Auckland Madrid
and associated companies in
Berlin Ibadan

Oxford is a trade mark of Oxford University Press

Published in the United States
by Oxford University Press Inc., New York

British Library Cataloguing in Publication Data
Data available

Library of Congress Cataloging in Publication Data
Pite, Ralph.
The circle of our vision: Dante's presence in English romantic
poetry / Ralph Pite.
Includes bibliographical references.
1. English poetry—19th century—History and criticism. 2. Dante
Alighieri, 1265-1321—Influence. 3. English poetry—Italian
influences. 4. Romanticism—Great Britain. I. Title.
PR457.P58 1994
821'.709—dc20 93-40171
ISBN 0-19-811294-7

1 3 5 7 9 10 8 6 4 2

Typeset by Graphicraft Typesetters Ltd., Hong Kong
Printed in Great Britain
on acid-free paper by
Biddles Ltd.,
Guildford and King's Lynn

TO HESTER JONES

Preface

ECHOES of other writing frequently occur in literature without being observed and a significant part of their effect is produced only so long as they remain hidden. Source-studies can, in consequence, often seem a laborious version of 'we murder to dissect'. The danger lies, however, less in the discovery of points of reference (which may be pleasurable and, sometimes, illuminating) than in the beliefs that attach to them once discovered. It is easy to overstate the significance of a newly discovered echo and, fearing this perhaps, many critics resign themselves to observing similarities and citing parallel passages. In this book I am attempting to do more than list parallels without making exaggerated or blinkered claims for their importance.

My explication of Dante's presence in English Romantic poetry is governed by the desire to increase our understanding of the poems where echoes of his work appears. This project involves locating the Romantic poets' echoes of Dante in the context of their other work and their literary, personal, and historical influences; in the context, therefore, of a poetic career and of a cultural climate. It cannot avoid including some topics that may appear at first to be off the point. These apparent digressions are designed to contribute to the explanation of Dante's presence in a writer's work: by showing the significance of the poems where these Dantean moments occur, and by outlining the connotations of the passages from Dante that are adopted, I aim to offer reasons for Dante's appearance in a particular place and to explain what his introduction might mean.

However, while it is bringing to light the purposes and methods of English Romantic writers when they refer to Dante, this book should also illuminate other writing and writers that are not mentioned (both Romantic but not Dantean and Dantean but not Romantic). It will be useful too, I hope, to those who have not read all the texts involved. I aim, in addition, to show that the purposiveness of Romantic allusion has been underestimated. In the works of Keats, Shelley, and Byron, I believe, the use of Dantean language and a frame of reference drawn from the *Commedia* is both intelligent and revealing. This is not to claim that the adoption is always fully deliberated or conscious. Neither need it be observed by the reader for its effects to be felt.

In Coleridge's case it is difficult to find any allusive quality in the moments of likeness between his work and Dante's. His references to Dante's work are always incidental and one cannot find him adopting or adapting extracts from the *Commedia* or *Vita Nuova* and refashioning them to his own ends. I argue, in his case, that there are parallels between the two writers (particularly between their projects in the *Commedia* and *The Friend*), and that these parallels help explain the idea of symbolism that underlies the complicated design of Coleridge's prose writing.

Coleridge's concern with symbolism links him to the common thread that runs through the other chapters and forms the central theme of this book. 'The circle of our vision' is a phrase taken from Henry Cary's introduction to his translation of the *Divina Commedia*, a translation itself entitled *The Vision,* and first published in 1814. Cary means the phrase pejoratively: Dante's 'solicitude', he says, 'to define all his images in such a manner as to bring them distinctly within the circle of our vision [. . .] sometimes renders him little better than grotesque, where Milton has since taught us to expect sublimity'. Dante tries too hard to make everything in Hell visible; his work suffers when it draws sublime incidents into the realm of our flawed, unpoetic, and uninspired vision.

Each of the poets considered in this book responds to Dante's work while they are thinking about the implications of such a critical judgement not only for Dante but for their own writing and for their role as writers and supposed visionaries. An effort to be precise and minute where their predecessors had been Miltonic and grand, to bring inspired vision into the light of common day, is accompanied by changes in their self-understanding as writers and a change in their relation to their public. Both of these influences encourage them to give more credence to the idea (epitomized at times by Dante's work) of bringing all their images distinctly within the circle of our vision. This change in turn alters their sense of 'vision' itself—creating an awareness of both its limits and its dependence on a community of perceivers.

R.P.
September 1993

Acknowledgements

THIS book began as a Ph.D. thesis. I am most grateful to my supervisors, Professor Martin Dodsworth and Dr Robin Kirkpatrick, for the encouragement and care they have given to both projects. I would like to thank the late Professor Ugo Limentani, Professor Timothy Webb, and Professor John Beer for examining the work at different stages; Eric Griffiths and Jeremy Maule for reading several chapters in earlier versions; and Emily Lincoln for reading proofs and checking references. My two anonymous readers at OUP were very helpful indeed.

While working on this project, I have learnt a great deal from discussions in the Romantic Period Graduate Seminar at Cambridge University and am particularly grateful to John Beer, Marilyn Butler, Nigel Leask, and Steve Clark. I am indebted to Trinity College, Cambridge, and Corpus Christi College, Cambridge, for their intellectual and financial support. Students at both places have made me think again, especially Stephen Cheek, Bill Jones, Kiri Lewin-Poole, Michael Osbourne, and Eric Woehrling. I have relied throughout on the advice and support of my parents and sisters; of Jonathan Coe, Alban Harvey, Judith Hawley, Hester Jones, John Kerrigan, Judith McLaren, Adam Piette, Adrian Poole, Peter Robinson, Peter Singer, Nick de Somogyi, Peter Swaab, Michael Tanner, Dave Taylor, and Robert Teed.

Contents

List of Plates

(between pages 112 and 113)

Abbreviations

Place of publication is London unless otherwise indicated.

Allott	*The Poems of John Keats*, ed. Miriam Allott (Longmans Annotated English Poets, 1970).
Anxiety	Harold Bloom, *The Anxiety of Influence: A Theory of Poetry* (New York, 1973).
Barnard	John Keats, *The Complete Poems*, ed. John Barnard (2nd edn., Harmondsworth, 1977).
BL	S. T. Coleridge, *Biographia Literaria, or, Biographical Sketches of my Literary Life and Opinions*, ed. W. Jackson Bate and James Engell, CC, vii, 2 vols.
Boyd	Henry Boyd, *The Divina Commedia of Dante Alighieri consisting of Inferno, Purgatorio, and Paradiso*, 3 vols. (1802).
Cary	*The Vision; or, Hell, Purgatory, and Paradise of Dante Alighieri*, trans. Henry Francis Cary, 3 vols. (1814).
Cary 1819	*The Vision [. . .]*, 3 vols. (1819).
CC	S. T. Coleridge, *The Collected Works*, gen. ed. Kathleen Coburn, in progress (London and Princeton, NJ, 1969–).
Circle	*The Keats Circle: Letters and Papers, and more Letters and Poems of the Keats Circle*, ed. H. E. Rollins, 2 vols. (2nd edn., Cambridge, Mass., 1965).
CL	*Collected Letters of Samuel Taylor Coleridge*, ed. E. L. Griggs, 6 vols. (Oxford, 1956–71).
CN	*The Notebooks of Samuel Taylor Coleridge*, ed. Kathleen Coburn, in progress (London, New York, and Princeton, NJ, 1957–).
Conv.	Dante Alighieri, *Il Convivio*, ed. Bruna Cordati (Classici Italiani Commentati, Turin, 1968).
CritH	*Keats: The Critical Heritage*, ed. G. M. Matthews (1971).
C&S	S. T. Coleridge, *On the Constitution of the Church and State*, ed. John Colmer, CC, x.
EHC	S. T. Coleridge, *The Poetical Works*, ed. E. H. Coleridge, 2 vols. (Oxford, 1912).
ELH	*ELH: A Journal of English Literary History*.

EOT	S. T. Coleridge, *Essays on His Times*, ed. David. V. Erdman, *CC*, iii, 3 vols.
Foster and Boyde	*Dante's Lyric Poetry*, ed. K. Foster and P. Boyde, 2 vols. (Oxford, 1967).
Friend	S. T. Coleridge, *The Friend*, ed. Barbara Rooke, *CC*, iv, 2 vols.
Gray	*The Poems of Thomas Gray, William Collins, and Oliver Goldsmith*, ed. Roger Lonsdale (Longmans Annotated English Poets, 1969).
Hazlitt	William Hazlitt, *The Complete Works*, ed. P. P. Howe, 21 vols. (London and Toronto, 1930–4).
JEGP	*Journal of English and Germanic Philology*
Jones	*The Letters of Percy Bysshe Shelley*, ed. F. L. Jones, 2 vols. (Oxford, 1964).
Keats	*The Poems of John Keats*, ed. Jack Stillinger (Cambridge, Mass., 1978).
K–SJ	*The Keats–Shelley Journal* (New York, 1952–).
Lay Sermons	S. T. Coleridge, *Lay Sermons*, ed. R. J. White, *CC*, vi.
Lectures 1808–19	S. T. Coleridge, *Lectures 1808–1819 On Literature*, ed. R. A. Foakes, *CC* v, 2 vols.
LJ	*Byron's Letters and Journals*, ed. Leslie A. Marchand, 12 vols. (London, 1973–81).
McGann	Lord Byron, *The Complete Poetical Works*, ed. Jerome J. McGann, 7 vols. (Oxford, 1980–93).
Marginalia	S. T. Coleridge, *Marginalia* [5 vols. projected], ed. G. M. Whalley, *CC*, xii.
Milford	Leigh Hunt, *The Poetical Works*, ed. H. S. Milford (Oxford, 1923).
Milton	John Milton, *Paradise Lost. A New Edition*, 2 vols. (Edinburgh, 1807).
Misreading	Harold Bloom, *A Map of Misreading* (New York, 1975).
PMLA	*Publications of the Modern Language Association of America*
Poems	*The Poems of Shelley*, ed. G. M. Matthews and Kelvin Everest, 3 vols. [projected] (London and New York, 1989–).
PP	*Shelley's Poetry and Prose*, ed. Donald H. Reiman and Sharon B. Powers (New York and London, 1977).
Prelude	William Wordsworth, 'The Prelude', *1795, 1805, 1850 [. . .]*, ed. Jonathan Wordsworth, M. H. Abrams, and Stephen Gill (Norton Critical Editions, New York, 1979).

PW   Shelley, *Poetical Works*, ed. Thomas Hutchinson,
                corrected by G. M. Matthews (Oxford and New York,
                1970).

Rollins   *The Letters of John Keats 1814–1821*, ed. H. E.
                Rollins, 2 vols. (Cambridge, Mass., 1958).

Sapegno   Dante Alighieri, *La Divina Commedia*, ed. Natalino
                Sapegno, 3 vols. (2nd edn., Florence, 1968).

Stevenson   *Blake: The Complete Poems*, ed. W. H. Stevenson (2nd
                edn., London and New York, 1989).

Table Talk   S. T. Coleridge, *Table Talk*, recorded by Henry
                Nelson Coleridge (and John Taylor Coleridge), ed.
                Carl Woodring CC, xiv, 2 vols.

Toynbee   Paget Toynbee, *Dante in English Literature from
                Chaucer to Cary (c.1380–1844)*, 2 vols. (1909).

Triumph   Donald H. Reiman, *Shelley's 'The Triumph of Life'*:
                A Critical Study, Based on a Text Newly Edited [. . .]
                (Urbana, Ill., 1965).

Vita Nuova   Dante Alighieri, *Vita Nuova—Rime*, ed. Freda
                Chiapelli (Milan, 1965).

Warton   Thomas Warton, *The History of English Poetry, from
                the Close of the Eleventh to the Commencement of
                the Eighteenth Century*, 3 vols. (1774, 1778, 1781).

Wittreich   J. A. Wittreich Jr. (ed.), *The Romantics on Milton:
                Formal Essays and Critical Asides* (Cleveland, Oh.,
                1970).

Wordsworth   William Wordsworth, *The Poetical Works*, ed. E. de
                Selincourt and Helen Darbishire, 5 vols. (Oxford,
                1940–9).

I
Introduction

'The archetype of all modern poetry'

Thomas Love Peacock, with his sharp eye for literary fashion, observed in 1819 that Dante had suddenly become required reading. The 'Honourable Mr Listless' in *Nightmare Abbey* remarks:

I don't know how it is, but Dante never came in my way till lately. I never had him in my collection, and if I had had him I should not have read him. But I find he is growing fashionable, and I am afraid I must read him some wet morning.

This rise in Dante's popularity was encouraged in part by Coleridge's influential lectures of 1818–19 and by articles in the *Edinburgh Review* of the same years by Ugo Foscolo. These combined promoted the *Commedia* so well that Henry Cary's translation, *The Vision*, which had appeared in 1814, was reprinted in 1819 and, for the first time, sold well. In the following few years, as Mr Listless languidly prophesies, Dante turned from a specialist interest into a necessary acquisition for the cultivated person.[1]

I discuss in the second chapter Foscolo's role in matching Dante's poetry to the aspirations of liberal opinion after Waterloo, and the bearing of his image of Dante on the work of Shelley and Byron. Coleridge's successful advocacy in the same period reveals, however, that Dante's appeal was not restricted to one school of political thought. I want to show in this chapter that Dante's writing gained

---

[1] *Nightmare Abbey* (1818), in David Garnett (ed.), *The Novels of Thomas Love Peacock*, 2 vols. (London, 1963), i. 379–80. See *Lectures 1808–19*, ii. 394–5, 397–403; *Edinburgh Review*, vols. xxix, xxx (Feb./Sept. 1818), repr. in Toynbee, ii. 161–5. Ginguené's *Histoire littéraire d'Italie* (1811–19) was also influential, along with: Jean de Sismondi, *De la littérature du Midi de L'Europe*, 4 vols. (Paris, 1813); and Henry Hallam, *A View of the State of Europe during the Middle Ages*, 2 vols. (London, 1818). See also Toynbee, ii. 253–9. Hazlitt reviewed Sismondi's work in the *Edinburgh Review* of 1815 and incorporated many of his remarks into the first of his 1818 *Lectures on the English Poets*; see Hazlitt, xvi. 31 ff.

in popularity because it offered a precedent for the poetic ambitions inherited, shared, and disputed by different Romantic writers; and, in particular, because he offered an example to those who sought, in Coleridge's words, to join 'a faithful adherence to the truth of nature' with 'the modifying colours of imagination' (*BL*, ii. 5).

When Coleridge declares that he is concerned to unite these two qualities, he is reformulating, from earlier in the *Biographia*, 'the marks which distinguish genius from talents'. These include the power:

to combine the child's sense of wonder and novelty with the appearances, which every day for perhaps forty years had rendered familiar; [. . .] so to represent familiar objects as to awaken in the minds of others [. . .] that freshness of sensation which is the constant accompaniment of mental, no less than of bodily, convalescence. (*BL*, i. 81)[2]

Coleridge's ideal demands an accurate wonder; the child's sense of novelty needs to survive in the adult's perception of routinely familiar things. But to lose the novelty in weariness at the ordinary is no more of a disadvantage than its opposite: sacrificing familiar appearances in order to create novelty. Though Coleridge and Wordsworth both lament the loss of childhood, they also strive to maintain that a child's 'freshness of sensation [. . .] is the *constant accompaniment*' (my emphasis) of a healthy maturity.

Wordsworth's 'Intimations Ode' epitomizes this endeavour and reveals the inevitable partiality of its success.[3] In Wordsworth's poem 'The glory and the freshness of a dream', lost since childhood, is approached once again through the details of landscape:

> I love the Brooks which down their channels fret,
> Even more than when I tripped lightly as they;
> The innocent brightness of a new-born Day
> > Is lovely yet.
> ('Ode', ll. 5, 193–6, Wordsworth, iv. 279, 285)

---

[2] Cf. *Friend*, i. 419; *Lectures 1808–19*, i. 326–7.

[3] Dante's nearness to the aspirations embodied in Wordsworth's poem can be shown from Charles Lamb's parody of the 'Intimations Ode', his essay 'Witches and Other Night-Fears' (first published in the *London Magazine*, Oct. 1821), in *The Works of Charles and Mary Lamb*, ed. E. V. Lucas, 7 vols. (London and New York, 1903–5), ii. 67 ff. See Gerald Monsman, *Confessions of a Prosaic Dreamer: Charles Lamb's Art of Autobiography* (Duke, NC, 1984), 68.

The loss of childhood's dreams provokes Wordsworth to focus his attention on external objects, on the 'Brooks which down their channels fret'. Earlier in the poem and in life, he saw these as streams 'Apparelled in celestial light'.[4] His adult perspective sees the rub, the water forming the channel and the channel directing the water; it sees that things are created by their relationship with an environment. The same principle and the same way of looking then apply to Wordsworth's younger self: 'Even [...] when I tripped lightly as they'. The child's step imitates the stream's but the adoption of it, in this line's lilting irregularity, demands a recognition (by reader and writer alike) of the speaker's distance from the child who enjoyed 'The innocent brightness of a new-born Day'. The continuing gap between the child and the man both limits and releases the poem's power to recreate a child's innocent point of view. Though Wordsworth seems, therefore, to have suffered the loss of celestial light, he introduces into the close of the poem a plainer diction that joins the discriminating and self-conscious 'powers of manhood' to the 'feelings of childhood'. Within this diction and rhythm, Wordsworth's feelings become, he says, 'Even more' intense despite the loss that his wording confesses: his inability as an adult to see everyday things clothed in celestial apparel.[5]

Bringing the feelings of childhood into the powers of manhood requires of Wordsworth qualities of mind and of writing that Dante came to exemplify. Dante's directness, the pictorial accuracy and vividness of his writing, correspond to a child's fresh percipience, while the organization of his experience according to self-consciously established categories of judgement reveals the powers of manhood at work. Both these qualities are discovered in Dante in the Romantic period and discovered more than they had been before. Dante's proximity to Romantic ideas of poetry is evident from the gradual reinterpretation and revaluation of his work that occurs in the critical writing of the late eighteenth and early nineteenth centuries. In this reassessment, moreover, Dante's

---

[4] 'Ode', l. 4, Wordsworth, iv. 279.
[5] The interactions between rhyme-scheme and line-length create some of the finest moments in Wordsworth's poem. Contrast the rhyme between 'fret' and 'yet' in these lines with the regularity of Wordsworth's opening stanza: 'It is not now as it hath been of yore;—| Turn wheresoe'er I may, | By night or day, | The things which I have seen I now can see no more.' (ll. 6–9, Wordsworth, iv. 279).

method becomes an object of special interest because it succeeds in being at once attached to the particular object or person and able to see it allegorically. His allegory is reread as the kind of symbolism that Coleridge aspired to when he described poetry as joining childhood and adulthood, freshness and familiarity.

As his allegory is reinterpreted, Dante's relation to his narrative is seen in a new light: where an allegorical writer remains aloof from an encounter with the figures whose meaning s/he knows in advance (and whose meaning cannot be qualified by anything surprising in the figure itself), the symbolic writer respects and attends curiously to the figure, discovering through the encounter a wider meaning. Changes in the account of Dante's role in the poem he narrates occur at the same time as changes in the understanding of his symbolic method and bring with them changes in the understanding of the reader's role. Where Dante remains aloof, so can the reader; where Dante is more vulnerably involved, the reader might also be under threat. When this change in perspective occurs it implies a change in Dante's relation to the reader, whom he is able to draw in and appear to endanger. Dante's symbolism consequently raises questions both about the responsibility the poet may have to his audience and about the possible worthlessness or destructiveness of poetry's powerful fictions. These questions and self-doubts occupy the centre of several major Romantic poems; studying Dante's role and status in the period should help in understanding them.

The following discussions of Dante's presence are, therefore, more ambitious than a source-study without being principally concerned to investigate the psychology of influence.[6] The Romantic poets' interest in Dante can, certainly, be read as the result of their anxiety to establish priority over a predecessor; in other words, it can be placed in line with the model of influence established by Harold Bloom. George Bornstein (in a study, influenced by Bloom, of Dante's bearing on Yeats) points out that, in general,

---

[6] On the presuppositions of 'source-study' see Claudio Guillén, 'The Aesthetics of Literary Influence', in *Influx: Essays on Literary Influence,* ed. Ronald Primeau (Washington, NY, and London, 1977), 54–6; for examples of Dante as a source in Romantic poetry, see Robert Gittings, *The Mask of Keats: A Study of Problems* (London, Melbourne, and Toronto, 1956), 31–2; John Livingston Lowes, '*Hyperion* and *Purgatorio*', *Times Literary Supplement* (11 Jan. 1936), 35. Cf. J. Drummond Bone, 'On "Influence" and on Byron's and Shelley's Use of *Terza Rima* in 1819', *Keats–Shelley Memorial Bulletin,* 4 (1981), 39.

'Poets who wrote in a different language can liberate later poets from the intimidations of their own immediate predecessors in their own language.'[7] The frequent comparisons between Milton and Dante made by Shelley and Keats appear to support the idea that in turning to Dante Romantic poets were finding a means of escape from the weight of Milton's achievement.[8]

Bloom's arguments assume that the demand for priority consistently (and irrevocably) governs Romantic and post-Romantic poetry, indeed any and all poetry written since Milton. Starting from this position Bloom frequently reveals competitiveness and hostility where previous critics had been deceived by an appearance of generosity. He cannot, however, see motives for disguise that do not derive from the need for priority. His readings ignore the variety of the motives that have at different periods prompted writers to allude to, echo, or suppress each other. Consequently, his studies iron out the differences between the forms of allusiveness found in different periods of literature.[9]

The primacy of priority in Bloom[10] contributes to his consistent historical model in which post-Miltonic writing comes after a decisive shift from benignant to malevolent forms of influence. Once this shift has taken place it cannot be reversed.

there was a great age before the Flood, when influence was generous (or poets in their innermost natures thought it so), an age that goes all the

---

[7] I discuss Bloom below. George Bornstein, *Poetic Remaking: The Art of Browning, Yeats, and Pound* (University Park and London, 1988), 6; cf. 74: 'Yeats could on occasion elevate him [Dante] beyond even Blake and Shelley, as a rebellious son will substitute a grandfather for a father in family romance.'

[8] See 'A Defence of Poetry', *PP*, 499–500; Rollins, ii. 212; the comparison is well established: see Toynbee, i. 470; Philip Neve, *Cursory Remarks on Some of the Ancient English Poets, Particularly Milton* (London, 1789), in *Milton 1732–1801: The Critical Heritage*, ed. John T. Shawcross (London and Boston, 1972), 351.

[9] Cf. Roger Lonsdale, 'Gray and "Allusion": The Poet as Debtor', in *Studies in the Eighteenth Century*, 4, ed. R. F. Brissenden and J. C. Eade (Canberra, 1979), 31–6; Christopher Ricks, 'Tennyson Inheriting the Earth', in *Studies in Tennyson*, ed. Hallam Tennyson (London and Basingstoke), 68; W. K. Wimsatt, 'Imitation as Freedom: 1717–1798', in id. *Day of the Leopards: Essays in Defense of Poems* (New Haven, Conn., and London, 1976), 117–39. Wimsatt's essay was written in 1968 and first published in *New Literary History*, 1 (Winter 1970). Bloom dedicated *Anxiety* to Wimsatt.

[10] See *Misreading*, 17–18: 'the poet-in-a-poet is as desperately obsessed with poetic origins, generally despite himself, as the person-in-a-person at last becomes obsessed with personal origins'.

way from Homer to Shakespeare [. . . .] every post-enlightenment master moves, not towards a sharing-with-others [. . .] but towards a being-with-oneself. (*Anxiety*, 122–3)[11]

Bloom's assessment of the Romantic period follows, therefore, W. Jackson Bate in thinking that a late-eighteenth-century attitude towards preceding poets became established and remained un-questioned.[12] The move 'towards a being-with-oneself' is seen as an unalterable and unaltering necessity.

Thomas Gray in 1757 apparently confirms the first part of this argument by linking his taste for primitive writing (from Celtic literatures and medieval Italian) to a desire for freedom from the burden of the English tradition; these primitive sources, he says:

leave an unbounded liberty to pure imagination, & fiction (our favourite provinces) where no Critick can molest, or Antiquary gainsay us.[13]

Bloom would read this desire as an instance of the imagination (of a succeeding 'strong' poet) demanding priority over its predecessor in order that it may attain 'unbounded liberty'. In his accounts of influence, this desire for freedom may be thwarted but it is never either overcome or forgotten, sublimated or replaced.[14] His central assumption is difficult either to disprove (since it is possible to interpret any form of address to another writer as a version or inversion of hostility), or to deny (because this will appear to be a revealing and weak repetition by the critic of the hostility s/he

---

[11] Bloom becomes more sceptical about the possibility of benevolent relations in later studies; this leads him sometimes to doubt the actuality of a period before the flood, though he continues to see the modern as belated; see Harold Bloom, *Poetry and Repression: Revisionism from Blake to Stevens* (New Haven, Conn., and London, 1976), 21–4, 88–9.

[12] See *Anxiety*, 8: 'The modern poet, as W. J. Bate shows in *The Burden of the Past and the English Poet* [London, 1970], is the inheritor of a melancholy en-gendered in the mind of the Enlightenment by its skepticism of its own double heritage of imaginative wealth, from the ancients and the Renaissance masters.' Cf. Dustin Griffin, *Regaining Paradise: Milton and the Eighteenth Century* (Cambridge, 1986), 3.

[13] Thomas Gray, *Correspondence*, ed. P. Toynbee and L. Whibley, 3 vols. (Oxford, 1935), ii. 534; quoted in Lonsdale, 'Gray and "Allusion"', 45.

[14] Bloom's exact position changes with respect to the degree of success with which a strong poet may 'achieve a style that captures and oddly retains priority over [its] precursors' (*Anxiety*, 141). Cf. his later reading of Keats (as a poet seeing through this claim to success when he rewrites *Hyperion*) in Bloom, *Poetry and Repression*, 130–5.

refuses to accept).[15] However, supposing the desire for unbounded freedom and priority to exist, it need not be the only influence at work nor, unless you accept Bloom's definition of 'sublimation', need it be an irremovable burden.[16]

Gray's formulation of his freedom suggests, moreover, that he is aware of its necessary limits, and that the impossibility of 'being-with-oneself' without also being (or sharing) with others defines his understanding of freedom. His last sentence echoes the Bible, most clearly the Sermon on the Mount: 'Lay not up for yourselves treasures upon earth [. . .] but lay up for yourselves treasures in heaven, where neither moth nor rust doth corrupt, and where thieves do not break through nor steal' (Matthew 6: 19–20); but also Luke 21: 14–15: 'Settle it therefore in your hearts, not to meditate before *what ye* shall answer: for I will give you a mouth and wisdom, which all your adversaries shall not be able to gainsay nor resist.' Gray's inclusion of the Bible in this sentence shares with his Romantic heirs a sophisticated awareness that allusiveness is a ruling condition of even the most direct forms of address. His resignation willingly concedes that the freedom his scholarly researches can offer falls short of the kingdom of heaven (or, taking 'gainsay' as a recollection of Luke specifically, of the unpremeditated, inspired utterance that Christ promises). Gray's amused self-deprecation is not, however, the secret expression of regret at this falling-short. He enjoys freedom from criticism while perceiving that such freedom is not absolute; the allusion to the Bible admits that his utterances and aspirations will

---

[15] See Bloom, *Poetry and Repression*, 115: 'Keats could not read Milton or Wordsworth without troping what he read, and we do the same to Keats'; *Anxiety*, 5: 'Weaker talents idealize'; Harold Bloom, *Agon: Towards a Theory of Revisionism* (New York, 1982), 16–18. Cf. Robin Jarvis, *Wordsworth, Milton and the Theory of Poetic Relations* (Basingstoke and London, 1991), 40: 'The most therefore that one can counterpose to Bloom is an alternative set of tropes, or an alternative reading of the same tropes, which is the same as saying an alternative act of will.'

[16] Whether the obsession with priority can ever be overcome hinges on whether sublimation continues or outgrows repression. Bloom is never as optimistic about sublimation as Freud sometimes is; cf. *Anxiety*, 8–9, 115, with Sigmund Freud, 'Family Romances' and 'A Special Type of Choice of Object made by Men (Contributions to the Psychology of Love I)', in *The Standard Edition of the Complete Psychological Works*, gen. ed. James Strachey, 24 vols. (London, 1953–74), ix (1959), 236–41; xi (1957), 163–75. Bloom modifies and refines his view of Freud; cf. Bloom, 'Freud's Concept of Defense and the Poetic Will', *Agon*, 119–44; Bloom, *Poetry and Repression*, 135.

be recognized insofar as they are held in common, yet he will not be gainsaid.

English Romantic writing, as has been emphasized in recent years, is notably eclectic. Interest in non-classical literatures (Scandinavian, Old High German, Medieval English and Italian, Oriental) bears witness to the continuance of the desires that prompted Gray's reading in Welsh and Gaelic. These impulses do not, however, go unqualified by changing literary and political concerns. Shelley's interest in Calderón and Dante, for example, coincides with his celebrations of political revolt in Spain and Italy; his literary eclecticism is, arguably, an aspect of the revolution he desired. It was thought of by Shelley both as the means to that revolution's swifter success and as a way of pursuing liberty in the face of political disappointment.[17]

In part because of their involvement in political agitation, the Romantic writers discussed below were at least as self-consciously aware as Gray of the limits to the freedom that could be gained from reading foreign or unfamiliar literature. They do not, generally speaking, find in or invoke from Dante an ideal benignity of relation to other writers, a 'matrix of generous influence' where Virgil 'moved his ephebe to love and emulation and not to anxiety'.[18] They do not re-enter, through reading Dante, the Earthly Paradise, though their interest when reading the *Commedia* is frequently focused on the possibility of such a paradise.[19] The dangers (as well as the pleasures) of not being gainsaid attract

---

[17] See Marilyn Butler, *Romantics, Rebels and Reactionaries: English Literature and its Background 1760–1830* (Oxford, New York, Toronto, and Melbourne, 1981), 113–37; Nigel Leask, *British Romantic Writers and the East: Anxieties of Empire* (Cambridge, 1993); Martin Aske, *Keats and Hellenism: An Essay* (Cambridge, 1985).

[18] *Anxiety*, 122. On Dante and Virgil, see also Ernst Robert Curtius, *European Literature and the Latin Middle Ages*, trans. Willard Trask (London and Henley, 1953), 359: 'The European spirit knows no situation of such affecting loftiness, tenderness, fruitfulness'; and Roger Sale, *Literary Inheritance* (Amherst, 1984); literary history finds pre-eminently in Dante 'one of the prized and celebrated abilities of older writers: to honour the predecessor, to let the predecessor be guide and creator' (p. 12). On why this idealization of Dante has taken place, see Gregory S. Jay, *T. S. Eliot and the Poetics of Literary History* (Baton Rouge and London, 1983), 127 ff.

[19] Dante's 'Earthly Paradise' cantos (*Purgatorio*, xxviii–xxxiii) are read and praised by all the writers discussed and by others; see Mary Shelley, *Mathilda* (written 1819), in *The Mary Shelley Reader*, ed. Betty T. Bennett and Charles E. Robinson (New York, 1990), 184, 241.

Romantic poets to the community of perception which allusions can imply when they appear as echoes.

This emphasis in Romantic readings of Dante is consistent, therefore, with the characteristics of their allusiveness in general. In 'Frost at Midnight', for instance, Coleridge does not use allusions to declare equality with an earlier writer so much as to establish the common ground of a shared endeavour.[20] His allusions imply the rejection of educated language as an index of worth (of allusions as a means of declaring one's ascent of Parnassus), and yet do not embrace either the ideal of a primitive language uncluttered by allusions, or its correlative, an idea of the poet as possessing simple sincerity and unique originality. Rather, Coleridge seeks to suggest the coexistence of earlier and later writer. This prevents the gentlemanly 'learned game: a kind of literary one-upmanship' which is characteristic of Augustan poetry from influencing its Romantic heirs.[21] Coleridge replaces it with a more complete appropriation of earlier texts: a more complete absorption, however, that depends upon the assumption that an inviolable distinctness is enjoyed by the writer quoted.

Coleridge defended his plagiarisms from Schelling in *Biographia Literaria* on the grounds that:

all the main and fundamental ideas, were born and matured in my mind before I had ever seen a single page of the German Philosopher.[22]

What he adopts coincides with his own creation. Although this claim may have been untrue, it is consistent with Coleridge's adoption of Shakespeare in his poetry:

> The Frost performs its secret ministry
> Unhelped by any wind. The owlet's cry
> Came loud—and hark, again! loud as before.
> ('Frost at Midnight', ll. 1–3, EHC, i. 240)

---

[20] For these as the characteristics of Augustan allusions, see: Christopher Ricks, 'Allusion: The Poet as Heir', in *Studies in the Eighteenth Century*, 3, ed. R. F. Brissenden and J. C. Eade (Canberra, 1976), 209–40; Reuben Brower, *Alexander Pope: The Poetry of Allusion* (Oxford, 1959).

[21] Lucy Newlyn, *Coleridge, Wordsworth, and the Language of Allusion* (Oxford, 1986), p. vii.

[22] *BL*, i. 161; see also pp. cxvii–cxx and *CN*, ii. 2375. Frances Ferguson, *Solitude and the Sublime: Romanticism and the Aesthetics of Individuation* (New York and London, 1992), 38.

'Owlet' is used only once by Shakespeare, in *Macbeth* (IV. i. 17, 'Lizards legge and Howlets wing'). Coleridge is thinking here of the nervous exchanges between Macbeth and Lady Macbeth in Act II:

LADY MACBETH.   Hark! Peace!
    It was the owl that shrieked [. . . .]
MACBETH. I have done the deed. Didst thou not hear a noise?
LADY MACBETH. I heard the owl scream and the crickets cry.
    Did not you speak?
MACBETH.   When?
LADY MACBETH.   Now.
MACBETH.   As I descended?
LADY MACBETH. Ay.
MACBETH. Hark!
                                        (*Macbeth*, II. ii. 2–3, 14–18)

Coleridge's lines open with a half-rhyme of 'ministry' and 'cry'. In what Coleridge describes as a 'strange | And extreme silentness' the sound of the rhyming cry breaks in and leaves the reader waiting for it to recur, as it does: 'hark, again! loud as before'.[23] The Shakespearean scene concentrates on listening, but the conspiracy and crime create in Macbeth and Lady Macbeth a panicky alertness to sounds and omens. Pragmatic fears and superstitious anxieties stifle their exchanges into, on the one hand, sharp, rapidly answered questions and, on the other, Lady Macbeth's watchful, unconvincing calm: 'I heard the owl scream and the crickets cry.' Coleridge's lines cannot be said to allude to Shakespeare; the reminiscence is much more remote than that. A reader who had no knowledge of *Macbeth* would still gain from 'Frost at Midnight' an impression of unusual quiet strangely reinforced by the noise that interrupts it. He or she would still be able to imagine the sound actually breaking on the ear. If a reader notices the similarity to Shakespeare, the literary reference seems to have been taken up into Coleridge's scene and absorbed into the consciousness of the poet. The scene from *Macbeth* is being repeated by the incident in the poem, without being either replaced or used as a point of reference, either competed with or submitted to. The educated reader is invited either to find the passage peculiarly resonant while not hearing the echo or to note a correspondence (between

---

[23] ll. 9–10, EHC, i. 240. Cf. Shakespeare, *Lucrece*, ll. 162–8.

Coleridge and Shakespeare) which implies the independent discovery of a common world of experience.

This inclusion of Shakespeare remains open, of course, to psychological readings along Bloomian lines: the avoidance of eighteenth-century allusive techniques can be taken as itself implying a swerve away from Pope and Swift; the tacit nature of Coleridge's reference can be seen as intensifying a claim to priority by claiming independent discovery. By this account, the supposedly common ground is made common only through a secret claim to possession made by the latecomer, Coleridge. Such readings underestimate the confidence with which Romantic poets felt that they could employ their predecessors' work as the starting-point for their own contribution to the 'general and gregarious advance of intellect':

A great Poem is a fountain for ever overflowing with the waters of wisdom and delight; and after one person and one age has exhausted all of its divine effluence which their peculiar relations enable them to share, another and yet another succeeds, and new relations are ever developed, the source of an unforeseen and unconceived delight.[24]

Recognizing the existence and influence of this ideal is not to idealize the poets who embraced it. There is a great deal of evidence that Romantic poets felt in competition with their predecessors, Milton especially, and felt more violently in conflict with their contemporaries.[25] The aspirations Shelley expresses here colour, nevertheless, the forms of exchange with their predecessors that Romantic writers invented and through which they sought to set competition aside. Though the Romantic poets, generally speaking, do not consider Dante to be the exceptional example of benignant influence, Shelley's *The Triumph of Life* adopts, in the relation between Shelley and Rousseau, elements of Dante's relation to his great forerunner, Virgil.[26] Shelley's structural echo of

[24] Rollins, i. 281; P. B. Shelley, 'A Defence of Poetry', *PP*, 500. See also *BL*, i. 164: 'I regard truth as a divine ventriloquist: I care not from whose mouth the sounds are supposed to proceed, if only the words are audible and intelligible.'

[25] See Keats on Milton (Rollins, ii. 167, 212) and his irritation at the poetry of 'Barry Cornwall' (B. W. Proctor) (ibid. 267–8). Also consult Wittreich on this topic.

[26] This is, naturally, an important matter in criticism of the *Commedia*. See e.g. Teodolinda Barolini, *Dante's Poets: Textuality and Truth in the 'Comedy'* (Princeton, NJ, 1984); Robin Kirkpatrick, *Dante's* Inferno: *Difficulty and Dead Poetry* (Cambridge, 1987); Robert Hollander, *Il Virgilio dantesco: tragedia nella* Commedia (Florence, 1983); and, more widely, Madison U. Sowell (ed.), *Dante and Ovid: Essays in Intertextuality* (Binghampton, NY, 1991).

Dante in that poem employs the tacit allusiveness that character-izes Romantic poetry and exhibits Shelley's idea of poetic rela-tions: *The Triumph of Life* forms one of the unforeseen delights which arise from *The Divine Comedy* as from any great poem. Shelley claims to be carrying on the succession, the chain of inter-relating texts which begins in prehistory and ends in infinity. His allusive method does not depend on Dante's example but implies the permanence of the relations that Dante describes. Shelley assumes, therefore, that the poetry in a great poem can remain untouched by the pressures exerted by historical circumstances. In eighteenth-century accounts of the *Commedia*, Dante had, by contrast, appeared as the characteristic writer of an unenlightened age.

The first English criticism to dwell on the *Commedia* at any length is Thomas Warton's *History of English Poetry* (1774–81).[27] Warton's historical model makes Bloom's sound derivative. Warton observes a lack of sophistication in Dante that makes him vivid and carelessly prolix; Dante comes 'before the great age' of en-lightened taste:

These shadowy inhabitants of hell-gate are conceived with the vigour of a creative imagination, and described with great force of expression. (Warton, iii. 241)

The opening of canto iii, which Warton uses here to epitomize the rest of *Inferno* was, and remained, the *locus classicus* of Dante's starkness and power. The period's changing understanding of 'a creative imagination'[28] is illustrated by the different praise lavished on the passage in 1814:

---

[27] See Joan Pittock, *The Ascendancy of Taste* (London, 1973), 208–11. Dante's absence from English literary culture during the seventeenth and early eighteenth centuries is general and remarkable. However, Judith Sloman, *Dryden: The Poetics of Translation* (Toronto, Buffalo, and London, 1985) argues that Dryden's late plays, *Love Triumphant* (1694) and *Cleomenes* (1690), respectively invoke Paolo and Francesca and Ugolino, and suggests that Dryden's translations conceive of a 'poetic community [. . . .] modelled on Dante's hierarchically ordered circles of the blessed in Paradise' (p. 50).

[28] See James Engell, *The Creative Imagination: Enlightenment to Romanticism* (Cambridge, Mass., and London, 1981); K. Wheeler, *The Creative Mind in Coleridge's Poetry* (London, 1981); M. H. Abrams, *The Mirror and the Lamp: Romantic Theory and the Critical Tradition* (New York, 1953). For Warton's similarity to his contemporaries, see below.

it is in the style and sentiments of the poet that his true originality consists; and where in the works of preceding and contemporary versifiers, could Dante have discovered any specimens of that severe, yet energetic tone, the voice of nature herself, by which the reader is irresistably struck even on approaching the vestibule of his immortal fabric? (Toynbee, ii. 12–13)

Warton admires a creative imagination for delineating these 'shadowy inhabitants' clearly and colourfully, shedding light and putting them in their best light. His own authoritativeness particularly enjoys condescending to Dante's controlling power, seeming at once surprised to find it and gratified by its limitations. He condemns a large proportion of the imagery as 'at once great and ridiculous', and finds it much improved by Milton's retention of 'the just beauties' and his avoidance of 'the childish or ludicrous excesses of these bold inventions'.[29] Milton's steadying influence matches Warton's judiciousness in seeing the need to temper Dante's childishness. The later reviewer is more easily impressed: 'childish excesses' are 'the voice of nature herself, by which the reader is irresistably struck' at the opening of the poem.[30]

The high regard paid to an impression made by nature implies a different point of view, in which imaginative participation replaces considered judgement. The reviewer is 'irresistably struck' so that he must follow Dante's *personaggio*, the character who goes through Hell, whereas Warton sees himself as enjoying the poet's (and more than the poet's) foreknowledge and composure. Warton is impatient with a vividness of detail he thinks the result of a barbaric age:

We are surprised that a poet should write one hundred cantos on hell, paradise and purgatory. But this prolixity is partly owing to the want of

[29] Warton, 245, 247. Cf. Nathaniel Howard, *The Inferno of Dante Alighieri* (1807), 249 (canto xv, l. 21 n.), 'a simile too ludicrous for the occasion'. Warton describes this comparison (of an old tailor squinting through the eye of a needle) as 'a comic one'. Howard's notes often give Gray as a possible comparison (whether for his translation or the original is unclear); see Howard, *The Inferno*, 227–8, 242, 244–5. I discuss the incident below.

[30] His preference for Milton fits with his belief that progress is the beginning of criticism: Warton, i, 'Preface'. On Warton's progress and primitivism, see Martin Aske, *Keats and Hellenism*, 21–2, 148. See also Arthur Johnston, *Enchanted Ground: The Study of Medieval Romance in the Eighteenth Century* (London, 1964). Admiration for Dante reflects the period's relocation of progress: see below; Boyd, i. 25; and Morris Ginsberg, *The Idea of Progress: A Revaluation* (London, 1953).

art and method: and is common to all early compositions, in which everything is related circumstantially and without rejection, and not in those general terms which are used by modern writers. (Warton, iii. 240–1)

The relationship between Warton's posture regarding the *Commedia* and his judgement of its structural unity is evident from the brusque dismissal of the 'infernal journey'. Insofar as Dante fails to fulfil an ideal of supremacy over his material, the poem is flawed.

In the most important translation of the Romantic period, Henry Cary begins by admitting objections to Dante that sound much like Warton's:

His solicitude, it is true, to define all his images in such a manner as to bring them distinctly within the circle of our vision, and to subject them to the power of the pencil, sometimes renders him little better than grotesque, where Milton has since taught us to expect sublimity. (Cary 1819, i, p. xl)

Cary's 'circle' is the range of mundane perception that all Dante's readers share. The only exception to a universal point of view is the poet of vision, like Dante, who should not establish too close a likeness between his own and his readers' perceptions.[31] Dante's 'solicitude' to bring everything down to our level transgresses the duty of 'sublimity' imposed on him by the poetic vocation. It is a kind of humiliating concern for our welfare that is embarrassing.

Cary, however, uses 'sublimity' with a different emphasis from Warton (who agrees that the *Commedia*'s 'absurdities often border on sublimity').[32] In Cary, Dante is seen as mistakenly subjecting his 'vision' to pictorial clarity, limiting its sublime power. For

---

[31] See Cary's criticism of Erasmus Darwin: 'It was, indeed, a notion he had taken up, that [. . .] the words expressive of those ideas belonging to vision make up the principal part of poetic language [. . . .] The admirers of poetry have not only eyes but ears and hearts also; and [. . .] harmony and pathos are required of the poet no less than a faithful delineation of visible objects.' *Lives of English Poets from Johnson to Kirk White [. . .]* (London, 1846), 267. Cary's essay-length 'Lives' were first published in *The London Magazine*, 1821–4.

[32] Cf. Hugh Blair's account of Milton's and Homer's 'sublimity': Homer's has 'fire and impetuosity'; Milton's 'a calm and amazing grandeur', *Lectures on Rhetoric and Belles Lettres*, published 1796, delivered 1759–60, in *Milton 1732–1801 The Critical Heritage*, 247. On the changing senses of 'sublimity' and the 'sublime' see Samuel H. Monk, *The Sublime: A Study of Critical Theories in Eighteenth-Century England* (London, 1935, repr. Ann Arbor, Mich., 1960); Ferguson, *Solitude and the Sublime*, 40–54.

Warton, Dante's project is merely foolish and his vividness admirable when it does not transgress communal expectation. When Cary chose *The Vision* for his title he in part continued that eighteenth-century view. *Vision* lifts Dante above the sordid demands of narrative, as Cary confirms in his introduction: 'the story (if story it may be called) ends happily' (Cary, i, p. viii). But he also intended his choice to defend and explain the way Dante relates his experiences 'circumstantially and without rejection'.[33] Cary concedes that this may rightly be no longer to modern taste, but commends it as a result of the visionary truthfulness that Dante could, wonderfully, attain in those 'early compositions'.[34]

Where eighteenth-century works invoked the idea of 'a vision' this usually indicated their employment of a (fictional) dream as the vehicle for allegory.[35] In his *Dictionary*, Johnson rejects the belief that humanity can attain the direct perception achieved by Dante's 'vision':

---

[33] Homer's and Dante's vividness are appreciated simultaneously. See William Cowper, *The Iliad and Odyssey, translated into English Blank Verse*, 2 vols. (London, 1791), p. xiv: 'HOMER [. . .] with all his sublimity and grandeur, has the minuteness of a Flemish painter.' Cary accommodates the same quality in Dante by elevating its clarity and prophetic truth above the reach of modernity. Cf. William Mickle's history of epic in his translation of Camoens: *The Lusiad; or, The Discovery of India. An Epic Poem* (Oxford, 1776), pp. cxxxix, clxvii.

[34] Cary found a precedent for the title in some early editions: *La visione. Poema di Dante [. . .]* (Vicenza, 1613; Padua, 1629). It is not known what text Cary used, nor how many, but he refers throughout to a Venetian edition of the complete works (1793). This is now rare, see *CN*, ii. 3014 n.

[35] Dreams are elided with visions and used allegorically in several papers of the *Spectator*. See *Spectator*, ed. D. F. Bond, 5 vols. (Oxford, 1965), i. 14–17, 270–3, 353–6; iii. 75–8. Addison places 'Fables, Dreams, Visions' in his list of the 'species of Wit' according to Locke's definition (ibid. i. 265; see John Locke, *An Essay Concerning Human Understanding*, ed. Peter H. Nidditch (Oxford, 1975), 156). Cf. Henry Fielding's allegorical 'The Opposition, A Vision', *The Complete Works of Henry Fielding*, ed. W. E. Henley, 16 vols. (repr. New York, 1967), xiv. 323–31. The mode was still, principally, satirical at the end of the century: see Theophilus Swift, *The Temple of Folly [. . .]* (1787); Alexander Thomson, *The Paradise of Taste* (1796). Mark Akenside, Joseph Warton, Thomas Gray, and William Collins in mid-century, like Coleridge in the 1790s, revived Miltonic and Pindaric forms in order to reinstate poetry's visionary claim. The claim remained, however, either internal to the genre or a sign of modern belatedness by comparison with primitive clarity. See E. L. Tuveson, *The Imagination as a Means of Grace: Locke and the Aesthetics of Romanticism* (Berkeley, Calif., and Los Angeles, 1960); P. M. Spacks, *The Poetry of Vision: Five Eighteenth-Century Poets* (Cambridge, Mass., 1967); Marshall Brown, 'The Urbane Sublime', *ELH*, 45 (1978), 236–54; Stephen Knapp, *Personification and the Sublime: Milton to Coleridge* (Cambridge, Mass., 1985).

A dream; something shewn in a dream. A dream happens to a sleeping, a vision may happen to a waking man. A dream is supposed natural, a vision miraculous; but they are confounded.[36]

Johnson's insistence that humanity cannot distinguish between deceitful dreams and true visions contributes to the avowed fictionality of 'visionary' writing. As late as Cary, the adjective implied a foolish willingness to give credence to one's own fantasies.[37] Cary makes Dante's poem miraculous: the unique example of truthful vision by contrast with the modern, customary device. His title is, therefore, primitivist, suggesting Dante's enviable clarity while still allowing his readers to read the work from a distance, not as a real narrative but as an instance of unrepeatable truth. The sublimity 'we have learned to expect' is generated by the remoteness of Dante, coupled with his authority; by his work's being the primal version of Milton's achievement. His introduction and translation correspond therefore to Burke's idea of sublime writing. '[O]dd wild grotesques', Burke states, are not 'capable of producing a serious passion'. Sublime poetry must appear to threaten, but must not overwhelm, its readers:

When danger and pain press too nearly, they are incapable of giving any delight, and are simply terrible; but at certain distances, and with certain modifications, they may be, and they are delightful, as we every day experience.[38]

---

[36] Samuel Johnson, *A Dictionary of the English Language* (London, 1755, repr. Oxford, 1978). Both editions are unpaginated. See also, however, Johnson's use of Locke's epistemology: 'The idea of any thing in our mind, no more proves the existence of that thing, than the *visions* of a dream make a true history.' (This quotation from Locke appears under the fourth definition of 'vision'.) Locke's theory of knowledge denies but cannot refute the identical status of ideas in our mind and visions in a dream. Cf. Addison's description of humanity 'at present delightfully lost and bewildered in a pleasing Delusion' (Bond, *Spectator*, iii. 546).

[37] Cary is 'inclined to believe' Rossetti's political readings 'not altogether visionary'; and he criticizes Landino as 'now and then, a little visionary in his interpretation' (Cary to Thomas Price, 8 Jan. 1825, see R. W. King, *The Translator of Dante: The Life [. . .] of Henry Francis Cary (1772–1844)* (London, 1925), 168–9; Cary 1819, p. xlix). On this topic and this word, compare James Beattie, 'On Dreaming', *Dissertations Moral and Critical* (Edinburgh, 1783), 215: 'If this conjecture trouble me in the day-time, it may also recur in sleep, accompanied with some visionary circumstances [. . . .] Surely, I have no more reason to consider it as prophetical, than to look upon the conjecture which gave rise to it as the effect of inspiration.'

[38] Edmund Burke, *A Philosophical Enquiry into the Origins of our Ideas of the Sublime and the Beautiful* (1757), ed. James T. Boulton (2nd rev. edn., Oxford,

Cary's translation shows the effect of sublimity (so defined) on a reading of Dante. Romantic writers' readoption of the vividness in Dante that Cary found distasteful, their entering 'the circle of his vision' to make it their own, is of a piece, therefore, with their attempt to make poetry both primitively clear and faithfully adherent to 'the truth of nature'.

The implications of Thomas Warton's judgement on Dante and its distance from Romantic reading can be shown by comparing two translations of the Ugolino episode: Thomas Gray's, probably written in 1737–8, and Thomas Medwin's of 1821, corrected by Shelley.[39] Gray thought of the episode in isolation from the rest of the *Inferno* but presents the central speech as something witnessed by an anonymous third-person narrator.[40] Dante's *personaggio* disappears and the narrative voice does not overhear so much as herald the speaker—attending dispassionately while endowing the speech with a heightened simplicity of emotional appeal. In Gray's view and in his own practice, the poet absents himself in order to exert unequivocal control. His verse is uncomplicatedly passionate, sustaining its interest through its richness of detail about the feelings involved. Ugolino's catching sight of his sons, for instance, confirms their estranged similarity:

> But oh! when I beheld
> My sons, and in four faces saw my own
> Despair reflected, either hand I gnawed
> For anguish, which they construed hunger.
> (ll. 61–4, *Gray*, 25)

'My own' is his own face and the faces of his own, of 'My sons', producing from self-pity and pity for one's children the despair that follows. The misunderstanding a moment later acknowledges

1987), 40. Cf. Lord Kames, *Elements of Criticism*, 2 vols. (Edinburgh, 1788), ii. 329: 'force of expression consists in raising complete images; which have the effect to transport the reader as by magic into the very place of the important action, and to convert him as it were into a spectator, beholding every thing that passes'. Cf. Angela Leighton: 'this imaginative view [. . .] is in a sense autonomous; the poet can see as freely as he chooses' (*Shelley and the Sublime: An Interpretation of the Major Poems* (Cambridge, 1985), 17).

[39] Cf. Warton's account with James Beattie's in 1783 and William Roscoe's in 1795 (Toynbee, i. 358, 528). The gradual dissent from Warton's views, coinciding with a shift from Ugolino to 'softer' incidents like canto v, has been neglected; see Steve Ellis, *Dante and English Poetry: Shelley to T. S. Eliot* (Cambridge 1983), 104.

[40] See *Gray*, 23, headnote para. 3.

the difference between one's self and one's children which vanishes
in Ugolino's utter despair, but it is a misunderstanding that leads
to reciprocal self-sacrifice: his children willing to lay down their
lives for him; he strengthened to resist the lust for self-destruction.
Gray's 'construed' finds the calm that Ugolino feels in remember-
ing his sons' endearing confusion and re-establishes relations be-
tween them that had been pressured out of existence just moments
earlier by what he had 'beheld'.

These manners of speech welcome the reader's sympathetic
pursuit of Ugolino's feelings but Gray prevents our fully identify-
ing with him, in part by placing at either end of the account lines
in the third person. These are spoken by Dante in the original,
where Ugolino also acknowledges Dante's presence:

> 'Quivi morí; e come tu mi vedi,
> vid' io cascar li tre ad uno ad uno'.
> (*Inferno*, xxxiii. 70–1, Sapegno, i. 366)

('With this he died; and just as you see me now, I saw the remaining three
fall one by one'.)

It is a curiously offhand source of disturbance. Just by urging the
veracity of his statement Ugolino recalls his own death and Dante's
contrasting liveliness, bringing to mind the difference between what
he has seen and what, despite the earlier horrors of Hell, Dante
will never see. The effect of watching your children die raises itself
as a question that separates the two of them. Gray's translation
has no equivalent to the remark and, at the close, draws more
closely into one the different dictions of Ugolino and the narrator:

> 'ond' io mi diedi,
> già cieco, a brancolar sovra ciascuno,
> e due dí li chiamai, poi che fur morti:
> poscia, piú che 'l dolor, poté 'l digiuno.'
> Quand'ebbe detto ciò, con li occhi torti
> riprese 'l teschio misero co' denti,
> che furo all'osso, come d'un can, forti.
> (Ibid., ll. 72–8)

('afterwards, already blind, I took to groping after each of them and for
two days called them after they had died: then hunger had greater power
than grief.' Having said this, he, with a grim frown, again took hold of
the miserable skull with his teeth, which were fierce on the bone like a
dog's.)

Thomas Gray ends his translation at this point in the original.

> 'For three days more I groped
> About among their cold remains (for then
> Hunger had reft my eyesight), often calling
> On their dear names, that heard me now no more;
> The fourth, what sorrow could not, famine did.'
> He finished; then with unrelenting eye
> Askance he turned him, hasty to renew
> The hellish feast, and rent his trembling prey.
>   (ll. 77–84, *Gray*, 25)

Ugolino's unwillingness to say exactly what he means is finely caught by Gray's version of the speech's last line as it snaps shut. The comma breaks co-operate with the assonance of 'fourth' and 'sorrow' to produce sudden acceleration in the short 'i's of 'famine did' and the alliterative sequence adds to this urgency so that the bald action, whatever it might have been, stands apart and threatens.

The relation is sustained as Ugolino returns, relentlessly, to Ruggieri. Gray certainly renders the cannibalism more palatable, removing the specificity of teeth and bones and introducing adjectival diversions. These interest his reader in Ugolino's mysterious motivations as aspects of a personality more than as the consequences of a punishment that destroys personality. 'The hellish feast' shields us from Hell, and 'rent his trembling prey' invites wonder and a quiveringly tender compassion for the underdog in the midst of this revenge. The attenuation of ferocity in Gray derives from the same impulse that irons out Ugolino's self-pity in such a way that his experiences become more pitiable; Dante's reflexive construction, 'io mi diedi [. . .] a brancolar', minutely emphasizes Ugolino's awareness of his enforced self-abandonment. There is a hint of self-congratulation about his description of the enduring devotion he showed at the time. In Gray's version he gropes about among their 'cold remains', both slightly ridiculous and horrible, as he fondles dead flesh. The surge of pathos in line 80, 'their dear names, that heard me now no more', overwhelms our horror and dislike, but it is difficult to respect him by the end.[41] One of the sources of our sympathy is Ugolino's unfortunate

---

[41] Cf. W. H. Auden, 'Earth, Sky, a few dear names', *Collected Shorter Poems, 1927–57* (London and Boston, 1966), 256.

loss of all right to respect, his reduction to a childish lack of decency and a childlike vulnerability.

Gray elides the two voices of the original because he has no qualms about the intervening presence of the writer or the likelihood of his imposing on the subject. (What applies to his understanding of Dante's position in the poem applies equally to his role as translator—his version shows no sign of the distance that persists or the difficulties overcome moving between Italian and English.[42]) This confidence defines the configuration of emotions in the poem and preserves the underlying invulnerability of the audience. Thomas Medwin's 1821 translation of the same episode, with Shelley's corrections, isolates Ugolino's speech entirely by giving nothing of the frame.[43] Their renderings focus more narrowly on Ugolino himself:

> 'When I
> *Heard locked beneath me, of that horrible tower*
>
> *The outlet, then into their eyes alone*
> *I looked to read myself*, without a sign
> Or word.'
> (Medwin, *Life of Shelley*, 20, ll. 29–33)

This enquiry is translated by Gray as dumb foreboding: 'Then on my children's eyes | Speechless my sight I fixed, nor wept.' Similarly Ugolino's anguish, 'when I beheld | My sons, and in four faces saw my own | Despair reflected', becomes sorrier and even petulant:

> 'but when to shine
> Upon the world, not us, came forth the light
>
> Of the new sun, and thwart my prison thrown,
> Gleamed thro' its narrow chink—a doleful sight—
> *Three faces, each the reflex of my own,*
>
> *Were imaged by its faint and ghastly ray*;
> Then I, of either hand unto the bone,
> Gnawed, in my agony'.
> (Medwin, *Life of Shelley*, 21, ll. 38–45)

---

[42] See T. R. Steiner, *English Translation Theory 1650–1800, Approaches to Translation Studies*, ii (Assen and Amsterdam, 1975); Timothy Webb, *The Violet in the Crucible: Shelley and Translation* (Oxford, 1976).

[43] The only surviving text of this translation was published in Thomas Medwin, *The Life of Percy Bysshe Shelley*, 2 vols. (London, 1847), ii. 19–22. Medwin uses italics to indicate Shelley's contributions.

Ugolino's greater isolation encourages, perhaps, the Gothic horror of '*faint and ghastly ray*' and the pointed self-attention that describes the sun as shining 'Upon the world, not us'. The reader is invited to share, however, Ugolino's separation from the world. Much of the pleasure in the passage is thought in this translation to arise from our alignment alongside him in Hell. One is able to imagine it really happening whereas, in Gray's version, one may entertain the thought of it, considering suffering as an instance rather than the specific and actual case.

The relationship between reader and translation in Shelley and Medwin's version corresponds, in fact, to that between Ugolino and the dream he has while in prison:

> '*it was a slumber deep*
> *And evil—for I saw, or I did seem*
> *To see*'.
> (Medwin, *Life of Shelley*, 19, ll. 9–11)

Gray introduces Ugolino's doubt about exactly what he saw as the defining feature of this dream (like any other), not as a momentary source of fascinated self-absorption; Dante's 'pareva a me' (*Inferno*, xxxiii. 28, Sapegno, i. 364) becomes 'methought' (l. 28, *Gray*, 24). As Shelley rewrites it, Ugolino's unwillingness to confine his dream to its appropriate fictional status, or to believe it, epitomizes our relationship with his dramatic monologue—we see, or seem to see, him, share, or seem to share, in his experience. Interest moves from what Ugolino saw in the dream to the arresting doubtfulness of the way he saw it; from what the dream may explicitly tell us to how we may discover things through it. As a result the landscape of the dream is bound up with Ugolino's suffering and becomes legible as an aspect of his mind. He dreams of a chase:

> '*up the steep*
> Ascent, that from *the Pisan is the screen*
> Of *Lucca*'.
> (Medwin, *Life of Shelley*, 19, ll. 12–14)[44]

He is confronted by and hunted up a physical barrier not, as in Gray, by an object that interrupts his perceptions:

---

[44] Cf. 'The Boat on the Serchio', ll. 39–40, *PW*, 655.

'I saw methought
Towards Pisa's mount, that intercepts the view
Of Lucca'.

(ll. 28–30, *Gray*, 24)

Ugolino is foiled by an intervening object beyond which his eye cannot rove, while in Shelley the inversion of the sequence of events and the use of '*screen*' at the end of a heavily assonant line places the speaker within the landscape. A landscape of the mind repeatedly disappoints his hopes of escape as the enjambement of 'steep | Ascent' enforces the presence of a steep slope. '[S]teep' is changed from a noun to an adjective only to qualify a synonym.

The differences between the two translations correspond to changes in critical judgement. In Shelley's version, Dante's centrality, the reader's opportunity to identify with him, and the suspicion that he generates a dream-world which manifests his nature (where in Gray the dream is an allegory of his situation), all make Ugolino resemble Friedrich Schelling's view of Dante himself:

So far as Dante himself may be looked upon as the hero, who serves only as a thread for the measureless series of visions and pictures, and remains rather passive than active, the poem seems to approach nearer to a Romance; yet this definition does not completely exhaust it.[45]

Schelling regards *The Divine Comedy* as the 'archetype of all modern poetry' because it creates 'a world by itself and wholly characteristic'. In doing so, the poem transcends genre distinctions and its 'measureless series of visions and pictures' represents Dante as a passive hero. The 'dialogues and adventures' of an 'infernal journey' are found to create a single world of their own in which Dante, like his creation Ugolino, is both the recipient of 'visions and pictures' and their creator. Schelling's revolutionary assessment of Dante's position in the history of poetry—as the first modern poet whom Warton treated as typically Medieval—carries

---

[45] I quote from a translation given in *The Divine Comedy: Purgatorio* translated by Henry Wadsworth Longfellow (London and New York, 1867), 484–5. See 'Über Dante in philosophischer Beziehung' (1803), *Schellings Werke*, ed. Manfred Schröter, 6 vols. (Munich 1927, repr. 1958), iii. 573: 'Inwiefern Dante selbst als die Hauptperson betrachtet wird, die nur als Band für die unermessliche Reihe von Gesichtern und Gemälden dient und mehr leidend als thätig sich verhält, könnte dieses Gedicht dem Roman sich zu nähern scheinen; aber auch dieser Begriff erschöpft es so wenig.' Cf. Nigel Leask, *The Politics of Imagination in Coleridge's Critical Thought* (London, 1988), 115–16.

with it a new view of his relationship to his work. The 'measureless series of visions and pictures' forms a world, characteristic of Dante, which he inhabits and passively perceives, but in being seen to create a world of its own the 'measureless series' establishes unity in the collection of individual pictures.

Dante's position as participant and creator enables him to provide a thread that links up the various encounters which Warton thought randomly organized. When this perspective moves the focus of interest in the poem from what Dante sees and who he meets to the process of seeing and meeting, the didacticism that Warton looked for is replaced by the pleasure and interest that are considered to be inherent in imaginative encounters. Schelling's account similarly realigns allegorical figures, giving emphasis less to their interpretation than to the possibility and consequences of meeting them:

There is no doubt, and the poet has himself elsewhere declared it, that Beatrice, for example, is an Allegory, namely of Theology. So her companions; so many other characters. But at the same time they count for themselves, and appear on the scene as historical personages, without on that account being symbols.[46]

Repositioning the narrator in relation to the story and reconsidering allegory so as to reinstate the 'historical personages' on which it depends co-operate in Schelling to produce a new appreciation of Dante's work as a whole. Moreover, because allegorical significance and historical reality are now thought to be indistinguishable in the *Commedia*, Dante is found able to make objects represent abstract qualities without such significance obscuring those objects or personages. They still 'count for themselves'. Dante's vividness and particularity are no longer simply a result of his primitive period nor the tasteless extravagances that Warton condemns; they make him into the archetype and precedent of characteristically modern art.

Some of these emphases are evident in the translation by Medwin and Shelley. Though he is interestingly hesitant by comparison

---

[46] The German reads: 'Es ist kein Zweifel, und der Dichter hat es selbst anderwärts erklärt dass Beatrice z.B. eine Allegorie, der Theologie nämlich, ist. So ihre Gefährtinnen, so viele andere Gestalten. Aber sie zählen zugleich für sich selbst, und treten als historische Personen ein, ohne desswegen Symbole zu sein' (Schröter, *Schellings Werke*, 575–6).

with Schelling, Coleridge largely shares this view of the *Commedia*'s distinctiveness in style:

I have deferred the consideration of Allegory; but I must not defer my reason—as respects Dante's Poem—. The Poem is a system of moral political, and theological Truths with arbitrary personal exemplifications— ⟨the punishments indeed allegorical *perhaps*—⟩ (*Lectures 1808–19*, ii. 400)[47]

William Hazlitt, in addition, sees allegorical meanings in Dante subsumed by symbolic values; in his reading, however, Dante's symbols demand the sympathetic participation of the reader in order to be understood.

Dante's great power is in combining internal feelings with external objects. Thus the gate of hell, on which that withering inscription is written, seems to be endowed with speech and consciousness, and to utter its dread warning, not without a sense of mortal woes. This author habitually unites the absolutely local and individual with the greatest wildness and mysticism [. . . .] All this, perhaps, tends to heighten the effect by the bold intermixture of realities, and by an appeal, as it were, to the individual knowledge and experience of the reader.[48]

Dante's 'intermixture of realities', then, contains inherently 'an appeal [. . .] to the individual knowledge and experience of the reader'. The poem's symbolism, which combines 'internal feelings with external objects', necessitates a reader's involvement.

Hazlitt, however, does not call this quality symbolic and Schelling rejects the term: Beatrice and the other figures are, he says, 'historical personages, without on that account being symbols'. Slippery definitions, though, do not entirely account for the hesitation to be found in Coleridge's lecture. More strongly than Schelling, Coleridge is preoccupied with 'personal exemplifications', with whether symbolic significance compromises an object's particularity. He becomes interested in the *Commedia* as a model of a symbolic style whose fusion of object and significance (that Coleridge saw

---

[47] See *Table Talk* 17 Aug. 1833, i. 426–7 where Coleridge decisively rejects Gabriele Rossetti's allegorical reading. See Gabriele Rossetti, *La Divina Commedia* [. . .] *con comento analitico*, vols. i, ii (London, 1826–7) and Toynbee, ii. 446.

[48] Hazlitt, v. 18. He is opposing Sismondi's version of the orthodoxy which states that Dante is 'the most loftily sublime' poet and that 'there is scarcely a stanza which might not be represented with the pencil'. Cf. ibid. 17, and Paul J. Alpers, *The Poetry of* The Faerie Queene (Princeton, NJ, 1967), 232–3.

as, in addition, a mixture of judgement and dream) was peculiarly and, perhaps inimitably, complete.[49]

Coleridge's interest in symbolism arises independently of his reading Dante, but it informs his account of Cary's translation. The translation itself implies a more passive reading posture than Coleridge usually recommends or than Hazlitt thinks is required of us by the very nature of Dante's text. This does not make it as triumphant and effortlessly successful as the Dante that Schelling presents. Paradoxically, Cary's version achieves a degree of fidelity to the original that was unique for the period but does so through an effort to avoid the appeal to the reader that Hazlitt regards as innate in Dante's 'intermixture of realities'. Cary's translation arises from the suspension of private judgement in favour of the original's authority.[50] A tension that must come into play in any translation (between an idea of fidelity and one of recreation) comes under increased strain in Cary's The Vision because (according to Hazlitt and others in the period) Dante's text will not be satisfied with fidelity; it makes appeals to and places demands on the translator's (like the reader's) individual experience.[51]

None of the writers discussed below was entirely ignorant of Italian and consequently none of them was entirely dependent on Cary's translation for their understanding of Dante. Keats is the one closest to Cary but even he, in his last writing year, read the original alongside the translation. On the other hand, they all read

---

[49] See below, Ch. 3. For other accounts of the Romantics reading allegories symbolically, see Samuel R. Levin, 'Allegorical Language', in *Allegory, Myth, and Symbol*, ed. Morton W. Bloomfield (Harvard English Studies, 9, Cambridge Mass., 1981), 23–38; Stephen Knapp, *Personification and the Sublime*, 10–23, 106–20. See also Paul de Man, 'Rhetoric of Temporality', *Blindness and Insight: Essays in the Rhetoric of Contemporary Criticism* (2nd rev. edn., London, 1983), 204–7.

[50] See his letter to Anna Seward, 5 Mar. 1789: 'The first object of translation is to give you the clearest and most intimate acquaintance with the original.' He dates the translation from 16 June 1797 to 8 May 1812 (Henry Cary, *Memoir of the Rev. Henry Francis Cary* [. . .], 2 vols. (London, 1847), 92, 28, 269). He published *The Inferno of Dante* [. . .], 2 vols. (1805–6) and included a parallel text; *The Vision; or, Hell, Purgatory, and Paradise* [. . . .] was published, privately, in 1814 in 32mo. See King, *The Translator of Dante*, 300; Toynbee, ii. 204. Comparison of Cary's 1805–6 and 1814 editions shows him moving closer to the original: see 'Hell', i. 24–9 and ii. 116–17 (Cary (1805–6), 5, 29; Cary (1814) i. 1–2, 8).

[51] On the general problem in translation, see Peter Robinson, *In the Circumstances: About Poems and Poets* (Oxford, 1992), 142–72. On Cary's version, see V. Tinkler-Villani, *Visions of Dante in English Poetry: Translators of the* Commedia *from Jonathan Richardson to William Blake* (Amsterdam, 1989), 125.

Cary and contested his version's success. The emphasis laid increasingly in the period on the encounters that take place in Dante's text and on the engagement which his text demanded of its readers frequently becomes clear when Romantic writers are in dispute with Cary, as if the absence of this quality from his text brought it to light in the original. I discuss the emergence of readings similar to Hazlitt's in more detail below; by looking at Cary's translation beforehand, I aim to show how the feeling, thought, and perspective of Dante's work are altered by Cary's redisposition of Dante's encounters.

Cary's preface to the first complete edition (of 1814) quotes from Coleridge's *The Friend*:

I do not regard those hours as the least happy of my life during which (to use the eloquent language of Mr Coleridge) 'my individual recollections have been suspended and lulled to sleep amid the music of nobler thoughts'. (Cary, p. vi)[52]

The authority of Dante's vision demands, for Cary, not a mixture of passivity and activity but a passive compliance with what has been shown. He saw translation as a humble self-surrender to the 'golden ages of our literature'.[53] In accordance with his title for the poem, Cary's willing suspension of judgement creates an exemplary Dante. His blank verse, which is Miltonic in some respects but also indebted to Cowper's translation of Homer, elevates the poem towards the sublimity 'we have learned to expect' since Milton, but in doing so Cary privileges the reader with a kind of detachment. Adherence, in other words, to the self-effacing but all-comprehending virtue of sympathy produces a translation that turns Dante's poem into a set of occasions when sympathy may be displayed.[54] These are often movingly written but they cannot include Hazlitt's appeal to the experience of the reader—that, in Cary's view, would be best suppressed in advance. This emphasis

---

[52] Quoting *Friend*, ii. 218. The passage was not reprinted in the 1818 edition of *The Friend*, but in *BL*, ii. 186.

[53] See Hazlitt, xvi. 102–3. Cary referred to the interest in Italian literature as 'a sign that we are so far willing to revert to the golden ages of our literature' (*London Magazine*, 1823, repr. in Toynbee, i. 488).

[54] Born in the same year as Coleridge, Cary started translating when Coleridge was composing his Miltonic 'Religious Musings' and his sonnets reminiscent of Bowles. The complete translation remained consistent with the aesthetic assumptions with which Cary began and, consequently, appeared in some respects old-fashioned by the time of its success in 1819.

in Cary alters more than the affective possibilities of Dante's poem: because the truth-content and the worth of the *Commedia* are taken to be self-evident, they cannot be tested by the reader in the process of reading.

Cary's version of the famous meeting between Dante and Brunetto Latini in *Inferno* xv brings out the differences between the two versions.

> e sí ver noi aguzzavan le ciglia
> come 'l vecchio sartor fa nella cruna.
> Cosí adocchiato da cotal famiglia,
> fui conosciuto da un, che mi prese
> per lo lembo e gridò: 'Qual maraviglia!'
> E io, quando 'l suo braccio a me distese,
> ficca' li occhi per lo cotto aspetto,
> sí che 'l viso abbruciato non difese
> la conoscenza sua al mio intelletto;
> e chinando la mia alla sua faccia,
> rispuosi: 'Siete voi qui, ser Brunetto?'
> (*Inferno*, xv. 20–30, Sapegno, i. 167–8)

(and they squinted at us as an old tailor squints at the eye of his needle. While being gazed at in this way by such a company, I was recognized by one, who grabbed my coat and called out, 'How marvellous!' And I, when he stretched out his arm to me, fixed my eyes on his baked features so that his scorched face did not prevent my mind from recognizing him and, inclining my face to his, I replied, 'Are you here, Ser Brunetto?')

Brunetto Latini, Dante's old teacher, is placed in the circle of those who did violence to nature. His punishment expresses the orthodox condemnation of homosexuality as consisting in an attack on the natural order.[55] Latini's 'violence' is punished by his being exposed to a rain of fire while walking through a desert. Dante and Virgil cross this circle by following one of the rivers of Hell which, at this point, is boiling hot: the steam rising from the water protects them by extinguishing each falling spark before it can land. Dante's features are and remain, therefore, strikingly recognizable: they are not 'cotto' (cooked or baked by the burning flakes) nor 'abbruciato' (scorched or singed). Where the body that Latini defiled is being deformed, Dante's intact face is a reminder both of life on earth and of the salvation that Latini is now denied. Because the

---

[55] Cf. however, *Purgatorio*, xxvi. 76–90, Sapegno, ii. 288–9, where among the lustful who are saved Dante puts both heterosexual and homosexual.

woman who clutched the hem of Christ's garment and the man whose withered arm Christ heals are both recalled when Latini clutches Dante, the meeting confirms the divide between the two characters which their mutual recognition appears, momentarily, to overcome.[56] In the same way, Dante's simile of the 'vecchio sartor' adds more than incidental interest because Dante is passing through the eye of a needle to enter the kingdom of Heaven from which Latini is debarred.

Dante's secure confidence in this undeniable truth about their opposite destinies is, none the less, threatened by the meeting. His initial wary and enquiring glance (the glance with which one habitually confronts strangers, looking less for recognition than for an assurance of mutual indifference) is turned by Latini's urgency into a fixed look. As much as his more concentrated attention removes the disguise created by Latini's charred physical features, it erodes Dante's protective hostility. 'La conoscenza sua' penetrates 'al mio intelletto' irresistibly: recognition and acknowledgement enter Dante's mind, so that he turns his face to meet the other's face: 'la mia alla sua faccia'. The change in wording (from 'viso' and 'aspetto' to 'faccia') also indicates a change in their relation, and a loss of descriptive self-confidence. When he is recognized, in other words, Dante is made to accept a mutuality which recognition implies. This does not mean, however, that he is swept up by Latini or entirely absorbed in looking at him. The question he asks is respectful, using 'voi' not 'tu', and immediately sets Latini back in his place: 'Are you here, Ser Brunetto' (rather than in Heaven)?[57]

The moment of recognition is followed, therefore, by the shocked realization that Latini is Latini in Hell. Exchanging looks with his friend and searching out from the scorched features of this damned soul the traces of a recognizable face do not recover those features and do not put Dante in Latini's place. Dante's likeness to Christ, in fact, entails a limit to his capacity for sympathy while Dante's awareness that he lacks Christ's power to free the damned from Hell adds regret to his compassion. Cary does not translate the form of determined hesitance that Dante imposed on his sympathy:

---

[56] Matthew 9: 20, Mark 5: 25, Luke 8: 43, Matthew 12: 10-13, Mark 3: 1-5, Luke 6: 6-10.

[57] Cf. T. S. Eliot's version of the question in 'Little Gidding', ii. 98: 'What! are *you* here?' and the wording in his draft: 'Are you here, Ser Brunetto?' (Helen Gardner, *The Composition of* Four Quartets (London and Boston, 1978), 174).

And toward us sharpen'd their sight as keen,
As an old tailor at his needle's eye.
  Thus narrowly explor'd by all the tribe,
I was agniz'd of one, who by the skirt
Caught me, and cried, 'What wonder have we here?'
  And I, when he to me outstretch'd his arm,
Intently fix'd my ken on his parch'd looks,
That although smirch'd with fire, they hinder'd not
But I remember'd him; and towards his face
My hand inclining, answer'd: 'Sir! Brunetto!
And art thou here?'
                    ('Hell', xv. 19–29, Cary, i. 63–4)[58]

Cary's syntax and lineation render very cleverly the reciprocations
that Dante is suggesting when the two characters look at each
other, when 'he to me outstretch'd his arm' and, Dante says, 'I
[. . .] Intently fix'd my ken on his parch'd looks'. This fidelity to
the original, however, becomes reverential when Cary ennobles
the lines in which recognition occurs. Cary turns the moment of
recognition into a recollection: 'But I remember'd him.' Originally,
Dante was no longer defended against the encounter by Latini's
deformity: ' 'l viso abbruciato non difese | la conoscenza sua al
mio intelletto'. In Cary, Dante is not subjected to the recognition
but unhindered in his remembering. He is not open to the same
affliction from the encounter as occurs in the original. The 'But'
of 'But I remember'd him' suggests an inevitable discovery, with
a hint of self-congratulation, and recalls rather grandly the mo-
ment at which recognition dawned. Dante's sense of a suddenly
established, and endangering, intimacy consequently slips into
heartiness and tactlessness. The naming of Latini turns into a
salutation. '"Sir! Brunetto! | And art thou here?"', Cary's Dante
excitedly calls after his teacher (as if surprised to find him invited
to the same party).[59]
  By altering the original's portrayal of Dante's intense attention,
Cary's version necessarily realigns the perspective of the reader,

[58] This is one of the few occasions when Cary alters the wording of the trans-
lation when revising it in 1819 (He systematically changes the orthography and
punctuation.) The last lines quoted read: 'My hand inclining, answer'd: "Ser
Brunetto! | And are ye here?"' (Cary 1819, i. 127).
[59] Cary's translation of l. 29, 'e chinando la mia alla sua faccia', by 'and towards
his face | My hand inclining' is the result of his choosing a reading of the original
text which gives 'mane' in place of 'mia'; see l. 29 n., Sapegno, i. 168.

tending to attenuate the appeal Dante makes to his or her individual experience. Later in *Inferno*, for example, the distance that Cary introduces (between Dante's *personaggio* and the suffering he witnesses in his journey through Hell) makes it difficult for a reader to participate in Dante's fear. In canto xxiii, Dante and Virgil seem to have escaped a crowd of enraged devils but, as they go on, Dante begins to realize that the demons may still be in pursuit:

> If anger then
> Be to their evil will conjoin'd, more fell
> They shall pursue us, than the savage hound
> Snatches the leveret, panting 'twixt his jaws.
> ('Hell', xxiii. 15–18, Cary, i. 97)

In Cary's translation, Dante's unspoken consideration of this danger proceeds measuredly towards the simile, reasoning his fears and accepting the consequences. The enjambement within the simile takes us from the chase to kill, to linger on the suffering of the prey; the dactyls of 'Snatches the leveret' combine with shortened vowels to make 'panting' into a slight pause of relief. While the verse takes us through the motions of capture in the sudden rapidity of its rhythms, it also sets up a division between the last gasps of the victim and its own more even, rhythmic pulse. '[P]anting 'twixt his jaws' sinks to rest, leaving the first word as the keystone of the line, and leaving the pain of the leveret's death as an object of attention.

Cary's version simultaneously softens the violence of Dante's image and fits it into a sequence of thought and feeling different from the original:

> 'Se l'ira sovra 'l mal voler fa gueffa,
> ei ne verranno dietro piú crudeli
> che 'l cane a quella lievre ch'elli acceffa.'
> (*Inferno*, xxiii. 16–18, Sapegno, i. 253)

('If anger gets tangled up with evil will, they will come after us more fiercely than a dog after the hare it snaps at.')

This is far less considered: 'gueffa' in the first line interferes with the abstract status of moral qualities by suggesting that they are entangled with the devils, not merely found together. The succession of phrases in the last line repeatedly prevents Dante from stopping the description, as if every time he has to go one step further, 'a quella lievre' and again, 'ch'elli acceffa'. The line seems to hear something at its back and a moment later Dante finds out what: 'e stava in dietro intento' ('and [I] stood looking back intently', l. 20). After this Virgil reassures him, first by celebrating the congruity of their thoughts and then by offering a means of escape. The whole incident is as sensitive about the degree of fear engendered by the mere belief that one is being pursued—as great and in some ways greater than that produced by knowing—as it is profound about the effort in putting behind one something that is chasing from behind, particularly when, like Christ, one has to put the Devil behind. But Virgil comforts a substantial fear as well as one whose meaning is allegorically complex. Dante's thoughts cannot dwell on the poignancy of being caught because he is too frightened—the image of the 'lievre' works as an intimation of speed.

Cary chooses 'leveret' for 'lievre' partly in an effort to use etymologically related words, but his diminutive also introduces greater pathos into his version. The Italian can mean 'leveret' but is used more often of the adult hare, that escapes predators by running, twisting, turning, and doubling back. Dante's line imitates the panic of the chase in its alliteration and elisions. Cary's cadence opens with similar haste but then offers a way of escape from the pressure of the Italian. Here (as elsewhere) Cary's expectations about how a poet should speak accommodate Dante's dramatic urgency far less well than they replicate the elegiac tone that Dante's Virgil can sometimes command.

Virgil's lament about humanity's perverse weakness at the end of *Purgatorio* xiv, for example, is stringently impassioned about a problem that is, in some respects, none of his concern:

> 'Ma voi prendete l'esca, sí che l'amo
>   dell'antico avversaro a sé vi tira;
>   e però poco val freno o richiamo.
> Chiamavi 'l cielo e 'ntorno vi si gira,
>   mostrandovi le sue bellezze etterne,
>   e l'occhio vostro pur a terra mira;
> onde vi batte chi tutto discerne.'
>   (*Purgatorio*, xiv. 145–51, Sapegno,
>   ii. 161)

('But you take the bait so that the hook of the old enemy draws you to him, and then curb or lure are of little use. Heaven calls you and wheels around you, showing you its eternal beauties, and your eye looks only on the earth; therefore He strikes you down, who sees all things.'

Virgil preserves some dislike amidst his sympathy: 'e l'occhio vostro' seems to despise humanity's refusal to attend but is not surprised by it; and, in the last line, Virgil's logic is slightly wearied by possible objections or protest. The repetition of 'richiamo' in 'Chiamavi', however, offsets his impatience with a sense of how divine mercy enduringly offers itself through the surroundings we disregard. This countermovement of sympathy attracts and reveals Cary's gifts:

> 'But your old enemy so baits his hook,
> He drags you eager to him. Hence nor curb
> Avails you, nor reclaiming call. Heav'n calls,
> And round about you wheeling courts your gaze
> With everlasting beauties. Yet your eye
> Turns with fond doting still upon the earth.
> Therefore He smites you who discerneth all.'
> ('Purgatory', xiv. 146–52, Cary, ii. 64)

'Heaven calls' finds God's grace as purely moving as in the original: it is neither challenging, bracing, nor rebuking in its generous appeal. Cary makes the intrusion of divine grace slightly more touching than in the original because he makes it an honour and portrays humanity as worthy of the honour. The opportunity to look at our condition from this perspective is, none the less, offered by Virgil's Italian.

Where Dante has to meet the damned this perspective is impossible. Because Farinata, in *Inferno* x, is damned for falsity of attention, his speech articulates the ideas about perception which underlie the *Commedia* and indicate the different assumptions of Cary's translation. Moreover, because in the original Farinata (in the same way as and to a greater degree than Latini) poses a threat to Dante's spiritual growth, the translation also shows how differently Cary conceives of the relationship between particular perceptions and the attainment of moral insight. Farinata explains the perceptions of the damned:

> 'Noi veggiam, come quei c'ha mala luce,
>   le cose' disse 'che ne son lontano;
>   cotanto ancor ne splende il sommo duce.

Quando s'appressano o son, tutto è vano
nostro intelletto; e s'altri non ci apporta,
nulla sapem di vostro stato umano.'
(*Inferno*, x. 100–5, Sapegno, i. 118)[60]

('We see, like those with defective vision, things'—he said—'which are distant from us; to that degree the ruler of all shines upon us still. When they approach or are present, our intellect is entirely useless; and if others do not bring us news, we know nothing of your human state.')

Cary translates the passage:

'We view, as one who hath an evil sight,'
He answer'd, 'plainly, objects far remote:
So much of his large splendour yet imparts
The' Almighty Ruler; but when they approach
Or actually exist, our intellect
Then wholly fails, nor of your human state
Except what others bring us know we aught.'
('Hell', x. 98–104, Cary, i. 42)

To some extent Farinata's speech explains a kind of blindness suffered by all the damned.[61] In the translation, however, the relationship between Farinata's inability to focus on the actual and his Epicurean materialism is lost. In the original, the affliction of his sight corresponds to the proud unbelief that underlay his particular heresy—unbelief, that is, in the deeper significance of the objects before his eyes and a consequent ordering of life by appearances alone. The self-centredness of this is intimated by the reduction of 'ne son lontano' to 'son': Farinata perceives objects at a distance and not those close at hand, but he has to find a relationship between himself and the object before seeing it. While the punishment reverses the order of Farinata's earthly perceptions the moral failing remains the same: the light of God continues to illuminate his vision as far as he allowed it to do while alive, but his determination to take things 'as they are', prevented and prevents the divine light from extending to the perception of immediate objects.

---

[60] For Dante's view of perception, see P. Boyde, 'Perception and the Percipient', *Italian Studies*, 35 (1980), 19–24.
[61] See Cary's note to l. 98, first added in his *Vision* (3rd edn., London, 1844), 50.

Farinata explains his position here rather than confessing it—stiffly enduring his affliction with an unexpected eloquence. One might readily feel unqualified admiration for his resilient clear-headedness, as one is grateful for his neatly outlining the ingenuity of divine retribution. Dante, however, interjects 'disse' in the second line to exacerbate a rhythmical unease it shares with the first. '[D]isse' reinstates a critical distance at risk in Farinata's uncontroversial opening and warns us of possible oddness despite the smoothness of what follows. Farinata begins by, uncomplicatedly, seeing things and steadily goes on to say, in 'nulla sapem di vostro stato umano', that he is no longer human. His ability to be so clear about what he is suffering while racked by physical pain hovers suddenly between admirable composure and unthinkable, inhuman self-detachment. He reaffirms his clarity with perfectly lucid utterance at the moment when the substance and manner of his speech need to be rapidly reassessed by his human audience. In this, 'vostro' and, in the previous line, 'nostro' form an abyss, crossed on occasion by 'altri' bringing news. The intimacy apparently implied by the pronouns in the first tercet ('Noi' and then 'ne' twice) breaks up as Farinata ceases to be one of us, and as it becomes clear that his way of seeing cannot conform to that incumbent on our 'stato umano': an attention to present matters (not future or past) which is made possible through divine illumination.[62]

Cary alters this sense of God's operation in our perceptions by translating 'splende' as 'large splendour yet imparts'. It sounds as if these objects offer some solace to Farinata in his misery. Cary's 'large splendour', however, imposes on Farinata's emotional life—he is either penitent, humbly praising what he had previously despised, or sarcastic and undignified. Furthermore, while trying to say that all human perception is engendered by God's light, Cary's verb 'impart' connotes a transfer where 'splende' shines. It seems, in Cary, more natural that Farinata should be distanced from God. As a consequence his intellect can fail rather than, with a different simplicity, fall.[63]

---

[62] Cf. Erich Auerbach, *Mimesis: The Representation of Reality in Western Literature*, trans. Willard R. Trask (Princeton, NJ, 1953), 174–202 (esp. p. 200).

[63] Cary's emphasis on intellectual failure weakens the sense of moral transgression; his 'evil sight' compensates for this by stressing the moral aspect of 'mala luce' (literally, 'bad vision', 'weak sight').

Cary's 'fails' translates 'tutto è vano': this phrase in Dante, joined with 'nulla sapem', excises knowledge and intellectual power rather than pointing to their failure. Similarly, Farinata prophesies that, after the Last Judgement, 'tutta morta | fia nostra conoscenza' (*Inferno*, x. 106–7, Sapegno, i. 118). This Cary translates as 'all | Our knowledge [. . .] shall expire' ('Hell', x. 105–6, Cary, i. 42). His version takes away the imposition of vacuity performed by Dante's word 'fia' (which reverses and completes the Creator's 'fiat'). The shift in emphasis here is paralleled in Virgil's warning from the previous canto:

> 'Volgiti in dietro e tien lo viso chiuso;
>   ché se il Gorgòn si mostra e tu 'l vedessi,
>   nulla sarebbe del tornar mai suso.'
>   (*Inferno*, ix. 55–7, Sapegno, i. 102)

('Turn round and keep your face hidden because if the Gorgon appears and you were to see her there would be no possibility of your ever returning back up to earth.')

Dante and Virgil, outside the City of Dis, are in danger of being forced to stay where they are eternally, or of going back the way they came. In the conflict, Virgil's disdain for the devils is contrasted directly with Dante's need to avoid looking at the forces of evil for fear of succumbing to their power.[64] If overpowered by their evil, he would have no chance of returning upwards (whether by turning back or going through Hell and out the other side). Dante's line 'nulla sarebbe del tornar mai suso' means, literally, 'there would be nothing of returning ever above'.[65] Cary's translation turns this extinction of possibility into a loss:

> 'Turn thyself round, and keep
> Thy count'nance hid; for if the Gorgon dire
> Be shown, and thou shouldst view it, thy return
> Upwards would be for ever lost.'
>   ('Hell', ix. 56–9, Cary, i. 36)

Cary works to avoid paraphrasing the original or excluding anything from it, even its apparent redundancy: his Virgil explains as

---

[64] On this passage's relation to the *Commedia* as a whole, see John Freccero, 'Medusa: The Letter and the Spirit', in *Dante: The Poetics of Conversion*, ed. Rachel Jacoff (Cambridge, Mass., 1984), 119–35.

[65] Cf. Longfellow, 'No more returning upward would there be', *The Divine Comedy*, i. 29.

carefully as Dante's that if the Gorgon is 'shown' and if it is 'viewed' then Dante will be in danger. Cary's lineation, however, labours the point (more than is done by Virgil's repetition within a single line of the original) and his verbs lose Virgil's fear of the meeting because they suggest that Dante is about to be threatened with something on display. Dante is imagined as being at once more passively receptive and more choosy than in the original. The interaction in the *Commedia* between what you see and what you might become involves a greater dependence in the human soul on the objects of its sight and, therefore, teaches a willingness to resist the things you see. Accordingly, the more detached viewpoint Cary introduces envisages the Gorgon simply as an interesting classical allusion. Its role as a symbol of those evil impulses uncontrollable by human reason diminishes because Cary's Dante stops looking at it in the same way.[66]

Two features of Dante's perception come out of these examples: from Farinata's affliction, the reliance of human vision on divine illumination; from Virgil's warning, the susceptibility of the soul to the objects of its sight. These two combine to produce Dante's particular allegorical method and the momentum of his narrative. Narrative movement, symbolic method, and the perspective of Dante's *personaggio* are, in addition, interconnected with a relation to Dante's text that his Romantic readers were distinctively willing to adopt.

When Dante first sees Farinata, Virgil urges him to pay attention:

> Ed el mi disse: 'Volgiti: che fai?
>   Vedi là Farinata che s'è dritto:
>   dalla cintola in su tutto 'l vedrai'.
> Io avea già il mio viso nel suo fitto.
>   (*Inferno*, x. 31–4, Sapegno,
>   i. 111–12)

(And he said to me: 'Turn round: what are you doing? See Farinata there, risen up; you can see all of him from the waist upwards.' I had already fixed my gaze on his)

---

[66] For other examples of Cary's translation differing from the *Inferno* cf. 'Hell', xi. 45–9, xiv. 89–94, xvii. 111–22 with *Inferno*, xi. 42–5, xiv. 94–9, xvii. 115–26 (Cary, i. 45, 60, 74; Sapegno, i. 125, 161, 197). Howard, *The Inferno*, is a helpful additional contrast; see cantos xiv. 89–95 and xvii. 111–24, pp. 82, 103.

Dante's fixity of attention here causes momentary cessation of movement both physically and in the verse. He uses the same term to describe lack of movement more generally, including the soul's inability to leave the confines of the body while alive. In *Purgatorio* xiv Dante meets the Envious whose punishment—their eyelids are sewn together—and whose sin resemble Farinata's. They too overestimated the importance of worldly appearances at the expense of divine realities, resentful of what other people possessed while all they truly desired was to be found in God. Dante is asked for his credentials:

> e disse l'uno: 'O anima che fitta
>   nel corpo ancora inver lo ciel ten vai,
>   per carità ne consola e ne ditta
> onde vieni e chi se''
>   (*Purgatorio*, xiv. 10–13, Sapegno,
>   ii. 151)

(and one said: 'O soul, who, still fixed in the body, art going towards heaven, pity us for charity's sake and tell us where you come from and who you are'.)

Dante's soul is 'pent in the body' as he 'tendest toward the sky' (Cary, ii. 60) in the same way as Satan is frozen solid:

> 'ov'è la ghiaccia? e questi com'è fitto
>   sí sottosopra? e come, in sí poc'ora,
>   da sera a mane ha fatto il sol tragitto?'
>   (*Inferno*, xxxiv. 103–5, Sapegno, i. 379)

('where is the ice? and how is it he there is fixed upside-down like that? and how, in such a short time, has the sun made its passage from evening to morning?')

As he crosses the world's centre of gravity Dante finds Satan below him upside-down. The two poets' escape from Hell produces a sudden change in perspective whose significance dawns on Dante as 'fitto' is replaced by 'fatto'. The sun's movement in the celestial sphere enters as an action rather than a state, a contrast assisted by the different auxiliary verbs, 'ha fatto' as against 'è fitto'. The change in Dante's focus of attention from the state of the immediate surroundings to a movement in heaven produces and implies a sense of liberation consonant with the realization of what he has escaped. His initial fear at the transformation ebbs away as he looks upward and as the lines lose the urgent emphases of 'sí sottosopra' and 'sí poc'ora' in the more rounded description of the sun, 'da sera a mane ha fatto il sol tragitto'. Satan's fixity, opposed to Virgil's and Dante's movement, and to movement in the world beyond, appears the opposite pole of a moral order, standing for powerlessness and constraint within the delineation of a posture or position. In his earlier meeting with Farinata, however, Dante seemed compelled by the man's grandeur and by Virgil's exhortation to fix his attention on him. His ability to do so seemed the natural advantage of a living, as opposed to a damned, soul. Dante's way of attending displays his physical humanity and his temporal life so that the living soul's restriction to the limitations of the body prevents it from taking an overall view. A human life, for Dante, consists in the freedom to see or avoid seeing—a freedom which will be taken away in the afterlife—but in which sight involves a momentary loss of freedom, an interpenetration of minds described in Dante's meeting with Farinata. Simply to view Farinata would not be to see him, and to see him alone would condemn the onlooker to the same sin and damnation. Dante's ascent towards the vision of God requires a series of such encounters, each one of which commits him for that moment, only to be transcended in the gradual achievement of a right spiritual commitment. This quality in Dante is cardinal to Romantic readings of him: these sought to sustain in their experience of the poem an appeal to their own experience; and to preserve in their reading what Coleridge named the 'waking dream'—the condition when a reader is entranced but not 'lulled to sleep amidst the music of nobler thoughts'.

2
Illustrating Dante

'to rouse the fancy and understanding to the fullest stretch
of which they are capable'

Illustrations of the *Commedia* began to appear in English circles
in the late eighteenth century. Sir Joshua Reynolds exhibited his
famous picture of Ugolino in 1773; Henry Fuseli returned from
Rome in 1778 with a collection of drawings based on Inferno; and
in 1793 John Flaxman published the first complete set of illustra-
tions to the *Commedia*.[1] This was not a passing fashion merely:
Fuseli and Reynolds exhibited further paintings with Dantean
subjects in the first decades of the nineteenth century, and in 1824
William Blake was commissioned to illustrate the *Commedia*. He
died in 1827 leaving the task incomplete. In this chapter I want
first to show how the three sets of illustrations (by Fuseli, Flaxman,
and Blake) follow a development in understanding Dante's work
that is similar to the one exhibited by his translators in the period,
and, secondly, to suggest that Blake's work constitutes a further
development which exemplifies a new, and distinctively Romantic,
way of approaching the *Commedia*.

Henry Fuseli, who was variously influenced by Winckelmann's
neoclassicism and German *Sturm und Drang*, creates, in several
respects, a painterly equivalent to Cary. Though the relations
between *Sturm und Drang* and the cult of 'sensibility' are clearly
complicated, they share a tendency to regard the highest good as
a form of sympathy that is both a source of artistic creativity and

---

[1] See Paget Toynbee, 'The Earliest English Illustrators of Dante', *Quarterly
Review*, 211 (1909), 395–417; *Dante in English Art: A Chronological Record of
Representations by English Artists (Painters, Sculptors, Draughtsmen, Engravers)
of subjects from the Works of Dante, or connected with Dante ('c'.1745–1919)*
(Cambridge, Mass., 1921). On Reynolds's picture, see F. A. Yates, 'Transforma-
tions of Dante's Ugolino', *Journal of the Warburg and Courtauld Institutes*, 14
(1951), 94–8.

socially alienating.[2] (Goethe's *Die Leiden des jungen Werther*, for example, can equally well be regarded as a product of *Sturm und Drang* or of 'sensibility'.) In Fuseli, as in Cary, sympathy's encounter with the other produces a highly ambiguous transformation of the self.

The ideal vision, which to Cary's mind was granted Dante by his period, is for Henry Fuseli an aspect of universal genius:

Genius, inspired by invention, rends the veil that separates existence from possibility.[3]

Fuseli's man of genius is identified with the 'idealist' (who is third and highest in his scale, above the 'copyist' and 'imitator'); the idealist 'by the "mind's eye" fixes, personifies, embodies possibility'.[4] To see how things could be, rather than dully what they are, requires an absorption in the subject:

Genius, absorbed by the subject, hastens to the centre; and from that point disseminates[,] to that leads back the rays: talent, full of its own dexterities, begins to point the rays before they have a centre.

True, rather than factitious, art is characterized by this absorption in the subject: 'The being seized by an enormous passion [. . .] is absorbed by the power of the feature that attracts it.' Metamorphoses, furthermore, represent an 'allegory of [the] sympathetic power' that effects this absorption. Yet Fuseli insists that the artist must remain true to himself: 'excursions into the deserts of mythology or allegory' or an academic training are equally fruitless because they separate the artist from his natural character. The sole means to valuable 'expression' in art is the sympathetic power

---

[2] See Robert Rosenblum, *Transformations in Late Eighteenth Century Art* (2nd printing, Princeton, NJ, 1969), 7–17; Hugh Honour, *Neo-Classicism* (Harmondsworth, 1969), 54 ff.; John Mullan, *Sentiment and Sociability: The Language of Feeling in the Eighteenth Century* (Oxford, 1988); Gerhard Sauder, 'Subjectivität und Empfindsamkeit im Roman', in *Sturm und Drang: ein literaturwissenschaftliches Studienbuch*, ed. W. Hinck (Kronberg, 1978), 163–74.

[3] Henry Fuseli, 'Aphorisms, Chiefly Relative to the Fine Arts', in *The Life and Writings of Henry Fuseli, Esq. M.A. R.A.*, ed. John Knowles, 3 vols. (London, 1831), iii. 61–150 (no. 51, p. 79).

[4] The 'Aphorisms' were composed in the last two decades of Fuseli's life and first published posthumously. He may have been influenced by Coleridge's distinction between 'copy' and 'imitation' but more probably drew on earlier discussion; see *BL*, ii. 73 n., and Fuseli's review of Richard Payne Knight, 'Landscape', *Analytical Review*, 19 (May–Aug. 1794), 179: 'neither to "copy" nor to "create" is the proper term for an art, the business of which is to imitate and to invent'.

whose mother is a delicate sensibility: 'How can he paint Beauty who has not throbbed at her charms?'; 'Shakespeare wept, trembled, laughed first at what now sways the public feature; and where he did not, he is stale, outrageous or disgusting'. How, though, can the chameleon poet remain true to himself? If this succession of sympathetic metamorphoses is as complete as Fuseli suggests, can a 'character' in the sympathizer be found?[5]

John Barrell has argued that Fuseli was profoundly self-divided, caught between 'the voice of the stoic guardian of public virtue, the gentleman [. . .] of comprehensive vision' and the 'second voice [. . .] of a man who knows himself to be the victim of history rather than its critic'. According to Barrell, these two poles govern Fuseli's changing taste: his praise of Michelangelo was replaced as he grew older by increasing admiration of Raphael, whose 'art of compromise' had renounced the epic denunciations of *The Last Judgement*. By 'a complex irony', Barrell states, 'the pronouncements of two different voices are often mingled and passed off as harmonious'.[6] From the 'Aphorisms', however, it appears that the presence of both voices is not so much harmonized, by ironic self-awareness, as comprehended by a single, self-contradictory idea, rooted in the paradoxes of 'sensibility'. The afflicted 'victim' is, in a limited sense, unceasingly 'stoic' because the assault of the world confronts an innate character that cannot be changed by sympathy. The sympathetic power is its nature.[7] Fuseli's self-division into victim and stoic is inherent in his notion of sympathy, and it provides one source for the historical model that opposes (as in Schiller) the naïve, epic Michelangelo to the sentimental, intuitively sensitive and delicate, Raphael.[8]

[5] 'Aphorisms', nos. 101, 119, 89, 163, 82, 200, in Knowles, *Henry Fuseli*, iii. 97, 105, 90, 126, 88, 137. On 'expression' see Corollary to no. 126, p. 108.

[6] John Barrell, *The Political Theory of Painting from Reynolds to Hazlitt: 'The Body of the Public'* (New Haven, Conn., and London, 1986), 260, 261–2.

[7] Fuseli is, therefore, nearer to Hazlitt: '[Hazlitt's] belief [. . .] is that there is in all people worth representing a self-identity, a consistency of the self as it is organised by one principle, which is the gift of nature, not of art' (Barrell, *Political Theory*, 332). Cf. Hazlitt, xvi. 8–9.

[8] Friedrich Schiller, 'Über naïve und sentimentalische Dichtung' (1795). Schiller restricts the 'naïve' to the Greeks, since the 'sentimental' characterizes all Christian art, including Michelangelo. Fuseli's historical model develops from Winckelmann's neoclassicism in the same direction, arguing that the naïve is irretrievable, though he relocates the time of its disappearance. Cf. Kathleen Wheeler (ed.), *German Aesthetic and Literary Criticism: The Romantic Ironists and Goethe* (Cambridge, 1984), 2–7.

Fuseli's illustrations, like Cary's translation, are intended to display Dante's sympathetic power, his noble genius absorbed in the horrors he sees.[9] In his illustration to *Inferno* xxiv–xxv (see Plate 1), Virgil's statuesque rigidity, lifted gaze, and his right forefinger—raised in warning while the hand rests comfortingly on Dante's shoulder—all contrast starkly with Dante's violent horror.[10] Dante's left hand, clutching his own right shoulder, and his recoiling posture both draw him back into the figure of Virgil, while his fixed gaze holds him to the damned soul, who is similarly convulsed on the right-hand side of the composition. The figure of Dante repeats postures of horror drawn from the nude youths in the Sistine Chapel; a second figure, again taken from Michelangelo, lies beneath the soul being transformed into a serpent. Sprawling horizontally, the second damned soul replicates *God Dividing Light from Darkness*. The sinners' metamorphoses are seen as traducing God's creative power, and its corollaries in the human arts of painting and writing.

The four figures—Virgil, Dante, and the two sinners—form a diagonal that follows Dante's gaze. He is at once transfixed and held in check, more fully modelled than either of the damned yet drawn back into an area of shadow while the sinners are harshly lit. The division between light and darkness applies in the picture

[9] Fuseli illustrated *Inferno*, v, x, xiii, xxiv–xxv, xxxiii (twice) and *Purgatorio* v (Gert Schiff, *Johann Caspar Füssli: 1741–1825*, 2 vols. (Zürich and Munich, 1973), nos. 419, 421, 423–5, 427, 429). The pictures date from his time in Rome (1770–8). See Nancy L. Pressly, *The Fuseli Circle in Rome: Early Romantic Art of the 1770s* (New Haven, Conn., 1979), 28–47. Fuseli drew several 'Köpfe aus Dantes Inferno' ('Heads from Dante's Inferno') to illustrate John Caspar Lavater, *Essays on Physiognomy* (London, 1792); see Schiff, *Füssli*, nos. 946, 959, 959a. His 1806 painting, *Ugolino und seine Söhne im Hungerturm* (Ugolino and his sons in the Tower of Famine) survives only in an 1809 engraving (Schiff, *Füssli*, no. 1200). His 1818 painting, *Dante entsteckt bei seinem Abstieg in die Hölle in einem Wirbelwind die Schatten von Paolo und Francesca* (As he descends into Hell, Dante discovers the shades of Paolo and Francesca in a whirlwind) is lost; see Schiff, *Füssli*, i. 653.

[10] On Fuseli's relation to Dante see David Irwin, *English Neoclassical Art: Studies in Inspiration and Taste* (London, 1966), 129–38. Virgil's right hand resembles that of the sculptured hand in Fuseli's *Der Künstler, verzwiefelnd vor der Grösse der antiken Trümmer* (The Artist, in Despair at the Grandeur of Ancient Ruins) (1778–80), Schiff, *Füssli*, no. 665. The gigantic foot in that picture reappears in the background of Fuseli's illustration to *Inferno* xxxiii, representing Dante's Titans. Fuseli may have seen Botticelli's similar illustration, but is concerned with Dante's endurance of the modern artist's despair. See Schiff, *Füssli*, i. 98. On hand gestures in the art of the period, see Janet A. Warner, *Blake and the Language of Art* (Kingston, Montreal, and Gloucester, 1984), 47–58.

as the separation between witness and sufferer. Dante appears, then, anguished and curiously secure: he is backing away from these sinners, as if warned by their postures against the dangers of sympathy and, from his security, continuing a receptive, sympathetic gaze.

Fuseli was an admirer of the *Commedia* throughout his life, but objected to Dante's notorious deception of Alberigo in *Inferno* xxxiii (ll. 115–17, 148–50): 'That is bad, you know,' Fuseli remarked, 'faith should be kept, even with a poor devil in Antenora.'[11] His remarkable picture of cantos xxiv–xxv is consistent with that complaint in assuming that Dante can always afford to be sympathetic with 'a poor devil'. Similarly in Fuseli's illustration to *Inferno* xxxiii (see Plate 2), Dante's troubled witness embraces Ugolino in a gesture of hopeless compassion. The genius of his sympathy offers the comfort of its gaze, as Ugolino raises his head and looks up towards him, yet the gaze is itself comfortless. As Gert Schiff remarks of the picture:

In the face of this most extreme punishment, Dante raises his arms in a gesture that conjures up all the suffering perceived. His strangely cracked face seems lifeless [. . .] yet even here Dante is passively afflicted, enduring dumbly the horror of those he sees.[12]

Dante's patient endurance acknowledges the horror as well as the pathos of Ugolino, but his power of acceptance confirms a nobility, an almost angelic compassion, that depends upon and also characterizes the artist's distance. Dante epitomizes the sympathetic witness of suffering: his sympathy is infinite because it continues in parallel with his experience, instead of altering with the self that alters.

Fuseli's pictures, therefore, grasp the intensity of Dante's gaze, his noble endurance of afflictions he does not idealize. They give unqualified praise, however, to that power of endurance. Fuseli was, politically, a disappointed radical, a defender of Rousseau

---

[11] Knowles, *Henry Fuseli*, i. 360; see Sapegno, i. 368–9, 370. Dante promises to break the ice off Alberigo's face so that he can weep again but then refuses to do so. Cary translates without comment: '["]But now put forth | Thy hand, and ope mine eyes." I oped them not. | Ill manners were best courtesy to him' (Cary, i. 149). Henry Boyd makes Dante obedient to Virgil's severity: ' "Far be the task prophane!" the Mantuan cry'd | Mute I obey'd my unrelenting Guide' (Boyd, i. 349).
[12] Schiff, *Füssli*, i. 102 (my translation).

against English conservative opinion and a member of J. Johnson's left-wing circle in the 1790s. He fervently praised *Childe Harold's Pilgrimage* and portrays Dante as a kind of 'Childe Harold': a troubled and responsive sensibility, withstanding the world whose horrors vex him and whose evils cannot be alleviated.[13]

The ideas of Dante that disturb Fuseli's perspective and help create Flaxman's and Blake's are best exemplified by John Taafe. This is because Schelling's and Hazlitt's arguments for the reader's participation in the *Commedia* become the distinctive concern of his earnest and long-winded commentary, *A Comment on the Divine Comedy of Dante Alighieri* (1822), which was read in manuscript by both Byron and Shelley. Taafe sees the difficulties of Dante's teaching and the brevity of his style as making peculiar, extreme demands on us which we should not evade. Like Hazlitt, Taafe defends the inscription on the gate of Hell in canto iii:

> GIUSTIZIA MOSSE IL MIO ALTO FATTORE:
> FECEMI LA DIVINA POTESTATE,
> LA SOMMA SAPIENZA E 'L PRIMO AMORE.
> (*Inferno*, iii. 4–6, Sapegno, i. 30)

(Justice moved my high creator; I was made by divine Power, the highest Wisdom and the original Love.)

Ginguené, the influential French literary historian whom Taafe attacks throughout, had demurred at this: 'mais on ne peut sans répugnance, y voir coopérer explicitement le *premier Amour*. Si l'on en excepte ce seul trait, quelle sublime inscription!'[14] Henry Boyd irons out the problem in his translation by making 'Love' restrain Justice: '*Unbounded pow'r the strong foundations laid,* | *And Love, by wisdom led, the Limits drew*'. Taafe is unwilling to let us have 'quelle sublime inscription' (with the help of some censorship) or to blur the harshness of what Dante says so as to make it more readily acceptable.

benignity [. . .] is conspicuous throughout his work, but perhaps nowhere more strikingly so than here where we are constrained to confess, it is the same principle of immeasurable love, which prepares everlasting felicity

---

[13] See Knowles, *Henry Fuseli*, i. 359 ff.; Henry Fuseli, *Remarks on the Writing and Conduct of J. J. Rousseau* (London, 1767); Eudo C. Mason, *The Mind of Henry Fuseli: Selections from his Writings with an Introductory Study* (London, 1951).

[14] Pierre-Louis Ginguené, *Histoire Littéraire d'Italie*, 9 vols. (Paris, 1811–19), ii. 35.

for the virtuous, that consigns the guilty to hopeless agony. To recall such a truth in such a circumstance is to rouse the fancy and understanding to the fullest stretch of which they are capable; is to take in at one view all that we can imagine of heaven, hell, and God—the remotest extremes and their common centre: and thus instead of lingering on details, we are engaged to collect and concentrate the whole resources of our intellect— joys and sorrows, delights and miseries, pleasure and suffering [. . .] and [. . .] express the entire in a single word, *love*, the love that is illimitable, the love of universal order.[15]

Taafe has the poem impose on and constrain its readers; at this moment pre-eminently it rouses 'the fancy and understanding to the fullest stretch of which they are capable'. One might differ with him about whether the love that Dante means is 'the love of universal order' but still admire his perception that 'lingering on details' in Dante cannot be separated from an effort to understand the whole. His paragraph dwells on this one word, love, in such a way that he does not linger on it but reorients around it the world-view of the poem; the world-view that a reader must stretch to grasp in order to do anything like justice to the work.[16]

Taafe's commentary argues that the imaginative participation which Dante asks of his reader cannot be accommodated by an aesthetic of the sublime. This belief corresponds to his dislike of allegorical readings that abstract meaning from the poetry. For similar reasons, he disapproves of scholarly distractions from the words themselves, while providing a good number himself. Allegory and scholarship, in Taafe's view, equally prevent Dante's readers from wrestling with the 'characteristic simplicity of Dante's text'. Ginguené had found this quality in the Italian wonderfully naïve:

il est toujours simple et vrai; jamais un trait d'esprit ne vient refroidir une expression de sentiment ou un tableau de nature. Il est naïf comme la nature elle-même, et comme les anciens, ses fidèles imitateurs.

---

[15] Boyd i. 109; [John Taafe], *A Comment on the Divine Comedy of Dante Alighieri* (London, 1822), i. 166 [no further volumes were published].

[16] Cf. Boyd's explanation: 'That Love to the general welfare that must induce a moral Governor to enforc [sic] his laws by the sanction of punishments' (Boyd, i. 109). Cf. also John Wesley Thomas, *The Trilogy; or Dante's Three Visions. Translated into English, in the Metre and Triple rhyme of the Original*, 3 vols. (London, 1859–66): 'Dante feels that there cannot be love, wisdom, or power without justice' (p. 26).

Against this patronizing effusion, Taafe argues that directness does not produce unequivocal feelings. Dante's portrayal of Francesca, he says, is 'more than ever expressive of an internal war of feelings, of sorrow, regret, contrition, disdain, satisfaction, and almost delight'. By confronting his reader with such complexity, Dante 'habituates us to weigh the poet's decisions'.[17]

Where Warton and Gray placed Dante outside the Hell he imagines, Taafe considers the *Inferno* as a pilgrimage whose end is in doubt, and he notices the irony of 'LASCIATE OGNI SPERANZA, VOI CH'ENTRATE' (*Inferno*, iii. 9: 'Abandon all hope, you who enter here'):

He can't have meant losing *all* hope because some get out of Limbo, and he has the hope of escaping himself.

He has the hope though not, as Taafe sees it, the certainty, and this doubt is made part of the exercise his reader must endure. The 'verbosity' (as he calls it) of Cary's translation and Leigh Hunt's *The Story of Rimini* makes it impossible to read Dante in this way. Taafe prefers the 'peculiar poignancy; which a literal version best conveys'. Translations are evaluated by how well they preserve the complexity that enforces a troubled engagement with Dante. The reader may even, in Taafe's account, reject him: the language 'habituates us to weigh the poet's decisions, and not hesitate to reverse them, whenever they appear unsatisfactory to ourselves'. This freedom is not the result of disregard; rather it implies a confident exchange between equals which Taafe, often comparing Dante with Rousseau, imagines Dante himself would welcome.

Taafe's work is one of the fruits of Dante's suddenly increased popularity in England after Waterloo.[18] His reading of the *Commedia* is a characteristically liberal one, congruent with the image of Dante offered by left-wing Italian exiles from the Restoration regime. Ugo Foscolo's comparisons of Dante and Petrarch,

[17] Ginguené, *Histoire*, i. 263; Taafe, *A Comment*, 322, 334–5.

[18] Dante's popularity is a European phenomenon: for French taste, see Michael Pitwood, *Dante and the French Romantics* (Geneva, 1985); for Italian taste, see C. P. Brand, 'Dante and the Middle Ages in Neo-Classical and Romantic Criticism', *Modern Language Review*, 81 (1986), 327–36. G. A. Scartazzini, *Dante in Germania* (Milan, 1883) provides a comprehensive index of German developments; see also T. Ostermann, *Dante in Deutschland* (Heidelberg, 1929); Werner P. Friedrich, *Dante's Fame Abroad [. . .]* (Rome, 1950), 359 ff.

for example, accuse the latter poet of succumbing to the injustices his predecessor resisted.[19] Petrarch's inwardness is compared unfavourably with Dante's public spirit and directness:

Dante, like all primitive poets, is the historian of the manners of his age, the prophet of his country, and the painter of his morals; and calls into action all the faculties of our soul to reflect on all the vicissitudes of the world. (Toynbee, ii. 170)[20]

The reflection that Dante prompts is a form of action whereas Petrarch's 'propensities [. . .] by keeping the heart in perpetual disquietude, paralize [sic] intellectual exertions'. Foscolo's preference is partly engendered by self-rebuke: his *Ultime Lettere di Jacopo Ortis* had followed *Die Leiden des jungen Werther* in portraying the paralysis and eventual suicide of one who, like Petrarch, had seen 'every thing through the medium of one predominant passion'.[21] Thomas Campbell's sardonic analysis of the taste for Dante shows, however, that it became authoritative in England after Waterloo. In defending Petrarch, Campbell says that the 'Dantists' (as controversy named them):

allege that Petrarch's amatory poetry, from its platonic and mystic character, was best suited to the age of cloisters, of dreaming voluptuaries, and of men living under tyrannical governments, whose thoughts and feelings were oppressed and disguised. The genius of Dante, on the other hand, they say, appeals to all that is bold and natural in the human breast, and they trace the grand revival of his popularity in our own times to the re-awakened spirit of liberty.[22]

Though Foscolo's is as partial and self-referential an account of Dante as Warton's or Cary's, it values the *Commedia* for rousing our minds. As the forerunner of Italian patriotism, Dante can become for English readers an image of the liberal poet continuing

---

[19] On the influence of Italian exiles, like Foscolo, on English taste, see C. P. Brand, *Italy and the English Romantics: The Italianate Fashion in Early Nineteenth-Century England* (Cambridge 1957), 58, 101.

[20] Quoted from Ugo Foscolo, *Essays on Petarch* (London, 1823), 183–4.

[21] Ibid. 170. Ugo Foscolo's *Ultime Lettere di Jacopo Ortis* was published in Italy in 1802. The first edition published in London appeared in 1811. The first English translation (*The Letters of Ortis to Lorenzo*) appeared in 1814 and reached a second edition in 1818.

[22] Thomas Campbell, 'The Literary Character of Petrarch', *Life and Times of Petrarch: With Notice of of Boccaccio and His Illustrious Contemporaries* (2nd edn., London, 1843), quoted from Beatrice Corrigan (ed.), *Italian Poets and English Critics, 1755–1859: A Collection of Critical Essays* (London, 1969), 150–1.

to work through his art towards the achievement of political ends that have otherwise been disappointed. His writing becomes an exercise for the reader in overcoming despair and, consequently, it begins to demand the reader's pursuit of the experience Dante undergoes.

This estimate of Dante's worth and Taafe's approach to reading him became familiar in the early 1820s and were directly influential on Byron and Shelley.[23] Dante is gradually reconsidered as a protagonist whose entry into a process of self-reform must be emulated by his true reader. Moreover, as much as Foscolo's praise of Dante is the repudiation of a younger self, Shelley and Byron are drawn to Foscolo's image and Taafe's reading by their sense of a life lived through time, and their relinquishing the perfections of 'sensibility'.

Dante's dispute with political orthodoxies is, for these readers, matched by his apparent dissent from Catholic orthodoxy. For Foscolo and other liberals, the spirit of liberty was opposed to 'the age of cloisters' as much as to 'tyrannical governments'. Political and religious opposition went hand in hand, in part because the Tory establishment was routinely but fiercely orthodox. Moreover, Evangelical beliefs (whose influence among the middle classes increased markedly in the period) were frequently employed to justify the harsh treatment of the poor. As Boyd Hilton has demonstrated, the period's *laissez-faire* economics were underpinned by Evangelical theology so that opposition to the first implied opposition to the second.[24]

Evangelical belief reasserted the actual existence of an afterlife of punishment: repentance was necessary, at least among the

[23] See C. P. Brand, 'Dante and the English Poets', in *The Mind of Dante*, ed. U. Limentani (Cambridge, 1965), 164; E. R. Vincent, *Byron, Hobhouse and Foscolo: New Documents in the History of a Collaboration* (Cambridge, 1949); Thomas Moore, *The Life, Letters and Journals of Lord Byron [. . . .]* (London, 1860), 268.

[24] Boyd Hilton, *The Age of Atonement: The Influence of Evangelicalism on Social and Economic Thought 1785–1865* (Oxford, 1988). Clearly some shades of liberal opinion wholeheartedly supported *laissez-faire* economics. The writers under discussion here were closer to the radical end of liberal opinion than to what later became crystallized in Liberal Conservatism, and they considered reform as demanding the amelioration of the condition of the poor. See Bianca Fontana, 'Whigs and Liberals: The *Edinburgh Review* and the "Liberal Movement" in Nineteenth-century Britain', in *Victorian Liberalism: Nineteenth-century Political Thought and Practice*, ed. Richard Bellamy (London and New York, 1990), 42–57.

prosperous, to avoid damnation, while the poor need not be helped in this world since their sufferings here made it less likely that they would suffer eternally. The pressure of such beliefs was felt by all the writers considered later in this study: Coleridge's conversion (from Unitarianism to Anglicanism) committed him to believing in Hell; Byron repeatedly failed to relinquish a suspicion that damnation might be his actual fate after death;[25] Shelley, like Blake, thought damnation to be a real condition of unreality, experienced before death, and the creation of the religion that pretended to condemn unbelievers to the pains it inflicted on itself. In the late eighteenth century, by contrast, Anglicans, Deists, and Freethinkers equally rejected the doctrine of eternal damnation.[26] That consensus became more difficult to sustain as Evangelical views became more influential. The possible truth of Dante's doctrine pressed more forcefully on his readers because the idea of Hell's existence was not any longer being rejected simply as a barbarous error or an instance of priestcraft.[27] For his early-nineteenth-century readers, generally speaking, Dante's Hell ceased to be an acknowledged fiction while, for many, it could not be accepted as an unquestionable truth. The 'liberal' poets, considered in what follows, could not dismiss the doctrine of eternal punishment, and were, in consequence, more disposed than their eighteenth-century predecessors, to participate in Dante's 'fiction'. At the same time, a comparable involvement in Dante's work was encouraged by their (present or past) allegiance to the political position they took Dante to represent.

Translators who either rejected or accepted Dante's doctrine of Hell outright avoided a comparable engagement. Henry Boyd's

---

[25] See Coleridge to Cottle, 27 May 1814, *CL*, iii. 498; Hilton, *Age of Atonement*, 29.

[26] See D. P. Walker, *The Decline of Hell* (London, 1964); Geoffrey Rowell, *Hell and the Victorians: A Study of Nineteenth-century Theological Controversies Concerning Eternal Punishment and the Future Life* (Oxford, 1974); Hilton, *The Age of Atonement*, 270–6.

[27] Cf. Fuseli's poem 'Hölle' (dated after 1803). It includes the familiar rational condemnations of the doctrine as the 'Phantom des Aberglaubens' and 'Unsinn dem Denker, Gespött des Freigeist' ('phantom of superstition', 'nonsense to the philosopher, absurdity to the free-thinker'). Yet 'Von deinem Odem angefacht, blendet uns | Die flamme Dantes' ('fanned by your breath, Dante's flame blinds us'); by contrast, Dante's flame is extinguished in the slumber of Paradise (Johann Heinrich Füssli, *Sämtliche Gedichte*, ed. M. Bircher and K. S. Guthke (Zurich, 1973), 93–4). Fuseli's account of Hell resembles St Paul's version of the cross: 'a stumbling-block to Jews and folly to Gentiles' (1 Cor. 1: 23).

eighteenth-century Anglicanism professes indifference about how one should consider Dante's punishments:

it is not very material whether we suppose the descriptions of their punishments [in *Inferno*] to be allegorical pictures of different species of confirmed depravity in this life, or exhibitions of their allotments in a state of retribution in the world to come.[28]

Consequently the poem can be admired as a morally instructive narrative describing '*The conversion of a sinner by a spiritual guide, displaying in a series of terrible visions the secrets of Divine Justice*'. Dante's portrayals of damnation, Boyd says, arouse and direct our 'sympathy', but that only means they 'interest the passions that enlist on the side of virtue; and appeal to our native notions of right and wrong'. The poem is to be admired for the exceptional variety of its punishments:

Every thing that is terrible in human nature is there brought to view successively; his corporal sufferings are variegated with more imagination, and described with more sublimity than any other poet, not excepting MILTON, who drew some of his most tremendous scenes evidently from DANTE.[29]

Dante's imagination is little more than ingenuity, and 'corporal sufferings' are simply representations of what is 'terrible in human nature'. Boyd disallows the suspicion or fear that these sufferings are real punishments which his reader may have to endure after death. Instead, Dante's torments are allegorical pictures of human nature; reading the *Commedia* implies our viewing the succession of images as they are 'brought to view': we witness them from a still point of vantage. The poem contains, therefore, a succession of tremendous scenes but implies no movement by the reader, who is in consequence left free to admire Dante's improving moral fiction.[30]

[28] 'Preliminary Essay on the Purgatorio of Dante', Boyd, ii. 3.
[29] Boyd, i. 4, 8, 23. He first published the essay in *A Translation of the Inferno [. . .]*, 2 vols. (Dublin, 1785), i. 25–73. The text of this edition is unreliable: see G. F. Cunningham, *The Divine Comedy in English: A Critical Bibliography, 1782–1966*, 2 vols. (Edinburgh, London, and New York, 1965–6), i. 16.
[30] This religious position naturally facilitates the form of sublimity that Burke admired: an impressiveness that never threatened the essential integrity of the observing self. On Boyd, see Tinkler-Villani, *Visions of Dante in English Poetry* (Amsterdam, 1989), 137: 'the contemporary reader enjoyed the pathetic story of Ugolino but objected to the lack of moral stature of Dante's hero. [. . .] [Boyd] highlights the pathetic, and adds the sublimity of darkness, space and loftiness, together with the characteristic sublime imagery'.

At the other extreme lies John Wesley Thomas's translation, *The Trilogy [. . .]*, 3 vols. (London, 1859–66). Thomas writes in the belief that Dante's portrayal of the damned represents an actual state of the afterlife. Curiously, however, his acceptance of the reality of damnation allows both him and his reader to look at it from the outside. Thomas, characteristically, triumphs over the damned, taking up the posture of an angel. In canto ix of *Inferno*, an angel opens the gates of Dis:

> Ahi quanto mi parea pien di disdegno!
> Venne alla porta, e con una verghetta
> l'aperse, che non v'ebbe alcun ritegno.
> 'O cacciati del ciel, gente dispetta,'
> cominciò elli in su l'orribil soglia,
> 'ond'esta oltracotanza in voi s'alletta?'
> (*Inferno*, ix. 88–93, Sapegno, i. 105)

(Ah, how much he seemed to me to be full of indignation! He came to the gateway and with a small staff he opened it, for there was no opposition. 'O outcasts of heaven, despised race,' he began, speaking from the horrifying threshold, 'how is it this opposition dwells in you?')

Thomas translates the passage as follows:

> Ah, me! what noble scorn sat on his brow!
> He reached the gate, which with a slender wand
> He opened, leaving there no hindrance now.
> 'Outcasts of heaven!' he said, as he his stand
> Sublimely took upon that horrid sill,
> 'Whence this presumption? despicable band!'[31]

In the original, the angel is enviably scornful of the damned, since, unlike Dante, he is not fearful of losing his eternal life. Dante's cry ('Ahi quanto mi parea pien di disdegno!') is as much alarmed as admiring: it registers the fear that Dante may be one of the outcasts of Heaven himself. Thomas's line, by contrast, is a moment of head-shaking awe. Wishful thinking (Would that I could be so scornful!) has occluded any personal anxiety. The narrator can admire the sublime posture of the angel instead of feeling compelled to listen to the speech.

Thomas's distance from the action fits with his portrayal of Dante as a proto-Protestant, holding to the true faith amidst

---

[31] Thomas, *The Trilogy*, i. 68 (canto ix. 88–93).

Catholic superstition. We recognize in Dante's religious opinions, he says, 'the ancient Faith, preserved in the midst of ignorance, error, and superstition, to reappear and triumph in the Reformation'.[32] In this account, Dante was left miraculously untouched by the hellish medieval world of ignorance and superstition. His *Inferno* may be read, therefore, as a scathing but unmoved attack on popery.[33] Because the sublimity of the angel approximates to Dante's stand, Thomas makes Dante's condemnation of papal wealth in *Inferno* xix unironic and impersonal: Dante prefaces the speech with an apology, 'I' non so s'i' mi fui qui troppe folle' ('I don't know whether I was too bold here'), which Thomas gives as 'I know not if too rashly I my mind | Expressed'. When he has finished, Dante looks to Virgil for approval and finds it in his look: 'con sí contenta labbia sempre attese | lo suon delle parole vere espresse' ('with such a contented smile he listened throughout to the sound of spoken truth'). Thomas's translation stresses what Dante accepts—the externality of this truth to Dante himself: 'Regarding always with so pleased a look, | The sound of those true words by me expressed'. In the original Dante wants to claim that his attack is justified because truthful, and to sound impetuous so that he does not appear presumptuous. He is embarrassed to find himself haranguing the Pope and even makes fun of his speech—'mentr'io li cantava cotai note' ('while I was singing him this tune'). The self-mockery sees the dangers of losing your temper with the successor to St Peter and so makes Dante turn more urgently to his guide. In Thomas, Dante's only doubt is whether it was politic at this moment to express what he had always thought; he never entertains doubt as to the rightness of his judgement, partly because he sees himself as the mouthpiece only of 'true words' that have a source outside himself. It is a dose of

[32] Ibid. i, pp. x, xlvii. Thomas has clearly been influenced in this by Gabriele Rossetti, *Disquisitions on the Antipapal Spirit which produced the Reformation*, trans. Miss Caroline Ward (London, 1834). The work was first published in Italian in 1832; Rossetti had outlined similar opinions in his edition *La Divina Commedia con comento analitico [. . .]* (London, 1826–7). See Thomas, *The Trilogy*, p. xli; Italian exiles like Rossetti represented Dante as a defender of liberty. Thomas reveals how close this role lay to the patriotic Englishman's self-image.

[33] On concepts of damnation in the period, see Michael Wheeler, *Death and the Future Life in Victorian Literature and Theology* (Cambridge, 1990); and the Roman Catholic tract, *Hell Opened to Christians; or, Considerations on the Infernal Pains, for Every Day in the Week, Illustrated by Plates Emblematic of the Infernal Agonies* (London, 1807).

'scriptural truth' he administers with cool disdain: 'And while into his ears these notes I pour'.[34]

Thomas's acceptance that Hell is real engenders, therefore, as comparable a distancing of 'danger and pain' as Boyd's assumption of Hell's non-existence.[35] Both translators differently admire the 'sublimity' of the *Commedia*—the quality in it that the writers and illustrators, discussed in what follows, reconsider when they acknowledge the 'press[ing] too nearly' of Dante's Hell. The unheroic and disturbing involvement of Dante in his narrative becomes the focus of liberal attention because it makes the poem an act of opposition to unexamined faith in either religious orthodoxy or the political establishment.[36] In other words, the ways of reading him alter as the relation between doctrine and poetry is pressured by, on the one hand, Romantic convictions about the creative mind and, on the other, an Evangelical conviction that essential truths have already been received and can only be accepted. The series of illustrations by William Blake shows the distinctive nature of this Romantic reading because it implicitly accuses Dante of taking up in his poem the position of a recording angel. The

[34] *Inferno*, xix. 88, 122–3, 118, Sapegno, i. 216, 219; Thomas, *The Trilogy*, i. 140. Cf. *Hamlet*, III. ii. 254 (stage direction): '*Powres the poyson in his eares*'. In Nathaniel Howard's translation, moralized disregard for the suffering of the damned becomes a Gothic delight in agonies that cannot be believed. See Howard, *The Inferno*, 5 (canto i. 97–9): 'Now follow me, thy friend and guide; thy steps | Darkling, shall sound th'eternal realms below. | Harsh in thy ears the yellings of despair | Shall ring, grating; meantime, from penal flames | Spirits shall shrieking rise, and vainly ask, | In second death, a respite from their pains [. . .]'. Cf. *Inferno*, i. 113–20, Sapegno, i. 14–15.

[35] Cf. Robert Pollok's epic of the afterlife, *The Course of Time: A Poem, in Ten Books*, 2 vols. [bound together] (Edinburgh and London, 1827), 21–2: 'Where'er the eye could light, these words you read, | "Who comes this way—behold, and fear to sin!" | Amazed I stood; and thought such imagery | Foretokened within, a dangerous abode. | But yet to see the worst a wish arose: | For virtue [. . .] all invulnerable fears no hurt. [. . .] and, poised on steady wing, | I hovering gazed.'

[36] Their approach is made more distinctive by contrast with E. H. Plumptre's Victorian liberalism. In his *The Commedia and Canzoniere of Dante Alighieri*, 2 vols. (London, 1886–7), Hell is not a dubious doctrine but the experience of doubt. Virgil 'removes the poet's doubt' in canto iii; in canto ix, 'The higher human wisdom represented by Virgil protects Dante [. . .] by hindering him from looking into the perilous depth of doubt' (Plumptre, *Commedia*, i. 13, 45). The angel in canto ix is full of 'scorn divine', but Dante's 'e sol di quell'angoscia parea lasso' (*Inferno*, ix. 84, Sapegno, i. 105: 'and he seemed wearied only by this effort [to clear the smoke from his eyes]'), becomes 'And with that anguish seemed his strength half-gone' (Plumptre, *Commedia*, i. 46). See Thomas, *The Trilogy*, i. 68, 'That labour seemed the sole fatigue he knew'. I discuss below Schlegel's treatment of this incident.

detachment that Thomas later ascribed to Dante, Blake condemned as the 'Cunning & Morality [which] are not Poetry but Philosophy'.[37] Blake's illustrations oppose Dante's theology by going through the worlds of the afterlife more susceptibly than, according to him, Dante did himself. He claims to improve on the *Commedia* by remaining vulnerable to its visions while being convinced that he is free to differ. Though later poets, with the probable exception of Shelley, had less clearly defined objections to orthodox theology, their readings of Dante parallel Blake's illustrations in their linking of participation and dispute.

Blake was a personal friend of Fuseli and of John Flaxman, both of whom may have helped him to understand Dante's original text. Flaxman's portrayal of the serpents in *Inferno* xxv is echoed in Blake's illustration of the canto, but this and other similarities only reveal how profoundly Blake's portrayal of the *Commedia* and his understanding of the artist's role depart from those of Flaxman and Fuseli.[38] Flaxman's outline illustrations, employing and harmonizing classical motifs, were especially popular in Germany and France: Goethe and A. W. Schlegel wrote admiring articles; David's paintings are the first of many examples in the nineteenth century where Flaxman's engravings provide the vocabulary of posture.[39] Their (for the period) revolutionary disruption of academic composition and their striking clarity made the illustrations peculiarly attractive and available. They could be adopted and transformed because Flaxman's conscious naïvety

[37] Blake's annotation to Henry Boyd, *The Inferno of Dante [. . .]* (London, 1785), 46.

[38] See Albert S. Roe, *Blake's Illustrations to the Divine Comedy* (Princeton NJ, 1953), 31; and see Anthony Blunt, *The Art of William Blake* (London, 1959), 40 (where he points out the similarity between Flaxman's and Blake's portrayals of *Inferno* xxiii), and 90 (on their illustrations of *Inferno* xxxi: Flaxman's is a 'tidy neoclassical version'; Blake 'uses every possible means to bring out the colossal size of the giant'). Blake also engraved Fuseli's painting, *Kopf eines Verdammten aus Dantes Inferno* (Schiff, *Füssli*, no. 946).

[39] See Sarah Symmons, 'French Copies after Flaxman's Outlines', *Burlington Magazine*, 115 (1973), 591–9. See J. W. Goethe, 'Über die Flaxmanischen Werke', *Propyläen* (1799) (J. W. Goethe, *Sämtliche Werke nach Epochen seines Schaffens*, ed. Karl Richter, H. G. Göpfert, N. Miller, G. Sander, in progress (Munich, 1985–), VI. ii. 144–5); A. W. Schlegel, 'Ueber Zeichnungen zur Gedichten und J. Flaxman's Umrisse', *Athanaeum*, 2 [1799], 193–246. Goethe praises Flaxman's 'Gabe sich in den unschuldigen Sinn der ältern Italiänischen Schule zu versetzen, ein Gefühl von Einfalt und Natürlichkeit' ('[his] gift for transposing himself into the innocent spirit of the Early Italian School, a feeling of simplicity and naturalness', Goethe, *Sämtliche Werke*, VI. ii. 144).

liberated the ambitions of later artists. At the same time, Flaxman's provision of a comprehensive anthology of antique forms fulfilled the characteristic neoclassical desire for freedom of invention within a regulated and, especially, a recognizable vocabulary. In his set text, artists like David found a common point of reference from which development was easy.

Schlegel's admiration similarly derives from Flaxman's combination of universality with a reader's freedom. As Sarah Symmons points out:

these linear designs [. . .] are in themselves the sort of expressive hieroglyphs which parallel the imaginary symbols used by both poet and artist.[40]

Schlegel was, in the 1790s at least, very close in his thinking to Schelling, whose description of Dante's world as self-contained and infinite attracts (and is attracted to) the portrayal Flaxman gives. In Flaxman's pictures Dante himself disappears almost entirely, while their simplicity gives ample room to the imaginative activity of his viewer.[41] Dante is not so much followed as displaced; the implicit drama of the exchange between his judgements and his reader's vanishes as the reader is perfectly identified with Dante's *personaggio*. Schlegel's translation of the *Commedia* (incomplete but ranging throughout the work) was begun at the same time as Flaxman's illustrations appeared and relishes the comprehensive and tacit freedom to appropriate which is implicit in Flaxman's technique.[42]

Schlegel remarks of *Inferno* iii, where Virgil briefly describes the structure of Hell:

Der allgemeine Plan hat nur seinem Verstande vorgeschwebt; er verliert ihn aus den Augen bei jeder einzelnen Scene [*sic*], die er dagegen mit seiner

---

[40] Sarah Symmons, 'John Flaxman and Francisco Goya: Infernos Transcribed', *Burlington Magazine*, 113 (1971), 511.

[41] Taafe also praised Flaxman's pictures (see *Comment*, p. xxxi). The unacknowledged tension in his account (between the demands Dante makes on his readers and the unqualified freedom to differ from him which they also enjoy) allows Taafe to praise illustrations that depart radically from one of the impulses behind his work.

[42] Schlegel translated passages from fourteen cantos of *Inferno*, from eight of *Purgatorio* (concentrating on the Earthly Paradise), and from nine of *Paradiso*, including canto ii, which Schelling translated as well. See A. W. Schlegel, *Sämtliche Werke*, ed. Eduard Böcking, 12 vols. (Leipzig, 1846–7), iii, *Poetische Uebersetzungen und Nachbildungen [. . .]: Erster Theil*, 199–349; and *Schellings Werke* iv. *Ergänzung Band*, 526–30. Schlegel's translations first appeared in 1791–7.

ganzen Einbildungskraft festhält und ergründet. Vertraut mit der Welt seiner Visionen wird er in seinem kargen Beschreibungen ihres Innern oft unverständlich, wie man bei der Schilderung einer Gebäudes, das man selbst bewohnt, leicht in Gefahr ist, etwas für den fremden Zuhörer Notwendiges auszulaßen.

(He has only a dim recollection of the general plan; this he loses sight of during the separate scenes, each of which, by contrast, he grasps and probes with all his imaginative power. Intimate with the world of his visions, he is often incomprehensible in his terse descriptions of its interior, as in the depiction of the building where you live there is often the risk of leaving out something that your listener, unfamiliar with the place, absolutely needs to know.)[43]

Dante's obscurities are understandable and unimportant: they reveal an intimacy with the place that his reader is drawn into. Lack of comprehension places the reader closer to what is important in the *Commedia*: the lively portrayals of character that, in Schlegel's view, are actually in conflict with the thought that created the structure.[44] The order of the whole, like its allegory and theology, receives less of Dante's imaginative attention and need not trouble his modern reader.[45]

Schlegel is, consequently, happier with Dante's uncertainty than Dante is himself:

> Umnachtet war es, tief und neblicht, so
> Daß, wie mein Blick auch durchzubohren strebte
> Doch unerkennbar alles mir entfloh.[46]

---

[43] Schlegel, 'Ueber Zeichnungen [. . .]', *Athanaeum*, 2, 238–9.

[44] See also Schlegel, *Sämtliche Werke*, iii. 244: 'denn nur in dem absoluten sittlichen Unwerth eines Menschen kann seine Verdammniß bestehen [. . . .] Allein aus eben dieser Inkonsequenz entspringt der ganze Reichtum des Gedichts an wahr und bestimmt gezeichneten Charakteren; so daß es scheint, als hätte sich hier der Denker gutwillig von dem Dichter einen Streich spielen lassen' ('for only in the absolute moral worthlessness of a man can his damnation consist [. . . .] From just this inconsistency alone arises the entire richness of the poem in true and distinctly drawn characters; so that it seems as if here the philosopher has willingly allowed himself to be tricked by the poet').

[45] Schlegel comments on *Inferno*, ix. 61–3, where Dante warns his reader of a difficult allegory, that 'In der That sind alle Bemühungen der Ausleger über diese Stelle sehr unbefriedigend.' ('In fact, all the efforts to explicate this passage are very unsatisfactory.') But 'Durch die Unmöglichkeit, die versteckte Bedeutung zu entziffern, wird die äußere Darstellung wieder in ihre Recht eingesetzt.' ('Through the impossibility of deciphering the hidden meaning, the external appearance is restored to its rightful position.'); ibid. 261.

[46] Ibid. 242. Cf. Schlegel's translation of *Inferno*, ix. 10–15, p. 257. Schlegel's translations use a modified *terza rima*, rhyming axa bxb cxc, the central line lacking

These lines translate Dante's in *Inferno* iv:

> Oscura e profonda era e nebulosa
> tanto che, per ficcar lo viso a fondo,
> io non vi discernea alcuna cosa.
> (ll. 10–12, Sapegno, i. 41–2)

(It was so dark, deep, and foggy that, straining my eyes to penetrate its depths, I did not discern anything there.)

Schlegel's 'wie [. . .] Doch' construction gives an impression of continuing exploration: 'as my gaze tried to penetrate [the obscurity], still everything, unrecognizable, escaped me'. His last line emphasizes this vanishing quality more than the absence of discernible objects. In Dante, Hell's lack of distinction proves its falsity where, in Schlegel, it gives the opportunity for further exploration. Dante's firmness resists the alarm that such obscurity threatens to arouse, while Schlegel remains contentedly looking over the abyss.

As one would expect from this, Dante's progress through Hell seems inevitable to Schlegel and has on occasion the jauntiness of an excursion. The angel in *Inferno* ix opens the gates of Dis and then departs:

> Dann wandt' er sich, ohn' uns ein Wort zu sagen,
> Zum Sumpf zurück, und war so anzusehn
> Wie einer, welchen andre Sorgen nagen
> Als um die Menschen, welche vor ihm stehn.
> Und wir, nun sicher nach der heil'gen Rede,
> Erhuben uns, um in die Stadt zu gehn.
> (ll. 100–5, Schlegel, iii. 260)

(Then he turned, without saying a word to us, back towards the marsh, and he appeared like one who is worried by other concerns and not about the men who stand in front of him. And we, now secure after the holy speech, started up to go into the city.)[47]

a rhyme. This preserves the triplet structure but abandons the implications of judgement that arise from its continual interconnections. This is a large topic in Dante criticism; see, for instance, John Freccero, 'The Significance of *Terza Rima*', *Dante: The Poetics of Conversion*, 258–71.

[47] Schlegel, *Sämtliche Werke*, iii. 260, translating *Inferno*, ix. 100–5, Sapegno, i. 106. Schlegel remarks on the sublimity of the angel: 'Es giebt eine erhabene Kürze im Thun wie im Reden. Es ist wahrhaft groß, nach einer erstaunlichen That sich nicht anders fühlen, als wenn man ein gewöhnliches Tagesgeschäft verrichtet hätte.' ('There is a sublime brevity in action and in word. It is truly great, after an astonishing feat to feel no different than if one had finished everyday business.'); Schlegel, *Sämtliche Werke*, iii. 265.

It is striking how this excellent translation loses Dante's tone in the last two lines: 'e noi movemmo i piedi inver la terra, | sicuri appresso le parole sante' ('and we moved our feet across the ground, in security after the holy words'). Schlegel moves Dante's last line inside the main clause with the result that this prerequisite is more easily passed over. Schlegel's angel has restored their confidence where Dante's exorcized the demons in their path.

Schlegel's translation loses the centrality of Dante's and Virgil's regained security because he continually enjoys the freedom of imagination. The *Commedia* generously provides the opportunity for Schlegel to meet startling characters vividly drawn. Its clarity, like Flaxman's drawings, sets off a reading which it never challenges or endangers, so that Schlegel's reader may ignore the argument by attending more closely to the characters. Indeed, this selective attention loosens the *Commedia* from the grip of doctrine. The 'dexterous manœuvre' whereby Shakespeare, in Schlegel's view of him, 'allows us an occasional glance at the less brilliant reverse' of a play's apparent argument, is achieved, in his version of Dante, by the characters in Hell: their virtues and energy contradict their state of damnation. In the same way that Shakespeare's ironic skill demonstrates that he 'is not tied down to the represented subject, but soars freely above it', Schlegel's Dante is a Romantic ironist whom his translator emulates.[48] If, as Schlegel and Schelling suggest, Hell is truly a world of its own, in which classical imagery is set in a modern order, then this ironic relation to the vision is appropriate for modern reader and Dante alike.

Though he hated the doctrine of eternal punishment, Blake (by contrast with Schlegel) gave credence to the idea of Hell. It was, in his view, the creation and the preserver of despotism, and afflicted the living with the punishments supposedly reserved for the damned. As a result, Blake would not transform the *Commedia* into an experience confined to the world of art. His illustrations make this objection to orthodox accounts of Hell explicit, by repeatedly contrasting self-righteousness (which engenders Hell) with the transforming force of love.

Blake's illustration to canto ix (no. 19) reveals this.[49] The angel

---

[48] A. W. Schlegel, 'On Dramatic Art and Literature' quoted from Wheeler, *German Aesthetic and Literary Criticism*, 215.

[49] The numbering is from Alexander Gilchrist, *Life of William Blake*, 2 vols. (London, 1880). The second volume contains W. M. Rossetti's descriptive catalogue of Blake's works.

crossing the marshy river Styx appears on the left, with the gate of Dis opposite. The angel can be made out within a vast wave rising from the marsh, looping round on itself at the shoreline, and shooting upwards to the top of the picture where, sketchily, it begins a second loop. This composition repeats Blake's illustration to *Inferno* v (nos. 10 and 103, see Plates 3 and 4) where the lustful are pulled by a whirlwind, first towards Dante and Virgil and then away again through a loop, to disappear through the top left-hand corner. In both pictures, a figure within the whirling motion has crashed against the ground, as if crucified, upside-down, while other figures rush past out of the picture and into the light. The motif occurs again in Blake's illustration to *Purgatorio* v and vi (entitled *The Souls of Those Who Only Repented at the Point of Death*, no. 75), where Dante and Virgil are found on a ledge of the mountain: one portrayed with arms raised joyfully and looking upward; the other turned to greet the souls who are rising to the ledge like mermaids. The souls are in a stream that begins in the bottom right, beyond Dante and Virgil, and runs above them, round the perimeter of the composition, before gathering at their feet. According to the *Commedia*, these 'late-repentant' souls cannot ascend the mountain until they have waited in Ante-Purgatory for a given length of time (which varies according to how many souls on earth intercede for them). Blake's illustration includes their delay (by contrasting it with Virgil's and Dante's continuing eager climb), and it suggests the souls asking for their prayers. The composition, however, creates harmony between delay and ascent: both are formed into a motif of movement upwards, as if (and this is what Dante himself declares) the delays forced upon the late-repentant are a necessary part of their eventual climb.

There is less sense of harmony in Blake's illustration to *Inferno* v. '[T]he effect of motion is intensified', as Anthony Blunt points out:

by the contrast with the static group on the right: the standing figure of Virgil, the fainting Dante prostrate at his feet, and the vision of the lovers at their first meeting, shown in a sun over the two poets. (Blunt, *Art of Blake*, 90)

Dante, however, lies beneath a flame that climbs between sun and whirlwind as if it rose out of him, like a dream. The flame, containing Paolo and Francesca (he looking back as he flies on;

she seeming to withdraw), peters out beyond Paolo, failing to repeat the escape achieved by the lovers further to the left. One of these, high up in the whirlwind, looks across towards the circle of light where Paolo and Francesca kiss, establishing a connection between the two conditions of love that the composition confirms. The right-to-left diagonal (of flame and whirlwind) is balanced by the left-to-right diagonal leading into the distant circle of light. Dante's stasis places him on a level with the crucified figure, and between the apparently complementary alternatives of upward escape and perfect seclusion.

Albert Roe argues that Blake deliberately opposes the anti-clockwise motion of the purgatorial spirits in no. 75 to the clock-wise movement in nos. 10, 19, and 103; the two directions are meant to reproduce, according to Roe, the ethical and mythical contraries of Blake's other writing. In fact, the 'late-repentant' are delayed on the other side of the world and, as Dante observes with some bafflement, nearly everything in *Purgatorio* goes round the wrong way. Roe's reading both allegorizes Blake's pictures—making them conform rigidly to the esoteric doctrine of the prophetic books—and oversimplifies them, ignoring both their fidelity to Dante's writing and their dissent from it.[50] Blake's illustration argues, in part, that it is Dante's judgement of Paolo and Francesca which prevents their love from completing its appointed task of liberating the soul. Instead of serenely inhabiting the heaven of love, or moving through love towards heaven, Paolo and Francesca are constrained by the belief that adultery is sinful. The flame that contains them curves as seductively as Francesca, whose alluring coyness draws Paolo back towards the earthly realm when he ought to be leading her towards the spiritual. All of this (Blake argues) is Dante's particular creation, since the image of it rises from his body; it suggests the destructively oppressive consequences of moral condemnation. On the other hand, the picture's central flame of unfulfilled love joins the circle and the whirlwind,

---

[50] Roe bases his argument for contrary motion on Blake's *Jerusalem*, pl. 77, where Jesus confronts 'the wheel of religion': 'Jesus died because he strove | Against the current of this wheel' (ll. 58, 61–2, Stevenson, 802; see Roe, *Blake's Illustrations*, 144). David Fuller points out well the wrong-headedness of Roe's approach: he gives 'the intellect something it can readily get hold of, a code which is a mechanically applicable key to significance once one has got up its intricate language'; this claims 'understanding where there is only a thin and intellectualized kind of knowing' ('Blake and Dante', *Art History*, xi (1988), 351, 353).

enabling the eye to move back and forth between the two. Dante's 'religious' view may destroy love, but it may also represent a necessary intermediate step between its two perfect forms. Blake tries, therefore, to show that Dante's judgement is false without condemning it. To judge Dante would be to repeat his mistake since, for Blake, '[true] Poetry is to excuse Vice & show its reason & necessary purgation'.[51]

The necessity of the central error in this illustration is confirmed by the ambiguous status of the lovers in the sun. Their serenity seems perfect and yet confined. Albert Roe points out that to Blake:

the concept of a globe implies bonds and indicates, therefore, deficiency of vision on the part of him who beholds it. In eternity everything must have infinite extension and hence no limits.[52]

Roe seems justified in taking this element of Blake's illustrations to be continuous with his other work. In the prophetic books Blake frequently opposes 'wheels' (Newtonian mechanism) with 'vortices'. The ideal 'wheel within wheel' of Eden creates a vortex and so offers access to eternity, while the 'wheel without wheel' is empty callousness. In *Milton*, it is Beulah, rather than Eden, that Blake represents as an encircled place of safety and rest:

> Beulah is evermore created around Eternity, appearing
> To the inhabitants of Eden around them on all sides.
> But Beulah to its inhabitants appears, within each district,
> As the beloved infant in his mother's bosom, round encircled
> With arms of love & pity & sweet compassion. But to
> The sons of Eden the moony habitations of Beulah
> Are from great Eternity a mild and pleasant rest.
>
> (*Milton*, pl. 30, ll. 8–14, Stevenson, 546)

Women and children may remain there while men must pass through (ibid., pl. 31, ll. 4–5, p. 546). Without onward movement, Beulah's safety will become imprisoning and self-righteous, the 'secluded place of rest | And a peculiar tabernacle' that Los perceives Jerusalem as having entered (*Jerusalem, the Emanation of the Giant Albion*, pl. 60, ll. 32–3, Stevenson, 758).

---

[51] Blake's annotation to Henry Boyd, *The Inferno of Dante [. . .]* (London, 1795), 46.
[52] Roe, *Blake's Illustrations*, 70.

However, while circles are certainly dangerous, the spirals of love can equally well prove destructive: misplaced, disordered passion will become serpentine. In *The Four Valas*, Orc:

> began to organize a serpent body,
> Despising Urizen's light & turning it into flaming fire,
> Receiving as a poisoned cup receives the heavenly wine,
> And turning affection into fury & thought into abstraction,
> A self-consuming dark devourer, rising into the heavens.
> ('Night the Seventh', ll. 152–6, Stevenson, 378–9)[53]

The serpentine can be rendered as the labyrinthine:

> Hence arose from Bath
> Soft deluding odours, in spiral volutions intricately winding
> Over Albion's mountains, a feminine indefinite cruel delusion.
> (*Jerusalem*, pl. 65, ll. 65–7, Stevenson, 766)

There are, therefore, true and false wheels, those of Eden and Newton, in which Blake opposes imagination and mechanism, love and callousness. He also includes, however, false versions of the true, Edenic condition. These are forms of perverted love: the serpentine passion of Orc or Vala, and the passionless love of Beulah, if by remaining there you take it for Eden.[54]

In his illustrations to *Paradiso*, Blake suggests that Dante is reaching the true form of the wheel, where the opposition of circles is overcome and made harmonious by the intervention of divine love. The distinctions present in his portrayal of Paolo and Francesca form the narrative which he discovers in the *Commedia*. This narrative shares some common ground with the religious views Blake articulated in his own prophecies and employs some of Blake's private imagery. He is, none the less (and here I differ from Roe) seeking to understand the poem by discovering his disagreements with it. In plate no. 93, *Beatrice and Dante in Gemini, amid the spheres of Flame*, he and Beatrice are found in the ellipse formed by two intersecting circles. Plate no. 94 shows Dante and Beatrice meeting a rather insidious-looking Peter

---

[53] See Milton Klonsky, *Blake's Dante: The Complete Illustrations to the* Divine Comedy (London, 1980), 370.

[54] The enclosed circles of Blake's illustrations suggest the relief and ambiguity of Beulah, by contrast with the vortices of passion which, although more dangerous, are necessary for entry into the divine vision. Blake also suggests Newtonian wheels in no. 29, illustrating *Inferno,* xvi.

(representative of the established Church); no. 95 shows Peter versus James in dispute, in a composition reminiscent of the devils battling in Hell (nos. 42 and 15);[55] no. 96 then shows this pair joined by St John. He swoops down between the two other saints and commands Dante's and Beatrice's complete attention. Peter and James are silenced, even abashed; Dante and Beatrice are held by John's love within a triangular shape instead of being excluded by opposing forces. Blake's argument in this series seems to be that Dante's and Beatrice's love for each other is true religion, opposed to the tyranny and dogmatism of the Church. St John (the disciple whom Jesus loved, and who catechizes Dante on love in *Paradiso* xxvi) represents and practises what is true in Christianity.[56]

The repetition of whirling spirals, in *Purgatory* and in the *Circle of the Lustful* in Hell, is consistent with the praise of love in Blake's illustrations to *Inferno* ii and *Paradiso* xxvi.[57] Beatrice, when she visits Hell, and the angel of *Inferno* ix, bring with them a force of love that does not emanate from God the Father, the angry God that created Dante's *Inferno*. The passionate movement of love, in Beatrice and the angel, overturns the circular hierarchies of Heaven and Hell. It creates a vortex instead of a sphere and, in addition, condemns Dante's posture, which is either rigidly upright or horizontal. In *Inferno* v Dante perceives Paolo and Francesca within a sacrosanct circumference of love. This may be an intuition of what love finally achieves, but its passion must break all bounds in order to create an intersecting harmony between persons—a form of relation that equally overcomes rigid opposition and

---

[55] No. 42 is engraved as no. 105.

[56] The pattern of this sequence repeats pl. 3, *The Mission of Virgil*, where Beatrice's compassion for Dante is contrasted with 'the angry God' whom Blake places at the top of the picture. Beatrice is portrayed on the left-hand side within a circle and weaving like Penelope. The drawing of Beatrice, assuming it is her, is very faint. See also *Jerusalem*, pl. 67, l. 4: 'for every female is a golden loom' (Stevenson, 777).

[57] Contrast no. 74, *Dante and Virgil ascending the Mountain of Purgatory* with no. 86, illustrating *Purgatorio* xxvii, *Dante and Statius sleeping, Virgil watching*. The ascent has an implicit spiral motion, whereas Dante's dream of Rachel and Leah (in no. 86) is portrayed as two figures within a circle that floats above Virgil's head. In the *Commedia* Dante has the dream and Virgil makes no reference to it. Dante's previous dreams (*Purgatorio* ix and xix) were interpreted by Virgil, but in *Purgatorio* xxvii Dante's dream foreshadows his surpassing of Virgil's wisdom. Probably the title, which is not Blake's, is a mistake. For Roe's reading of no. 86, see Roe, *Blake's Illustrations*, 161.

splendid isolation. Only in Heaven (as Blake suggests in his picture of St John) has Dante approached the kind of perception and the kind of love that is true religion.[58]

Blake's Hell can be read, therefore, as an analysis of the false perception that creates the doctrine of punishment. In no. 16 (*Goddess of Fortune*, omitted by Gilchrist in his list of illustrations), Blake represents canto vii of the *Inferno*, where the Miserly and the Prodigal are punished by having to roll heavy stones. Dante says that when these stones crash into each other the souls cry out '"Perché tieni?" e "Perché burli?"' (*Inferno*, vii. 30, Sapegno, i. 79: '"Why hoard?" and "Why spend?"'). They then return the way they came to clash again on the other side of the circle. Blake sketches in the punishment but names the stones 'Celestial Globe' and 'Terrestrial Globe'. He then names the Goddess Fortune 'the Devils Servant' (who dwells in 'The Hole of a Shithouse'). In Dante's canto, Virgil explains that people blame Fortune quite unfairly for their disappointments. God in fact, Virgil says, 'ordinò general ministra e duce | che permutasse a tempo li ben vani | di gente in gente' (ibid. 78–80 Sapegno, i. 83: 'ordained her [as] general minister and guide, who should shift in due time empty wealth from one race to another'). These punishments are created by Dante, following the evil doctrines of orthodoxy, because, in Blake's view, Dante sees the 'Celestial' and 'Terrestrial' globes as opposite and irreconcilable. That division derives from his acceptance of Fortune which is a corollary of his making 'for Tyrannical Purposes [. . .] This World the Foundation of all, & the Goddess Nature Mistress; Nature is his Inspirer & not the Holy Ghost' (Blake's inscription to no. 7). To claim Fortune as an inscrutable agent of God is, for Blake, to submit to the world and its judgement and so to obscure the coincidence of the terrestrial and the celestial. That submission is, furthermore, to subordinate imagination to reason, revelation to the institutions of the world.

Blake's half-dozen illustrations to *Inferno* xxiv–xxv, where the condemned thieves are turned into serpents and back into thieves again, make this attack on Dante's theology (and its resultant politics) imply a condemnation of Dante's attention. The metamorphoses of *Inferno* xxiv–xxv offer, in Blake's view, a perverse account of the transformation through love that true Christianity

---

[58] See Fuller, 'Blake and Dante', 362; Klonsky, *Blake's Dante*, 361.

demands. But the perversity in this derives from Dante's perception, not from the wickedness of the thieves themselves. In plate no. 51, engraved as no. 106 (see Plate 5), Dante averts his gaze, while the damned souls are both more frightened by the punishment and more sympathetic. All the damned stand on the same level and the bodies of those watching twist round towards the victim. Dante looks obliquely upwards, wistfully and with a tragic consciousness that disregards the sufferer. Virgil, in profile, gazes unperturbed. Similarly in no. 53 (engraved as no. 107), Dante reveals shock and almost prudish horror by contrast with one sinner's agony and the other's compassion and endurance. Blake's pictures imply that Dante is at fault for accepting the judgement of God the Father on these 'sinners', a judgement that Vanni Fucci defies and Capaneo (one of the Blasphemers, to whom Blake gives his grandest portrait, no. 27) impassively resists.[59] Blake does not include Brunetto Latini in his illustrations, nor Ulysses' account of his life (indeed the dramatic monologues of the *Commedia* are barely illustrated).[60] These and similar incidents in the poem, where Dante finds himself in conflict with the judgements of God, are replaced by the sinners who condemn divine punishment and, by implication, condemn the false imagination of the poet who has sought to vindicate the tyranny of God the Father.

Blake's dispute with Dante's judgemental attention (in both its particular condemnations and its mode of condemnation) is extended in his use of human figures caught in the rocks of Hell. These appear in no. 109, illustrating *Inferno* xxxii (where the poem's description of sinners caught in ice might have suggested Blake's figures), and in nos. 34 and 108, illustrating *Inferno* xviii and xxix–xxx (where Dante gives no pretext for Blake's invention). In nos. 34 and 108 (*The Devils under the Bridge* and *The Pit of Disease*; see Plate 6), the bridges that cross the ditches of Dante's Malebolge are formed of human flesh; this vantage-point for surveying the damned can be gained only by treading on humanity. Moreover, Dante and Virgil, who are standing on one of

---

[59] No. 49, *Fucci 'making the Figs' against God*, shows a snake twisting upwards around Fucci's left arm, following the line of his defiant gesture, as if this resistance to divine judgement is a version of love. See Blake's annotations to Boyd, *The Inferno of Dante [. . .]*, 46: 'The grandest Poetry is immoral the Grandest characters Wicked. Very Satan. Capaneus.'

[60] There is one sketchy illustration to Ugolino: no. 68, *Ugolino in Prison*.

the bridges, shade into it while the damned souls beneath are reflected in the twisted shapes of the rock opposite. Dante's and Virgil's graphic rectitude implies a self-righteousness of spirit that is no more than the inevitable opposite of the twisted tortures it creates. Dante's doctrines are, therefore, in accordance with the 'laws of moral virtue' (*Jerusalem*, pl. 4, l. 30, Stevenson, 635). His perception divides the world into warring opposites of chastity and punishment.[61]

The rocky landscape of these illustrations is the result of following 'moral virtue' and accords exactly with Blake's description of 'Natural Religion'. In 'the building [of] Natural Religion' and on the 'altars [of] Natural Morality', Albion (manifested as Luvah) is sacrificed by his children, the daughters of Albion:

> They pour cold water on his brain in front, to cause
> Lids to grow over his eyes in veils of tears, and caverns
> To freeze over his nostrils.
> (*Jerusalem*, pl. 66, ll. 30–2, Stevenson, 774)

These 'rocks are opaque hardnesses covering all vegetated things' (ibid., pl. 67, l. 5, Stevenson, 777). The rocks that Blake places in Dante's Hell evoke this blind and frozen world (where human reason claims priority over revelation) in order to suggest that Hell is itself created by that error. The human forms in the rocks of Hell are an example of when 'The cities & villages of Albion became rock & sand unhumanised' (ibid., pl. 63, l. 18, p. 766)— of the divided creation formed when justice denies the resurrection and withholds love's liberating and transforming power.[62]

According to Blake's illustrations, then, Dante's work reveals the contradictions inherent in his theology, and shows him, occasionally, grasping truths that are at odds with his system. Blake's pictures argue that Dante's account of the universe contradicts

---

[61] Within the *Commedia* Dante handles the opposition between self-righteous spectator and tortured victim that Blake sees as the poem's major fault. In *Inferno* xiii the souls of the suicides are trapped inside trees while their opposite, the profligate, are torn apart by bloodhounds. The canto recalls Ovid's opposites, Echo and Narcissus: the self-enclosed and the dissipated, one trapped and the other dismembered. Dante's breaking of a branch (*Inferno*, xiii. 31–3), which makes the suicide speak, is an action, moreover, that questions Dante's right to scrutinize, let alone judge, the damned.

[62] Cf.: 'Therefore thy mountains are become barren, Jerusalem; | Thy valleys, plains of burning sand; thy rivers, waters of death.' (*Jerusalem*, pl. 60, ll. 25–6, Stevenson, 757).

itself because it does not assimilate the truth it contains. Blake accepts, therefore, the detachment that Flaxman's drawings ascribe to Dante, and makes it the focus of a critique. His work passes by the self-criticism that the *Commedia* develops because his pictures exclude the conflicts in perception experienced by Dante's *personaggio*. Dante's encounters with the damned, however, are transformed into Blake's contention with Dante's portrayal of the damned. What Flaxman composedly portrayed (as a settled object readily available for imitation), Blake determinedly rewrites. To settle for representation, as in Blake's view Flaxman did, would be to accept the mystified, inscrutable authority of dogma and so succumb to the false judgement of Dante's Hell. The disruptive power of love in Blake's pictures, that parallels the defiance of Dante's blasphemers, parallels also the energy of his engagement with the poem. His unsubmissive fidelity to the original text makes possible a resistant encounter with it. This interpretative re-reading of the *Commedia* contends with its peculiarities without obscuring them. The same method is at work, as I have shown, in some passages of Cary's translation; it is partially foreshadowed also by Taafe's description of Dante's characteristic 'rousing' effects. Blake's dissenting involvement in the *Commedia*, however, is paralleled more closely and developed more profoundly in the late works of Keats, Shelley, and Byron.[63]

[63] Cf. Roe, *Blake's Illustrations*, 37: 'Dante's progress through Hell, Purgatory, and Paradise does not altogether fit with the Circle of Destiny of Ulro, generation, Beulah, and Eden, in spite of all that Blake could do to seek for correspondence' and Fuller, 'Blake and Dante', 350; Fuller's more sympathetic account tends to exaggerate Blake's craftsmanlike submissiveness in reaction to Roe's exaggeration of his self-will.

3

Coleridge, Dante, and The Friend

Symbols in a Waking Dream

Coleridge's vast and eclectic reading included the *Commedia* and other poems by Dante at several points, early and late in his career. Often, however, his subsequent allusions to Dante are incidental or ornamental. In this chapter I want to argue that significant parallels appear between Coleridge's and Dante's work in two periods of Coleridge's life: first, between 1804 and 1807 when Coleridge travelled to Malta and southern Italy; and, secondly, around 1818, when he was occupied in rewriting his periodical, *The Friend*, for publication in its three-volume edition. At this later period, Coleridge read Cary's translation for the first time.

In Malta, Coleridge's idea of symbols changes considerably and in ways that are paralleled by developments in Dante's thought that occurred when he was exiled from Florence. These similarities between Dante and Coleridge are illustrated most clearly by the canzone 'Tre donne al cor mi son venute', which Dante wrote in exile and Coleridge read with particular interest while abroad. In the second period under discussion, Coleridge reorganizes the essays for *The Friend* (that he had written in 1809–10), revises, and adds to them. These changes are in part the consequence of his having thought through the nature of symbolic writing. But the purpose and design of his new arrangement become more apparent when placed alongside the features of Dante's *Comedy* that Coleridge chose particularly to praise in his lectures from the same date. In neither period, then, am I arguing for Dante's influence on Coleridge; the comparisons illuminate Coleridge's work but no claim is made to have discovered the causes of his development. This chapter is more concerned to argue that the 1818 version of *The Friend* successfully put into practice Coleridge's idea of symbolic writing; that its neglect when published (and, by and large, since) has obscured one of Coleridge's best achievements; and that comparison of Dante and Coleridge helps to show the exact nature of Coleridge's success.

Coleridge first read Dante in 1796 in Henry Boyd's version, but at the time Dante's Hell provided little more than a shorthand euphemism for the torments inflicted by the slave-trade:[1]

I will not mangle the feelings of my readers by detailing enormities, which the gloomy Imagination of Dante would scarcely have dared attribute to the Inhabitants of Hell.[2]

Coleridge's time in Malta between 1804 and 1806 led him to read the original text with more attention than he had devoted to Boyd. On leaving he asked Wordsworth for a copy of the complete works and an Italian dictionary; ten years later he could compare the original, which he quoted from memory, with Cary's translation.[3] Sections of Dante's treatise *De Vulgari Eloquentia* and several of the *canzoni*, both genuine and spurious, were copied into Coleridge's notebooks after his return. These transcriptions suggest a long-standing interest and, on several occasions all restricted to authentic work, they disclose a perturbed engagement with the poetry.[4] The transcriptions are, however, the only materials to hand: until 1817 and the lecture series of the following spring, Coleridge's corpus furnishes barely a single reference to Dante and his work. Later in life, Coleridge quotes from him more

---

[1] See, however, J. L. Lowes, *The Road to Xanadu* (London, 1951), 263. This early reading may have contributed to Coleridge's rapidly improving poetry. *CN*, i. 170 reads 'Poem in ~~three~~ one Books in the manner of Dantè on the excursion of Thor'. Coleridge had come across Thor in Amos Cottle, *Icelandic Poetry, of The Edda of Saemund* (Bristol, 1797). This poem may be one of the projects realized in 'The Rime of the Ancyent Marinere'. From Boyd's translation, Coleridge could only have gained a sense of Dante's structure, but Wordsworth had read parts of the original; see Toynbee, ii. 3.

[2] Coleridge, *The Watchman*, *CC*, ii. 133. See also *Lectures 1795 On Politics and Religion*, *CC*, i. 156, 238; *CN*, i. 56, 170. For Coleridge's conventionality cf. Warton, iii. 254, and *A New Review*, 10, ed. Henry Maty (July 1786), 39. For his reading see George Whalley, 'The Bristol Library Borrowings of Southey and Coleridge 1793–8', *The Library*, 5th series, 4 (1949), 114–31.

[3] See *Marginalia*, ii. 131–2. On Dante's importance to Coleridge's experience of the voyage see Patricia Adair, *The Waking Dream: A Study of Coleridge's Poetry* (London, 1967), 80–1. Cf. William Empson and David Pirie (eds.), *Coleridge's Verse: A Selection* (London, 1972), 53.

[4] See his letters to Wordsworth, *CL*, ii. 1059 and to Cary, *CL*, iv. 782; for transcriptions see *CN*, ii. 3011–14, 3017–19. Coleridge quoted *De Vulgari Eloquentia* in *BL*, ii. 30, 56.

frequently and discusses him, occasionally at some length, confident that his audience is likely to be familiar with the *Comedy* at least.[5] Between 1807 and 1817, however, Dante largely drops from sight.[6]

Coleridge's influence on the sudden improvement of Dante's English reputation in the 1820s cannot, therefore, prove Dante's contribution to the development of the aesthetic by which he came to be appreciated. Rather, Coleridge's interest in *The Divine Comedy* in 1817 seems to have been awakened when he found that Dante's manner suited the understanding of poetry which he had reached independently. For Coleridge, Dante provided further evidence to support opinions he had formed and reformulated with increasing clarity since the beginning of the century. In this respect, Dante's example illuminates particularly the revised version of *The Friend* that Coleridge published in 1818.[7] Its organization and its perspective on the authorial self approximate, respectively, to the overarching structure of the *Comedy*, and the relation created in the poem between *poeta* and *personaggio*.

Earlier and more generally, however, Dante's work can reveal the dangers inherent in Coleridge's account of symbols. Both writers describe and pursue a form of attention that creates symbols by linking the general and the particular without subordinating either. In this they are seeking a kind of attention that joins captivation and detachment. In Dante, each individual object is discovered to participate in a universal truth, to express and embody

---

[5] See *C&S*, 184–5; *CL*, vi. 713–15; *Marginalia*, i. 134–6. The first of these may have influenced Henry Hallam's description of 'Paradiso' in his *Introduction to the Literature of Europe* (London, 1837–9); see Toynbee, ii. 262–3. Coleridge's late poems occasionally appear to draw on events in the *Commedia*: see, 'The Garden of Boccaccio' (1828) and 'Ne Plus Ultra' (1826), EHC, i. 478–81, 431. Coleridge's 'Limbo' (1817) adopts elements from Dante's Limbo (*Inferno*, iii. 19–69, Sapegno, i. 31–5) and, more distinctively, features of Dante's 'Old Man of Crete' in *Inferno* xiv. Cf. esp. 'Limbo', ll. 26–30, EHC, i. 430, and *Inferno*, xiv. 103–5, Sapegno, i. 162.

[6] Coleridge mentions Dante in 1811 (*Lectures 1808–19*, i. 361–2, cf. *BL*, ii. 21). In 1812 he plans to include Dante and Ariosto in a lecture series (*CL*, iii. 364); he plans in 1816 to publish 'a Review of old Books', including Dante (*CL*, iv. 648). See *CN*, iii. 3611 (1809), and 4211 (June 1814); cf. *CL*, iv. 561. In *BL*, ii. 147 he quotes Dante's *canzone*, 'Voi, che intendendo, il terzo ciel movete', first read by him in 1807–8 and copied into *CN*, ii. 3219.

[7] *The Friend* was first published in periodical numbers in 1809–10. Barbara Rooke's *Friend* prints 1818 in vol. i and 1809–10 in vol. ii. I refer to parallel passages following quotations and, where Coleridge's organization is noteworthy, to the numbers of 1809–10 or the sections of 1818.

it, while preserving its own identity intact. Beatrice, for example, does not only explain Christian theology in *Paradiso*; she is an incarnation of its truths while remaining a recognizable person. Dante's ascent to the vision of God in the Empyrean entails his growing to see her more clearly. Her individuality becomes more distinct the more deeply he perceives her identity with God. Dante asserts this dual existence with startling force:

quella Beatrice beata che vive in cielo con li angeli e in terra con la mia anima. (Conv., II. ii. 1, 52)

(that blessed Beatrice who lives among the angels in heaven and on earth within my soul)

Coleridge, I will argue, understands true, purified perception in broadly similar terms; and he describes poetry leading to the same balance between attention to the personal and the comprehension of particulars as part of God. Dante's narrative, in its separate incidents and taken entire, progresses to the vision which is the goal Coleridge sets for the motions, varied and continuous, of a poetic style.

This goal for his style can be inferred from his definition in *Biographia Literaria* of a 'just poem'; it cannot be:

on the one hand [. . .] a series of striking lines or distichs, each of which absorbing the whole attention of the reader to itself disjoins it from the context, and makes it a separate whole, instead of an harmonizing part; and on the other hand [it cannot be] an unsustained composition, from which the reader collects rapidly the general result unattracted by the component parts. The reader should be carried forward, not merely or chiefly by the mechanical impulse of curiosity, or by a restless desire to arrive at the final solution; but by the pleasureable activity of mind excited by the attractions of the journey itself. (*BL*, ii. 14)

Coleridge's praise of Cary's translation repeats this opposition:

both your Metre and your Rhythm have in a far greater degree, than I know any other instance of, the variety of Milton without any mere *Miltonisms*—[. . .] the Verse has this variety without any loss of *continuity*—and [. . .] this is the *excellence* of the Work, considered as a translation of Dante—that it gives the reader a similar feeling of wandering & wandering onward and onward. (*CL*, iv. 781)

The separate lines of Cary's translation are variously interesting in themselves but such attractions do not distract from the interest of the whole; they do not prevent 'continuity' from carrying the reader forward, hardly noticing his progress as he finds pleasure in the journey itself. The easy progress Coleridge enjoys when reading Cary is implicitly set against what the *Biographia* describes as an 'unsustained composition' in which 'meaning' separates from wording. Without 'variety', the reader 'collects rapidly the general result'. For Coleridge, like Dante, the component parts of verse must possess sufficient 'force of expression' to arrest but not divert attention. The striking particular that absorbs 'the whole attention of the reader' must somehow be joined to 'the general result', so that each separable element of poetry resembles a symbol: it makes up part of the whole without being lost in it.

The pursuit of symbolic forms unites Coleridge and Dante, and helps explain the nature of Coleridge's interest in the *Commedia*. Moreover, comparing the two reveals the particular difficulties Coleridge encountered when he attempted to see particulars as part of a greater whole while not losing them in that whole. The problems he faced can be seen in his definition of the symbol. A symbol exhibits, Coleridge claims:

a translucence of the Special in the Individual or of the General in the Especial or of the Universal in the General. Above all by the translucence of the Eternal through and in the Temporal. It always partakes of the Reality which it renders intelligible; and while it enunciates the whole, abides itself as a living part in that Unity, of which it is the representative. (*Lay Sermons*, 30)

Dante, by contrast, sounds matter-of-fact about the coincidence that Coleridge celebrates. Coleridge emphasizes so strongly that the particular continues to exist within the reality it expresses because he is concerned to establish a distinction between allegory and symbol. The intensity of that concern derives from the importance of the distinction to Coleridge's faith and poetics. In the explication, however, Coleridge starts losing the particular in a celebration of particularity.[8]

---

[8] The same difficulties are implicit in the figural realism that Auerbach describes in Dante and finds rediscovered in Stendhal and Balzac. See Erich Auerbach, *Mimesis: The Representation of Reality in Western Literature*, trans. Willard R. Trask (Princeton, NJ, 1953), 191–202, 554–5; A. C. Charity, *Events and their Afterlife: The Dialectics of Christian Typology in the Bible and Dante* (Cambridge, 1966), 161 n. Coleridge's writing, I argue, sometimes succumbs to this danger and sometimes responds to his awareness of it. The problems in Auerbach's account are

Coleridge's ascent through successive orders of generality—from individual, to species, to 'genera', and beyond—leads to its highest term, 'the Eternal', which is both 'above all' the others and pre-eminent within them. The sequential structure of Coleridge's sentence seeks to realize the 'translucence of the Eternal through and in the Temporal'.[9] Coleridge's movement up the scale leads his reader to imagine acquiring true vision and enacts its attainment. He goes, through the sentences, towards the perception of a supervening 'Reality'. From that higher perspective—and this is part of its attraction—Coleridge can enjoy the affecting vulnerability of separate things, defending them while he glories in their true magnificence. His effort to gain imaginatively the highest point of view consequently runs the risk of merely producing an intellectual and literary context, where he may have his feelings and keep them inviolable.

This is apparent at the end of the sentence, where Coleridge employs a less intellectualized vocabulary: his intricate clause, 'abides itself as a living part of that Unity', departs from the expository precision of 'which it renders intelligible' and 'while it enunciates the whole'. Coleridge's writing makes the survival of the living particular, that 'abides', appear endangered, as if its minuteness required protection from greater surrounding powers. Meanwhile, 'translucence' lifts the symbolic object into union with the reality it represents, and displays its miraculous nature as part of God. A peculiar, unmixed quality of poignancy attaches to the particular, despite Coleridge's absolute confidence that it could not be safer. His confidence may indeed have made possible the unqualified poignancy; were the particularity of symbolic objects genuinely under threat within this 'Unity', Coleridge could not attend to their vulnerability with such pleasure. The warmth of his feeling comes from gratitude and relief that the single object is

---

explained and contextualized very well in Gregory S. Jay, *T. S. Eliot and the Poetics of Literary History* (Baton Rouge and London, 1983), 127–8. Cf. Harold Bloom, *Poetry and Repression*, 87–9.

[9] 'Translucence', meaning 'the act or fact of shining through' (*OED*, definition 1) is Coleridge's own usage, invented when 'translucent' was changing from its original sense of 'transparent' to its modern one of 'semi-transparent'. He places the symbolic object between those two meanings: it is felt to be present but perfectly unobstructive. The *OED* gives Coleridge's first use in 'The Two Founts' (1826, 1st pub. 1827), l. 27 (EHC, i. 455).

able to appear vulnerable precisely because it lies at the centre of a benevolent universe.[10]

In *The Statesman's Manual* definition, then, the symbolic object's fragility is more touching for Coleridge when that object is seen to be invulnerable. Early and late in his career, Coleridge can be found seeking to derive falsely secure comfort in and from the imagination.[11] My emphasis on Coleridge's writing in the middle period of his life (in exile and in *The Friend*) makes the claim that, as a prose writer at least, Coleridge's best work is his most un-self-confident. I aim to demonstrate that his avowedly complex style could avoid bombast and obscurity to create the accommodating and hesitant relation to symbols that his beliefs demanded.

Coleridge sailed for Malta in April 1804 and remained abroad, there and later in Sicily and Italy, until August 1806. His public motive for going was to improve his health by living in a warmer and drier climate:

Heat in a hot climate is the only regular & universal Stimulus of the external world; to which if I can add Tranquillity, the equivalent, & Italian climate, of the world within, I do not despair to be a healthy man. (To Robert Southey, 17 Feb. 1803, *CL*, ii. 930)

He had mooted the project on several occasions since his illness in the winter of 1800–1 but dropped the plan, usually pleading lack of money. At least as strong an influence on his staying was his attachment to Sara Hutchinson. The decision to leave, finally, was largely motivated by his resolve to interrupt his devotion to her. He aimed as well to substitute for the irregular, private stimulus of opium, the 'regular and universal' one of Mediterranean heat.

---

[10] Symbolic forms are precious in part because they enable the frailty of particulars to be considered more lovingly once their security is guaranteed. There are hints of this difficulty in 'Dejection: An Ode', see ll. 130–6 (EHC, i. 368) where, arguably, Coleridge is gathering excessive comfort from Asra's absolute security.

[11] The dangers in Coleridge's understanding of symbolic forms are paralleled in his sometimes blurred perceptions of suffering and of evil. The afflictions that bow Coleridge down to earth in 'Dejection' (l. 82, EHC, i. 366) are thought of earlier in his career as beneficial, see 'Religious Musings', ll. 213–20, EHC, i. 117 (and its variant version in *The Watchman*, CC, ii. 131); 'The Destiny of Nations', ll. 80–8, 459–69, EHC, i. 134, 146–8; Empson and Pirie, *Coleridge's Verse*, 20–1; *CL*, ii. 1000–1; and *CN*, i. 87. On this question see Emmanuel Levinas, 'Transcendence and Evil', *Collected Philosophical Papers*, trans. Alphonso Lingis (Dordrecht, Boston, and Lancaster, 1987), 175–86.

While intending to rescue his health, Coleridge was equally in search of the tranquillity which he attributed to an Italian climate.[12]

In this letter, characteristically, he describes good health as consisting in a match between such a climate within and the actual one without. He can prevent incipient despair about his health by rediscovering the relation to Nature which, in 'Dejection' he had wished for Sara. Coleridge's complaints about his state of mind when leaving for Malta support the idea that his search for tranquillity entailed the effort to regain such harmony.[13] 'Miss S. Wedgewood is a truly excellent woman', he writes in 1802 when visiting the family, 'her whole Soul is clear, pure, & deep, as an Italian Sky'.[14] He would prefer himself to be scattered to the winds:

My Spirits are low: and I suffer too often sinkings & misgivings, alienations from the Spirit of Hope, strange withdrawings out of the Life that manifests itself by existence—morbid yearnings condemn'd by me, almost despis'd, and yet perhaps at times almost cherish'd, to concenter my Being into Stoniness, or to be diffused as among the winds, and lose all individual existence   (To Sir George and Lady Beaumont, 6 Apr. 1804, *CL*, ii. 1122)[15]

This deadened silence, instead of peace, hovers around Coleridge's hopes for improved health and renewed strength as he sails into exile. To be 'diffused as among the winds' repeats one of Coleridge's fundamental desires: to 'wander like a breeze | By lakes and sandy shores'.[16] In the letter this wish shifts, all too easily, towards an

---

[12] Coleridge's is a conventional belief; cf. Shelley, 'the loveliness & serenity of the sky made the greatest difference in my sensations' (Jones, ii. 3); John Edmund Reade, *Italy: A Poem, In Six Parts: With Historical and Classical Notes* (London, 1838), 9: 'O thou loved land which still art Paradise! | Thou that embodiest all the Poets dream! | Thou, that art bathed, as in a fount, by skies | Of Heaven's own tincture'. Cf. Coleridge's 'Ode', ll. 8–10: 'And ah! he sigh'd—that I might find | The cloudless Azure of the Mind | And Fortune's brightening Hue', EHC, i. 35, and *The Watchman*, 141.

[13] See his letter to Sir George and Lady Beaumont, 1 Oct. 1803, *CL*, ii. 1000: 'For what is the nature & the beauty of Youth? [. . . .] to make ideas & realities stand side by side, the one as vivid as the other, even as I have often seen in a natural well of translucent water the *reflections* of the lank weeds, that hung down from it's sides, standing upright, and like Substances'. Cf. 'The Picture; or, The Lover's Resolution' (1802), ll. 92–106, EHC, i. 372; and *CN*, ii. 2557.

[14] To Thomas Poole, 17 Dec. 1802, *CL*, ii. 900.

[15] Cf. his letter to William and Dorothy Wordsworth, 4 Apr. 1804, *CL*, ii. 1115–16.

[16] 'Frost at Midnight', ll. 54–5, EHC, i. 242. See also 'France: An Ode', ll. 99–105, ibid. 247; *EOT*, iii. 78.

entire (and secure) loss of self within external things. Exile itself, however, and the distance from Sara Hutchinson it inevitably brought about, proved that his longed-for tranquillity was unobtainable, and, at the same time, helped to counter the 'morbid yearnings' he fostered and loathed. This was because Sara's absence could account for the blankness of his feelings and provide a focus for his desire to be diffused.

Why an't you here? This for ever | I have no rooted thorough thro' feeling—& never exist wholly present to any Sight, to any Sound, to any Emotion, to any series of Thoughts received or produced | always a feeling of yearning, that at times passes into Sickness of Heart. (*CN*, ii. 2000)

This is the whole of an entry written while Coleridge was on board ship in 1804. Its unrelenting question concentrates on a single person, on one 'you' in whose absence he is made absent from himself, 'never wholly present' to anything 'received or produced'. The syntax reveals an indifference as to whether these thoughts are his own or other people's. He cannot comprehend his thoughts properly as he endures a slackening disengagement from the world. Acknowledging this extreme self-division leads him to apply the mournful enquiry 'Why an't you here?' to himself. Her absence begins to question his presence, and the equal applicability of the words to both of them suggests a form of union; a meeting which is made possible only when their separation makes itself felt most powerfully. That separation, on the other hand, is unmistakable because 'Why an't you here?' (when spoken to Coleridge), sounds like a riposte, answering the rebuke implicit in his version of the question. As he observes his attachment to Asra in particular, he imagines her independent nature. This independence makes her appear more real, of course; it brings her closer in imagination, but Coleridge accepts that such closeness does not reduce the physical distance separating them.

The structure of this entry foreshadows the passage in *Lay Sermons* defining symbols. Coleridge heaps up in the notebook a succession of increasingly weighty terms, 'any Sight [. . .] any Sound [. . .] any Emotion [. . .] any series of Thoughts', in order to reach a principle: '*always* a feeling of yearning' (my emphasis). Having made this declaration he can retreat from it into the more familiar and mundane affliction: 'that at times passes into Sickness of Heart'. He moves from self-definition towards a suggestion of 'the actual' within a structure that heightens its pathos. The later sentence works in the same way: 'while it enunciates the whole, abides itself as a living part in that Unity'. The mention of temporality in both: 'at times' and 'while'; their use of verbs—'passes' and 'abides'—that are, at once, straightforward and imposing, reveals a similar technique. If, however, the later passage suffers from an excessively confident poignancy, the notebook's evocation of self-pity avoids mawkishness by its avoidance of self-assurance. At the end of the entry, 'passes', within the progressing drama of the sentences, is moving towards the last description but does not lend it outstanding authority nor make it appear that the final act of definition will clear up the difficulty. The reader is left with 'this for ever': self-questioning mixed up with and counterbalancing the assured self-assessment and calculable pathos of 'Sickness of Heart'.

A better understanding of love and interdependence was, perhaps, the essential discovery Coleridge made in exile. The sensitivity it creates in this entry contrasts violently with his treatment of his wife before going away.

My Love is made up 9/10ths of fervent wishes for the permanent *Peace* of mind of those, whom I love, be it man or woman; & for their Progression in purity, goodness, & true Knowlege [*sic*]. Such being the nature of my Love, no human Being can have a right to be jealous. (To Mrs S. Coleridge, 22 [23] Nov. 1802, *CL*, ii. 887)

Coleridge had gone to visit the Wedgewoods and provide company and entertainment for Thomas, his depressive patron and friend. This call of duty came, probably, as a welcome relief from his wife's increasing resentment about Sara Hutchinson, who was living nearby with the Wordsworths at the time. Coleridge's answer to her implicit accusation seeks to rise above it—'fervent wishes for the permanent *Peace* of those, whom I love' obviously restrict his affection to benevolence, fitting Coleridge for the role of saint and intercessor.

His fervour is so earnest and so false because other people's peace of mind ensures his, so that his dispassionate benignity is part of a bargain. He constructs his time with the Wedgewoods so that it proves him in the right about 'the nature of my Love':

What sweeter & more tranquillizing pleasure is there, than to feel one's self completely innocent among compleatly [*sic*] innocent young Women—! (To Mrs S. Coleridge, 4 Dec. 1802, *CL*, ii. 890)

There is no question here of flirtation, 'no human Being can have a right to be jealous', because although Coleridge surrounds himself with people who share his nature, they leave him, essentially, untouched. His pleasure lies in the opportunity for conscious self-praise provided by these circumstances, by the encircling girls whose innocence allows one 'to feel one's self completely innocent'. This 'tranquillizing pleasure' appreciates the sisters insofar as they form a landscape that conforms to the needs of Coleridge's inner being: 'Miss S. Wedgewood [. . .] is clear, pure & deep, as an Italian sky.'

Mrs Coleridge is left with disadvantageous comparisons: asked to wonder how much her husband needed peace and quiet, after living in such discord with her; led to notice how easy it is to restore him to the state of innocence he lost in her company. Coleridge's exclamations are, of course, rebuking and at some level a calculated attack. The repetition of 'compleatly innocent' attempts to make her fears look sordid as well as unfounded, but in doing so the repetition contradicts the perfection he desires. This perfection extends, nevertheless, the impervious kindness Coleridge understands by love, so establishing his lofty indifference to the people and places where he lives. He is not 'concentered into Stoniness' but more gaily self-absorbed, inaccessibly seeking tranquillity there.

Consequently, in views of love Coleridge propounded before going abroad 'fellow-feeling' is used to describe the recognition of similarity, at the expense of a movement of sympathy. His version of sympathy does not participate in another person's life so much as absorb it. He exists 'almost wholly within myself' and is 'connected [. . .] with my especial friends, by an intense delight in fellow-feeling, by an intense perception of the Necessity of LIKE to LIKE'.[17] How deeply he wanted to make himself invulnerable to, and yet remain within, human relations is shown by his grasping unsuccessfully at the same form of possession when in exile:

the truly Beloved is the symbol of God to whomever it is truly beloved by!—but it may become perfect & maintained lovely by the function of the two | The Lover worships in his Beloved that final consummation ⟨of itself which is⟩ produced in his own soul by the action of the Soul of the Beloved upon it, and that final perfection of the Soul of the Beloved, ⟨which is in part⟩ the consequence of the reaction of his (so ammeliorated

---

[17] Cf. his letter to Mrs Coleridge, 13 Nov. 1802, *CL*, ii. 882.

[*sic*] & regenerated) Soul upon the Soul of his Beloved | till each contemplates the Soul of the other as involving his own, both in its givings and its receivings. (*CN*, ii. 2540)

In the first sentence, the object of love remains a means. Like the Wedgewood girls, 'the truly Beloved' is defined perfectly by 'whomever it is truly beloved by'. The notebook, however, smoothes away this assertiveness by capping the familiar truth with a further one: 'but it may become perfect & [be] maintained lovely by the function of the two'. As he goes on to explain, love demands an exchange of gifts.

The interaction between love and beloved threatens to continue the self-centredness in which it begins. The 'Lover worships in his Beloved that final consummation of itself' which is, simultaneously, 'produced in his own soul'. What he loves in her (let us say) is himself made perfect in her.[18] Because he is thinking of love as contemplation, Coleridge does not mention desire but, all the same, he introduces an idea of self-love:

The Lover worships [. . .] that final perfection of the Soul of the Beloved, (which is in part) the consequence of the reaction of his (so ammeliorated & regenerated) Soul upon the Soul of his Beloved.

The angle brackets indicate a later insertion, 'which is in part'. Love, and fellow-feeling, are seen to rely on the otherness of 'the Beloved'. Without the insertion, 'That final perfection' of the beloved would be solely 'the consequence' of the lover's effect, owing nothing to her innate qualities or personal, historical nature. Difference and distance between lover and beloved allow gratitude and appreciation, expanding 'love' beyond the algebraic reciprocations that Coleridge's terms have detailed until this point. Just as 'it *may* become perfect' replaces 'the truly Beloved *is* the symbol' (my emphases), so the definition suddenly acquires a purpose and a goal: 'The Lover worships [. . .] till each contemplates the Soul of the other as involving his own'. The uncertainty of their reaching perfection leads Coleridge to depict a gradual process, in which lovers do not stand admiring themselves in each other, but are progressively led to achieve mutual comprehension. So they are 'maintained lovely' by continuing in their 'givings and receivings'.

---

[18] Cf. Simone Weil, *First and Last Notebooks*, trans. Richard Rees (London, 1970), 284.

The echo of the marriage service ('either to other, in the giving and receiving of a ring') further enlarges the definition beyond predictable consequences into a realm of interdependence. Coleridge's hesitation accepts that, just as perfect love depends on an independent *other*, so particular examples of a truly loving relation cannot be represented within an idealist terminology. Their substance must outreach the logic which anatomizes them. He evokes the otherness of such relations and, at the same time, their familiarity by adopting the *Book of Common Prayer*, dropping his authoritative stance in order to replace his reader's assent with recognition.

The symbolic quality of the person one loves, though granted from the outset, is itself recognized more perfectly when seen as part of a process; when it is reconsidered within sentences that enact the process. In other words, the 'function of the two', the reciprocality of loving relations, requires the *otherness* that love seeks to overcome, suggesting a further sphere—out of reach but intuitively understood—where interchange becomes union and symbolic meanings are directly perceived. The otherness of the beloved prevents the self-containment that Coleridge's idea of tranquillity desired, and so ensures that perfect harmony extends beyond our grasp. As a result it provokes a style of prose that directs the reader towards the next stage, towards the unattainable coexistence of ideas and realities, the elevated position where symbols are comprehended absolutely.[19]

Understanding a symbol's true meaning, like union through love with another person, begins to appear something that must always be postponed.

O Sara! gladly if my miserable Destiny would relax, gladly would I think of thee and of me, as of two Birds of Passage, reciprocally resting on each other in order to support the long flight, the awful Journey.   (*CN*, ii. 2556, fo. 75ᵛ)

Love is an action of comfort that allows you to be comforted in return and, analogously, it is a place of rest that allows you to travel. Loving behaviour creates the variety and continuity that

---

[19] Coleridge does not consistently recognize this reciprocality and interchange; see *CN*, ii. 2530: 'I love her as being capable of being glorified by me & as the means & instrument of my own glorification | In loving her thus I love two Souls as one, as compleat'.

underlie Coleridge's ideas of 'just poetry' and methodical action. He imagines an entirely mutual exchange where neither person is the means to advancement, but both provide it for the other. And he imagines this reciprocity in their relationship, while accepting that it does not subsist, either in fact or necessarily; he knows it to be true and yet not the case, to be a fact, perhaps, but not a thing. Although, to some extent, he makes it true by thinking it (gathering comfort in his awful journey by imagining Asra's support), his repeated conditionals admit that the thought itself does not relax his miserable destiny. Even more, this destiny is seen to prevent his imagining their reciprocal support as wholeheartedly or, perhaps, as single-mindedly as he otherwise would. The more he realizes that he cannot think 'of thee and of me' in the way he would like, the more he succeeds in imagining their relationship properly, and the sort of comfort her presence would give.[20]

His dependence on a distinct *other*, which Coleridge discovered while in exile, makes him more deeply aware of a self that will not be accommodated by imaginative consolations. This self-recognition forms the point of comparison between Coleridge's exile and the one Dante describes in his *canzone*, also written in exile, 'Tre donne al cor mi son venuto'. This was the one among Dante's poems Coleridge found most interesting in 1806:

Canzone XIV, fra le Rime di Dante is a poem of wild & interesting Images, intended as an Enigma, and to me an Enigma it remains, spite of all my efforts. Yet it deserves transcription, and translation. (*CN*, ii. 3014)

Coleridge's lack of confidence in interpreting the poem is unaffected and understandable. The *canzone* is, as he says, highly enigmatic. It is usually assumed that Dante wrote 'Tre donne' to counter the political disaster of exile and, in particular, a succession of military defeats suffered by the exiles soon after their expulsion from Florence in 1302.[21] Its narrative describes three women visiting the 'Amore' that dwells in Dante's heart; the first of these is named 'Drittura' (Justice), who is followed by her

---

[20] Cf. his letter to George Fricker, 9 Oct. 1806, *CL*, ii. 1192.

[21] The exact date is unknown, either 1302 or 1304 (after Dante quarrelled with his allies). Dating is made more difficult by the presence in some manuscripts of an additional *congedo* (not printed in Coleridge's edition.) *Canzoni* consist of several stanzas followed by a shorter *congedo*, formed out of the stanza's rhyme-scheme. 'Tre donne''s extra *congedo* differs in its rhyme-scheme and is more humble. If it is therefore an afterthought, the rest of the poem may be earlier, say 1302.

daughter and granddaughter. The debate between 'Amore' and the 'Tre donne' forms the substance of the *canzone*.

The poem's difficulty is illustrated by the dispute surrounding the allegorical meaning of the three women. Scholars now seem in agreement that Dante intends by them a complex idea of justice: natural justice ('Drittura') descends from God into earthly things and there engenders human ideas of justice (Drittura's daughter); these in turn produce the institutions of the law (her granddaughter).[22] The enigma of the poem lies, however, less in its precise allegorical significance (if there is only one) than in its shifts between allegory and symbol, between treating the women as the personification of abstract qualities and perceiving them to be aspects of Dante's experience.[23]

Dante says nothing in the poem until the conversation between Amore and Drittura finishes with their taking comfort in being separate from the sublunary world. Here he intervenes, declaring his inability to take heart, bound as he is to his exile. The first *congedo* which follows addresses the poem itself, as is conventional, and demands its secrecy: if it should come across a sympathetic listener, the poem may then speak out. Dante's hesitation foresees the reluctance with which his complaints will be heard by political opponents, and fears the unrecognizability of goodness in a world where moral categories are confused and Justice appears in rags. He is the more cautious, however, because in the last stanza he has admitted so fully the degree of his sufferings in exile. His humility and weakness demand compassionate attention:

> E io, che ascolto nel parlar divino   1
> consolarsi e dolersi
> così alti dispersi,
> l'essilio che m'è dato, onor mi tegno:
> ché, se giudizio o forza di destino   5
> vuol pur che il mondo versi
> i bianchi fiori in persi,

[22] See Plumptre, *The Commedia and Canzoniere* [. . .], 2 vols. (London, 1886–7), ii. 297 n., rejecting Gabriele Rossetti's political allegory, and 432–4. On the growth of a scholarly consensus, see *Rime della Maturità e dell'Esilio*, ed. M. Barbi and V. Pernicone (Florence, 1969), 586 n.

[23] Coleridge's interest is consistent; he plans to 'insert for their singularity' Dante's 'Di donne io vidi una gentile schiera' and 'Un dì si venne a me Melancolia'. The second of these closely resembles 'Tre donne' in its portrayal of abstractions entangled and in conflict with a self. See *CN*, ii. 3019; Foster and Boyde, i. 74, 80.

cader co' buoni è pur di lode degno.
　E se non che de gli occhi miei 'l bel segno
per lontananza m'è tolto dal viso,   10
che m'have in foco miso,
lieve mi conterei ciò che m'è grave.
Ma questo foco m'have
già consumato sì l'ossa e la polpa
che Morte al petto m'ha posto la chiave.   15
Onde, s'io ebbi colpa,
più lune ha volto il sol poi che fu spenta,
se colpa muore perché l'uom si penta.   18
　　(*Canzone* xiv, Foster and Boyde, i. 180)[24]

(And I, listening to the noble exiles using divine language to console themselves and grieve, I count as an honour the exile I have been given; because, if either judgement or the power of destiny dictate that the world turns white flowers to black, the only praiseworthy act is to fall with the good. And if it were not that distance had taken from view the cynosure[25] of my eyes, to place me in fire, I would happily accept what weighs me down. But this fire has consumed so much my bones and their marrow that Death has put his key to my breast. Even if I have been at fault, the sun has been revolving for many months since it was cancelled, if crimes die when a man repents.)[26]

The point that Dante's construction of the stanza leads us to dwell on is the unusual 'm'have' construction which he repeats in lines 11 and 13, on the second occasion fitting it into the rhyme-scheme at a peculiarly prominent point. Line 13, 'Ma questo foco m'have' (But this fire has), produces an unusually close couplet rhyme with line 12, 'lieve mi conterei ciò che m'è grave' ('I would happily accept what weighs me down'). This seven-syllable line completes the rhyming couplet more quickly than the equivalent instance in lines 8 and 9, and across a wider syntactical division than between lines 10 and 11. In doing so it initiates the closer interweaving of

---

[24] These are ll. 73–90 of the poem. To avoid confusing my analysis of the formal construction I have numbered the lines as part of the stanza.

[25] 'Bel segno' means literally an object of love, 'segno' combining 'sign' with 'goal', 'focus', or 'aim'. See Foster and Boyde, i. 197–8; ii. 290.

[26] The final lines are disputed. 'Colpa' may mean a crime, or the blame that attaches to it; Dante may appear self-abasing, or slightly hostile to criticism. Charles Lyell, *The Canzoniere of Dante [. . .]* (London, 1835) adopts the first: 'Should fault then have been mine, | Months hath the sun revolved since 't was redeemed; | If guilt expire when man sincere repents' (repr. in *CN*, ii. 3014 n.). See Foster and Boyde, ii. 290–1.

rhymes, crossed by alternating lines and half-lines, which distinguishes the second half of the stanza, the *sirima*.[27] 'M'have' is a Sicilian verb-form and usually reserved for the first person while Dante gives the standard form, 'm'ha', to Morte in line fifteen. He reinvokes for his own speeches the language of the first love-poets who wrote in the Italian vernacular. Their dialect carried the authority of an earlier, nobler period before Dante's exile and the corruption of Florence. In the Sicilian poets, private feelings came under intense intellectual scrutiny that sought out the extent of their conformity to ideal patterns of conduct. Dante's verb-form tries his feelings at the moment of declaring them because he declares in the same breath his subjection to the Sicilian judgement of feeling. By recalling a precedent, 'm'have' also loads Dante's physical disintegration through exile with a grandeur of inevitability. It appears unavoidable, but neither sordid nor banal, when its admission seems to demand Dante's self-effacement within a distant and ennobled diction. Though elevated in its diction, the line's place in the stanza lends it stridency, and this suits the discomfort with which its directness is thrown into contrast with the balance of the preceding line, 'lieve mi conterei ciò che m'è grave'. The Sicilian verb-form seeks an abrupt weightedness of personal declaration that will do justice to, and allow justice to be done to, the potential embarrassment of his confession.

This running together of daring personal admission and conventional impersonality carries on in the images of 'l'ossa e la polpa' and of Death, personified, setting his key to Dante's breast. The lines present in miniature the two elements of the poem that Kenelm Foster identifies: the 'dramatic and self-dramatising manner [which] foreshadows the *Comedy*'; and its opposite, the 'allegory conceived according to "lo modo de li poeti", that is, by covering truth with fiction'.[28] The intervention of 'E io, che ascolto nel parlar divino' into the exchanges between personified abstractions (Love, dwell-

---

[27] The first half, the *frons*, divides into two equal *pedes* rhyming abbc abbc, scanning 11/7/7/11 11/7/7/11. In the *sirima* symmetry is suggested but not established. The rhymes begin a third quatrain, cdde, but in its last line the rapid couplet rhyme begins a new pattern, efefgg. The rhyme-scheme is counterpointed by metre 11/11/7/11/7/11/11/7/11/11. The last six lines can divide into two groups of three, as in the final stanza; or, as in the preceding one, syntactical divisions may fall between ll. 10–11, 14–15, to create two half-heard quatrains.

[28] Kenelm Foster, 'Dante's Canzone "Tre donne [. . .]" ', *Italian Studies*, 9 (1954), 68.

ing in Dante's heart, and Justice, visiting), begins self-consciously to mediate between the two modes which in Foster's reading are seen simply to coexist. Dante's verb-forms and their position in the rhyme-scheme, that is to say, understand the extent to which abstractions apply personally. His stylistic acuity acts within the poem's wider structure to further the account of discovering that a single 'I' lies beyond, as well as within, the convention of personification in which it finds itself.[29]

Dante's first person interruption appears more startling because it answers the speech of reassurance and encouragement which Amore addresses, at the end of the preceding stanza, to Justice and her children.

> Però, se questo è danno,   65
> piangono gli occhi e dolgasi la bocca
> de li uomini a cui tocca,
> che sono a' raggi di cotal ciel giunti;
> non noi, che semo de l'etterna rocca:
> ché, se noi siamo or punti,   70
> noi pur saremo, e pur tornerà gente
> che questo dardo farà star lucente.
>   (*Canzone* xiv, Foster and Boyde,
>   i. 178)

(And so, though this is dreadful, let the eyes weep and the lips mourn of the men whom it touches, men who are bound to the beams of such a heaven, not we whose life is set on the eternal rock; because, although now we are cut to the quick, we are immortal and a people shall return who will make this arrow shine brilliantly again.)[30]

Amore offers two comforts to Justice and her daughters: first, because they really belong in the eternal city of the heavenly Jerusalem, they are invulnerable to transitory earthly suffering; secondly, their immortality means they can rest their hopes in a future which Dante himself may never see. The second implies a

---

[29] Cf. the use of 'mendicando'. Amore reassures the ladies: 'Larghezza e Temperanza e l'altre nate | del nostro sangue mendicando vanno' (ll. 63–4, Foster and Boyde, i. 178, 'Generosity and Temperance and the others born of our blood go around begging'). See Dante's harshest complaint, 'per le parti quasi tutte a le quali questa lingua si stende, peregrino, quasi mendicando, sono andato' (*Conv.*, I. iii. 4, p. 14, 'through nearly all the regions where this language extends, like a pilgrim or even a beggar, I have gone'). See also *Paradiso*, vi. 141.

[30] The 'dardo' is one of Love's two arrows, rusty through lack of use. See Foster and Boyde, ii. 288, l. 59 n.

persisting engagement with the world which the first denies, as is gently acknowledged in the concessionary admissions which Amore opens with each time: 'se questo è danno' and 'se noi siamo or punti'. Aloof contempt for sublunary affairs (which one might expect to be most ferocious in Justice treated unjustly) is restrained by the indicative verbs. These reconfirm pain's continuing independence from the means of its alleviation. Amore's compensating hopes and distractions may help to outweigh the sorrow of exile, but cannot deny or disregard it. In the following stanza, Dante is moved towards recognizing the truth of that, brashly declaring his agreement with what they have known all along. He starts by finding his exile all the more honourable for being shared with these 'alti dispersi' (l. 75) and seeks to retire from the inconstancy of the world into the received formulations of tragic heroism, 'cader co' buoni è pur di lode degno' (l. 80). The collapse of this heroic alignment brings him to accept the insinuating temperateness of Amore's earlier speech.[31]

The close of the poem, then, exiles Dante from the wandering personifications to place him in the world of men, and this further exile leads him to admit the same weaknesses in himself as are assumed by the tact and urbanity of Love. Where originally Justice and her daughters vindicate Dante by suffering the same exile, their movement away from earth comes to appear the true meaning of his punishment. Dante finds he has entered the human world where, as perhaps he should have known before, natural justice is in tatters and, inexplicably, black turns to white and white to black.[32] His exile is imaged in their affliction and then consists in their ability to leave, because that departure provokes the recognition of his isolated self. The self can then face its humiliating vulnerability to experience in the same way that Coleridge

---

[31] Cf. Wilfred Owen, 'My friend, you would not tell with such high zest | To children ardent for some desperate glory, | The old Lie: Dulce et decorum est | Pro patria mori.' His rhyme of 'zest' and 'est' considers the reality of the deaths hidden within the acceptance of them that is supposed by the Latin tag (Wilfred Owen, *The Complete Poems and Fragments*, ed. Jon Stallworthy, 2 vols. (London, 1983), i. 140).

[32] Drittura resembles the classical goddess Astraea, the last of the immortals to leave the earth. Christian interpreters understood her leaving as a consequence of the Fall. Dante's poem rebukes his innocent surprise at the wickedness of the world and checks his desire to claim equality with the unfallen. See C. S. Singleton, 'Virgo or Justice', *Studies in Dante 2: Journey to Beatrice* (Cambridge, Mass., 1958), 184–203; and Kenelm Foster, *The Two Dantes and Other Studies* (London, 1977).

after Malta could acknowledge more steadily the pressure of circumstances on his thought. The susceptibility to experience which Dante can no longer deny creates, therefore, a self that stands between inner and outer worlds; what had been invisible within the 'allegory of the poets' asserts its independence of the allegory in order to declare itself equivalent to the virtues. Then, in the breakdown of its heroic aspirations, the self is exiled into a more truthful similarity to personified abstractions—a similarity which, in turn, makes these abstractions look more human.

Discovering truth through suffering, as Dante appears to do in this poem, immediately threatens to lessen the actuality of suffering by serving as a compensation. Dante's poem withholds such consolation. In part this is the consequence of his closing the last stanza in a gesture of abandonment: 'se colpa muore perché l'uom si penta' (l. 90). But the ambiguity of 'colpa' in the last stanza draws attention to the lack of confidence with which he can rehearse this familiar assumption. Although Dante's conversation with these abstractions may have moved him towards clearer self-consciousness, this makes him only more hopelessly dependent on the forgiveness of his fellows.[33] It is taken for granted that contrition leads to the forgiveness of sins but, because he is still held in disgrace by Florence, forgiveness seems at best theoretical. Dante attacks his opponents' hostility, certainly, by implying that it stultifies, as well as contradicts, the mercy of God; but, though a restoration to innocence *may* be brought about by exile, this does not happen, either within the poem or in a future it can predict with certainty. Dante may put a purgatorial construction on his experience and see it retrospectively as redemptive, but he denies that interpretation immediacy by distancing himself from the point of vantage it requires. Exile seems to consist, most of all, in the division between the point of view that gives coherence to experience—a point of view Dante can envisage perfectly well but not adopt—and the unhappily self-doubting attitude that circumstances force him to take up.

After his return from Malta, Coleridge's new understanding of imaginative consolations corresponds to the distinctive features

[33] He offsets it also by refashioning a vocabulary from his earlier poetry that likened love's trials to those of banishment and self-banishment. Cf. 'Tre donne', ll. 9–12 (Foster and Boyde, i. 176) with *Vita Nuova*, xiv, §§8 and 12, pp. 36–7; *Conv.* II. xii. 2, p. 82; and with *Vita Nuova*, xv, §§5–6, vii, §1, pp. 38, 25.

of 'Tre donne''s symbolism. In thinking about Asra, Coleridge ac-
knowledges more consistently that a symbolic object persists unto
itself, within and, as it were, despite its symbolic value. Moreover,
in his writing after 1806, Coleridge recognizes that the truths dis-
covered in or through poetry are themselves symbols of higher
truths outside the grasp of language. The perception of symbolic
forms demands that one attend to them as indications of some-
thing unattainable; if the higher truth were seen entire, it would
be seen in advance.[34] Only the continual postponement of dis-
covery (which is seen at the end of 'Tre donne' to be a precondi-
tion of discovery), enables *otherness* to endure and, consequently,
prevents symbols from turning into allegories. As we shall see, this
subtle idea of symbols, which is approached in Dante's 'Tre donne'
and in Coleridge's later prose, brings with it the danger that a
tactic of postponement will become familiar. If that happens, the
symbol will sustain the pre-emptiveness which its very nature
supposedly denies.

Coleridge faces up to this difficulty most fully when rewriting
The Friend in 1818. Earlier in his career, however, his new under-
standing of symbols alters his idea of his role as a writer. *The Friend*
grew out of 'The Comforts and Consolations'—a projected set of
essays first mentioned in November 1803 and from then on fre-
quently alongside 'The Soother of Absence', which he had been
planning earlier. Thought of, at first, as a long poem and later as
an anthology (to include the *canzoni* by Dante, transcribed in 1806–
7) 'The Soother of Absence' was gradually abandoned in favour
of the essays that went to make up *The Friend*. The substitution
of 'consolation' for 'soothing' epitomizes Coleridge's gain in moral
understanding as a result of exile. The collection of poems, that is,
was intended to administer solace medicinally; the essays start
from the assumption that it is self-defeating to attempt doing so.
The importance of exile to this change emerges from his plans for
the work, before and after visiting Malta. In 1804 he wrote to Sir
George Beaumont full of enthusiasm for the new idea.

The 'Consolations' are addressed to all in adversity, sickness, or distress
of mind | the first part entirely practical—the second in which I consider

---

[34] The changes in Coleridge's idea of symbolism affect his theology and his view
of history. This is a large subject. On religion, see his letter to Thomas Clarkson,
13 Oct. 1806, *CL*, ii. 1193–6; *CN*, ii. 2405; on history, see 'Letters on the Span-
iards', ii and vi, *EOT*, ii. 49, 75–8.

distress of mind from gloomy Speculation will, of course, be speculative, & will contain a new Theodicee, & what will perhaps appear to many a new Basis of Morals | the 'Comforts' are addressed to the Happy & Prosperous, attempting to open to them new & perhaps better—at all events, more numerous & more various Sources of Enjoyment.—Of this work every page has & will come from my Heart's Heart— (1 Feb. 1804, *CL*, ii. 1053)

In the plan 'Consolations' (Coleridge's own work aimed at resolving predominantly intellectual 'distress') are to be coupled with what sounds like a further anthology, the 'Comforts' that offer 'more numerous & more various sources of Enjoyment'. The combination is a precedent of his interspersion in *The Friend* of miscellaneous amusements among the passages of argument. When these plans are set out again as part of Coleridge's 'Prospectus' to the 1809–10 version, the two audiences he aimed at originally are no longer separated and, accordingly, the twin projects of his letter are seen to arise out of each other:

Sources of consolation to the afflicted in Misfortune, or Disease, or Dejection of Mind, from the Exertion and right Application of the Reason, the Imagination, and the moral Sense; and new sources of enjoyment opened out, or an Attempt (as an illustrious Friend once expressed the Thought to me) to add Sunshine to Daylight, by making the Happy more happy. In the words 'Dejection of Mind' I refer particularly to Doubt or Disbelief of the moral Government of the World, and the grounds and arguments for the religious Hopes of Human Nature. (*Friend*, no. 1, ii. 18–19)

Because Coleridge's semi-colon divides the two activities but not, at first, their prospective audiences, the 'Comforts' appear to continue what the 'Consolations' achieved. The 'new sources of enjoyment' in 1809 are opened out to 'the afflicted' who then appear the beneficiaries of Coleridge's adding 'Sunshine to Daylight'. The explanation that follows disrupts this connection but does not sever it. Instead, 'the afflicted' and 'the Happy' are gradually taken together, lending the work more universal appeal—one can imagine reading it in both states of mind—and, standing at opposite ends of the sentence, they unobtrusively point towards the movement from affliction to consolation which is the aim and effect of the work as a whole. Although the intermixture of both aims enables Coleridge to make this implication (that he can raise the afflicted to happiness), he simultaneously tones down his claims for the project. In 1809, the misery caused by 'gloomy Specula-tion' is included among other circumstantial things and so it be-comes biographical: 'Dejection of Mind' recalls his own 'Dejection'; the slightly patronizing 'gloomy Speculation' is made into more persistent and nagging 'Doubt and Disbelief'. Similarly, the 'Con-solations' have become 'Sources of consolation' that require some kind of answering 'Exertion' before they will yield their comfort and by no means '*contain* a new Theodicee' (my emphasis) even if they may, under some circumstances, lead to greater under-standing of God's ways.[35]

In the later version of his proposals, then, Coleridge both re-stricts his desire to dispense wisdom and gives it freer rein. In 1809 the afflicted and the happy become confused so that the second may appear to take over, and Coleridge may seem intent on leading us from one to the other. Intent on leading, not dra-gooning, since the movement is made to depend on his audience's efforts. Coleridge's new respect for his readers' self-will in apply-ing or not applying what he says equals the acceptance in his theology and history of an irremovable difference between self and other—the consequent aim of offering 'material for reflection' leaves its mark on the style itself. The rather high-pitched self-deprecation of his letter to Sir George—'new & perhaps better—at all events, more numerous [. . .]' and 'what will perhaps appear to many a new Basis of Morals'—is lost in a tone of command that adopts examples instead of seeking approval for form's sake. Coleridge's self-importance and his concern to ensure the reader's freedom of response create in *The Friend* his high estimation and often accomplished practice of a mediating role.[36]

In 1818, however, Coleridge's difficulties were of a further order of magnitude because the end-point of his arguments was,

---

[35] See *Friend*, i. 283, 'It was part of my plan to allot two numbers of *The Friend*, the one to a selection from our prose writers, and the other from our poets'. Coleridge also repeats his terms of comfort and instruction in introducing 'The Story of Maria Eleonora Schöning', see ii. 173 (i. 342).

[36] His success in *The Friend* contrasts with the embarrassed mediation of *Biographia Literaria*. Cf. K. M. Wheeler, *Sources, Processes, and Methods in Coleridge's* Biographia Literaria (Cambridge, 1980), 157 ff. and John R. Nabholtz, '*My Reader My Fellow Labourer*': *A Study of English Romantic Prose* (Columbia, Mich., 1986), 97–128. See also Jerome Christensen, *Coleridge's Blessed Machine of Language* (Ithaca, NY, and London, 1981), 104–8; Paul Hamilton, *Coleridge's Poetics* (Oxford, 1983), 20–2, 25–6.

by now, known in advance (if only to their expositor, Coleridge). What had been, perhaps, 'a regular stepping of the Imagination towards a Truth' was being recomposed from the outside and with the benefits of hindsight. In the rest of this chapter, I want to show first how the problem inherent in rewriting *The Friend* may be seen repeated in Coleridge's ideas about dreaming, in particular in his concept of the 'waking dream'. Secondly, I want to suggest that Dante's *Commedia* requires and employs the same kind of self-division as Coleridge has to create in order to solve the problems of rewriting and to preserve in it the tentativeness and integrity of symbolic prose. This will lead me to dwell on the characteristics of Coleridge's style and structure in the 1818 version, characteristics which, in turn, reveal the shortcomings of critical writing on *The Friend*.

The problem and its solution can be seen in outline, however, in his idea of the 'waking dream'. Coleridge's interest in dreams was lifelong, but he concerned himself with the waking dream only in his middle years. Later in life, dreams offer a freedom that may be disturbing or delightful; in 1805, they are dangerous:

But Fancy and Sleep *stream* on; and [. . .] they connect with them motions of the blood and nerves, and images forced into the mind by the feelings that arise out of the position & state of the Body and its different members. (*CN*, ii. 2543)[37]

Coleridge's imaginings cannot resist the inclinations of the body and so, as he goes on to say, they lose their innocence: in the waking state, on the other hand, 'outward Forms and sounds' are our 'Sanctifiers' and 'Strengtheners'. The 'new influxes from without' (made possible by sensory awareness of the external world) are continually 'counteracting the Impulses from within, and *poising* the Thought' (ibid.).

A 'waking dream' is 'poised' by the external world, without becoming as absorbed in appearances as we are in everyday life. This makes the experience as vivid as a nightmare without its being delusory.

---

[37] Dreams reveal the 'wild activities and restless chaos' of our sinful nature (*CL*, vi. 715) or they create seclusion: 'when we sleep the mind acts without interruption' (*Table Talk*, 1 May 1823, i. 53). This reveals the same opposition that controls Coleridge's desire 'to concenter my Being into Stoniness, or to be diffused among the winds' (see above).

the Night-mair is not a mere Dream, but takes place when the waking
State of the Brain is re-commencing, and most often during a rapid alter-
nation, a *twinkling* as it were, of sleeping and waking [. . . .] [W]e unite
the Actual Perceptions, or their immediate Reliques, with the phantoms
of the inward Sense—and thus so confound the half-waking, half-sleeping
Reasoning Power, that we actually do pass a positive judgement in̶ for the
reality of what we see & hear.   (*Lectures 1808–19*, i. 135–6)

Nightmares are terrifying because we believe the events are actu-
ally happening. We unite, without realizing it, 'Actual Perceptions
[. . .] with the phantoms of the inward Sense'. During a nightmare
and when we are awake, the inner and outer realms are brought
together as the one interrupts the other; but everything depends on
how they are joined. When awake, internal and external somehow
counteract, giving 'poise' to our thoughts; in nightmares, the two
spheres coalesce. Coleridge implies, nevertheless, that our night-
mares' '*twinkling* as it were, of sleeping and waking' can be illu-
minating. This oscillation may be confusing or simply normal, but
it can also give access to a higher truth.

'Waking', however, occurs both within the dream and at the
moment when it ends. It signifies both a state and the moment of
transition from one state to another. This feature of Coleridge's
idea prevents him from claiming to possess a vision of truth. Its
true nature will be revealed when he wakes. At the same time,
'waking' ensures that what is seen in a dream is, none the less,
true. Its symbolic power is not reduced by its remaining secondary
to the true reality, because the dream's continual waking has in-
troduced and intermingled reality already. The concept allows
Coleridge to see the eternal as translucent in the temporal and to
follow through the consequences of that. A waking dreamer per-
ceives the eternal within the sequence of time; but because his
experience does not escape that sequentiality he cannot be conclu-
sive about the truth he has perceived. The human perception of
truth can neither possess it nor renounce its possession; it must
continue to move towards what is seen already.

The alternation of sleeping and waking, which brings us to a
point of true vision, demands that Coleridge wakes:

As a man who having walked in his Sleep by rapid openings of his eyes
too rapid to be observable by others or rememberable by himself sees and

remembers the whole of his Path, mixing it with many fancies ab intra.— & awaking remembers, but yet as a Dream. (*CN*, ii. 2584)[38]

The oscillation between sleeping and waking is continued in his conscious recollection of the dream 'yet as a Dream'. The waking dream may have led him to within sight of the truth, but in order to see that it has done so he must step away. The opposing case of the nightmare illustrates this: its terrifying delusions frighten us only so long as we sleep. When we wake up, of course, they vanish and we calm down. Because in a waking dream we are unconsciously percipient of the outside world—because we are unconsciously awake—the moment of waking has the opposite result: it makes us aware of the truth. It repeats the action that secures us from deception while we are having the dream: the 'rapid openings of his eyes too rapid to be observable [. . .] or rememberable'.

As we wake we see the dream for what it is, and so we carry on into waking consciousness the movement between inner and outer which forms this kind of dream. This means that what is both preliminary to the truth, and a true representation, may remain without question the latter by being reconsidered as the former. So, on waking, we are enabled to secure the truth-value of our dreams by granting that they are only dreams. While the dreaming mind streams on, the nightmare sufferer, similarly, only unites and never redivides the external and the internal. The watcher of his own waking dreams (where inner and outer are mingled but not fused) can wake to observe the otherness of his own imagined perceptions.[39] 'Waking', therefore, provides a form of perception symbolic enough to understand symbols, and a form of self-consciousness that transforms private experience into a symbolic language.

Such a recognition involves a pause—the 'Reason and Reality'

---

[38] This complex entry suggests that waking up from such a dream is comparable to entering an afterlife. The succession of intermediate states between earth and heaven does not include memories of death itself but only those of a previous life 'Something like a Dream' (ibid.). Our eternal being continues a sequence of existences. The waking dream, therefore, gives an intimation of eternity that is, surprisingly, identical to our immortal life. In dreaming and in dying, our entrance into eternity remains a temporal process.

[39] Cf. 'I felt myself in pleasurable bodily feeling half-asleep and interruptedly *conscious* of being sweetly half-asleep | and I felt how strongly, how apart from all concupiscence' (*CN*, ii. 2495, fo. 39ᵛ; see also 2302, 2441).

which are always 'poising' the thought of the waking mind 'can stop and stand still' (*CN*, ii. 2543)—and pausing is essential to Coleridge's idea of good writing. He describes poetry in the *Biographia* as successful when it produces 'the liveliest image of succession with the feeling of simultaneousness!' (*BL*, ii. 25) and Cary's translation is praised for combining 'variety and continuity' (for moving onward and standing still). The same consideration also determines Coleridge's judgement of good reading and good watching. During nightmares people do 'pass a positive judgement for the reality' of what they see, but watching a play requires more sceptical and more self-conscious collaboration:

a sort of temporary Half-Faith, which the Spectator encourages in himself & supports by a voluntary contribution on his own part, because he knows that it is at ~~any~~ all times in his power to see ~~it~~ the thing as it really is. (*Lectures 1808–19*, i. 134)[40]

'[T]emporary Half-Faith' begins 'that willing suspension of disbelief for the moment which consitutes poetic faith' (*BL*, ii. 6). The dramatic principle is later extended to all literary experience and the balancing-point that defines the waking dream—a point of balance which is portrayed also as a continual movement between extremes—becomes a criterion central to Coleridge's thinking about true representation in art.[41] It is a criterion, however, open to the same difficulties as Coleridge's conception of symbols and symbolic perception.[42]

[40] Cf. *CN*, ii. 2274: 'Hard to express that sense of the analogy or likeness of a Thing which enables a Symbol to represent it, so that we think of the Thing itself— & yet knowing that the Thing is not present to us.' See also the continuation of the *Lectures 1808–19* passage (p. 136).

[41] Erasmus Darwin and Herder may have been influential on Coleridge's thinking and, more remotely, Lord Kames (*Lectures 1808–19*, i. pp. lvii, 134 n.). Elisabeth Schneider in *Coleridge, Opium and Kubla Khan* (Chicago, 1953), argues for Darwin's exclusive influence; Alethea Hayter in *Opium and the Romantic Imagination [. . .]* (London, 1968, rev. edn., 1988), puts it down to drugs. See Adair, *The Waking Dream*, 52–5, on the importance of Andrew Baxter, *An Enquiry into the Nature of the Human Soul*, 2 vols. (London, 1745). Adair recognizes 'the dream-like method of [Coleridge's] composition, a mingling [. . .] of conscious and unconscious processes' and 'the dream-like haunting quality' of his best work. But discussion always stops here. She adds that later in life 'a more conscious awareness' took the place of Coleridge's dreams. By neglecting Coleridge's intellectual framework and stylistic methods she can assume more easily that his dream-like manner could not endure self-awareness (Adair, *The Waking Dream*, 8, 196).

[42] 'Waking dream' and 'the suspension of disbelief' are familiar phrases in Coleridge criticism and the relationship between the two has been observed before.

The twin dangers of tranquillity and oblivion reappear in Coleridge's assessment of art. '[T]emporary Half-Faith' slips easily into complete submission to the great works of, pre-eminently, Shakespeare. The great artists are then elevated above the world into a visionary calm so that they can no longer remain engaged, continually, with 'the thing as it really is'. The hero-worship that moves Coleridge to these complementary extremes is itself the opposite (and twin) of his desire for Shakespearean (or Words-worthian) authority. His formulation of dramatic experience as 'a sort of temporary Half-Faith', for instance, hovers too confidently on the brink of claiming that the watcher only entertains belief, while s/he knows 'that it is at all times in his power to see the thing as it really is'.[43] The continuance of this awareness is the only guarantee that he feels and sees the truth that is revealed by drama. But to continue in a posture of receptivity and hesitance involves becoming self-conscious about the need for self-restraint. Such self-consciousness runs the risk of defeating receptivity, usurp-ing the 'Half-Faith' by presuming to know its nature. *The Friend* is an attempt to put into practice deliberate self-restraint. It is, in some respects, Coleridge's response to Wordsworth's completed *Prelude* and aims, like the poem, to establish Coleridge's author-ity as universal because not his own. He idealizes the elevation of Shakespeare or Milton, but tries himself to practise a method that makes him the friend, not the teacher, of his readership. This policy requires that Coleridge's predetermination of events does not destroy the progressiveness of his writing. The 'waking' of the waking dream must be employed to keep Coleridge within the sequence he has already completed.

Coleridge's revision of *The Friend*, then, needed to preserve this wakeful 'Half-Faith' in particularly difficult circumstances. The problems he confronts when restructuring the work correspond, however, to the aims at its centre, because the 'waking dream' describes symbols and the perception of symbols. In the 1809–10 version Coleridge was already trying to encourage his readers to take up the point of view of a 'waking dream' because his essays were concerned with a particular kind of symbol, the principle.

The difficulties Coleridge encountered in holding himself at this mid-point of en-gaged attention are less well accounted for.

[43] See *Friend*, ii. 217–18, not reprinted in 1818, but in *BL*, ii. 186. Cary quotes this passage at Cary, p. vi.

It is my object to refer men to PRINCIPLES in all things; in Literature, in the Fine Arts, in Morals, in Legislation, in Religion. (*Friend*, no. 1, ii. 13)[44]

'PRINCIPLES', as Coleridge defines them in *The Friend*, form the mid-point between prudential maxims and a tyrannical system, mid-way therefore between Burke and Rousseau, and similar in their nature to symbols.[45] Rousseau's system (according to Coleridge's hostile description) paid no attention to contingencies; English 'Realpolitik' (stemming, perhaps falsely, from Burke) ignored every-thing bar the immediate. Coleridge believed his readers must make their judgements depend neither on events seen in isolation, nor on presuppositions independent of circumstances. To perceive prin-ciples and to have his reader perceive them, Coleridge must write in the way he recommends in *Biographia Literaria*, avoiding both the striking lines which absorb 'the whole attention of the reader' and 'an unsustained composition from which the reader collects rapidly the general result' (*BL*, ii. 14).[46]

To find a way between these two extremes commits Coleridge to making his reader a fellow-labourer who thinks through the arguments Coleridge presents, instead of passively accepting them. This co-operation is inherent in Coleridge's political position, be-cause both of the positions he wants to avoid engender passivity in writer and reader alike: accepting 'Realpolitik' condemns the artist to the role of entertainer (since events, not thought or opinion, entirely determine policy); proclaiming a system means imposing an authority the reader cannot resist. Thought is therefore neces-sitated by resisting either alternative, and demands a style that

---

[44] See also *Friend*, ii. 27. Neither of these passages remained in the 1818 version, whose opening presentation of a 'bill of fare' gathered material from nos. 1, 11, and the 'Supernumerary'. The exclusion of 'reference' happens consistently in 1818. The work that distinguishes *The Friend* sees 'principles' as elevating and replacing the 'maxims of prudence' while avoiding the tyranny of a system—resisting Uni-tarian self-confidence and the self-immolation of a Roman Catholic. Remaining between these extremes involves the establishment of a relation between the prin-ciples and the person who holds them. It resembles the form of faith that (unlike the Unitarian's or Roman Catholic's) is engaged with its objects of worship. This need governs Coleridge's writing in *The Friend* and determines its manners to-wards the reader.

[45] Coleridge changed his sense of principles and their relation to circumstance as he wrote the 1809–10 version: see ii. 132 (i. 201). For a longer account of Coleridge's political project, see Deirdre Coleman, *Coleridge and* The Friend (*1809–10*) (Oxford, 1988).

[46] *Friend*, i. 176–202 (ii. 103–9, 122–33); see above, p. 71.

makes collaboration possible. Only by ensuring the reader's participation will Coleridge prevent his principles from appearing universal (but superficial) maxims of prudence, or from appearing merely his own, private judgements inflated into a system. The collaboration Coleridge requires is made possible by a style that pauses, avoiding both the 'skipping, unconnected, short-winded asthmatic sentences' of the 'true modern taste' and, equally, the 'strutting and rounded periods, in which the emptiest truisms are blown up into illustrious bubbles by help of film and inflation'.[47] These are the styles of empirical maxims and empty systems. By stopping and starting, Coleridge's style enacts the process of the mind properly at work and approaching the truth: as in reading a genuine poem, Coleridge, like his reader, 'at every step [. . .] pauses and half recedes, and from the retrogressive movement collects the force which again carries him onward'.[48] His writing aims to reproduce the fusion of judgement and receptivity that defines both a waking dream and Shakespeare's art.

In 1817 Coleridge's praise of Dante's style discovers in it the qualities of the waking dream—the retrogressive movement that allows both further forward motion and a conjunction between foreknowledge and immediacy. Dante exemplified these qualities because his writing created 'Topographic REALITY' out of the 'thousand delusive forms' of Nature. Dante's pre-eminently 'picturesque' poetry never enters the sublime realm of Shakespeare but implies more consistently, therefore, the aesthetic of the 'waking dream'. His descriptions conjoin 'Topographic' particularity with 'REALITY', elevating objects so that they are seen in truth, while representing them as accurately as possible.[49] Dante's 'fidelity in the representation of objects' avoids Wordsworth's *'matter-of-factness'* by remaining faithful to 'REALITY', *'truth operative [. . .] who hath not her existence in matter, but in reason.'*[50] The meeting-point in 'Topographic REALITY' between ideal and real

[47] *Friend*, i. 26; on 'Thought' see i. 16, 114 (ii. 277, 81 n.). Coleridge defines his style against that of fashionable Gallic prose at i. 21 (ii. 151).

[48] *BL*, ii. 14. See also Coleridge's image of the water-insect's 'alternate pulses of active and passive motion', i. 124; and cf. *CN*, i. 1590.

[49] Cf. H. N. Coleridge's simplified version of this remark: 'Very closely connected with this picturesqueness, is the topographic reality of Dante's journey through Hell', *Coleridge's Miscellaneous Criticism*, ed. T. M. Raysor (Cambridge, Mass., 1937), 155. Cf. *CN*, iii. 4498 and n.

[50] *BL*, ii. 126, 127, quoting William Davenant against *The Excursion*.

ensures the co-existence of variety and continuity, so that Coleridge can find himself 'wandering & wandering onward and onward'.[51] The phrase suggests the progressiveness Coleridge admired because it divides into three: 'wandering', '& wandering onward', 'and onward'. While the parallelism, 'wandering & wandering', 'onward and onward', suggests infinity, the ampersand in the first half gives the last addition, 'and onward' the impression of going one step further even as you go on for ever. Dante's varied movement runs counter to the sublime self-assurance Coleridge idealized in other artists. Because of this, his manner is made into an example of the pausing style necessary for the communication of truth.

The passage from Cary that Coleridge selects for his lectures reveals, however, that such onward movement, the 'Topographic REALITY' of a waking dream, is combined in the *Commedia* with continual foreknowledge:

We the circle cross'd

To the next steep, arriving at a well,
That boiling pours itself down to a foss   105
Sluic'd from its source. Far murkier was the wave
Than sablest grain: and we in company
Of the' inky waters, journeying by their side,
Enter'd, though by a different track, beneath.
Into a lake, the Stygian nam'd, expands   110
The dismal stream, when it hath reach'd the foot
Of the grey wither'd cliffs. Intent I stood
To gaze, and in the marish sunk descried
A miry tribe, all naked, and with looks
Betok'ning rage.   115

('Hell', vii. 103–15, Cary, i. 30)[52]

The change from 'we [. . .] journeying' to 'Into a lake, the Stygian named' at the beginning of line 110—from first person to third, and past to present—exactly follows the original's disruption of the narrative by an authorial comment. Spoken by Dante as *poeta*, the lines momentarily separate the reader from the poet's journey and free him to consider the meaning of this name.[53] They

---

[51] *Lectures 1808–19*, ii. 402; *CL*, iv. 781. For Dante's picturesque power see *BL*, ii. 21; *CN*, iii. 4498 (repr. in *Lectures 1808–19*, ii. 401 ff.).

[52] See *Inferno*, vii. 100–11, Sapegno, i. 84–5.

[53] Cf. Hazlitt's remark about *Inferno* xi: 'In the midst of the obscure and shadowy regions of the lower world, a tomb suddenly rises up with the inscription, "I am the tomb of Pope Anastasius the Sixth" ', 'On Poetry in General', Hazlitt, v. 18.

deliberately bring the general into the particular and give 'the thousand delusive forms' of Dante's Hell a more long-standing significance than that of the passions they may excite. The loss of narrative drive, however, matches a hesitation in the story itself when, at the foot of the cliff, Virgil and Dante have another, broader vista opened to them. The intervening poetic voice cannot therefore provide an escape into contemplation or visionary calm, but is reinvolved in the progress of the narrative. In Coleridge's terms, the pause offers a moment of aftersight and foresight that makes the story, as it resumes, intelligible as a symbol. The reader acquires the perspective from which Hell is a space, previously defined, and in which he may wander, but as a result, he is able to see its details with a precision that knows the reality behind the appearance.

The example from *Inferno* vii is particularly happy because its pause and Dante's perspective on himself co-operate so fully. In the poem as a whole, Dante's self-division makes a continuous interruption that runs alongside his paralysing encounters with the other speakers of the poem—Virgil, the damned, Farinata, Beatrice, and so on. Dante is always re-attending to the self-assessments that form the poem's narrative so that, while he can attend to his earlier actions as points in a predictable narrative, his angle of attention makes these events happen again and again. The characteristics of his self-attention are implied by his idea of true vision and accord with the poetry that creates it. The judgement suspended in an encounter, and the judgement needed in the effort to avoid being captivated by the damned, are themselves objects of Dante's judgement and his involvement. In writing and rereading, he carries on the purification the poem narrates. At the same time, the separation between Dante's two roles prevents the poem's re-enactments from becoming self-forgetful repetitions, or merely a wandering among events, unaware of the destination towards which they are moving.

The distinctive features of Coleridge's revised version of *The Friend* correspond to this quality in Dante. The 1818 version's conjunction of foreknowledge and immediacy (its practice of a style that parallels the 'waking dream'), is based upon the same perspective as the one Dante adopts in the *Commedia*. The changes between 1809–10 and 1818, and the subtle intellectual coherence that Coleridge achieved in the revised version, can be seen in his altered sense of pausing. Pausing becomes a continuous process, occurring at every moment and creating a sequence out of those moments.

Antecedent to all History, and long glimmering through it as a holy Tradition, there presents itself to our imagination an indefinite period, dateless as Eternity, a State rather than a Time. For even the sense of succession is lost in the uniformity of the stream. (*Friend*, i. 7)

This new opening paragraph begins the revised version with a different idea of how the golden age is remembered. It appears in 1809 as 'the tradition which the self-dissatisfied Race of Men have every where preserved and cherished' (*Friend*, ii. 11). In 1818 the knowledge of an ideal past intrudes on subsequent historical experience less steadily, at intervals 'glimmering through it as a holy Tradition'. History is punctuated by this perception of a prehistorical and prelapsarian eternity; man, within historical time, comes to expect that perception. Consequently, 'Tradition' applies both to the estimation of this earlier eternity, its traditional or mythical perfection; and to the repeated occurrence of that estimation within time. Coleridge's phrase succeeds in combining the instant of glimmering insight (into a traditional state of bliss) with the tradition of such insight. The timelessness of the golden age intervenes in a historical sequence from without, and is seen to persist within it all the time. The contrast between a momentary, retrospective view of bliss and the suffering of fallen experience itself creates a source of variety. This distinguishes our fallen world from uniform and invisibly successive paradisal existence, enabling us to perceive temporal movement by contrast with eternity. The further sense of 'tradition' as an ever-present possibility then appears to offer continuity within this variety so that 'glimmering' re-expresses the dual perspective Coleridge looks to find in poetry.

Looking back produces the same intelligent insight; the tradition presents to our imagination perfect successiveness invisible to the blessed themselves. The double sense of 'Tradition' means that paradisal innocence may be regained and left behind at the same time; the self's pause of thought recaptures the past and creates it anew, just as it observes an unbroken stretch of time by including it as a sudden break. The perceived interruption dislocates and fits into the self's life in time. Coleridge's landing-places in 1818 produce on a large scale the hiatuses in which forward movement is made possible by retrospection. Punctuation has the same effect:

In short, I look on the stops not as logical Symbols, but rather as dramatic *directions* representing the process of Thinking & Speaking conjointly—either therefore the regulation of the Breath simply [. . .] or as the movements in the Speaker's Thoughts makes [*sic*] him regulate his Breath, pause longer or shorter, & prepare his voice before the pause for the pause [. . . .] He pauses—then the activity of the mind, generating upon its generations, starts anew—& the pause is not [. . .] at all *retrospective*, but always prospective—that is, a the pause ~~does~~ is not affected by what ⟨actually⟩ follows, but by what anterior to it was foreseen as following. (CN, iii. 3504, fos. 8–8ᵛ)[54]

His punctuation aims to allow thought and utterance to coincide. The 'process of Thinking' engenders pauses of its own, which, once built into the flow of speech, facilitate a self-conscious understanding of one's own thought, that can see its end-point during its advance. Consequently, one can 'prepare his voice before the pause for the pause'. Coleridge's own punctuation in this note suggests an infinite regress towards the unattainable first hesitation. '[B]efore the pause, for the pause' would be more decisive and single-minded, but pins down too definitely where the process begins. The thought of it would outrun and subordinate speech. If their subdivisions were so entirely and restrictively comprehended beforehand, the stages of an argument would not flow into one another or contain within themselves their principle of growth.

The long example Coleridge gives in this note moves from outrage at the horrors of slavery to awareness of the general law—the distinction between things and persons—which is flouted by the trade. The general truth is fundamental to indignation at the particular crime 'but the former might be, & is gracefully regarded as the whole, at the commencement in the Speaker's view' (ibid.). Each pause comes at the completion of an argument which then turns out to be the beginning of a further argument. This is what Coleridge means by the distinction at the end of the note: pauses are not retrospective because they are not introduced in the light of later events, but by the intimation in advance of what is to come. This entails a different kind of self-consciousness that asks the writer continually to reperuse his previous thoughts and to distribute punctuation marks so that they allow writer and reader to re-enact the sequential reassessment that generates thought. The written version becomes, therefore, a further stage in the generation

[54] Cf. the description of methodical behaviour as a form of punctuation in *Friend*, i. 450.

of thought because it creates through pausing the occasion of another reassessment. By being part of the process, composition ensures that the writer remains continuous with the discovering self he writes for while it necessitates a division between the two. The relationship between Coleridge's two selves becomes dramatic—like that between playwright and actor in a one-man show.[55]

Other aspects of the work are affected by the changes in Coleridge's approach to and intentions for his writing: in the revised version, examples or anecdotes are no longer final proof but a point of certainty that facilitates contention, 'doubt and self-questioning'. Remembering, therefore, does not follow and confirm a proof by logic but is the beginning of debate. In consequence, the objects of memory retain their independence more entirely.[56] Likewise, exemplification, while it may alter one's views, is essential as the means whereby the self can recognize its own opinions —a recognition that allows the views to alter the self. Self-consciousness and the proper understanding of principles are both at work, then, during Coleridge's successive revisions, when he sees his writings as a record of experience and a tacit autobiography.

When annotating a passage in the 1809–10 version he was never satisfied with and finally cut, Coleridge refers his reader to 'Appendix C' of the *Statesman's Manual* and, while apologizing for its difficulty, urges the reader to account for that from the writer's point of view:

I beseech you, do not be discouraged if [. . .] you do not understand me at the first two or three Readings. Consider, how many years I have been toiling thro' mist and twilight; but I have not a fuller conviction of my own Life than I have of the Truth of my present convictions. They have taught me the difference in *kind* between the *sense* of certainty and the *sensation* of positiveness. (*Friend*, no. 5, ii. 76 n.)[57]

---

[55] 'Affected' in the note seems to mean 'brought about by, effected'. For this idea of pauses, cf. *BL*, ii. 14.

[56] Cf. on this point the anecdote recounted in *Friend*, ii. 31 and repeated in i. 35–6. In 1818 Coleridge adds a new paragraph, 'To a creature so highly, so fearfully gifted'. The addition is a self-rebuke directed against Coleridge's earlier ardent confidence. 'Truth' Coleridge now adds, 'is self-restoration', truth that must be 'without alloy and unsophisticated' (i. 36–7). The revision is made into a reassessment that requires the earlier anecdote and needs to correct it.

[57] *Lay Sermons*, 59–93, esp. 67–9. The note appears in Copy R, probably annotated in Sept. 1816 (*Friend*, i, p. lxxxi, ii. 388). Cf. what convictions have taught him here with what he plans to prove about them in no. 1, *Friend*, ii. 7.

From Coleridge's present standpoint, his earlier views appear foolishly enthusiastic and his whole way of holding opinions a sensory deception—unintelligent and visceral. But this self-knowledge is not itself 'positive' or insistently self-distanced in the same way. His '*sense* of certainty' is born of convictions external to him and yet as integral as his sense of life—he recognizes, that is, how he learnt from these convictions while, at the same time, he sees them as similar in nature to the belief in one's own existence which is one of the fundamental, indigenous assumptions of the self, however open it might be to philosophical analysis. The play between the two senses of 'conviction' draws certainty away from asseveration—the reader's difficulties reading Coleridge cannot be removed without destroying the connection between the '*sense* of certainty' and 'the conviction of my own Life', so that although he has reached a point of perfect confidence in the truth of his opinions he is still 'toiling thro' mist and twilight'—continuing to write his arduous prose and reflecting upon its difficulty; convinced of the truthfulness and intermediate status of each moment both of writing and of thinking.

In the 1809–10 version Coleridge never joins so fluidly certainty and doubt, self-composure and enquiry—in 1818, the convictions that teach us how to be certain are reproduced as the principles that guide our faith.

We live by Faith, says the philosophic Apostle; and faith without principles is but a flattering phrase for wilful positiveness, or fanatical bodily sensation. Well, and of good right therefore, do we maintain with more zeal, than we should defend body or estate, a deep and inward conviction, which is as the moon to us; and like the moon with all its massy shadows and deceptive gleams, it yet lights us on our way, poor travellers as we are, and benighted pilgrims. With all its spots and changes and temporary eclipses, with all its vain halos and bedimming vapors, it yet reflects the light that *is* to rise on us, which even now is *rising*, though intercepted from our immediate view by the mountains that enclose and frown over the vale of our mortal life. (*Friend*, i. 97)

An 'inward conviction [. . .] lights us on our way' and, though we persist in doubt and hesitations, our most deeply held beliefs—private and always possibly mistaken—can be an augur of what is to come. The light 'which even now is *rising*' is reflected back upon us from beliefs we cling to and zealously defend. This paradox depends on the same self-consciousness as earlier—the same reappraisal of our convictions that observes their doubtfulness in order to gain for them greater authority. Without this exchange with the principles that must accompany our faith (an exchange that distinguishes them from maxims and the dictates of fashion) we would be reduced to fanaticism. True faith involves continual reassessment: the moon that 'lights us on our way', a moment later 'reflects the light that *is* to rise on us'—as soon as we consider private convictions to be separate from ourselves their guidance turns into a sign of our destination. Their light is not their own and the pilgrimage not ours alone but paralleled in the approach towards us of what we seek. The advance of truth is not, nevertheless, only signalled by but revealed in the convictions that we hold most strongly; the inner light does not indicate something other that is to come, but is immediately transformed into part of the illumination, into a forerunner and an instance. What 'even now is *rising*' cannot be seen directly but is seen in truth, despite the surrounding darkness and the interruptions of circumstance.[58]

It is a most beautiful passage: the succession of qualifications shares the steadiness of the progress Coleridge describes but is not preternaturally calm. The high style of its sentence-structure is crossed by an urgency of emphasis (on '*is* to rise' and 'is *rising*') that breathes a sense of surprise and idiosyncrasy into Coleridge's grand, public voice and yet does not deride it. The indistinguishability and continual distinction of what is to come and what already exists, what is promised and what is a fact, controls the harmony within the prose between a constructive principle and an intuitive realization—the harmony, that is, between the elegance of its composition and the insight it brings about. Because private beliefs are here gradually taken for symbols—in a process of reassessment that is appropriate to symbols—they become part of the truth and are always being reassessed. The certainty that private beliefs are, to some extent, true denies the possibility of universal tolerance (as the essay argues throughout), but the form of that certainty generates an unending vulnerability to judgement. His balance between the conflicting demands is achieved through a process of self-reappraisal that involves self-consciousness about its necessity. He is, therefore, consistently eager to 'maintain with

---

[58] Cf. Sara Maitland: 'hope is the learning of, the integrating into dailiness of, a vision of what we might be and be in the process of becoming.' (*Independent*, no. 2,018, 8 Apr. 1993, 28.)

more zeal [. . .] a deep and inward conviction'. His zeal must be maintained and this persistent determination to be committed joins reason and passion, forethought and immediacy, so that convictions may become beliefs and persuasions, matters of assent and elements in a life.[59]

The need for self-consciousness controls, as we have seen, Coleridge's discrimination between various kinds of dream—the nightmare differs from the waking dream in not enabling us to see it for what it is or to have convictions about our convictions. In 1818 his acceptance that 'principles' were realized in existence and had to be reconsidered as such, in an endless process of self-conscious revision, gives his prose a new quality of balance between urgency and measure and promotes within it a different relation between exemplification and argument. The wider reorganization of the later version is governed by these priorities—as is suggested by his changing view of dreams. In no. 8 of the 1809–10 edition Coleridge argues that, like convictions, our dreams need to be seen as external and yet as internally generated; if we can be self-conscious about them, they start to reveal their truth; otherwise they are deceptive—a 'fanatical bodily sensation' (*Friend*, i. 97) misconstrued as revelation. He couches all this as a summary of future numbers:

I defer till then the explanation of the mode in which our Thoughts, in states of morbid Slumber, become at times perfectly *dramatic* [. . .] and by what Law the form of the Vision appears to talk to us its own thoughts in a voice as audible as the shape is visible.   (*Friend*, ii. 117–18 (i. 145))

In 1818 the final clause reads, 'and by what Law the *Form* of the vision appears to talk to us its own thoughts [. . .]'. The change in emphasis reduces the immediacy of imaginative production in dreams—the worthless vessel of 'vision', its 'form', becomes the focus of attention once the perception itself is in doubt. Coleridge's alteration finds the vision to exist in forms; in the movement of self-consciousness that arouses us to notice the truth in dreams, we are led to notice the way they appear as a source in themselves of the reality they point towards. Coleridge's revision of all the issues in 1818 similarly considers the overall form of the work as fundamental to its project. Out of the relative disorganization of

---

[59] Cf. *CN*, ii. 2540 and see above pp. 78–9.

the periodical numbers, Coleridge designs a sequence that leads to 'The Third Landing-Place' and its 'Sketches of the Life of Sir Alexander Ball', the exemplary man of principle.

Issue no. 8, on Erasmus and Voltaire, Luther and Rousseau, ghosts and apparitions, is a good example of this process at work. In the 1818 edition it is divided up, tidied into sections, and given titles, but is otherwise unaltered, and forms the first three essays of 'The Landing-Place'. This comes between the opening set of essays, concerned with the possibility, worth, and means of Coleridge fulfilling his aims, and 'Section the First', entitled 'On the Principles of Political Knowledge'.[60] The other two essays of 'The Landing-Place' respectively summarize the preceding essays and add a discussion of the distinction between Reason and Understanding. The first of these is an addition, the second transferred from no. 21. Originally, no. 7 began the discussion of politics as had been promised in no. 6. In order, Coleridge says there, to begin the new topic with a new number, he closes no. 6 with 'The Three Graves' in the additional hope of giving 'relief and amusement' to his readers. Issue no. 8, as it first appeared, interrupted the march of Coleridge's political arguments—the movement from no. 7, which analyses the three underlying types of political system, to the attack in no. 9 on Rousseau's in particular—by trying to show the similarity between Luther and Rousseau, Erasmus and Voltaire. This interruption implicitly fits the justification he gives for enquiring into a political system he believes to be debasing. Rousseau's theoretical bias and resulting lack of attention to the demands of expedience prevent him from possessing, Coleridge argues, the historical sense. It is this sense that suggests to Coleridge the similarities, which Rousseau would be blind to, in the charitable but unflattering comparison with Luther. Coleridge's comparison is obviously directed against Rousseau but, by being so lenient to his opponent (by granting Rousseau's close resemblance to the heroic Luther), he seeks to suggest that the habit of energetic comparison moderates prejudice. In 1818 there is no such interruption: no. 9's equivalent follows on from no. 7 in the sequence of 'Section the First', and no. 8 forms part of the 'Essays

---

[60] The first set reproduces with slight rearrangements nos. 3–6 of 1809–10, which originally made up one essay entitled, 'On the Communication of Truth and the Rightful Liberty of the Press in Connection with It' (*Friend*, ii. 38). See *Friend*, i. 163 n. for the change in title.

interposed for Amusement Retrospect and Preparation', as he subtitles 'The Landing-Place'.[61]

By replacing one interlude with another, removing 'The Three Graves' and putting no. 8 in its place, Coleridge provides a break from the effort of following his argument that is consonant with it. Luther and Rousseau are less pointed examples when, as in 1818, they precede the essay in which Coleridge defends his mentioning him at all, and so the polemic against Rousseau's philosophic self-involvement is tempered though not muted. So, for instance, no. 8, which begins with the concluding passage of the essay forming no. 7, gives as the third motive for including an attack on Rousseau the example he sets of mistakenly thinking oneself personally exempt from 'the universal necessary Laws, and Pure IDEAS of Reason'. Rousseau's political activity manifests the errors of personal vanity where, in truth, knowledge of our real duties demands 'that by an energy of continued self-conquest, we might establish a free and yet absolute Government in our own Spirits' (*Friend*, ii. 110–11 (i. 185)). This ideal may appear to modern eyes either dubious or inaccessible. Coleridge, however, believes the activity of contrasting Luther and Rousseau (performed by his readers as much as by Coleridge himself) will stimulate those readers and so help them approach the ideal condition of 'free and yet absolute' self-government. In 1809 the power to make the comparison is introduced as a type of self-questioning, a reversion from the temptations of Rousseau. In 1818 the same point of view is taken in advance of the debate. One considers the three systems of no. 7, i–iii (forming essays of 'Section the First') with Rousseau's attractive similarity to, and dangerous dissimilarity from, Luther already in mind and already providing an unsettling and invigorating double opposite to his own pretensions. This means that the 'energy of continued self-conquest' is gained from the pause itself and, as Coleridge reorders it, 'Amusement' ('The Landing-Place', essays i–iii), 'Retrospect' (iv), and 'Preparation' (v) are linked to create their own momentum. Without the breather of 'Amusement', the introduction of two essays made up of summary and preparatory material would only relocate the division

---

[61] *Friend*, ii. 88. See the collation tables in *Friend*, 'Appendix D', ii. 395–403 for details of these alterations. Cf. also his introduction of Charlemagne and Buonaparte as sources of comparison in no. 6, ii. 62–6 n. (i. 84–90).

between sections to the point between the two of them. Because of the digression, the summary is more of a resumption, and because the digressive material turns out to be so congruent with what follows, the hesitation on 'The Landing-Place' appears a turning-point and a stepping-stone.

The construction of 'The Landing-Place' is designed to let it enact in small the progress achieved by the entire work while still appearing to be a particular stage in the progression. The perspective implied by this opportunity to look forward and back makes 'what *is* to rise' appear 'already *rising*', both in the sense that the destination of the whole work is already being reached, and that what one might consider a possible future is seen to be impending. Being involved in the series and perpetually re-enacting one's arrival at the end of it are equally products of Coleridge's pauses —they take the reader out of his arguments for a moment and so allow him to pursue them both more actively and more dispassionately. Because, I would say, the 'Amusements' shadow his arguments so closely, the alternation between the two in the experience of reading is as uninterrupted as the hovering on the borders of sleep that occurs in the 'waking dream'. On the other hand, this uninterruptedness is made possible by a pause, a moment of waking, that reveals the limited truth one has acquired so far, as if from a higher vantage-point. This fresh point of view on one's thinking is brought about by stopping to think, but appears to be authoritative—it seems final, but implies another series, a further point of vantage, similar, and yet an advance.

Coleridge creates such a series out of the three landing-places in the 1818 version. The name is taken from a childhood memory of visiting 'THE GREAT HOUSE' nearby:

Beyond all other objects, I was most struck with the magnificent staircase, relieved at well proportioned intervals by spacious landing-places, this adorned with grand or shewy plants, the next looking out on an extensive prospect through the stately window [. . .] while from the last and highest the eye commanded the whole spiral ascent with the marbled pavement of the great hall from which it seemed to spring up as if it merely *used* the ground on which it rested.   ('The Landing-Place', essay iv, *Friend*, i. 148–9)

The intervals of the 1818 version are neatly but not rigidly proportioned—there are sixteen essays in the introductory section,

five in 'The Landing-Place', sixteen in 'Section the First', four
in 'The Second Landing-Place', eleven in 'Section the Second',
prefaced by a long introduction, and finally six in 'The Third
Landing-Place'. The metaphor from this passage implies the whole
structure—Coleridge must have had it planned all along—and
informs its sense of progress. Had the first set of essays been
numbered as such, followed by the first landing-place, the coupling
of section and landing-place would have been static throughout:
first section, first landing-place, second section, second landing-
place and so on. As it is, the landing-places both end and begin
movement as 'Essays Interposed' in the structure; 'The Third
Landing-Place', partly because of this numbering and partly be-
cause its essays are 'Miscellaneous' not 'Interposed', appears es-
pecially final and so resembles more closely the lofty retrospective
of 'the last and highest' position on Coleridge's 'stair-case'. But,
again, in thus commanding the whole ascent, Coleridge finds it
curious and magnificent in a way invisible before—the stairs ap-
pear no longer to climb but to spring from the ground that would
naturally appear their foundation and support. According to this
image, the end of the work comprehends but also reconsiders its
beginning, returning to it is a further step forward because it
aspires to the effortlessness revealed in looking back. From the
point of highest elevation, one looks down meditatively and resumes
the journey, this time within 'the very perfection and final bliss of
the glorified spirit' which St Paul represents 'as a plain aspect, or
intuitive beholding of truth in its eternal and immutable source.'[62]

The dynamic of this relationship governs the 1818 revision,
which relies on and produces Coleridge's gradual self-effacement—
his self-recognition as an instance of universal rules but not as a
model of principled behaviour. In both versions he looks forward
to anonymity:

---

[62] *Friend*, i. 104–5 (ii. 71). Cf. Erasmus Darwin's use of three 'interludes' be-
tween the four cantos of 'The Loves of the Plants'. Darwin places the discussion
of intellectual questions in the prose interludes, restricting the cantos to *'pure
description'*; the numbering is, by comparison with Coleridge's, conventional: after
'Canto i', Darwin places 'Interlude'; after 'Canto ii', 'Interlude ii'; after 'Canto iii',
'Interlude iii'. See Erasmus Darwin, *The Botanic Garden [. . .]*, 2 vols. (London,
1791), ii. 40, 40–50, 83–8, 119–32. Cf. the full title of Ann Radcliffe, *The
Mysteries of Udolpho, A Romance; Interspersed with some Pieces of Poetry*, 4 vols.
(London, 1794).

I can with strictest truth assure my Readers that with a pleasure combined with a sense of weariness I see the nigh approach of that point of my labours, in which I can convey my opinions and the workings of my heart without reminding the Reader obtrusively of myself.   (*Friend*, i. 26–7 (ii. 32))

In 1809 this assurance follows a brief history of his political opinions. In 1818 it follows the introductory and impersonal 'bill of fare'. As a result, in the revised version his gradual eclipse does not appear to depend so much on the exclusion of the personal but rather more on a shift in emphasis around the first person; the 'I' remains in 1818 but its history is unimportant. Coleridge's disappearance depends less on making clear exactly who he is, as seems the implication in 1809, than on his gradual integration into the general case. This implies unanimity with his readers: his unobtrusiveness will be the product of agreement, reached in the future and reflected in the reader's developing ability to identify with the 'I' of the essays. It will further help continuity to persist between his present self and his past; ensuring his self-descriptions remain actions of self-pursuit. In consequence the 1818 version changes *The Friend* into a devotional work for both writer and reader, circular in its structure and so properly infinite in its reaching after moral purity.

Coleridge's self-effacement compels him to win rather than command agreement: in the essay on tolerance added in 1818 he limits it to 'conscientious toleration of each other's intolerance'. To go beyond these limits is self-destructive because self-contradictory, yet there is a more obstinate contradiction inherent in any attempt to reach consensus:

For that must appear to each man to be *his* reason which produces in him the highest sense of certainty; and yet it is *not* reason, except as far as it is of universal validity and obligatory on all mankind.   (*Friend*, i. 97)

Agreement between the two aspects of reason demands their intersection: the personal conviction must acquire 'universal validity', and yet leave the person most fully realized when no longer at odds with anybody else. This ideal intersection lies at an infinite distance, but its attainment consists in continual alternation between the forms of reason. This is a version of the waking dream that requires the single identity to be involved in 'all mankind'. To guard certainty from positiveness, you have to think of yourself both as part of the audience and as an individual; as a friend to the audience whose private convictions gather integrity from being persuasive. Respect for the audience extends to self-respect, and the self-consciousness gained from the work turns it into the ideal friend. The work becomes the means whereby one can see oneself in the first and third persons, and so endlessly approach the point where they meet. Only the completeness of the self-division guarantees advancement towards reunion, and, accordingly, the audience cannot be presumed on. Coleridge's method closes in this self-limitation:

> This elevation of the spirit above the semblances of custom and the senses to a world of spirit, this life in the idea, even in the supreme and godlike [. . .] this it is which affords the sole sure anchorage in the storm [. . . .] This alone belongs to and speaks intelligibly to all alike, the learned and the ignorant, if but the *heart* listens. For alike present in all, it may be awakened, but it cannot be given.   (*Friend*, i. 524)

For Coleridge, then, the creation of symbols is made possible within a particular relationship between a writer and his readers— a relationship that defines the self as dependent for its true existence on establishing agreement with others and so, for its fullest self-expression, on sounding most like them. The Bible offers access to such universality, and Coleridge's various uses of its language— quotation, allusion, and imitation—characterize his symbolism, defining the project and its moments of success.[63] When he rewrites, for instance, a 1799 letter to his wife to make the 'Christmas Out of Doors' passage in *The Friend* (*Friend*, ii. 257–8; i. 367–8), the Bible no longer circumscribes material objects, limiting them to their point of resemblance to revealed truth, but offers a context of possible likenesses. A restraining qualification enters all the comparisons Coleridge makes: the ice that 'represented an agitated sea' appears again 'in shape like an agitated sea'; at sunset in 1799 'all the scattered islands of *smooth* ice were *blood*; intensely bright *Blood*'; in 1809 they change to 'an intensely bright blood colour—they seemed blood and light in union!' Figuring a

---

[63] Cf. *CN*, ii. 3078, where Coleridge uses biblical quotations to corroborate and go beyond the principles they expound. He uses words from the Bible as conclusive maxims that direct the reader's attention towards a further and unstated step in the argument, that is, the step of faith. For the precariousness of this attempt, cf. Coleridge's rewriting of material from *The Friend* in the *Lay Sermons* (*Friend*, ii. 70–1, 73; *Lay Sermons*, 48, 25).

union replaces a transformation, as if mystic insight was more amenable to poised, conversational uncertainty. Representation becomes similitude as the truth of natural objects is seen to consist in their being illuminated by, and united with, the light of divinity instead of absorbed in its 'life'.[64]

The mist, divided by the rising sun, originally became the Red Sea:

the Mist broke in the middle; and at last stood as the waters of the red Sea are said to have done when the Israelites passed—& between these two walls of Mist the Sun-light *burnt* upon the Ice in a strait *road* of golden Fire, all across the lake—intolerably bright, & the walls of Mist partaking of the light in a multitude of colours. (*CL*, i. 461-2)

In revision the explicit parallel disappears: 'the mist broke in the middle, and in a few seconds stood divided, leaving a broad road all across the Lake; and between these two Walls [. . . .]' The similarity is left to us to notice, in what Coleridge describes as 'our second frost', coming after a storm whose 'thunders and howlings' were dreadful because sublime:

Sounds more sublime than any Sight *can* be, more absolutely suspending the power of comparison, and more utterly absorbing the mind's self-consciousness in it's total attention to the object working upon it. (*Friend*, ii. 257)

This amplification of 'sublime' introduces explicitly a fullness of attention that should have been brought about already, as Coleridge states, by his earlier veiling of the resemblances. In our dwelling on the scene he describes its nearness to the escape from Egypt should gradually emerge and the truth of the similarity be felt even while the power of comparison is suspended. Were Coleridge to give chapter and verse, as he does in 1799, the reader would know more readily what to think, but be allowed to consider it with more approving and self-approving detachment. On the other hand, by placing the description of sublimity and its implicit instance in reverse order, Coleridge aims at a further self-consciousness about representation. The sounds, that affect us more deeply than any sight '*can*', withhold immediacy from any verbal description, setting perfection at a further remove. The second occasion (the

[64] To Mrs S. T. Coleridge, 14 Jan. 1799, *CL*, i. 462; *Friend*, ii. 257.

1. Henry Fuseli, *Die Strafe der Diebe* (1772) (The Punishment of the Thieves). See p. 42. Illustrating *Inferno*, xxiv–xxv.

2. Henry Fuseli, *Dante and Virgil on the Ice of Cocytus* (1772). See p. 43.
Illustrating *Inferno*, xxxiii.

3. William Blake, *The Circle of the Lustful: Paolo and Francesca*. Illustrating *Inferno*, v. See pp. 59–60. Blake sketched a nearly complete set of illustrations in pencil, adding water-colour washes to some (as here) and using them as the basis for engravings (see Plates 4–6).

4. William Blake, *The Circle of the Lustful: Paolo and Francesca* (1827), engraved copper plate. Illustrating *Inferno*, v. See pp. 59–60. The reversed plate produced engravings with the same right-left orientation as Plate 3.

5. William Blake, *The Circle of the Thieves: Agnolo Brunelleschi Attacked by a Six-Footed Serpent* (1827), engraving. Illustrating *Inferno*, xxv. See p. 65. This (and Plate 6) are engravings (not the engraved plates) and consequently they are not reversed.

6. William Blake, *The Circle of the Falsifiers: Dante and Virgil Covering their Noses because of the Stench* (1827), engraving. Entitled *The Pit of Disease: The Falsifiers* in Gilchrist's catalogue. Illustrating *Inferno*, xxix. See p. 65.

second frost, coming first) moves towards the remove. The passage arrests attention and then doubles back (against the dynamic of a reader's enquiry) to keep him or her judging, placing out of reach what has already been gained.

The rewriting of this letter typifies the processes that distinguish both versions of *The Friend*. Its personal testimony tapers into universal experience, at the expense of neither itself nor the other, and its symbols make a more tactful appearance but are neither lessened in importance nor blunted in definition.[65] To read the passage and its revision in this way is to oppose most recent critics of Coleridge's prose. Jerome Christensen's deconstructive reading believes the revision of this letter shows Coleridge withdrawing from 'the ontological pretensions of the symbol', in a compulsive denial of the incarnations he had seen and declared when younger: 'At the moment of transfiguration an allegorical figure of difference intrudes on the symbolic union'. Each removal of a first-person exclamation from the revised version is, Christensen says, 'an accommodation of writerly desire to the hygiene of the symbol'.[66] Because Christensen defines the symbol not only in opposition to allegory but as the opposite of allegory, this leads him to argue that Coleridge thought symbolic union was once available and is now withheld.[67] Human frailty, adulthood, Coleridge's personal failings, transcription itself may be held responsible for the 'difference', but the secondariness is final. In *The Friend* as a whole, Coleridge:

acts out the dilemma [...] that 'it is difficult to explain Words to the Bottom by Words; perhaps impossible.' He does so by, in effect, giving up a quest that might open up an infinite and infinitely debilitating regress. For that search, however, Coleridge has simply substituted its proper

---

[65] Coleridge's placing of this passage continues his arrangement of personal experience within a context of the universal. Cf. *Friend*, i. 341–73 with its sources in ii. 172–82, 285–7, 271–2, 256–9, 154–6, 308–9.

[66] Jerome Christensen, 'The Symbol's Errant Allegory: Coleridge and his Critics', *ELH*, 45 (1978), 645, 651, 649. Cf. Jean-Pierre Mileur, *Vision and Revision: Coleridge's Art of Immanence* (Berkeley, Calif., Los Angeles, and London, 1982).

[67] The distinction is from Paul de Man: see 'The Rhetoric of Temporality', in *Blindness and Insight: Essays in the Rhetoric of Contemporary Criticism* (2nd, rev., edn., London, 1983), 191–3, and 'The Epistemology of Metaphor', in *On Metaphor*, ed. Sheldon Sacks (Chicago, 1979), 11–28. M. Jadwiga Swiatecka convincingly demonstrates the anachronism of these views in *The Idea of the Symbol: Some Nineteenth-Century Comparisons with Coleridge* (Cambridge, 1980), 59–60.

metaphor, a thoroughly marginal method. Entirely rhetorical, Coleridge's own metaphors have no philosophical content.[68]

Accordingly, when Coleridge does unambiguously take on 'philosophical content', Christensen sees the 'fine point of [Coleridge's] discourse' blunted by his 'waxing ardor for the mysteries of trinitarianism, which corresponds to the congealing of his rhetoric into the oracular style of the 1825 *Aids to Reflection*'.

There is some truth in both Christensen's criticisms: Coleridge was over-cautious about committing himself to any assertion or a proof (so much so that he can sometimes appear to be marginalizing his own claims deliberately); moreover, the writing from his last decade sounds 'congealed' (exactly as Christensen describes it). Christensen's taste in both areas rests, however, on a simple idea of 'rhetoric', which he wants to place opposite 'content' in the same way that he opposes allegory to symbol. These consistent oppositions have the effect of restricting the range of tones available to Coleridge. Christensen finds in Coleridge's prose a continual yearning whose intensity rests on Coleridge observing (and only observing) that it cannot be fulfilled.[69]

As Christensen sees it Coleridge (who has accepted the impossibility of putting symbolic perception into words) writes always to describe the process of disappointment and is, in consequence, unable to treat rhetoric as an aspect of philosophy. An opposite critical view, most clearly represented by J. Robert Barth, finds Coleridge confidently asserting the presence of divine realities within symbols. This position makes the same assumption: by dividing Coleridge's use of language from the task he sets himself, Barth transforms symbols into sacraments. Raimonda Modiano observes this division among critics of 'Coleridge's philosophy of symbolism' and blames both sides for a failure to see the interaction of the two projects:

critics [. . .] emphasize either Coleridge's attachment to the transcendental source of the symbol at the expense of its material existence, or his belief in the full power of the particular to embody the universal.[70]

---

[68] Christensen, *Blessed Machine*, 116, quoting Hartley, *Observations on Man* [. . .], 2 vols. (1749, repr. New York, 1971), i. 277. See also Christensen, *Blessed Machine*, 46, and Bishop C. Hunt, jun., 'Coleridge and the Endeavour of Philosophy', *PMLA*, 91 (1976), 829–39.

[69] Christensen, *Blessed Machine*, 116 n; see also 115.

[70] Raimonda Modiano, *Coleridge and the Concept of Nature* (London and Basingstoke, 1985), 78; see also p. 224. For Barth see 'Symbol as Sacrament in Coleridge's Thought', *Studies in Romanticism*, 11 (1972), 320–31. See also

This categorization cleverly embraces a large proportion of Coleridge studies, but Modiano's own work cannot free itself from the same dichotomy.

Coleridge's substitution of love objects for natural objects fulfils his tendency to uproot the symbol from its material existence and push it firmly towards its transcendent abode. [. . .] Sara appears as a spiritual presence.

However, in *The Friend* in practice (and elsewhere in theory), Coleridge preserves the sense that this movement towards the transcendent abode can occur only through language or another medium—paint, stone, harmony—each of which continues to possess a material quality. Modiano, none the less, makes a restrictive (and in some respects false) understanding of Coleridge's impulses into the governing feature of his literary practice. Coleridge's stance in the *Biographia*

would suggest that the purest symbol is the symbol that destroys itself in order to merge with the inexpressible, just as the most eloquent page of writing would be the page that becomes blank.

This is the end-point shared by Christensen, Barth, and Modiano. Symbols in language are seen as being pushed by Coleridge firmly out of language in order to reach their fullest meaning. Transparency of language is made equivalent to its extinction. These assumptions, and the readings that follow from them, obscure the possibilities and dangers of Coleridge's foreknowledge, his considered employment of language as itself a symbol, to be regarded for itself and as a means to its true nature, which is the union of light and blood. These critics have missed, that is to say, *The Friend*'s effort to replace an ideal blankness with a perfect and advancing circle.[71]

Douglas Brownlow Wilson, 'Two Modes of Apprehending Nature: A Gloss on the Coleridgean Symbol', *PMLA*, 87 (1972), 42–52; Swiatecka, *The Idea of the Symbol*, 54–5.

[71] Modiano, *Concept of Nature*, 86, 80. He quotes from the third essay 'On the Principles of Genial Criticism' (1814, 1st pub. 1837). See *Biographia Literaria*, ed. J. Shawcross, 2 vols. (Oxford, 1907), 219–46. Modiano does not give the different date and misreads Coleridge's explanatory metaphor: see Shawcross, *Biographia Literaria*, ii. 238. Cf. Edward Kessler, *Coleridge's Metaphors of Being* (Princeton, NJ, 1979), 55–6. John Coulson's presentation of Coleridge's views is more accurate: 'In religion, as in poetry, we are required to make a complex act of inference and assent, and we begin by taking *on trust* expressions which are usually in analogical, metaphorical, or symbolic form, and by acting out the claims they make', *Newman and the Common Tradition* (Oxford, 1970), 4.

I do not mean to deny the confused tendencies in Coleridge's temperament and in his work, nor the transcendentalism of his later years—his succumbing 'finally to exhaustion, and then to torpor and silence' while the 'voice of God fills the void left by the vain words of the understanding'.[72] I would agree, however, that sacramentalist critics have tended, as Deirdre Coleman points out, 'to endorse Coleridge's rhetoric of unity automatically'. Coleman's formulation is undeluded and rightly challenges the idea that Coleridge's symbols create miraculous unity. However, Coleman sees this endorsement not as a misinterpretation of Coleridge's work but as an uncritical acceptance of the terms Coleridge sets.

Coleman's book consequently declares this 'rhetoric of unity' to be Coleridge's invention, designed to 'support the status quo and the Tory government'.[73] That political position places Coleridge in continual retreat: 'The movement [in *The Friend*]', Coleman says, 'is one from politics to principle, from the local and the temporary to the general and permanent, from activism to quietism.'[74] By assuming, heavily, that discovering principles implies quietism, she makes Coleridge's project imply throughout the defence of the Establishment. Her apposition of these phrases ('politics to principle [. . .] local [. . .] to the general [. . .] activism to quietism') also contends that any movement away from immediate circumstances (towards underlying trends or general rules) involves political apostasy and produces writing in bad faith. This need not follow: Coleman's argument has accepted the transcendental assumptions of a rhetoric of unity (as much as sacramentalist critics have endorsed them), only she believes these transcendental symbols to be a damaging illusion. Coleridge tried to resist the delusory power of the imagination but, equally, he tried to avoid the position that Coleman outlines here, where 'politics' is opposed to 'principle' and the only alternative to 'activism' is 'quietism'. Her sentence recalls Coleridge's definition of the symbol in *The Statesman's Manual* but its syntax ignores the searching and

[72] David R. Sanderson, 'Coleridge's Political "Sermons": Discursive Language and the Voice of God', *Modern Philology*, 70 (1973), 324.

[73] Coleman's study is as reductive as Christensen's, though less wistful: where Christensen sees in Coleridge the lame effort to half-acknowledge and half-obscure a loss of faith, Coleman sees the deployment of a flawed and deceptive rhetoric (whose limitations Coleridge knew perfectly well) in the service of political reaction.

[74] Coleman, *Coleridge and 'The Friend'*, 19 n., 13, 16.

problematic interplay (between local and general, temporary and permanent) that exists in Coleridge's definition of his project and in his subsequent practice.[75]

Coleman is repeating the accusation, first levelled at Coleridge by Hazlitt, that the changes in his political views were a feeble compromise intended to curry favour with possible patrons. This argument equates *The Friend* too readily with 'A Lay Sermon' (directed at 'the Higher and Middle Classes'), ignoring its equality with its audience and the distinctiveness of its symbolic method.[76] As I hope I have shown, *The Friend* avoids the reactionary movement Coleman describes by eschewing transcendental symbols, by continually working to involve the particular in the principle, and by making truth translucent in contingencies. Its undeniable difficulty is engendered by Coleridge's effort to re-perform the approach to (and postponement of) full perception, to repeat the 'eddying narrative' that structures our discovery of truth instead of proving its elusiveness.[77] The work's continued re-enactment of that pattern is devoted, self-effacingly, to the moral improvement Coleridge believes it to involve and represent.

The Friend parallels the endeavour of Dante's *Commedia*, therefore, in its employment of the forms of attention and self-attention, at once engaged and detached, that are required of symbolic prose. The results are at moments strikingly similar to the surprised discoveries once characteristic of his poetry:

> The owlet's cry
> Came loud—and hark, again! loud as before.
> ('Frost at Midnight', ll. 2–3; EHC, i. 240)

Were it louder, the cry would intrude more pointedly, betraying the poet's design upon us. As it is, the owlet is more persuasively heard in this strange and extreme silentness, because it disappoints. 'Loud as before', being anticlimactic, encourages the reader to listen more closely, at once to hear and to puzzle out

---

[75] Cf. David G. Riede, *Oracles and Hierophants: Constructions of Romantic Authority* (Ithaca, NY, and London, 1991); Ralph Pite, 'Brackets and *Authority* (my emphasis)', *English* 41 (1992), 175–88.

[76] For the problems in Coleridge's address to his audience in *Lay Sermons* see John Colmer, *Coleridge: Critic of Society* (Cambridge, 1959), 132–5.

[77] The phrase is Jerome Christensen's, from 'The Symbol's Errant Allegory', 655. See Coleridge's apparently contradictory evaluations of 'eddying' in *BL*, ii. 136 (about Wordsworth's defects) and 'Dejection', l. 136 (EHC, i. 368).

what importance it may have. In *The Friend* absorbed attention and detached enquiry with similar tact 'Fill up the [. . .] momentary pauses of the thought', articulated and stimulated as that is by the steps and turns of symbolic prose.[78]

[78] Ibid., ll. 9–10, 46–7; EHC, i. 240, 242. In Ch. 1, I discuss the echo of Shakespeare here. Cf. also the ending of Coleridge's 'To William Wordsworth': 'Scarce conscious, and yet conscious of its close | I sate, my being blended in one thought | (Thought was it? or aspiration? or resolve?) | Absorbed, yet hanging still upon the sound— | And when I rose, I found myself in prayer.' (ll. 108–13, EHC, i. 408). Coleridge's passive listening inspires actions, his private aspirations, and resolves, and the balance between activity and passivity is preserved by being interrupted in the closing act of prayer.

4

The Fall of Hyperion

'Morti li morti e i vivi parean vivi'

Keats probably came across Dante first when he read Leigh Hunt's
The Story of Rimini (1816).[1] Hunt's poem, written while he was
imprisoned, expands Dante's episode of Paolo and Francesca into
a full-length poem (of four cantos and more than 1,700 lines).
Byron read the poem in manuscript and admired much of it; Keats
wrote a sonnet in its praise, quoted it in his letters, and used
an extract for an epigraph.[2] His early poems, as has been observed
before, frequently make use of the diction that characterizes Hunt's
The Story of Rimini.[3] Keats's poems, however, differ from Hunt's
in their consideration of poetic self-awareness. As Keats adopts
Hunt's style he recognizes the adopted status of his consequent
writing, but he does not see that status as the exception or as
applicable only to derivative juvenilia. Instead, his writing high-
lights the artificial quality of all poetic effects—an artificiality which
Hunt's writing sought to disguise and claimed to avoid.

[1] See Clarice Short, 'The Composition of Hunt's *The Story of Rimini*', *K–SJ*,
21-2 (1972-3), 207-18. Keats owned a copy of Cary's translation of *Inferno*
(1805-6) and may have read all or parts of it either before or while reading Hunt.
The copy is now lost. Keats's 1818 annotations to his copy of Cary's 1814 trans-
lation focus on cantos i, ix–xv, and xxii–xxvii. They may be patchy simply because
Keats was reading Cary while on a walking-holiday but, perhaps, he already knew
some of the cantos well from his earlier reading. Keats quotes from Cary's version
of *Inferno* iv in 1817, comparing Edmund Kean to Dante's Soldan; see the
Champion, 21 Dec. 1817, p. 405. See Bhabatosh Chatterjee, *John Keats: His Mind
and Work* (New Delhi, 1971), 257-60, 470-1, on Cary's possible influence in
Endymion, iii, composed Sept. 1817.
[2] For Byron's notes (made in 1815 before publication), see Milford, 668-78;
Byron later remarked that *The Story of Rimini* was 'good poetry at bottom, dis-
figured only by a strange style' (To Tom Moore, 1 Dec. 1818, *LJ*, vi. 45). Byron's
notes focus on Hunt's canto iii and, though enthusiastic, show already his distaste
for Hunt's style. Byron underlines 'leafy' and 'tear-dipped' in 'And leafy dreams
affords me, and a feeling | Which I should else disdain, tear-dipped and healing'
(Milford, 13, 670). See *Keats*, 79, 92; Rollins, i. 396.
[3] See W. J. Bate, *The Stylistic Development of Keats* (New York and London,
1945), 8-28; Allott, 36-42; and Barnard, 541-2.

Keats's dissent from Hunt (which I discuss at greater length below) is repeated in some respects when he reads Milton in 1818 and 1819. Again, Keats's admiration is followed by imitation—his adoption in *Hyperion* of 'Miltonic inversions'.[4] Partly for biographical reasons, however, his use of *Paradise Lost* aimed to ignore the implications for the self of making such an imitation. *Hyperion*, unlike Keats's earlier work, therefore, attempts to forget the artificiality of poetry. Keats's rereading of Dante in the summer of 1819 (using a copy of the original Italian for the first time) contributed to his rewriting of *Hyperion* as *The Fall of Hyperion*.[5] In particular, Dante's narratorial position reminds Keats of his self-implication (in and by the act of writing) which the earlier version had sought to disregard.[6] This self-implication, I will argue, changes Keats's portrayal in *The Fall of Hyperion* of the suffering Titans. It draws Keats's attention to two aspects of Dante's style (his highly particularized but unheroic similes and his use of repetition) whose imitation cannot become a moment of self-forgetfulness for the poet imitating. The same underlying motive also contributes, I believe, to Keats's interest in Dante's *Purgatorio* when he was writing *The Fall of Hyperion*.[7]

Leigh Hunt creates in *The Story of Rimini* a retreat from earthly concerns, a place 'of nestling green, for poets made' whose seclusion protects the sinful lovers from prying criticism.[8] Paulo and

---

[4] Rollins, ii. 167. See also ibid. 139, 146.

[5] The Dantean quality of *The Fall of Hyperion* has been noticed before: see F. R. Leavis, *Revaluation: Tradition and Development in English Poetry* (London, 1936, repr. Harmondsworth, 1972), 251; J. L. Lowes, 'Moneta's Temple', *PMLA*, 51 (1936), 1098–113, and '*Hyperion* and the *Purgatorio*', *Times Literary Supplement* (11 Jan. 1936), 35; John D. Rosenberg, 'Keats and Milton: The Paradox of Rejection', *K–SJ*, 6 (1957), 87–95; Stuart Sperry, 'Keats, Milton and *The Fall of Hyperion*', *PMLA*, 77 (1962), 77; J. V. Saly, 'Keats's Answer to Dante: *The Fall of Hyperion*', *K–SJ*, 14 (1965), 65–79; Kenneth Muir, 'The Meaning of *Hyperion*', in *John Keats: A Reassessment*, ed. Kenneth Muir (Liverpool, 1969), 112; Harold Bloom, *The Visionary Company: A Reading of English Romantic Poetry* (2nd, rev., edn., Ithaca, NY, and London, 1971), 391; James Land Jones, *Adam's Dream: Mythic Consciousness in Keats and Yeats* (Athens, Ga., 1975), 181; John Barnard, *John Keats* (Cambridge, 1987), 129.

[6] This view links *The Fall of Hyperion* to *Endymion*, a link confirmed by Keats's referring once again to Chatterton in letters of 1819; see Rollins, ii. 212 and *Endymion*'s dedication, *Keats*, 102–3.

[7] Cf. Saly, 'Answer to Dante', 75, which attributes Keats's interest in the Earthly Paradise cantos to Hunt's encouragement.

[8] Keats used this line (*The Story of Rimini*, iii. 430, Milford, 22) as his motto to 'I stood tip-toe upon a little hill' (Dec. 1816), *Keats*, 79. Cf. Rollins, i. 170.

Francesca entered a separate world of love when, reading, they 'came upon the part | Where' Geneura and Lancelot kiss.

> Only he felt he could no more dissemble,
> And kissed her, mouth to mouth, all in a tremble.
> Sad were those hearts, and sweet was that long kiss:
> Sacred be love from sight, whate'er it is.
> The world was all forgot, the struggle o'er,
> Desperate their joy.—That day they read no more.
> (*The Story of Rimini,* iii. 598–9, 603–8, Milford, 26)[9]

As Paulo and Francesca forget the world, so they find peace with themselves, no longer dissembling the love that declares itself beyond their power to resist. The single passion overwhelms them so that 'whate'er it is' can appropriate to itself the terms of moral judgement within the world it defines. And this elevated world enhances the reader's recognitions. The universal, 'love [. . .] whate'er it is', is apparent here, mysterious and all-powerful. The reader is kept at a respectful distance but asked to practise the sympathy that suspends judgement.[10]

That sympathy precludes judgement is implied by the way Hunt attends to events as they occur. When he describes the garden at Rimini, Hunt has his readers discover it as they go:

> So now you walked beside an odorous bed
> Of gorgeous hues, white, azure, golden, red;   405
> And now turned off into a leafy walk
> Close and continuous, fit for lovers' talk;
> And now pursued the stream, and as you trod
> Onward and onward o'er the velvet sod,
> Felt on your face an air, watery and sweet,   410
> And a new sense in your soft-lighting feet;
> And then perhaps you entered upon shades,

Hunt's Rimini resembles his Hampstead: see his 'Sonnets to Hampstead', Milford, 235–8. Cf. also his 'To John Hamilton Reynolds: On his lines upon The Story of Rimini', Milford, 246.

[9] See Keats's letter to Reynolds, 17–18 Apr. 1817 Rollins, i. 133: 'I had become all in a Tremble from not having written anything of late'. 'Paulo' is Hunt's spelling throughout. Keats used it too: see Rollins, ii. 91.

[10] This is implicit in Hunt's separating the story from the *Commedia*. See Sapegno, i. 65 n., and C. P. Brand, 'Dante and the English Poets', in *The Mind of Dante*, ed. U. Limentani (Cambridge, 1965), 191: 'as elsewhere a whole plane of Dante's poetry is lost by a distortion of the point of vision'.

> Pillowed with dells and uplands 'twixt the glades,
> Through which the distant palace, now and then,
> Looked lordly forth with many-windowed ken;   415
> A land of trees, which reaching round about,
> In shady blessing stretched their old arms out,
> With spots of sunny opening.
>   (*The Story of Rimini*, iii. 404–18, Milford, 22)

The finest part of the garden, Hunt goes on to say, lies "twixt the wood and flowery walks, halfway' (ibid. iii. 434, p. 22) but his description prefers discovery to layout.[11] One finds oneself here, wanders by walks and streams before, perhaps, going on into the wood. Hunt adds to this next stage deliberate doubt, making it implicitly dependent upon discovering 'a new sense' that allows entry upon the shades. The mysterious but unthreatening causality of 'So now' becomes a suggestion of initiation, as if this garden requires delicacy in the explorer before giving up its beauties. And one rediscovers, on going further, things seen before: 'shades' (l. 412) nearly repeats the previous rhyme-word 'shade' (400) as the 'circling pines' (401) appear again in the land of trees that are 'reaching round about' (416). The doubtful new departure leads to a deeper rediscovery because of this distant rhyming. In that process the 'new sense' avoids idiosyncrasy while remaining an intensification. '[O]nward and onward' appears random and care-free exploration that leads, as if providentially, into the hidden recesses of the garden. Coleridge's description of reading Cary— the 'feeling of wandering & wandering onward and onward'— applies again here and is made an even more secure pleasure. Fulfilment is bound up with Hunt's design as much as the absence of any need to be guided is part of the pleasure.[12]

Keats's early diction is obvious in these lines: 'leafy' (406) and 'watery' (410); 'soft-lighting' (411) and 'opening' (418) are all characteristic. The present participles, however (as roots for adverbs and nouns, and in themselves) are most indicative of the two poets'

---

[11] Cf. Short's more hostile account of these features in 'Composition of *The Story of Rimini*', 212: 'Yet the whole remains as graphic and unmapable as the landscape in a dream [. . . .] Hunt never entirely solved the problem of point of view.'

[12] The garden in Rimini has become a version of Dante's Earthly Paradise. See *Purgatorio*, xxviii–xxxiii, esp. xxviii. 1–33, Sapegno, ii. 305–7, and, below, Keats's later consideration of these cantos. On this aspiration in Hunt, cf. John Hamilton Reynolds, 'The Eden of Imagination' (1814), in *John Hamilton Reynolds: Poetry and Prose*, ed. G. L. Marsh (London, 1928), 56–66.

shared interests.[13] The participles are coincident with the line-endings at the centre of this extract, whose fluidity and intimations of discovery give a pleasure in ease.

> And now pursued the stream, and as you trod
> Onward and onward o'er the velvet sod,
> Felt on your face an air, watery and sweet.

Hunt removes all strain from 'pursued' by having the lines step lightly: the dactylic opening of 'Onward and onward' lifts the weight of 'as you trod' with little effort; and their lightness is rounded off by the neat rhyme of 'trod' and 'sod'. Against this finish, 'Felt' strikes suddenly and surprisingly as if impinging on the mind. Similar effects are employed in what immediately follows:

> And all about, a lovely sky of blue
> Clearly was felt, or down the leaves laughed through.
> And here and there, in every part, were seats,
> Some in the open walks, some in retreats;
>
> • • • • • • • • •
>
> Places of nestling green, for poets made,
> Where when the sunshine struck a yellow shade,
> The slender trunks, to inward peeping sight
> Thronged in dark pillars up the gold green light.
> (*The Story of Rimini*, iii. 424–7, 430–3, Milford, 22)

'Clearly' is intended here both to intensify the feeling and suit it to a clear sky. 'Thronged' takes its energy from the specialness of 'inward peeping sight' in the previous line.[14]

The attempt to write poetry which represents rather than describes experience was recognized by contemporary readers of *Endymion*:

There is another objection to its ever becoming popular, that it is, as the *Venus and Adonis* of Shakespeare, a *representation* and not a *description* of passion [. . .] Mr Keats conceives the scene before him, and represents it as it appears. This is the excellence of dramatic poetry; but to feel its truth and power in any other, we must abandon our ordinary feeling and

---

[13] There are more remote connections: 'She was a gordian shape of dazzling hue' ('Lamia', i. 47, *Keats*, 453) flickers in the vowels of 'an odorous bed | Of dazzling hue'.

[14] See also *The Story of Rimini*, iv. 92–5 and 119–22, ii. 146–8 and 158–62, and MS version of i. 127–31, Milford, 28–9, 11, 664.

common consciousness, and identify ourselves with the scene. Few people can do this. (*Champion*, 7 June 1818, *CritH*, 465)[15]

Keats's project of '*representation*' is pursued through the technical achievements of Hunt's poetry and, to some extent, it shares in Hunt's claim to have regained access through these innovations to 'a region of his own': a region of originality, independence and directness.[16] Keats's sonnet, 'This pleasant tale is like a little copse' (written in February 1817, probably a month before 'On *The Story of Rimini*') finds for the reader of the medieval poem a similar 'region of his own'. Keats, however, immediately locates this place in the lines themselves.

> This pleasant tale is like a little copse:
>   The honied lines do freshly interlace,
>   To keep the reader in so sweet a place,
> So that he here and there full hearted stops;
> And oftentimes he feels the dewy drops
>   Come cool and suddenly against his face.
>   ('This pleasant tale is like a little copse',
>   ll. 1–6, *Keats*, 92)[17]

Keats's assertion of an identity between the narrative, in which the speaker enters a copse, and its formal construction, in which the lines create an interwoven barrier like the branches of a wood, declares the poetic and articificial nature of the effect as a whole. The lines are 'honied', sweet and sweetened by labour, but inter-lace 'freshly' as if found anew. The stanzaic form of 'The Floure and the Lefe' (not written by Chaucer but employing his seven-line rime royal stanza) halts the reader's progress through the wood and in Keats's reading the rhythms of exploration and of poetic

---

[15] The review was probably written by Woodhouse; see *CritH*, 87. Cf. *BL* ii. 25–8.

[16] Cf. Hunt's review of Keats's first volume, which concentrates on passages using verbs of motion as he does himself and links these stylistic innovations to a restoration of Eden: the *Examiner*, 6 and 13 July 1818; see *CritH*, 60. Byron claimed to have seen through the project early: '[Hunt] has persuaded himself into a belief of his own impostures, and talks Punch in pure simplicity of heart' (*LJ*, vi. 45). This usage ('talk Punch') is not listed in *OED*, though sb. 5c refers to 'Punch's voice', 'a peculiar bell-like, or ringing tone of voice [. . . .] heard among the insane' (1894). Cf. 'You talk Utopia', *Julian and Maddalo*, l. 179, *PP*, 117.

[17] The sonnet was also entitled 'Written on a Blank Space at the End of Chaucer's Tale of "The Floure and the Lefe"'. Keats's reading of other poetry was frequently similar in its preoccupations to his reading of Hunt.

composition are indistinguishable. The 'stops' allow a full and
fresh experiencing of the imagined place when the 'drops | Come
cool and suddenly'—the intrusive sensation that authenticates
Hunt's landscape is repeated by Keats with a greater insistence
on the thing that strikes. 'Cool' followed by 'suddenly' (rather than
the other way round) similarly adopts and improves on Hunt's
method, moving convincingly through a sequence of perception
from the bare sensation to the recognition that it is a sudden
feeling. The suddenness is represented 'as it appears' and more
inwardly than in Hunt's description of Paulo and Francesca who
'felt with leaps of heart | Their colour change'.[18]

In a similar way, 'I stood tip-toe upon a little hill' explores
the same landscape that Hunt portrays in his garden of love, but
makes clear that the exploration is imaginary:

> Linger awhile upon some bending planks
> That lean against a streamlet's rushy banks,
> And watch intently Nature's gentle doings:
> They will be found softer than ring-dove's cooings.
> How silent comes the water round that bend
> • • • • • • • • •
>   How they [the minnows] ever wrestle
> With their own sweet delight, and ever nestle
> Their silver bellies on the pebbly sand.
> If you but scantily hold out the hand,
> That very instant not one will remain;
> But turn your eye, and they are there again
> • • • • • • • • •
> Sometimes goldfinches one by one will drop
> From low hung branches; little space they stop;
> But sip, and twitter, and their feathers sleek;
> Then off at once, as in a wanton freak:
> Or perhaps, to show their black, and golden wings,
> Pausing upon their yellow flutterings.
> Were I in such a place
>   ('I stood tip-toe upon a little hill', ll. 61–5, 75–80,
>   87–93, *Keats*, 81–2)

---

[18] *The Story of Rimini*, iii. 598–9, Milford, 26. The possibility of combining pro-
gressiveness and closure is one of Keats's reasons for employing stanzas in *Isabella*.
Coleridge's interest in moments of pausing demonstrates the congruence between
Keats's (and Hunt's) concerns and those of the period. See also James Beattie's
introduction to *The Minstrel; or, The Progress of Genius [. . .]* (London, 1771),
p. vii; and Byron's introduction to *Childe Harold's Pilgrimage*, McGann, ii. 4–5.

The imperatives invite participation but will not shrink into a social tic; the presence of things is made to depend on the speaker's or reader's co-operative action. The future tenses—Nature's sweet doings 'will be found' and goldfinches 'will drop'—combine with the imperatives of 'Linger' and 'watch' so that events are apparently caused by a reader's attention while s/he discovers those events as naturally occurring. Keats's lines employ their rhymes and enjambements to create a rhythm of perception: the goldfinches 'one by one drop | From' the branches, 'stop' and then carry on, 'sip' taking up where the pause left off. The formal isolation of 'little space they stop' accentuates a pause just as the enjambement of 'drop | From' enacts the birds' descent.

In *Endymion*, a comparable concentration on the protagonist's mind accompanies a style that charts perceptions as they come to light and seeks to present particular objects with surprising immediacy.

> The same bright face I tasted in my sleep,
> Smiling in the clear well. My heart did leap
> Through the cool depth.—It moved as if to flee—
> I started up, when lo! refreshfully,
> There came upon my face, in plenteous showers,
> Dew-drops, and dewy buds, and leaves, and flowers,
> Wrapping all objects from my smothered sight,
> Bathing my spirit in a new delight.
> (*Endymion*, i. 895–902, *Keats*, 128–9)

Endymion, visiting the secret well 'Whose patient level peeps its crystal eye | Right upward, through the bushes, to the sky' (ibid., ll. 871–2, p. 128) catches sight of a cloudy Cupid reflected there and is on the point of leaving the place 'To follow it upon the open plain' (l. 892). The leap of his heart into the cool depth of the well repeats, therefore, his pursuit of Cupid through heaven and earth. Oddly, though, the leap of feeling seems to move his body and, in consequence, the 'bright face [. . .] Smiling' towards him (which moves when he desires to move) threatens to become a reflection. Endymion starts away as if to avoid the fate of Narcissus.

Endymion's leap of heart looks like a transgression (that is punished by the face's self-protective and chaste recoil), yet, by mentioning the immediate countermovement, Keats couples the risk of encroaching with the danger of self-reflexiveness. These possibilities are raised by the passage because Keats allows Endymion's perceptions to be tempting. Though Endymion does not actually move, his heart reaches down to discover and grasp what is already seen; because his exploration risks violation, the process of perception acquires undefined moral significance. Similarly, the refreshing drops are not labelled (either as a reward for Endymion's restrained turning away or a providential comfort for his loss), but the reader starts to wonder what they may mean.[19]

In *Endymion*, therefore, Keats is using the patterns of realization he found in *The Story of Rimini* to reveal the moral possibilities and possible dangers of poetry.[20] In Hunt's work, these are disregarded, because poetic pleasures are accepted without question. Hunt's work combines techniques of immediacy with an ideal of naturalness or simplicity—an ideal which ensures his exclusion of the difficulties that surround immediate representation. Keats's idea of 'negative capability' is a pursuit of Hunt's immediacy which does without the artful ironies Hunt employs to keep his aims at arm's length. Keats's earnestness in this is, characteristically, both callow and astute. His later *Hyperion* poems repeatedly probe 'negative capability', questioning the responsibilities and dangers which attend the claim that Hunt's poetry so blithely makes: the claim to have represented another person's experience at once accurately and inwardly.

The first version of the poem was written in reaction to the ambitions Hunt (by the autumn of 1818) had come to represent for Keats. *Hyperion*'s neoclassicism, the statuesque rigidity of its figures and the Miltonic elevation of its writing were, in part, influenced by Haydon's heroic aspirations by contrast with Hunt's domestic sentimentalism. Keats was reacting against the anti-intellectualism that Hunt, an educated man, embraced with impunity and from a position of strength. To these impulses was added the pressure that his brother Tom's illness brought to bear on Keats:

His identity presses upon me so all day that I am obliged to go out—and although I intended to have given some time to study alone I am obliged

---

[19] Cf. *Endymion*, ii. 376–86, *Keats*, 144, and their draft version (ibid. 144 n.).
[20] Wordsworth's *The Excursion* (1814) was also influential on the progressiveness and self-awareness of *Endymion*'s visions. Cf. Book iv. 738–59 (Wordsworth, v, 132–3), and 'Ode to a Nightingale', l. 26 (*Keats*, 370). See K. Allott, 'The "Ode to Psyche"', in Muir, *John Keats: A Reassessment*, 87–8.

to write, and plunge into abstract images to ease myself of his counten-
ance his voice and feebleness—so that I live now in a continual fever—
it must be poisonous to life although I feel well.   (To Dilke, 21 Sept. 1818,
Rollins, i. 369)[21]

Tom's dying brought home 'the eternal fierce destruction' of Keats's
verse-letter to Reynolds. In this poem, of March 1818, he had
already proclaimed his withdrawal from the grim strife of nature
into a world of poetry, and justified it as an attempt to correct the
egotism he finds in his own and Wordsworth's poetry.

> Do you get health—and Tom the same—I'll dance,
> And from detested moods in new romance
> Take refuge.
>> ('Dear Reynolds, as last night I lay in bed',
>> ll. 110–12, *Keats*, 244)

To escape from his own moods and to preserve himself against the
pressing identity of his brother, Keats turns to poetry: the 'new
romance' of the poem and the 'abstract images' of the letter are
distinguished by the urgency with which Keats turns to them but
the impulse is identical. The increased desperation of the Septem-
ber letter, where Keats cannot self-assuredly '*Take* refuge' but is
'obliged to [. . .] plunge into abstract images', begins to face up
more fully to the difficulty of meeting 'his countenance his voice
and feebleness'. Keats returns to Tom as he describes the process
of distracting himself from him. 'Ease myself of' (instead of 'ease
myself out of' or 'rid myself of'), similarly, makes Tom's weakness
appear the burden it is. Keats's decisive, hurried self-assertion (his
'plunging') over-compensates for Tom's 'feebleness'. He seems to
know that he is turning himself into a parallel (or parody) of his
brother, putting himself into the fever his brother actually and
passively endures. This cannot be avoided but may be fatal. The
abstractions he resorts to are, he declares the next day, his 'only
life' but do not provide relief from and probably exacerbate the
'continual fever' which 'must be poisonous to life although I feel
well'.[22]

The 'abstract images', the 'march of passion and endeavour

---

[21] Cf. his later contentment, *Rollins*, ii. 209.
[22] To Reynolds, 22(?) Sept. 1818, *Rollins*, i. 370.

[which] will be undeviating', the 'naked and grecian Manner' all bespeak an attempt on Keats's part to separate himself from the processes he describes.[23] The new poem will make him invulnerable to criticism because it originates in his absorption into the composition. Keats will succeed in distinguishing himself from Hunt and Hunt's circle by embarking on a project that demands his self-erasure. Although, therefore, the new style is pressed upon him by circumstances, it also provides an escape from them because it works less by 'sensation and watchfulness' than by a calculated abandonment to 'beauty in the abstract'. In the letters of autumn 1818 Keats is already wary about what feels too much like a necessity; a year later, when revising *Hyperion*, he is convinced that this approach had robbed the poem of what he calls 'the true voice of feeling'.[24] His revision of the poem seeks to reinstate the combination of watchfulness and sensation that governs *Endymion* (and is in some respects its subject). By contrast, the origin of *Hyperion* in a desire to plunge into abstractions divides it between the two poles of description and representation 'as it appears', the poles of observation and participation. These opposing attitudes correspond to, respectively, Keats's reading of Milton's 'sublime pathetic' and his reading of Cary.

Keats writes in his edition of *Paradise Lost*:

Milton is godlike in the sublime pathetic. In Demons, fallen Angels, and Monsters the delicacies of passion living in and from their immortality, is of the most softening and dissolving nature. It is carried to the utmost here—Others more mild—nothing can express the sensation one feels at '*Their song was partial &c.*' (Milton, i. 44–5; Wittreich, 557)[25]

He is annotating Book ii. 552 ff. where some of the devils retire from their fall to sing:

---

[23] To Haydon, 23 Jan. 1818, *Rollins*, i. 207. This letter is the first recorded reference to *Hyperion*. Cf. Keats's praise of 'Grecian grandeur' in 'On Seeing the Elgin Marbles', l. 12, *Keats*, 93. On Keats's neoclassicism, see Martin Aske, *Keats and Hellenism: An Essay* (Cambridge, 1985); Michael Rossington, '"The Voice which is Contagion to the World": The Bacchic in Shelley', in *Beyond Romanticism: New Approaches to Texts and Contexts 1780–1832*, ed. Stephen Copley and John Whale (London and New York, 1992), 101–17.

[24] *Rollins*, i. 374, 373; ii. 167.

[25] Keats's copy may be consulted at Keats House in Hampstead. Wittreich indents quotations but otherwise his transcriptions are accurate. He does not refer to the large number of passages without marginal notes but underlined.

> Others more mild,
> Retreated in a silent valley, sing
> With notes angelical to many a harp
> Their own heroic deeds and hapless fall
> By doom of battle; and complain that fate
> Free virtue should inthrall to force or chance.
> Their song was partial, but the harmony
> (What could it less when Spirits immortal sing?)
> Suspended Hell, and took with ravishment
> The thronging audience.
>   (*Paradise Lost*, ii. 546–55, Milton, i. 44)

Keats underlines here 'Their song was partial [. . .]' and 'Suspended Hell' but not the parenthesis in between. Milton's line interrupts the ravishment he describes with a rhetorical question that is also a speculation. The reader is invited at once to imagine the ineffable beauty of angelic harmony and to think on the theological implications of angels singing out of tune. Keats's underlining leaves out the urbanity of Milton's eloquence while catching in this suspension of Hell's pains the ravishment that Milton intends.

He is concerned to locate in the lines the sources and nature of Milton's 'sublime pathetic'—those feelings Milton is peculiarly able to render because the leading characters of his epic are immortals—and the techniques he employs to render them. Eternal sorrow and infinite regret are softening and dissolving; they overpower a reader's sense of his or her self. Keats, reading, can absorb himself in these abstract, imaginary interests. He can both witness these elevated passions, seeing them to be recognizably human while lifted up into an immortal sphere, and he can believe that poetry itself may relieve infernal suffering, providing a refuge within the silent valley that is a retreat from Hell.

Keats takes particular pleasure in the 'vales' and 'valleys' Milton places in his spiritual worlds. These not only offer reminders of earthly realities when the poem is presenting intangible superhuman events, they effect the same transformation and elevation of the earthly as is achieved in Milton's portrayal of suffering.

There is a cool pleasure in the very sound of vale. The english word is of the happiest chance. Milton has put vales in heaven and hell with the very utter affection and yearning of a great Poet. It is a sort of delphic Abstraction—a beautiful—thing made more beautiful by being reflected and put in a Mist. The Next mention of Vale is one of the most pathetic

in the whole range of Poetry. Others, more mild, Retreated in a silent
Valley &c. How much of the charm is in the Valley! (Milton, i. 12;
Wittreich, 554)

Milton's introduction of earthly vales into Heaven and Hell not
only gives 'cool pleasure' to the reader, it beautifies the vale.[26] The
reader gains from their obscurity the same yearning and affection
which moved Milton to mention them. In the same way, the 'sub-
lime pathetic' enables Milton's reader to yearn after the delicacies
of passion he portrays.[27]

The 'sublime pathetic', however, works in both directions: it
makes sources of mere pathos somehow sublime, and finds in the
angelic beings of *Paradise Lost* the signs of sorrow. Keats admires
most of all in the poem the invocation to Book vii: '*Nor could the
Muse defend her son*', and the Ceres passage in Book iv: '*which
cost Ceres all that pain to seek her through the world*'.[28] Power-
lessness and pain in the gods is a source of the wonder that then
comes to dominate *Hyperion*'s presentations of divine suffering.
When the Titan, Thea, wakes the fallen Saturn at the beginning of
Hyperion, Book i, Keats makes her into a 'delphic Abstraction':

> Her Face was large as that of Memphian sphinx,
> Pedastal'd haply in a palace court,
> When sages look'd to Egypt for their lore.
> But oh! how unlike marble was that face:
> How beautiful, if sorrow had not made
> Sorrow more beautiful than Beauty's self.
>   (*Hyperion,* i. 31–6, *Keats,* 330)

Thea's passionate immortality makes her into a reminder of earthly
idols, such as the Memphian sphinx, and an image that goes beyond
them in beauty and beyond 'Beauty' itself. This extraordinary figure
denies sorrow any element of pain. The stillness of the tableau
made by Saturn and Thea avoids the difficulty of sorrow by making

---

[26] As above, this is both an excellent insight into Milton's 'yearning' and one
oddly uncluttered by the demands of drama. See Keats's note to *Paradise Lost,* ix.
179–91, 'Whose spirit does not ache at [Satan's . . .] smothering and confinement'
(Milton i. 80; Wittreich, 560). Cf. Coleridge's reading of Shakespeare, particularly
Lectures 1808–19, i. 377–90.
[27] The attractiveness of an obscure 'delphic Abstraction' is also felt by Keats
when reading Homer (To Reynolds, 27 Apr. 1818, Rollins, i. 274).
[28] Milton, i. 92–3; Wittreich, 559. Cf. *Hyperion,* ii. 52–5, *Endymion,* i. 943–5,
Keats, 342, 130; and letter to Bailey, 18 and 22 July 1818, Rollins, i. 340–5.

it more than charming, by making it contemplative and a focus of our contemplation.[29]

In revising the poem, Keats cut these lines about a more beautiful sorrow but kept what follows—the moment where Thea assumes a more recognizable (rather than adorable) posture:

> One hand she press'd upon that aching spot
> Where beats the human heart, as if just there,
> Though an immortal, she felt cruel pain:
> The other upon Saturn's bended neck
> She laid
>
> (Ibid., ll. 42–6, p. 330)

Saturn is seated, his right hand nerveless on the ground 'While his bow'd head seem'd list'ning to the Earth, | His ancient mother, for some comfort yet' (ibid., ll. 20–1, p. 329). Thea clutches her heart and stretches her hand towards his neck in a conventional gesture of heartfelt sympathy. It is striking, however, because of the persisting strangeness of a goddess exhibiting 'living delicacies of passion'. The lines cannot say quite what is happening, but point out the features of her gesture and venture an interpretation: 'as if just there | Though an immortal, she felt cruel pain'. Keats makes her into Ceres: a goddess who reveals (and possibly is at this moment discovering in herself) 'that aching spot | Where beats the human heart'.

In the first version of the poem, this humanity is astonishing and awe-inspiring; it makes her express all the more distinctively a sorrow that is transformed into something more beautiful than beauty's self. In *The Fall of Hyperion* Keats notices Thea's human qualities in a different way and to different effect.

> Then came the griev'd voice of Mnemosyne,
> And griev'd I hearken'd. 'That divinity
> Whom thou saw'st step from yon forlornest wood,
> And with slow pace approach our fallen King,
> Is Thea, softest-natur'd of our brood.'
> I mark'd the goddess in fair statuary
> Surpassing wan Moneta by the head,
> And in her sorrow nearer woman's tears.
>
> (*The Fall of Hyperion*, i. 331–8, Keats, 486)

---

[29] See Nancy Moore Goslee, *Uriel's Eye: Miltonic Stationing and Statuary in Blake, Keats, and Shelley* (University, Ala., 1985), p. xii.

At this point *The Fall* returns to the account given in *Hyperion*; Keats seems deliberately to have left out the passage in the original version from 'She was a goddess of the infant world' to 'Sorrow more beautiful than Beauty's self', replacing it with these woman's tears that contrast with 'wan Moneta'. The revised lines move from the surpassing fair statuary to the heavy back-stress (nearly trochaic) of the last line: 'And in her sorrow nearer woman's tears'. Keats's observation changes from 'marking' her stature and statuesque quality to a less assured description of her 'sorrow'. The new 'nimbleness' with which Keats perceives 'the depth' of Thea's sorrow seems, at this point, to commit his poetry to her: the eye that marks her changes into the soul that pervades (is dissolved into and occupies the same space as) the other it is observing.[30]

This attentiveness in the revised version depends on a change in Keats's use of repetition. Where the delphic abstraction is a beautiful thing, 'made more beautiful by being reflected and put in a mist', Keats's repetitions in *The Fall of Hyperion* no longer elevate but participate in and pursue. Mnemosyne is grieved and the poet listens responsively by being equally grieved. As I hope to show, they also allow such participation to remain self-aware and unpresuming, helping to create a form of sympathy whose intimacy with its object does not pretend to be identification. In *Hyperion* itself, however, 'the cruel pain' in 'that aching spot' distinctively follows on from Keats's declaration that her sorrow is beautiful. The poem discovers intense suffering while imagining an intensity of endurance, and the moments of pain then acquire a heightened pathos which Keats abandoned in revision.[31] Within the 'sublime pathetic', therefore, and as Keats is overwhelmed by the human touches in a divinity, there exists in the poem an extraordinary dispassionateness. This is, in part, an implicit necessity of Keats's ambition. Sorrow can become more beautiful than beauty only if it remains an abstraction to the perceiver. The latent 'disinterestedness'

---

[30] Cf. *Hyperion*, iii. 113–18, 'Knowledge enormous makes a God of me [. . . .]', and the description of godlike perception in *The Fall of Hyperion*, i. 302–6: 'Whereon there grew | A power within me of enormous ken, | To see as a God sees, and take the depth | Of things as nimbly as the outward eye | Can size and shape pervade' (*Keats*, 355–6, 485); see also Arthur H. Bell, ' "The Depth of Things": Keats and Human Space', *K–SJ*, 23 (1974), 77–94.

[31] Cf. *Hyperion*, i. 135–41, *Keats*, 333 (cut in *The Fall of Hyperion*) and *Hyperion*, ii. 21–7, *Keats*, 341 (which Keats did not revise).

of *Hyperion* is more fully apparent, however, when Keats's detachment becomes clinical. At the beginning of Book ii, where Keats places the fallen gods in a 'nest of woe', he sees Cottus:

> Next Cottus: prone he lay, chin uppermost,
> As though in pain; for still upon the flint
> He ground severe his skull, with open mouth
> And eyes at horrid working.
>
> *(Hyperion,* ii. 49–52, *Keats,* 342)

Cottus' behaviour is perhaps odd but not bewildering because Keats's 'As though in pain' sounds a note of supercilious curiosity or technical interest. Cottus' actions become symptoms.[32] As he describes them, they become gradually more horrid and horrible to imagine, but the description manages the effect without considering its subject, without meeting Cottus' 'eyes at horrid working'.[33]

In moving, then, from sumptuous pathos to an unconcern designed to have its horrific effect, the poem seems to be shifting from Milton's sublime pathetic to the diagnostic eye which Keats especially noticed when reading Cary's version of 'the brief pathos of Dante'.[34] In his copy of Cary's 1814 edition Keats annotates quite closely cantos i, ix–xv, and xxii–xxvii of 'Hell'. It is not possible precisely to reconstruct the course of his reading from this evidence nor, as I have said, to be sure about his earlier familiarity with the work. But these annotations almost certainly date from the summer and autumn of 1818, around the same time as his notes on Milton.[35]

In his reading of Cary, Keats always notices the similes that

---

[32] See Hermione de Almeida, *Romantic Medicine and John Keats* (New York and Oxford, 1991), 51–3, 280–5.

[33] Keats underlines Milton's lazar-house passage, whose influence on *Hyperion* ii is evident, but leaves unmarked Adam's reaction: 'Adam could not [behold], but wept [. . .]'. Similarly he underlines the description of the flood but not Adam's speech 'O visions ill-foreseen [. . .]' (*Paradise Lost,* xi. 477–92, 495 ff., 745–52, 763 ff., Milton, ii. 158–9, 266–7).

[34] Milton, i. 92–3; Wittreich, 559.

[35] See Gittings, *Mask of Keats,* 5–44, for an effort to form Keats's annotations into an indisputable biographical sequence. Clearly, however, Keats read and remembered much he did not mark. He quotes from 'Hell', xvii. 101 (unmarked) in a letter to Dilke, 20 Sept. 1818, Rollins, i. 368. Keats's relations with Dante and Milton are complicated by Milton's own indebtedness to Dante, see Toynbee, i, pp. xxv–xxvii, 120–8, 200–2, 587–98; 'A Comparative View of the INFERNO [. . .]', Boyd, i. 23–5; and A. J. Smith, *The Metaphysics of Love: Studies in Renaissance Love Poetry from Dante to Milton* (Cambridge, 1985), 14–28, 140–5.

offer reminders of earthly existence; of a world remembered with something of the 'very utter affection and yearning' that underlies Milton's deepest feelings. In canto xiv, for instance, Dante and Virgil reach the plain of burning sand where the violent against God, nature, and art—the blasphemers, sodomites, and usurers— are punished.

> O'er all the sand fell slowly wafting down
> Dilated flakes of fire, as flakes of snow
> On Alpine summit, when the wind is hush'd.
> ('Hell', xiv. 25–7, Cary, i. 58)

Keats underlined the last two lines here and put two lines down the margin beside them. His markings of Cary consisted of single, double, and very occasionally triple lines down the margin and the underlining of at most five consecutive lines.[36] His marking here reveals considerable interest in the comparison that momentarily hushes the world of agonies it describes. Cary makes that hush the product of a moment, 'when the wind is hush'd', whereas Dante allows the stillness to appear lasting, though it is recalled only for the space of one tercet.

> Sovra tutto 'l sabbion, d'un cader lento,
>   piovean di foco dilatate falde,
>   come di neve in alpe sanza vento.
>   (*Inferno*, xiv. 28–30, Sapegno, i. 156)

(Over all the sand, gently falling, rained down broad flakes of fire, like those of snow in the mountains without wind.)

The repeated '-e' ending in these lines—'dilatate falde', 'come', 'neve', and 'alpe'—combines with the unusual regularity of the rhythmical pattern, especially in the final line, to produce an un-hurried and continuous movement in the lines themselves, a 'cader lento' that allows the falling of both snow and fire to appear unchanging while the resemblance between the two is introduced into the infernal world for only a moment. Cary reshapes the sudden stillness of Dante's lines in a manner that is, partly, pro-voked by the predispositions of blank verse: without the division

---

[36] Gittings, *Mask of Keats*, app. A, 152. Keats's copy is in private hands. His practice when annotating seems to have been the same as it was in his editions of Shakespeare and Milton. He may have underlined less and made fewer marginal comments because Cary's 1814 volumes were so small.

between individual three-line units, both produced and countered by Dante's rhyme-scheme, Cary cannot as easily suggest a momentary permanence. In Dante, the continuousness in the falling of the snow and fire extends to the permanence of the comparison between the two, although that comparison is mentioned very briefly. In Cary, this memory of earth leads to the evocation of a particular moment, within which the reader lingers as the imagined silence of the wind's hush meets the pause at the end of the line.

The difference between how they present this simile alters the moment when recollection gives way to narrative, when the poem turns back to Dante's infernal surroundings. In canto xiv Dante goes on to compare the burning sand with a legend about Alexander the Great's invasion of India. Under similar fiery rain Alexander ordered his men to trample the flakes as they landed to prevent fire spreading across the sand. The simile taken from this story extends over nine lines (ll. 31–9, Sapegno, i. 156–7) before Dante looks at the damned who are unable to stop themselves being burned.

> Sanza riposo mai era la tresca
>   delle misere mani, or quindi or quinci
> escotendo da sé l'arsura fresca.
>   (Ibid., ll. 40–2, p. 157)

(There was never a pause in the dance of wretched hands, now here, now there, beating away the fresh burning.)

After the classical simile, that immediately followed the image of snow among windless mountains, the ceaseless agitation of the damned recalls both: 'Sanza riposo' echoes and denies 'sanza vento' while 'Sanza riposo mai' and 'or quindi or quinci' establish the eternal present of damnation—a perpetual repetition of appropriate pain moment by moment—whereas Alexander could act effectually in a particular 'historical' time and place. The passage leads to this more intent consideration of the damned themselves, focusing on them within the landscape that has been described at gradually closer quarters, but the memory of 'sanza vento' in 'Sanza riposo' becomes a felt contrast between two states of being.

Keats leaves the simile concerning Alexander unmarked (as is usually the case with Dante's classical similes), but he draws a line in the margin alongside the description of the damned:

> Unceasing was the play of wretched hands,
> Now this, now that way glancing, to shake off
> The heat, still falling fresh.
> ('Hell', xiv. 37–9, Cary, i. 59)[37]

The persisting and connecting contrast in Dante's original between the mountain snow and the damned is lost in the translation, despite its quality. The suffering of the damned reasserts itself as an object of contemplation less qualified by recollection or informed by circumspection, allowing a 'brief pathos' to attach to the damned which is independent of the immediate verbal context. In that contemplation, Cary's lines, which move us to consider a point out of their reach, the instant 'when the wind is hush'd', confront the unqualified physicality of the damned: 'the play of wretched hands'. Keats seems to have been impressed by this bodily quality, finding it integral to the 'brief pathos' that Cary's translation makes more absolute.

Compare, for example, Farinata's stature in canto x:

> Meanwhile the other, great of soul, near whom,
> I yet was station'd, chang'd not count'nance stern,
> Nor mov'd the neck, nor bent his ribbed side.
> ('Hell', x. 71–3, Cary, i. 41)

Keats underlined the last line here, and from 'when' to 'cheek-bone' in the following passage from canto XII:

> We to those beasts, that rapid strode along,
> Drew near, when Chiron took an arrow forth,
> And with the notch push'd back his shaggy beard
> To the cheek-bone, then his great mouth to view
> Exposing, to his fellows thus exclaim'd
> (Ibid. xii. 73–7, p. 50)

In the opening of the same canto, Keats marks in the margin the description of the Minotaur:

---

[37] Keats marks canto xiii, ll. 1–10 but not the reference to the Harpies that follows. In canto xxvi he underlines the simile that compares Ulysses to a flame murmuring in the wind, but ignores references to the *Odyssey*. He seems uninterested in Hell's topography: see his notes to cantos xi and xiv (Cary, i. 53, 114, 45–6, 60–1; Gittings, *Mask of Keats*, 150, 160, 147–8, 151–2).

> and there
> At point of the disparted ridge lay stretch'd
> The infamy of Crete, detested brood
> Of the feign'd heifer: and at sight of us
> It gnaw'd itself, as one with rage distract.
> To him my guide exclaim'd.
>
> (Ibid., ll. 11–15, p. 48)

Though none of these provide a specific source, the bones of the centaur, Chiron's human face, Farinata's ribs, and the Minotaur's writhing in self-inflicted physical pain all contribute to Keats's description of Cottus in *Hyperion,* Book ii. The intrusiveness with which the physical aspects of a damned soul appear in Cary's translation is a source, therefore, of the bodily suffering endured by several of the Titans in *Hyperion.*[38] Keats seems to have drawn on the translation for the same effects that he found in Milton's 'lazar-house' of *Paradise Lost,* Book xi. Yet he notices as well the instances in *Inferno* when Dante's presence disturbs the damned, when the dispassionate observation of torment is interrupted by Dante's awareness of his own intrusiveness. The Minotaur gnaws itself 'at sight of us' ('quando vide noi', *Inferno,* xii. 14, Sapegno, i. 132) and in canto xxiii, Caiaphas (who lies like Cottus outstretched on his back) writhes in pain when he notices Dante looking at him.

> 'O friars!' I began, 'your miseries—'
> But there brake off, for one had caught mine eye,
> Fix'd to a cross with three stakes on the ground:
> He, when he saw me, writhed himself, throughout
> Distorted, ruffling with deep sighs his beard.
>
> ('Hell', xxiii. 111–15, Cary, i. 100)

Keats underlines only the last phrase here, 'ruffling with deep sighs his beard' but underlines on the opposite page the shock with which the damned notice Dante's life.[39]

---

[38] Cary's work bears also on *Hyperion,* i. 318 and ii. 3, 359; see 'Hell', i. 111. Cf. also *Hyperion,* i. 354–7 to 'Hell', xvii. 111–14 and to *Paradise Lost,* v. 266–8 (*Keats,* 339, 340, 351; Cary, i. 4, 74; Milton, i. 126).

[39] The phrase may be heard in *Hyperion,* i. 93–4, and *The Fall,* i. 450–1 (*Keats,* 332, 489).

> Soon as arriv'd, they with an eye askance
> Perus'd me, but spake not: then turning each
> To other thus conferring said: 'This one
> Seems, by the action of his throat, alive.'
> (Ibid., ll. 86–9, p. 99)

Keats pays more attention to Chiron's exclamation in canto xii, though with the same interest in view:

> 'Are ye aware, that he who comes behind
> Moves what he touches? The feet of the dead
> Are not so wont.' My trusty guide, who now
> Stood near his breast, where the two natures join,
> Thus made reply: 'He is indeed alive,
> And solitary so must needs by me
> Be shown the gloomy vale.'
> (Ibid. xii. 78–84, p. 50)

There are other examples to show the consistency of this interest in Keats's reading, but the double-line Keats puts in the margin beside ll. 79–80 ('Moves what he touches [. . .] I Are not so wont [. . .]') reveals its focal point most vividly.[40] The movement Dante causes when he touches objects, defines his living nature as well as displaying it and Cary in a moment of literal translation— 'move ciò ch'el tocca' (*Inferno,* xii. 81, Sapegno, i. 136) means simply 'moves that which he touches'—produces a phrase that would be richly suggestive to Keats when read in a Dantean context. Dante's living inhabitation of the world of the dead is an exception and a privilege. His presence contravenes the laws of Hell, denying to the Minotaur, Chiron, and Minos the authority they possess over everybody else. For that reason Dante provokes the Minotaur to gnaw itself in rage and Minos to remonstrate.

Vanno Fucci (in a passage also underlined by Keats) makes the same complaint:

> It grieves me more to have been caught by thee
> In this sad plight, which thou beholdest, than
> When I was taken from the other life.
> ('Hell', xxiv. 131–3, Cary, 105)[41]

---

[40] See 'Hell', xxiii. 95–7, and xxvii. 70–1 (Cary, i. 99, 119) marked by Keats in cantos he scarcely noted otherwise (Gittings, *Mask of Keats,* 156, 149, 161).

[41] Gittings, *Mask of Keats,* 157.

The earthly world is remembered once again by this but immediately dismissed, by Vanno Fucci at least, in his claim that the pain of leaving it was less intense than the shame of being seen. Vanno Fucci's insuperable pride may have got the better of his judgement here, but the implications of what he says are severe:[42] Dante's witnessing becomes an acknowledged and complex involvement with them. The puns on 'moves' and 'touches' produced by the simplicity of Cary's phrasing are not similarly prominent in the Italian, but still emphasize momentarily the proximity of Dante's extraordinary living presence among the dead to the influence he wields among them.[43] His physical presence prompts a startled and often anguished response among the damned, that denies the detached observation with which Keats describes Cottus, although the infernal pain Cottus suffers remains indebted to the physical agonies of Dante's damned.[44]

Dante's bringing together of clarity and involvement governs Keats's descriptions of suffering in *The Fall of Hyperion*. In the first version, Saturn is discovered, fallen in a twilit vale. Thea wakes him and describes their utter defeat, but Saturn refuses to give up hope though he knows there is nothing to be hoped for. He has 'left | My strong identity, my real self, | Somewhere between the throne, and where I sit | Here on this spot of earth'. Still, he urges Thea to help him find himself again: 'Search, Thea, search! and tell me, if thou seest | A certain shape or shadow, making way | [. . .] to repossess | A heaven he lost erewhile' (*Hyperion*, i. 113–16, 121–4, *Keats*, 332–3). He does not insist on being the same—a 'certain shape or shadow' will do—because purposefulness and self-certainty will guarantee the presence of his true self. The concession, however, with its hint of false modesty, allows him to be more confident that the return is inevitable. He claims any shape or shadow as the type of himself and conjures up his old power

[42] Dante can defend himself against the rebuke by recalling the deceitfulness of the devils, which was affirmed at the end of the previous canto (*Inferno*, xxiii. 142–8, Sapegno, i. 261).

[43] This creates a paradox Dante returns to on several occasions: see *Inferno* xxxii. 85–123, x. 61–72, Sapegno, i. 358–9, 114–16.

[44] Vanni Fucci speaks self-pityingly in Cary and with harsh self-certainty in Dante: see *Inferno*, xxxiv. 133–6, Sapegno, i. 272. Cary's translation, as in the passage from 'Hell' xiv discussed above, moderates the hostility between Vanni Fucci and Dante. Both parties are ennobled beyond embarrassment.

to inhabit and control the universe. As he does so, he begins to believe that this power exists:

> [']Yes, there must be a golden victory;
> There must be Gods thrown down, and trumpets blown
> Of triumph calm, and hymns of festival
> Upon the gold clouds metropolitan,
> Voices of soft proclaim, and silver stir
> Of strings in hollow shells; and there shall be
> Beautiful things made new, for the surprise
> Of the sky-children; I will give command:
> Thea! Thea! Thea! where is Saturn?'
>
> (*Hyperion*, i. 126–34, *Keats*, 333)

His speech sounds self-deceived and valiant at the same time. Like King Lear, he seems pathetically unable to fathom his changed circumstances and likely to burst out in furious defiance against his enemies and persecutors. He thinks his power will be restored naturally, in a 'triumph calm', though he is shouting to make himself heard. The grand gestures he makes may be founded on pride and self-delusion but they still win respect. His inflexibility implies that he has a nature which cannot change, a 'real self' which he has departed from and yet can always return to. The idea he has of the essential Saturn offers a focus for him; imagining its restoration enables him to protect himself from the suffering of his fall. Such protection is a self-fulfilling prophecy of victory and self-restoration.

Even though Saturn strikes one as someone whose defiance of his affliction consists in just denying it, his determination looks powerful. It is possible to be half-cheered by the strength he displays in separating himself from circumstances even while suspecting that the strength originates in wilfulness or capriciousness. Since enough of a self has survived in him to order and interpret the experience of self-loss, the reader is made to consider whether he may also be able to withstand it. Saturn's imagining a state of composure and stability implies the survival of a 'real self' that preserves itself independent of events. Although this may be a hopeless mistake, it seems at once an act of heroism and a necessity. The half-sublime, half-petulant resistance Saturn puts up keeps both reader and, implicitly, writer, like Saturn, withdrawn from what surrounds them. Afflictions are felt, then, as a violation of self and a disruption

of distance; they are overcome by the imagination. Saturn finds
comfort and power in his own convictions in the same way that
Keats's poetry makes sorrow into something beautiful.

As we have seen, Keats revises Thea in *The Fall of Hyperion* so
that he lessens her grandeur without reducing her stature. She is
still tall ('Surpassing wan Moneta by the head'), though no longer
of such a height as to beggar comparison. Keats now keeps her
within the range of description where, in the first version, she had
embodied the power of the sublime to overwhelm description.
Because Thea remains on a scale that includes Moneta, who in-
troduces her, Keats's claim that she is 'nearer woman's tears'
remains a statement of relative proximity. She may be as near as
one can conceive, but that does not make her into an embodiment
of the human tears she reveals. The revised version's characteristic
plainness excludes the transformation of sorrow into beauty that
had been Keats's earlier aim. However, that plainness does not
itself pretend to be an exact representation of ordinary, unbeautified
sorrow. Such a claim would itself begin to transform the sorrow.
Where earlier Keats's descriptions had embraced the indescribable,
they now acknowledge that they can go only so far towards the
experience they address.

This change and its implications are visible in Keats's descrip-
tions of Saturn. His voice grows much weaker and much less able
to command the lines of verse.

> I have no strength left,
> Weak as the reed—weak—feeble as my voice—
> O, O, the pain, the pain of feebleness.
> (*The Fall of Hyperion*, i. 427–9, *Keats*, 488–9)

His cries and repetitions sound like attempts to start his voice. It
will not go and his 'real self' will not return, not even in the minor
key of anguish. Neither can he successfully imagine a return to
power although he tries:

> let there be
> Beautiful things made new for the surprize
> Of the sky children.'—So he feebly ceas'd,
> With such a poor and sickly sounding pause,
> Methought I heard some old man of the earth
> Bewailing earthly loss; nor could my eyes
> And ears act with that pleasant unison of sense

> Which marries sweet sound with the grace of form,
> And dolorous accent from a tragic harp
> With large limb'd visions.
>
> (Ibid., ll. 436–45, p. 489)

'Let there be', not any longer, 'there shall be'. Saturn pleads for help for as long as he can until the words peter out. Instead of witnessing absolute resistance with a kind of stunned respect, Keats and his readers now go along with Saturn's gradual collapse.

The nature of the altered alignment which Keats establishes in the revised version between reader and suffering god can be observed again in his comparisons. As these come to mind, Keats's presence becomes more strongly felt: 'Methought I heard some old man of the earth | Bewailing earthly loss'. The first-person narrator is highlighted here but offers no guidance about the appropriate response. We do not know whether he was appalled or profoundly moved by Saturn's condition: in fact the comparison which springs to his mind appears to follow from a moment of contempt. The 'poor and sickly sounding pause' rhymes internally and alliterates so sharply as to sound momentarily disgusted. Keats's next words, however, withdraw from any judgement, giving the reader this comparison with an earthly man. He seems set on describing him without, as far as possible, predetermining his reader's reaction. Saturn's 'awful presence there' (ibid., l. 448, p. 489) stops him, he says, from enjoying his usual confidence as a poet in marrying 'sweet sound with the grace of form'. He cannot any longer find the 'dolorous accent' that would suit or marry with his 'large-limb'd visions'. Something of his poetic power has 'feebly ceas'd'. So, Keats's narrator makes explicit here that the loss of imaginative consolations is being experienced by the observer at the same time as it is suffered by Saturn. In consequence, the detachment and self-involvement of the first version is exchanged for a dispassionate portrayal of the case. This no longer separates the self from what is seen, protecting the self and using it as a form of protection. Instead, the poem relies on the presence of a witnessing narrator to establish credibility. To find a way of representing sorrow as it was in itself and without reference to the observer's feelings, Keats made himself into a witness, trying at all points to give a clear account of what he saw. This accurate version could not help being, however, a personal one; in fact, it has to imply a self watching in order to avoid being self-concerned.

The 'large-limb'd visions' disappear and Keats goes on: 'More
I scrutinized' (ibid., l. 445, p. 489).[45] His second look discovers
feelings which had been hidden even from Saturn himself by what
he said:

> only his lips
> Trembled amid the white curls of his beard.
> They told the truth, though, round, the snowy locks
> Hung nobly, as upon the face of heaven
> A midday fleece of clouds.
> (*The Fall of Hyperion*, i. 450–4, *Keats*, 489)

Keats notices this flicker of life and fear betraying itself in the
middle of Saturn's noble beauty. In the original version, Saturn
speaks 'As with a palsied tongue, and while his beard | Shook
horrid with such aspen-malady' (*Hyperion*, i. 93–4, *Keats*, 332).
His appearance had been emblematic and informative; in the re-
vision, his inner self lies hidden and his composed features are a
deliberate disguise. Keats, by looking as intently as he can, sees the
betraying marks of feeling that again disturb his writing: 'They
told the truth, though, round, [. . . .]' The successive interruptions
of these monosyllables contrast markedly with the grandiloquent
fluency of his following comparison. The line sounds nervous and
defensive about a claim it will not give up.

Keats's portrayal of Saturn employs repetition to admit the
ordinariness of a god's suffering: its likeness to what we might
expect and its continuing independence. Saturn does not react to
him, in the same way that Vanni Fucci does or Chiron, but Keats's
way of describing him continues to imply a self watching. His
pervading sympathy is never final or domineering but does its best
to portray what is there. Keats rewrites Saturn's lament so that he
ceases to be just an example of or an occasion for pathos, and
stops being a creation whose nature and effect Keats can entirely
control. The antics of Saturn's grand passion (in the first version)—
his weighty perspiration and wild gesticulations—are presented by
someone fascinated by the results of being consumed by passion.
In the second, Keats is prepared to be dismissive. Saturn's sickli-
ness is so marked that Keats is willing to think him just a feeble

---

[45] Cf. Beckett's use of 'scrute' in *Ill Seen Ill Said* (1981): 'With in second sight
the shack in ruins. To scrute together with the inscrutable face. All curiosity spent.'
(Samuel Beckett, *Nohow On* (Paris, London, and New York, 1989), 94.

old wreck. But Keats's coolness is both more self-respecting and more respectful: the old man of the earth might have been bewailing his petty sorrows—this seems for a moment the hostile tone of 'poor and sickly'—but is actually seen to be enclosed in recognizable 'earthly loss'. The repetition ensures that the familiarity of his suffering (and its likeness to the ordinary) does not allow Keats to become presumptuous about it.

Moneta, in the 'Induction' insisted on this attitude:

'None can usurp this height,' return'd that shade,
'But those to whom the miseries of the world
Are misery, and will not let them rest.'
  (*The Fall of Hyperion*, i. 147–9, *Keats*, 481)

The poem's descriptions have absorbed the implications of this command, as is evidenced by the restlessness of Keats's eye and the poem's reluctance to find much consolation in discovering what misery consists in. What Keats has invented in describing Saturn's sorrows may prove to true, but the correspondence between his imagination and 'the miseries of the world' alleviates nothing.[46]

For Keats to understand Moneta she must make 'comparisons of earthly things' and the revised version frequently introduces brief similes: 'Like a Silenus on an antique vase', 'Like a stunt bramble by a solemn pine', 'Like a vast giant seen by men at sea | To grow pale from the waves at dull midnight'.[47] Obviously, the first version included some similar comparisons;[48] what is distinctive in *The Fall of Hyperion* is their necessity (because of Keats's incomprehension) and the range of feeling they evoke. He embraces the potentially comic comparisons that Dante made and

---

[46] Cf. the iteration in Keats's letter from Italy about Fanny Brawne: 'The thought of leaving Miss Brawne is beyond every thing horrible—the sense of darkness coming over me—I eternally see her figure eternally vanishing' (To Charles Brown, 30 Sept. 1820, Rollins, ii. 345). He is caught in the short cycle of her appearance and disappearance, unable to rest because she will neither stay nor go.

[47] *The Fall of Hyperion*, ii. 3 and i. 56, 293, 457–8, *Keats*, 490, 479, 485, 489. Cf. ibid. ii. 18: 'For as upon the earth dire prodigies', with the *Hyperion* version: 'For as among us mortals omens drear' (i. 169, *Keats*, 490, 334).

[48] See e.g. 'that yielded like the mist | Which eagles cleave upmounting from their nest' (*Hyperion*, i. 156–7, *Keats*, 334), but note Keats's exclusion from the revised version of ll. 27–30, p. 330. Keats underlined several comparisons of this kind in Cary: see 'Hell', xxiii. 62–3 and xxv. 57–9 (Gittings, *Mask of Keats*, 155, 158).

Nathaniel Howard, like Thomas Warton, thought 'too ludicrous for the occasion'.[49] Their earthliness, in the *Inferno* and *The Fall of Hyperion*, continually draws attention to the watcher's position and perspective. Readers of both works notice who is watching so that their own attention is made self-aware.

Keats's opening to *The Fall of Hyperion*, however, seems to accuse Dante of the self-protectiveness that he struggles to avoid himself:

> Fanatics have their dreams, wherewith they weave
> A paradise for a sect
>   •   •   •   •   •   •   •   •
> [Poesy] With the fine spell of words alone can save
> Imagination from the sable charm
> And dumb enchantment.
>   (*The Fall of Hyperion*, i. 1–2, 9–10, *Keats*, 478)

The 'sable charm', like the 'ruby grape of Proserpine', will 'drown the wakeful anguish of the soul'; the 'strenuous tongue' of poetry, the 'wreath'd trellis of a working brain', are Keats's only guards against the false paradise equally offered by 'careless hectorers in proud bad verse' and by fanatical religion.[50] Milton's epic detachment is, therefore, a symptom not only of his style but of the religious security that he shared with Dante.

The Fall of Hyperion, then, uses a Dantean style to redirect the narrative of Dante's *Purgatorio* because Keats is determined to avoid the artist's humour—the concentration on aesthetic pleasures that made Milton's perspective invulnerable and Leigh Hunt's earthly paradise into a pleasure-garden. Dante becomes a model to Keats for the avoidance of such self-content but one he is committed to challenging and searching out. Not to do so would be for Keats to risk losing himself in the style he had adopted and so to repeat the artistic self-enclosure that had been unsatisfactory before.[51]

In summer 1819 two sections of the *Purgatorio* drew Keats's

---

[49] See above p. 13. Howard, *The Inferno*, 249 (canto xv. 21 n.) and 247 (canto xv, 38–9 n.).

[50] 'Ode on Melancholy', ll. 4, 10, 27; 'Ode to Psyche', l. 60; *The Fall of Hyperion*, i. 208 (*Keats*, 374–5, 366, 483).

[51] Keats is nearly always in an interchange with his influences. Where he is not his work becomes derivative and the 'influence' more easily located. The early 'To a Friend who Sent me some Roses' and 'Written in disgust of Vulgar Superstition' are barely distinguishable from Leigh Hunt's style and sentiments (*Keats*, 54–5, 88).

particular notice: the Earthly Paradise cantos and cantos ix–xii
where Dante enters Purgatory itself and sees the sculptured wall
on the terrace of the proud. At the end of *Purgatorio* xxvii Virgil
proclaims Dante's perfection—the sinlessness that proves his
readiness to regain the Earthly Paradise: 'libro, dritto e sano è tuo
arbitrio' (*Purgatorio*, xxvii. 140: 'your own will is free, right and
whole', Sapegno, ii. 303). This praise seems utterly misplaced when,
in the Garden of Eden that he enters, Dante meets his most power-
ful accuser, Beatrice. Although he has had his sins purged on the
terraces of Purgatory, Dante must now be penitent once more and,
apparently, confront particular, personal crimes. The biographical
self of his past history has to be purified. This self-confrontation
implies a further degree of involvement: *Purgatorio* differs from
Inferno in demanding Dante's submission to the same punish-
ments as those endured by the shades he meets. The Earthly Paradise
cantos argue, in part, that the rituals of penance (which purged
the seven deadly sins) must be completed by Dante's acknowledg-
ing each act of sin.

Beatrice's unveiling of herself follows Dante's confession of dis-
loyalty to her. Penitence, therefore, begins the transformation in
Dante that is continued as he enters Paradise.[52] Moneta, the
goddess whom Keats meets in the opening section of *The Fall of
Hyperion*, unveils herself to Keats when he has confessed he is
unworthy to be in her presence. She questions his self-confidence,
his sense of purpose and identity as a poet, before revealing
the vision of Saturn and Thea. The past 'dreaming thing' that is
a 'fever of thyself' must be purged, before Keats can begin to
practise the poet's vocation through what he subsequently beholds.[53]
A parallel movement governs both poems: in each, authoritative
perception of history (the history of the Church or of the Titans)
depends upon admitting one's unworthiness to witness it; and
insight into matters of universal concern brings with it continued
self-scrutiny.

In the Earthly Paradise Dante is made to watch two pageants
which present allegorically the revelation of the gospel and the
history of the Church. In these depictions of truth, however, he

---

[52] She is unveiled at *Purgatorio*, xxxi. 139–45; her accusation and Dante's
confession occupy xxx. 73–145 and xxxi. 1–69; Dante is 'transhumanized' (like
Glaucus) in *Paradiso*, i. 67–72; see Sapegno, ii. 348–9, 335–45 and iii. 9.
[53] *The Fall of Hyperion*, i. 169–70, *Keats*, 482.

sees most acutely into his own past.[54] A similar relation between
seer and seen gives rise to Keats's enquiring descriptions. He sees
Saturn's weakness and secret fears, unable to turn them into a
portrait of recognizable feeling that could be formulated within
the conventions of tragedy. None the less, his avoidance of a clear
response does not turn into another acceptable and static position.
He is compelled to go on scrutinizing the awful presence. Con-
tinuing the activity becomes the only guarantee of integrity and
accuracy—two qualities that seem now to coincide.

In this respect, again, Keats draws near to Dante. Beatrice rep-
rimands her lover in the Earthly Paradise for looking at her too
fixedly and too fixatedly.[55] Dante must look further and into the
pageant that will reveal, among other things, what he is truly like.
Similarly, on the terrace of the proud, Dante's eyes explore the
depths of the bas-relief sculpted on the wall: he 'takes their depth'
and meaning as nimbly as Keats. Even so, Virgil orders him to
look again and to look beyond: 'Non tener pur ad un loco la mente'
(*Purgatorio*, x. 46, Sapegno, ii. 109: 'Do not concentrate your mind
on one place alone'). In each scene depicted on the wall Dante sees
its 'visibile parlare' (ibid., l. 95, p. 113), imaginatively recreating
the drama God has put into the carvings.[56] This epitomizes his work
as a poet of piecing together the infinite number of speaking pic-
tures that God, who sees everything and sees Himself in everything,
has already created. To do this properly, he must go on doing so
indefinitely: delightedly perceive these things and create a self from

---

[54] The pageants occupy *Purgatorio*, xxix. 43–154; xxxii. 109–60, Sapegno, ii.
319–27, 357–60. Peter Dronke studies the autobiographical element of the alle-
gory in *Dante and the Medieval Latin Traditions* (Cambridge, 1985), 8, 55–81. See
also his 'The Procession in Dante's Purgatorio', *Deutsches Dante-Jahrbuch*, 53/54
(1978–9), 18–45, repr. in K. Foster and P. Boyde (eds.), *Cambridge Readings
in Dante's Comedy* (Cambridge, 1981), 114–37. For opposing views see C. S.
Singleton, *Studies in Dante, 2: Journey to Beatrice* (Cambridge, Mass., 1958),
141–287; R. Hollander, *Allegory in Dante's* Commedia (Princeton, NJ, 1969),
1–56, 149–74.

[55] *Purgatorio*, xxxii. 7–9: 'quando per forza mi fu volto il viso | ver la sinistra
mia da quelle dee, | perch'io udi' da loro un "Troppo fiso!"' (Sapegno, ii. 351:
'when my face was turned forcibly to the left by those divine things [Beatrice's
eyes] because I heard them say "Too fixed!"'). See also ibid. xxix. 61–3, pp.
321–2.

[56] In canto xii Dante notices the engraved figures on the floor of the terrace:
Satan, Briareus, Nimrod, and Niobe among others. I am grateful to Jane Everson
for pointing this out. See *Purgatorio*, xii. 25–69, Sapegno, ii. 131–5. I discuss the
canto below.

the process of perception which is ever more like God and able to see as a god sees.

When Dante's repentance and forgiveness is complete, Beatrice urges him to be more confident:

> Ed ella a me: 'Da tema e da vergogna
> voglia che tu omai ti disviluppe,
> si che non parli piú com' om che sogna'
> (*Purgatorio*, xxxiii. 31–3, Sapegno, ii. 363)

(And she to me: 'From fear and shame I wish you now to divest yourself, so that you no longer speak like someone dreaming'.)

He must rouse himself in order to fulfil his duty as a writer:

> Tu nota; e sí come da me son porte,
> cosí queste parole segna a' vivi
> del viver ch'è un correre alla morte.
> (Ibid., ll. 52–4, p. 365)

(You take note; and as they come from me, in that way repeat my words to the living whose life is a race towards death.)

Beatrice, like Moneta, knows she must adapt her speech to the narrowness of Dante's conceptions ('Veramente oramai saranno nude | le mie parole', ibid., ll. 100–1, p. 368: 'Truly my words will now be naked'). Dante's Earthly Paradise not only offers Keats a model of sympathetic attention and its cost, but connects that to the observant attentiveness that a poet must bring to everything. Dante, like Keats, must stop being such a dreamer in order to become a poet even though the Earthly Paradise, like *The Fall of Hyperion*, represents a dream.[57] Part of the interest for Keats lies in this being the moment in the *Commedia* when Dante wakes from a dream to find it truth.

Dante dreams only in Purgatory, and his ability to dream appears an aspect of his living humanity (by contrast with the limited humanity of the damned and the saved). The three dreams he has in the second section of the *Commedia* chart a development towards

---

[57] The poem is subtitled *A Dream*. Woodhouse writes in Aug. 1819 that he is 'embodying some of the principal events of my life in a "dream" (like) upon the Plan of Ld Byron's' (Rollins ii. 152). Keats may have looked at Byron's poem *The Dream* (1816). Cf. 'Herself the solitary scion left | Of a time-honour'd race'; 'As if its [her eye's] lid were charged with unshed tears' (ll. 67–8, 135, McGann, iv. 25, 27) with *The Fall of Hyperion*, i. 288, 220–1, *Keats*, 485, 483.

prophetic authority: at the opening of canto ix he dreams of an eagle that lifts him up from Ante-Purgatory to the gate of Purgatory itself. Upon waking Dante is told by Virgil that, in fact, St Lucy descended from heaven during the night and carried Dante up the last slope while he was still asleep. Dante's dream comes to appear a response to events that were actually taking place. At the opening of canto xix, when he is about to enter the third and final region of Purgatory, Dante dreams again, this time of a Siren. She seems to symbolize the need to purge the excessive love of secondary things that occurs on the higher terraces of the mountain. But the dream's meaning is less clear than Dante's first. Within it, Virgil is called by 'una donna [. . .] santa e presta' ('a lady, holy and vigilant', *Purgatorio*, xix. 26, Sapegno, ii. 207) to reveal the true horror of the Siren whom Dante's rapt stare has gradually transformed into something beautiful. When Dante wakes, Virgil says he has been trying to rouse him repeatedly. The woman's voice calling Virgil within Dante's dream is made suspiciously like Virgil's voice calling Dante—the dream seems to be a response to, and a rearrangement of, external events, as well as a symbolic insight into the excessive love Dante must chasten. In canto xxvii Dante dreams for the third time:

> giovane e bella in sogno mi parea
>   donna vedere andar per una landa
>   cogliendo fiori; e cantando dicea:
> 'Sappia qualunque il mio nome dimanda
>   ch'i' mi son Lia, e vo movendo intorno
>   le belle mani a farmi una ghirlanda'
>   (*Purgatorio*, xxvii. 97–102, Sapegno,
>   ii. 300–1)

(in a dream I seemed to see a young and beautiful woman going through a meadow gathering flowers; and singing, she said: 'Know, anyone who asks my name, that I am Leah, and I go busying my beautiful hands here and there to make myself a garland'.)

Leah and her sister Rachel, the two wives of Jacob in the book of Genesis, became types of the active and contemplative lives, rather like the New Testament figures, Martha and Mary. Leah exactly conforms to this reading of herself: by gathering flowers that will become her garland she seeks glory from action rather than contemplation. In the following canto this dream comes true:

e là m'apparve

· · · · · ·

una donna soletta che si gía
   cantando e scegliendo fior da fiore
   ond'era pinta tutta la sua via.
     (Ibid. xxviii. 37, 40–2, pp. 307–8)

(and in that place appeared to me [. . .] a solitary woman, who went singing and picking flowers from the flowers with which her whole path was painted.)

Dante's purgation during his ascent up the mountain lends his dreams ever greater prophetic power; he enters the Earthly Paradise to find his imagination effortlessly prophesying truth.

    Matilda, whom Dante meets here, resembles Leah as she appears and, in what follows, she is pre-eminently an agent, carrying Dante across both rivers of the Earthly Paradise in cantos xxxi and xxxiii. The identification of the woman he meets with the active life is confirmed by what follows, but Matilda's presence also transcends that identification.

Ella ridea dall'altra riva dritta,
   trattando piú color con le sue mani,
   che l'alta terra sanza seme gitta.
     (Ibid. xxviii. 67–9, pp. 309–10)

(Standing upright, she smiled from the other bank, arranging in her hands more of the coloured flowers which the high country produces spontaneously without seed.)

The glories of the Earthly Paradise amplify the dream. Dante's repeated, fascinated attention to exactly what Matilda is doing directs him and his reader to the particularity of the person in whom he finds that dream fulfilled and surpassed. Matilda will explain how it is that the flowers grow without need of seeds, as she will prove for certain to be an example of the perfect active life, but Dante responds, first of all, to the very fact of her presence in all its wonder.

    In a similar manner, Beatrice, whom he has always expected to meet at last in the Earthly Paradise, appears, confirming and baffling his hope. She appears on the chariot drawn by the Griffin and surrounded by the company of the pageant described in canto xxix that depicted God's revelation.

> dentro una nuvola di fiori
> che dalle mani angeliche saliva
> e ricadeva in giú dentro e di fori,
> sovra candido vel cinta d'uliva
> donna m'apparve, sotto verde manto
> vestita di color di fiamma viva.
> E lo spirito mio
>
> •   •   •   •   •
>
> sanza delli occhi aver piú conoscenza,
> per occulta virtú che da lei mosse,
> d'antico amor sentí la gran potenza.
>   (Ibid. xxx. 28–34, 37–9, pp. 332–3)

(within a cloud of flowers which rose from the angels' hands and fell back down inside and outside [the chariot in which Beatrice is placed] a woman appeared to me, wreathed with olive over a white veil and, under a green cloak, clothed in the colour of living flame. And my spirit [. . .] without gaining further knowledge from my eyes, by the hidden virtue which came from her, felt the great power of old love.)

The moment when Beatrice appears is allowed to interrupt the sequence of circumstances in which she appears and then immediately to take its place within that sequence. Dante's prompt recognition that this is Beatrice herself becomes part of the way in which he describes her appearing. The phrasing of 'donna m'apparve' echoes 'e là m'apparve' from the scene where Matilda appears but dwells on the woman whom Dante sees rather than on the fact of his seeing her.[58] Beatrice insists on this:

> 'Guardaci ben! Ben son, ben son Beatrice.
> Come degnasti d'accedere al monte?
> non sapei tu che qui è l'uom felice?'
>   (Ibid. xxx. 73–5, p. 335)

('Look closely! I am indeed Beatrice. So you deign to ascend the mountain? Do you not know that here mankind is happy?')

Beatrice justifies her ferocity towards Dante, whom the watching angels seem to pity, by telling them of his desertion of her after

---

[58] Dante was about to turn to Virgil and say 'conosco i segni dell'antica fiamma' ('I recognize the signs of the old flame'), a line that echoes the *Aeneid*. Beatrice's speech disrupts this exchange of learned compliments. (See *Purgatorio*, xxx. 48 and n., Sapegno, ii. 333).

her death ten years previously.[59] Dante must confess and repudiate the false goods of the world which he pursued in that period, neglecting her memory which was the epitome of all true good. The public humiliation which he suffers, and the attention he must pay to his earthly life as a result, begin, however, in Beatrice's command, 'Guardaci ben!' Within this paradisal world, that continues his prophetic dream by fulfilling it, Dante must pay absolute attention to Beatrice in order to see his own actions in their true light. His way of viewing Beatrice's first appearance, and the earlier enthusiasm with which he first saw Matilda, differ, and in their difference suggest his self-forgetful concentration on what he sees. Dante's subsequent contrition accepts the truth of her view of him and his past; at the same time, it involves the vision she demands. Dante sees more clearly into himself by looking more intently at her. The repeated fulfilment and disruption of Dante's dreams make this larger moral development equal to the ability to have a dream that is true. By looking so hard into Beatrice's face Dante can continue to dream prophetically and truthfully.[60]

Keats's 'Induction' evidently addresses what Dante is concerned to resolve in the Earthly Paradise. To do any 'benefit [. . .] To the great world' Keats recognizes that a poet must do more than dream. The alternatives Moneta offers him are either to 'seek no wonder but the human face; | No music but a happy-noted voice' or, as a true poet, to 'pour out a balm upon the world'. She insists that the dreaming Keats took for poetry is in fact nothing like poetry:

> 'Art thou not of the dreamer tribe?
> The poet and the dreamer are distinct,
> Diverse, sheer opposite, antipodes.
> The one pours out a balm upon the world,
> The other vexes it.'
>   (*The Fall of Hyperion*, i. 163–4, 198–202,
>   Keats, 482–3)

---

[59] Beatrice died in 1290 when Dante was about 25; the events of the *Commedia* are depicted as taking place at Easter 1300, though Dante wrote the poem between c.1309 and 1321.

[60] The difficulties of dreaming and the dreamlike quality of events in the Earthly Paradise are considered again in canto xxxii; see ll. 70–93. It is the prerequisite of Dante's writing, see ll. 100–5 (Sapegno, ii. 355–7).

Keats's response to this is as repentant as Dante's reply to Beatrice and it begins to 'note' his dream in the same way as Dante does. Keats first declares that he is not one of the 'large self worshippers, | And careless hectorers in proud bad verse'. The dreamer who vexes the world may be a poet, but only one of the 'mock lyrists' whom Keats condemns. When he turns from invective, Keats asks Moneta more straightforward questions:

> Though I breathe death with them it will be life
> To see them sprawl before me into graves.
> Majestic shadow, tell me where I am:
> Whose altar this; for whom this incense curls:
> What image this, whose face I cannot see,
> For the broad marble knees; and who thou art,
> Of accent feminine, so courteous.
> (Ibid., ll. 209–15, p. 483)[61]

Though Keats is convinced he will find 'life' through destroying these 'mock lyrists', his denial of any allegiance with them is infected with the feverishness Moneta has condemned in him before. His fever disappears when this implacable and predatory 'life' becomes present and doubtful: 'Majestic shadow, tell me where I am'. His ignorance accompanies the sudden care with which he attends to each object in turn (to 'this' altar, 'this incense' 'this' image), as if (in Keats's terms) the true poet, to discover his true life, must keep watch even in his dreams.[62]

Yet Moneta is not the same as Beatrice: she is an immortal not a human soul and when, like Beatrice, she unveils herself, Keats is not forgiven by someone he betrayed, nor does he receive a revelation of truth and divine love. Dante's purgation concludes (in canto xxxiii) with his reception into the heavenly order that vindicates as well as making possible his ambition to speak prophetically. Keats never enters that sectarian paradise and sees instead in Moneta's eyes only 'a benignant light' shining in the eyes of 'a wan face'. The eternal knowledge that Moneta intimates is

---

[61] The change in tone may be the result of further revision. Lines 187–210 were marked by Woodhouse for possible exclusion. See *Keats*, 672; Brian Wicker, 'The Disputed Lines in *The Fall of Hyperion*', *Essays in Criticism*, 7 (1957), 28–41.
[62] *The Fall of Hyperion*, i. 207–8, *Keats*, 483.

insupportable and comfortless, but her eyes 'held [him] back'. Dante sees in Beatrice the 'isplendor di viva luce etterna' (*Purgatorio*, xxxi. 139, Sapegno, ii. 348, 'the splendour of the living, eternal light'), recognizing her more completely because recognizing her identity with the God who created her. Keats sees only a mystery he can perhaps trust, and whose indifference is beyond him. She is the truly 'fore-seeing god' whose wisdom Keats can do no more than pursue and whose 'blank splendour' makes him ache to know more.

> As I had found
> A grain of gold upon a mountain's side,
> And twing'd with avarice strain'd out my eyes
> To search its sullen entrails rich with ore,
> So at the view of sad Moneta's brow,
> I ached to see what things the hollow brain
> Behind enwombed: what high tragedy
> In the dark secret chambers of her skull
> Was acting, that could give so dread a stress
> To her cold lips, and fill with such a light
> Her planetary eyes; and touch her voice
> With such a sorrow.
> (*The Fall of Hyperion*, i. 271–82, *Keats*, 485)

She keeps him avaricious for knowledge, impartially receptive to whatever he may have to learn. His eagerness becomes sensitivity as it moves from her 'skull' and 'cold lips' to her continuing voice of 'sorrow' rather than 'high tragedy'. As Keats, in these lines, looks more and more closely, he stops using epithets so that 'dark secret', 'dread', and 'cold' become 'such' and 'such'. The repetitions cherish her indefinable nature by holding back his voice. 'That could give so dread a stress' makes 'and fill with such a light' seem almost predictable so that 'and touch her voice', rhyming 'such' with 'touch' but further shortening the half-line, interrupts the confidence of Keats's movement and still makes him carry on. The internal rhymes make him render 'such a sorrow' without measuring it (as 'high tragedy') and without transforming its immeasurability into the sublime.

The encounter with Moneta declares Keats's dissent from Dante's faith, as much as from Milton's, and corrects both in the light of 'the general and gregarious advance of intellect' that casts doubt on 'Dogmas and superstitions': 'those resting-places and seeming sure points of Reasoning' in an earlier age.[63] The truth that Dante can dwell in and (given space) could describe indefinitely, Keats without 'resting-places' may only struggle towards perpetually. Yet, by using Dante's style, Keats can remain in these sure points.[64] The iterations in The Fall of Hyperion ('some old man of the earth | Bewailing earthly loss', 'Then came the grieved voice of Mnemosyne | And grieved I hearkened', 'and fill with such a light | Her planetary eyes; and touch her voice | With such a sorrow') imply the reciprocity that exists between Dante and his shades, and employ something of his method.[65] In Purgatorio xii, where Dante sees Satan and the fallen Titans carved on the pavement of the terrace, he acclaims the greatness of the artistry: 'Morti li morti e i vivi parean vivi: | non vide mei di me che vide il vero' (ll. 67–8, Sapegno, ii. 135, 'the dead seemed dead and the living living: | seen no more clearly by Him who saw the truth than by me'). The sculpture allows Dante to see as God sees, portraying living beings with a degree of accuracy Dante can emulate only through repetition.

True poetry for Dante is no different from dictation: he must note what Beatrice says and repeat it when he gets back to earth.[66] Such artistry is the form of proper sympathy: in Purgatorio xiv Dante meets two souls talking to each other, one of whom then listens to the other's prophecy.

[63] See Susan J. Wolfson, The Questioning Presence: Wordsworth, Keats and the Interrogative Mode in Romantic Poetry (Ithaca, NY, and London, 1986), 359; Wolfson describes 'Keats's uncertain situation in an age that lacked confidence in the grand schemes of redeemed suffering to which Milton's and Dante's epics could appeal. Is Negative Capability an adequate recompense? Perhaps.'

[64] R. S. White, Keats as a Reader of 'Shakespeare' (London, 1987), 214–17, 220–1, argues that the revision of Hyperion arises from Keats's reading of King Lear; that Cordelia's compassion informs Moneta's and Thea's. The 'precious, post-tragic awareness' (hinted at by the endings of Shakespeare's tragedies) lends Keats, in White's view, a comparable 'point of visionary refuge and inner peace, itself the product of powerful, humanistic and humane sympathy'. Though I am not convinced that Keats's sympathy implies 'inner peace', this is well seen and well put. White's chapter offers little account of Keats's changed style. The two 'sources' (Shakespeare and Dante) are really complementary: the narrative of Dante's Earthly Paradise indicated to Keats the difficulty of becoming like Shakespeare.

[65] See Paul D. Sheats, 'Stylistic Discipline in The Fall of Hyperion', K–SJ, 17 (1968), 83.

[66] See the discussion with Bonagiunta da Lucca, Purgatorio, xxiv. 52–63, Sapegno, ii. 266–8.

Com'all'annunzio di dogliosi danni
si turba il viso di colui ch'ascolta,
da qual che parte il periglio l'assanni,
cosí vid'io l'altr'anima, che volta
stava udir, turbasi e farsi trista,
poi ch'ebbe la parola a sé raccolta.
(*Purgatorio*, xiv. 67–72, Sapegno, ii. 156)

(As at the announcement of impending sorrow, the face is troubled of him who listens, no matter from what quarter the danger threatens him, so I saw the other spirit, who was turned to listen, trouble himself and become sad when he had absorbed the speech.)

The shade (Rinieri da Calboli) will himself, of course, not be hurt by the disasters, though they include the sins of his grandson (Fulcieri da Calboli). Though unaffected, Rinieri makes himself respond, 'turbasi e farsi trista'. On earth, that reaction is forced on a listener, 'si turba il viso'; in Purgatory, as Dante emphasizes in the reflexive verbs, 'l'altr'anima' moves itself to pity. Yet the perturbation is no different in feeling: the saved soul, out of danger, willingly experiences the anxiety of the victim to the full. By repeating the word, 'si turba', 'turbasi', Dante makes Rinieri's sympathy appear complete while still asserting, as he must, that it is deliberate. Rinieri's commitment to what he is told means that he replicates the experience of suffering by a form of willed passivity.[67]

Perhaps Keats read these passages either in Cary or the original: they are close to others he must have read[68] but reveal, in any case, a feature of Dante's writing that recurs.[69] The end of *Inferno* v contains the instance perhaps most important for him:

[67] Hence the force of 'da qual che parte il periglio l'assanni': the panic of earthly fears ignores the source of danger, whereas, in Purgatory, sympathy is consciously indiscriminate. It is liberal without being disinterested. See 'To Georgiana Keats', 15 Jan. 1820, Rollins, ii. 243: 'The more I know of Men the more I know how to value entire liberality in any of them.'

[68] Cf. The Fall of Hyperion, i. 90 ff. and ii. 51–3 with *Purgatorio*, ix. 94–102 (*Keats*, 480, 491; Sapegno, ii. 100–1). See also *Purgatorio*, xxx. 76–7, Sapegno, ii. 335.

[69] See e.g. *Purgatorio*, xxxi. 68–9, Sapegno, ii. 344–5. Cary's translation of these passages is as follows: 'Dead the dead, | The living seem'd alive; with clearer view | His eye beheld not who beheld the truth' ('Purgatory', xii. 60–2); 'As one, who tidings hears of woes to come, | Changes his looks perturb'd, from whate'er part | The peril grasp him, so beheld I change | That spirit, who had turn'd to listen, struck | With sadness, soon as he had caught the word.' (xiv. 71–5); '"If, but to hear thus pains thee, | Raise thou thy beard, and lo! what sight shall do!"' (xxxi. 65–6) (Cary, ii. 52, 62, 145).

Mentre che l'uno spirto questo disse,
l'altro piangea, sí che di pietade
io venni men cosí com'io morisse;
e caddi come corpo morto cade.
(*Inferno*, v. i. 139–42, Sapegno, i. 65)

(While the first spirit was saying this, the other wept, so that, out of pity,
I became almost as if I had died and fell as a dead body falls.)

Though the canto is unmarked in Keats's edition of Cary, he
would not have ignored this most famous of Dante's encounters
and the source of Leigh Hunt's *The Story of Rimini*. Probably,
he had read it before in his 1805–6 volumes of Cary's *Inferno*
that are lost. In April 1819 he certainly read it again: he writes to
George and Georgiana Keats 'The fifth canto of Dante pleases me
more and more' and then transcribes his sonnet 'As Hermes once
took to his feathers light'.[70] When first published, this was en-
titled, 'A Dream, after reading Dante's episode of Paolo and
Francesca'.[71] Cary's translation reads:

> While thus one spirit spake,
> The other wail'd so sorely, that heart-struck
> I through compassion fainting, seem'd not far
> From death, and like a corpse fell to the ground.
> ('Hell', v. 135–8, Cary, i. 22)

Dante's 'corpo morto' is the seemingly banal completion of 'com'io
morisse' and, when he falls, the comparison is again short-circuited
by repetition: 'caddi [. . .] come [. . .] cade'.[72] Cary's adornments

---

[70] For discussions of this sonnet see Jerome McGann, *The Beauty of Inflections:
Literary Investigations in Historical Method and Theory* (Oxford, 1985), 42; John
Barnard, *John Keats*, 94–6. Both critics read the sonnet as opposing the lovers
to the outside world, the ideal dream to reality. Its central ambiguity ('lovers need
not tell | Their sorrows' (ll. 11–12)) may, however, endanger the ideal by meaning
that the lovers' condition is obvious and needs no explanation, rather than that the
lovers can choose silence (see Allott, 500 n.). This alternative would correspond to
Keats's reading of the Earthly Paradise cantos.

[71] See Rollins, ii. 91; *Keats*, 326. The sonnet's 'flaw of rain and hail-stones' (ll.
10–11) uses Cary's translation of *Inferno* vi: 'Large hail, discoloured water, sleety
flaw' ('Hell', vi. 9, Cary, i. 23).

[72] The line draws attention to its repetitiveness by echoing the end of canto iii:
'e caddi come l'uom che 'l sonno piglia' (l. 136, Sapegno, i. 39, 'and I fell as a man
overcome by sleep'). For a discussion of these turns of phrase in Dante, see Eric
S. Mallin, 'The False Simile in Dante's *Commedia*', *Dante Studies*, 102 (1984),
15–36; Richard Lansing, *From Image to Idea: A Study of the Simile in Dante's
Commedia* (Ravenna, 1977).

('so sorely' and 'heart-struck | I') explain Dante's collapse as pro-
portionate and preserve the integrity of the sympathizing self. The
last comparison ('and like a corse fell to the ground') must, there-
fore, lose the point of Dante's obviousness. In the original, 'caddi'
and 'cade' lend the comparison as little breadth or expansiveness
as Keats finds when he describes Saturn as a 'man of the earth |
Bewailing earthly loss'. There is in both a comic incapacity to
avoid banal-sounding repetitions. The iterations point towards the
object's inscrutability and towards the struggling poet whose de-
scriptive powers are being overwhelmed. The latter focus reminds
the reader of the watcher's presence and, consequently, of his or
her own presence, preventing the plainness from claiming finality.
It is nearly a ludicrous effect, as risky as Dante's startling, incon-
gruous similes.[73]

Dante's attention is by no means perfect, at the stage of his
progress he has reached in *Inferno* v. This repetitive structure,
however, suggests the compassionate identification which Dante,
like the souls of the saved, achieves in the *Purgatorio*. In the later
section, and in a state of grace, however, this compassion can
leave the sympathizing person unmoved. Insofar as the *Commedia*
narrates an education in sympathy, *Inferno* v presents an initial
version which needs to be renounced in order to be regained. As
in *Purgatorio* xiv, Dante is witnessing a dialogue. Most frequently
in the *Inferno*, Dante is directly involved while Virgil looks on.
'Pietade' becomes more inappropriate the further Dante descends
and the more he is threatened with damnation. With Paolo and
Francesca 'pietade' is possible precisely because Dante is a third
party, enjoying the perspective he must learn, through Hell, to
preserve in relation to himself because that perspective is the eye
of God. With such self-detachment he will begin to be as unmoved

---

[73] Christopher Ricks finds similar effects much earlier in Keats's career. He says
of *Endymion*, i. 337–43: '[the lines] embody a generosity that can accommodate
a truthful recognition (and not be mesmerized), evoked through the repetitions
which are like those of grief itself and so are in companionship with grief' (Ricks,
Keats and Embarrassment (Oxford, 1974), 9). This is a fine description of Keats's
aim, but being similar to what you observe does not necessarily put you 'in
companionship with' it. The repetitions in *Endymion* are, I think, mesmerized,
and consequently they appropriate the victim's separate grief. In reaction to that,
The Fall of Hyperion is troubled by the reciprocity between witness and object.
Cf. Ricks's view of *Endymion*, i. 264–71 (ibid. 191). See also my 'The Watching
Narrator in *Isabella*', *Essays in Criticism*, 40 (1990), 287–302.

and yet as loving as God.[74] Keats's 'Induction' is a search for that point of view. The 'benignant light' of Moneta's eyes can, therefore, be seen as promising the dispassionate sympathy that Dante feels to be the natural consequence of grace. It does not promise anything more than that. In setting aside Milton and, more distantly, Leigh Hunt, *The Fall of Hyperion* establishes and practises Keats's belief that justifiable writing demands a continual exploration of 'dark passages', with sympathy as endangered and unrelenting as Dante's was, but in the absence of Dante's (eventual) assurance of escape.[75]

[74] Cf. Dante's different relationship with the Popes in *Inferno*, xix. 64–126 and *Purgatorio*, xix. 97–145, Sapegno, i. 215–19 and ii. 211–14.

[75] To Reynolds, 3 May 1818, Rollins i. 281. Keats may have been thinking of *Inferno* v in his description of climbing the steps to Moneta's altar: 'One minute before death, my iced foot touched | The lowest stair; and as it touched, life seemed | To pour in at the toes' (*The Fall of Hyperion*, i. 132–4). In canto vi Dante wakes up, freed suddenly from one affliction to witness more: 'novi tormenti e novi tormentati | mi veggio intorno' (*Inferno*, vi. 4–5, Sapegno, i. 67: 'new torments and new tormented ones I see all around'). Characteristically, Keats seems to be fusing Dante's climb up the steps of Purgatory (which, though representing repentance, is surprisingly easy) with his journey through the successive afflictions of Hell.

5

'The Lucifer of that starry flock'

Shelley in Purgatorio

Shelley's *The Triumph of Life* may have been influenced by Keats's first version of *Hyperion*. When Apollo meets Mnemosyne he has seen her before in the natural world of Delos: 'Sure I have heard those vestments sweeping o'er | The fallen leaves [. . . .] Surely I have traced | The rustle of those ample skirts' (ll. 53–6, *Keats*, 354). Shelley's *Alastor*, similarly, pursues the Arabian maid and finds a Spirit, who 'seemed | To stand beside him—clothed in no bright robes | [. . .] But, undulating woods, and silent well, | And leaping rivulet' (ll. 479–85, *PP*, 81). The 'shape all light' of Rousseau's narrative in *The Triumph of Life*, 'waned in the coming light' but can still be sensed:

> 'So knew I in that light's severe excess
> The presence of that shape which on the stream
> Moved, as I moved along the wilderness,
> More dimly than a day appearing dream[']

This 'day appearing dream' is comparable to Coleridge's 'waking dream' and shares in his attempt to combine realities and transcendent truth. Whether the 'shape all light' is, in fact, deceitful or revelatory, Rousseau declares her presence to be 'A light from Heaven' still visible within 'the sick day in which we wake to weep'.[1] Rousseau's experience, moreover, parallels the narrator's; the 'waking dream', as Shelley calls it, in which he sees the 'Triumph' of the Chariot of Life and meets Rousseau, is the result of 'a strange trance':

> Which was not slumber, for the shade it spread
> Was so transparent that the scene came through
> As clear as when a veil of light is drawn
> O'er evening hills they glimmer [. . . .]
> (ll. 42, 29–33, *Triumph*, 138)

---

[1] ll. 424–7, 429, 430, *Triumph*, 194.

The light of evening (and morning) brings out the contours of hills while irradiating them with colour. They are seemingly obscured but actually more clearly revealed. Their 'glimmer' (a word Rousseau uses for the shape's presence as well) epitomizes not only their faintness but the proper perception of them: their real nature shines through when light illuminates them and clothes them in itself. Shelley's narrator, at this point, seems privileged to see the 'many-coloured glass' of the phenomenal world more clearly, not less, because it is bathed in the 'white radiance of Eternity'.[2]

Whether truth can be revealed within actual things, or whether the actual world can only obscure the world of forms, is one way of putting the issue central to *The Triumph of Life*. Shelley's discussion of it is more vexed than in *Alastor* and more sceptical than *Hyperion*, Book iii. But, as in Keats and Coleridge, the idea of a 'transparent shade', a visionary perception that continues to reveal the earthly scene, is bound up with Shelley's sense of himself as a poetic and political agent. In reconsidering, through his narrator and Rousseau, the desire to claim a true perception of actual things, Shelley is reviewing his political hopes and poetic ambitions. Both of these rested on the assumption that a poet, as one of the 'unacknowledged legislators of the World' and an 'awakener of entranced Europe', could promote the betterment of society, its gradual transformation into the ideal state perceived in poetry.[3]

Curiously, if *The Triumph of Life* is in part a response to Keats's *Hyperion*, it redirects the poem in the same way as Keats did himself in *The Fall of Hyperion*. Shelley's work is similarly wary of the aloofness that can afflict anyone who claims visionary authority. And, as in *The Fall of Hyperion*, this wariness is made possible through Shelley's employment of Dante's style while his suspicion extends to Dante himself. In resisting too lofty a claim for poetry without renouncing its value, *The Triumph of Life* makes use of several elements from Dante: the world created by *Purgatorio*; the role of Virgil as an admired predecessor (like Rousseau) whom Dante may (like Shelley) surpass; and the compassionate detachment made possible both by Dante's status in the afterlife and by the nuances of *terza rima*. These aspects of the *Commedia* reveal to Shelley how a Faustian aspiration need not be self-destructive

---

[2] *Adonais*, ll. 462–3, *PP*, 405.   [3] 'A Defence of Poetry', *PP*, 508, 499.

and need not prove that life is a dream. Dante's work orients, I will argue, Shelley's eclectic poem, that is dense with the shadows of Goethe, Calderón, *Comus*, and Petrarch as well as of the *Commedia* itself.[4]

Shelley knew Dante's works better than any of the other Romantic poets did. As well as reading *Inferno* and *Purgatorio*, he was one of the first English readers to appreciate both *La Vita Nuova* and *Paradiso*. He also translated the first canzone of the *Convivio* and, as early as 1815, for the *Alastor* volume, the little-known sonnet 'Guido, vorrei che tu e Lapo e io'.[5] Critics have already considered the relation between Dante's redemptive narrative and those in Shelley's *Prometheus Unbound* and *Adonais*. Dante's idealization of love in *La Vita Nuova* has, similarly, been seen as an influence on *Epipsychidion*.[6] These analyses depend on large-scale similarities in structure or narrative more than on the comparison of verbal detail, whereas the stylistic similarities between Dante and *The Triumph of Life* have been recognized since the beginning of the century.[7] Whether the Dantean style of Shelley's last poem informs its elusive design has hitherto been largely neglected.[8]

---

[4] See also Edward Duffy, *Rousseau in England: The Context for Shelley's Critique of the Enlightenment* (Berkeley, Calif., Los Angeles, and London, 1979).

[5] The sonnet had already been translated by William Hayley in his 'Notes' to *An Essay on Epic Poetry [. . .]* (London, 1782), 171. Shelley's interest is probably independent.

[6] On *Prometheus Unbound* see C. S. Lewis, 'Shelley, Dryden, and Mr Eliot', *English Romantic Poets: Modern Essays in Criticism*, ed. M. H. Abrams (London, Oxford, and New York, 1960), 266; Steve Ellis, *Dante and English Poetry: Shelley to T. S. Eliot* (Cambridge, 1983), 19; Alan Weinberg, *Shelley's Italian Experience* (London and Basingstoke, 1991), 122–34. On *Adonais*, see R. H. Fogle, 'Dante and Shelley's *Adonais*', *Bucknell Review*, 15 (1967), 11–21; Ross Woodman, *The Apocalyptic Vision in the Poetry of Shelley* (Toronto, 1964), 158–77; Weinberg, *Shelley's Italian Experience*, 173–201. On *Epipsychidion*, see Earl Schulze, 'The Dantean Quest of *Epipsychidion*', *Studies in Romanticism*, 21 (1982), 191–216.

[7] A. C. Bradley. 'Notes on Shelley's "Triumph of Life"', *Modern Language Review*, 9 (1914), 441–56; E. Melian Stawell, 'Shelley's "Triumph of Life"', *Essays and Studies by Members of the English Association*, 5 (1914), 104–31; T. S. Eliot, 'What Dante Means to Me', *To Criticize the Critic* (London, 1965), 130.

[8] Similarly, in Shelley's *The Cenci*, allusions to Dante form part of the design: Beatrice in Act I, scene iii, says to the guests: 'I do entreat you, go not, noble guests [. . . .] What, if 'tis he who clothed us in these limbs | Who tortures them, and triumphs?' (*PP*, 251) recalling Ugolino's children: 'e disser: "Padre, assai ci fia men doglia | se tu mangi di noi: tu ne vestisti | queste misere carni, e tu le spoglia".' (*Inferno*, xxxiii. 61–3, Sapegno, i. 366: 'and said, "Father, it will give us far less pain if you eat us: you clothed us in this miserable flesh, so you should tear it from

Leavis and Eliot both claimed that the Dantean elements in the poem reveal the chastening of Shelley's ardent, immature idealism. Dante's supposed power to 'make us *see more definitely*' creates in *The Triumph of Life*, 'a new and profoundly serious concern for reality'.[9] This judgement has become normal: Miriam Allott states that Dante's influence produces, in *The Triumph of Life*, an 'unflinching scrutiny' of 'the painful realities of existence'.[10] William Keach has shown how Shelley's reading of the *Commedia* focused on Dante's 'fusion of the physical and the psychical' and pays less attention to the clarity and definition which Eliot admired.[11] Keach's observation is confirmed by its corollary in *The Triumph of Life*: the absence of an 'unflinching scrutiny' that is submissive to realities. The perspective and tone which Shelley acquires from his redisposition of Dantean techniques is less compromised by the world than Leavis or Allott suggest, in part because Dante himself is.

Shelley's rewriting of Dante no more submits to his authority than it confesses the priority of 'the world as men know it'. His wariness and self-questioning remain, however, far from disdain

us".'.) Cenci has just rejoiced in the death of his sons and assumes that he has every right to demand what Ugolino's children offer their father. From here, Ugolino's example begins to inform Cenci's behaviour: Beatrice thinks of her treatment in similar terms at III. i. 43–50, *PP*, 262; Giacomo's alienation from his family recalls Ugolino again in III. ii. 81–3, *PP*, 273. Cenci's tyranny attacks the one source of comfort that Ugolino finds. His rape of Beatrice starts to resemble Ugolino's eating of Ruggieri.

[9] See T. S. Eliot, 'Dante', *Selected Essays* (3rd edn., London, 1951), 244; F. R. Leavis, *Revaluation: Tradition and Development in English Poetry* (London, 1936, repr. Harmondsworth, 1972), 215–16; see also T. S. Eliot, 'The Metaphysical Poets', *Selected Essays*, 288.

[10] Miriam Allott, 'The Reworking of a Literary Genre: Shelley's *The Triumph of Life*', *Essays on Shelley*, ed. id. (Liverpool, 1982), 240. See also Jerome McGann, 'The Secrets of an Elder Day: Shelley after "Hellas"', *Shelley: Modern Judgements*, ed. R. B. Woodings (London, 1968), 259; Carlos Baker, *Shelley's Major Poetry: The Fabric of a Vision* (Princeton, NJ, 1948), 218. Peter Manning, *Reading Romantics: Texts and Contexts* (New York, 1990) argues lucidly for the *symboliste* foundation of Eliot's views.

[11] William Keach, *Shelley's Style* (New York and London, 1984), 59. For Shelley's markings, see W. E. Peck, *Shelley: His Life and Work*, 2 vols. (London, 1927), ii. 355–9. *Inferno*, i–xxi are annotated, mostly with marginal brackets. The date of the markings is uncertain. The second volume (*Purgatorio*) is unmarked except for the first lines of several *rime* written on the inside front and back covers. Shelley's interest in the corrupting power of money is evident: xvi. 73–5, xvii. 70–8, xxi. 40–3 are all marked. He notes also Dante's denunciations: xix. 58–84, 86–91 are marked, the second with special emphasis.

either for Dante or the world. The poem's reassessment of a person's relation to events and to poetic language does not coolly explore the possibilities. Paul de Man, for example, has argued that Shelley's concern with his own processes of figuration (which de Man divides from an interest in 'painful realities') produces in *The Triumph of Life* an 'altogether tantalising' poem. For de Man, the poem's total elusiveness becomes proof that Shelley attained the higher wisdom which sees all patterning as a falsification of random events. His poem is the result of an enviable serenity that de Man's studiedly casual writing seeks to imitate.[12]

If the poem is thought to be characterized by serenity, the Dantean elements in it become parodic of Dante. For Alan Weinberg the 'shape all light' seems 'to parody Dante's ladies' because, as he understands the poem, Shelley is replacing Dantean stability with Petrarchan instability; Earl Schulze reads 'Rousseau's allegorical vision' similarly—as solely 'Antithetical to Dante's Purgatory, perversely redeploying its imagery'.[13] These readings are facilitated by their assumption that the *Commedia* is a distinctively authoritative text which Shelley feels able (and/or compelled) to displace. Such a status for Dante's work is neither unequivocally present in the Romantic period nor the focus of Shelley's attention, but by supposing its existence these critics simplify Dante's bearing on *The Triumph of Life*.[14] The variety of Shelley's allusions and their apparently indiscriminate use of all three *cantiche* are taken to prove his disagreement with Dante's ordering of existence; his distinctive *terza rima* becomes an index of his dissent from hierarchical authority.[15]

[12] Paul de Man, 'Shelley Disfigured', in Bloom *et al.*, *Deconstruction and Criticism*, 53. See also pp. 45, 60, 69.

[13] Earl Schulze, 'Allegory against Allegory: *The Triumph of Life*', *Studies in Romanticism*, 27 (1988), 44; Weinberg, *Shelley's Italian Experience*, 236; see also p. 132.

[14] According to Trelawny Shelley described Shakespeare as 'the lion in the path'. Jonathan Bate takes this phrase to typify Shelley's combative relation to Shakespeare. He misses its echo of *Inferno* i where a lion blocks Dante's way: 'la vista che m'apparve d'un leone' (l. 45, Sapegno, i. 9, 'the sight which appeared to me of a lion'). Shelley, typically, does not try or fail to displace one writer with another; he uses eclecticism as a means of placing himself within a tradition of writers in order to change competition into emulation, imitation into co-operation. See Jonathan Bate, *Shakespeare and the English Romantic Imagination* (Oxford, 1986), 202.

[15] See also Harold Bloom, *Shelley's Mythmaking* (London, 1959), 254–5. The assumption that Dante is authoritative seems to derive from Eliot's view of the

Jerrold Hogle's reading of *The Triumph of Life* shares this view of Shelley's dissent, and takes it to be characteristic of his unwillingness to dictate conclusions.[16] *The Triumph of Life*, he says, defends and articulates the recognition that all thought refigures previous thoughts, so preventing any formulation from gaining absolute and repressive authority. The ambiguity of Shelley's parody allows his reader, therefore, to enter the reverie in which, Hogle claims, we are made free to practise freedom. This freedom is established when Shelley overturns Dante's theocratic authority:

Shelley's opening-out of *terza rima* in the poem [. . .] can now be noticed more and revealed as an insistence on the deferral of figure in defiance of older attempts to make verbal triads betoken centered trinities.

Paul de Man's pleasure in Shelley's denial of meaning is changed by Hogle into a pursuit of non-authoritative utterance. His reading is, therefore, much closer to Shelley's philanthropy and zeal. None the less, it underestimates (in my view) Shelley's sense of being involved in his experience. For Hogle, *The Triumph of Life*'s 'oscillation between rhetorical modes or stances' is valuable because it is the means whereby Shelley can create in his audience an openness to questions. The poem offers us, he argues, the opportunity to confront uncertainty. We are asked, and can ourselves ask, whether:

the discourse-patterns in which we usually fashion and extend ourselves [are] to be regarded as powerfully entrenched or constantly open to revision?[17]

Hogle's analysis of the poem finishes with a succession of similar either–or questions because, in his view, Shelley's poem makes this process of self-questioning possible. Shelley challenges his readers,

Commedia. Dante's cultural centrality was not assured in the England or Italy of Shelley's day. Shelley's letters (see below) suggest that he read him alongside, rather than above, the wide range of ancient and medieval writers he studied. On Shelley's *terza rima*, see Donald H. Reiman, *Shelley's* The Triumph of Life: *A Critical Study* (Urbana, Ill., 1965), 89; Richard Cronin, *Shelley's Poetic Thoughts* (London, 1981), 204–7.

[16] Jerrold E. Hogle, *Shelley's Process: Radical Transference and the Development of his Major Works* (New York and Oxford, 1988), 394, see also 335. Where Hogle and Schulze read Shelley as disrupting Dante's authority, Weinberg sees him in conflict with Dante's serenity (see Weinberg, *Shelley's Italian Experience*, 240).

[17] Hogle, *Shelley's Process*, 337, 398, 342.

Hogle argues, by creating the awareness of such questions. The uncertainty in Shelley's position seems right: *The Triumph of Life* is so elusive because it refuses to assert the victory of either oppression or liberty. But Hogle makes its difficulties strangely untroubling. If, in other words, he had posed questions in the way that Hogle imagines, Shelley could have entertained a readership indefinitely.

As I see it, Shelley in *The Triumph of Life* thought of liberty and oppression, sympathy and selfishness, as inevitably conjoined. He would use both–and where Hogle gives either–or:

Are the discourse-patterns in which we usually fashion and extend ourselves to be considered as both powerfully entrenched and constantly open to revision?

Supposing the answer is 'yes', the question implies another one ('Is this paradox sustainable?' for example, or 'How may it be sustained?') and implies it more rapidly and urgently than Hogle's version of the poem allows. Phrased like this, Shelley's question takes up a different relation to the experiential contradiction (in language, historical events, and personal conduct) that it presents and, consequently, it remains self-doubting. By making his enquiries refer back to and unsettle the enquirer, Shelley's *The Triumph of Life* cannot advocate a speculative liberalism. The value of speculative activity seems itself to be more open to question than Hogle's account of the poem admits (in which it questions everything except its own questioning). Furthermore, I argue, this unsettling of reader and writer alike gives meaning and purpose to the 'opening-out' of Dante's *terza rima*.

Writing to Leigh Hunt in 1819, Shelley denied that Michelangelo was the Dante of painting, because he had no gentleness: 'where shall we find [. . .] the Spirit coming over the sea in a boat like Mars rising from the vapours of the horizon, where Matilda gathering flowers' (*c.*20 Aug. 1819, Jones, ii. 112).[18] Mary Shelley thinks that the passage in *Purgatorio* ii where the spirit comes over

___

[18] Shelley's notes to *Inferno* ix, similarly, follow the angel advancing through Hell. He brackets ll. 60–3, 64–72, 73–84, 85–90, as if each stage of the description struck him as he read through it (Peck, *Shelley: Life & Work*, ii. 357). Cf. Leigh Hunt on *Purgatorio*, ii (see Toynbee, ii. 119) and Byron on Dante's gentleness, 'Ravenna Journal', 29 Jan. 1821, *LJ*, viii. 39–40. See below p. 201.

the sea was Shelley's 'most favorite passage'.[19] Whether or not that was always true is difficult to judge because of the breadth of Shelley's reading in Dante over a long period. In 1821–2, none the less, Shelley's interest in the *Commedia* appears to draw away from the ideal love and the ecstatic vision of *La Vita Nuova* and *Paradiso* towards the uncertainty and hope of *Purgatorio* and the 'Limbo' of *Inferno* iv.[20]

Shelley places his narrator, at the beginning of *The Triumph of Life*, on the sea-shore at dawn:

> before me fled
> The night; behind me rose the day; the Deep
>
> Was at my feet, & Heaven above my head
> (*Triumph*, ll. 26–8, p. 138)

As Charles Robinson has pointed out, these lines echo Goethe's *Faust*.[21] Yet the stasis and centrality which Faust enjoys place Shelley's narrator within the circling successiveness of life in time. By occupying the geometric centre, Shelley may appear uninvolved in the changes he observes, a still point in the turning world. He

---

[19] *The Letters of Mary Wollstonecraft Shelley*, ed. Betty T. Bennett, 3 vols. (Baltimore, 1980–8), ii. 283. The passage may have influenced *Alastor* where the sinking crescent moon shrinks to 'two lessening points of light' that 'Gleamed through the darkness' from 'the horizon's verge'. Alastor's death plays in reverse the new beginning of Dante's life: as the angel flies closer, two points of light appear over the horizon and a moment later can be recognized as wings (*Alastor*, ll. 654–5, 603, *PP*, 85, 84; *Purgatorio*, ii. 22–6, Sapegno, ii. 16).

[20] His letter to John Gisborne, 18 June 1822, rejects *Epipsychidion* ('the person whom it celebrates was a cloud instead of a Juno'), and later recommends 'the finest scene in the "Purgatorio", or the opening of the "Paradiso" or some other neglected piece of excellence' (Jones, ii. 436, 434). This contrasts with a year before: 'The acutest critics have justly reversed [. . .] the order of the great acts of the "Divine Comedy" in the measure of the admiration which they accord to the Hell, Purgatory and Paradise' ('A Defence of Poetry' (1821), *PP*, 497). See also Jones, ii. 258. See Timothy Webb, *The Violet in the Crucible: Shelley and Translation* (Oxford, 1976), 317. As the *Alastor* passage suggests, the *Purgatorio* is not a new interest for Shelley in 1822 but the revival of an old one. See Weinberg, *Shelley's Italian Experience*, 125–31 on *Prometheus Unbound* and *Purgatorio*.

[21] Charles E. Robinson, *Byron and Shelley: The Snake and the Eagle Wreathed in Fight* (Baltimore, 1976), 222–3. Goethe's lines are 'Vor mir den Tag und hinter mir die Nacht, | Den Himmel über mir und unter mir die Wellen' (*Faust: Eine Tragödie: Erster und Zweiter Teil*, ll. 1087–8: 'Before me the day and behind me the night | Heaven over me and under me the waves'). Shelley alters this, as Robinson points out, by facing the darkness not the dawn. His lineation also denies the unselfconscious centrality Goethe creates from the symmetry of these lines.

seems, at least, to have been granted the authoritative point of view enjoyed by his infant 'Spirit of the Earth' in Act IV of *Prometheus Unbound*. However, his wording threatens the sanctity of that position: Shelley is in the vanguard of dawn, so that night flees before him and day rises behind him like an army he leads. The heroism of this posture places the whole world at his feet, even 'the Deep'. 'Heaven', by contrast, cannot be taken up so readily since it is still 'above his head'. The poise of the narrator's centrality is implicit in the balance of the writing. That balance sounds glib at the moment when Heaven, by standing directly over him, seems to confirm his centrality. Because it is so easy, the position seems suddenly contrived. Rather than being at the centre of the universe, he is making the world revolve around him. The narrator is actively engaged in forming a particular perception of the world—probably to the same degree (we gather from his leading the day), as he is taking part in the historical process.[22]

So, while the narrator appears to have escaped the pressure of time, his wording reveals the temporal life of his self-descriptions. The lines are suspicious of his claim to have found himself perfectly positioned, though they do not dismiss such a claim. They intimate, instead, the necessity we suffer of continuing to run after shadows of the eternal, even though an impersonal objectivity can never be attained.[23] The narrator is, therefore, neither faultlessly convincing nor hopelessly self-deceived. Indeed, the continuance of truth-perceptions within the temporal sphere proves them right while seeming to deny their claims to transcendence. The narrator is granted the degree of authority appropriate to human perceptions.

At the time Shelley complained that people were too eager to confer authority on the masters of their day:

---

[22] I discuss further below the nearness of *Purgatorio*, i to the opening of *The Triumph of Life*.

[23] See Shelley's letter to John Gisborne, 'I think one is always in love with something or other; the error, and I confess it is not easy for spirits cased in flesh and blood to avoid it, consists in seeking in a mortal image the likeness of what is perhaps eternal' (18 June 1822, Jones, ii. 434). Hogle reads Shelley's oscillation between rhetorical stances as continuous with his hovering between Jane Williams and Mary Shelley, while still being drawn to ideals like Emilia Viviani (see Hogle, *Shelley's Progress*, 398). My purpose in disagreeing with Hogle is to show how this letter, like *The Triumph of Life*, (necessarily) continues to seek the resolution it cannot find. Cf. Shelley's earlier, more blithe account of love's benefits: 'On Love' (1818), *PP*, 474.

all, more or less, subdue themselves to the element that surrounds them, & contribute to the evils they lament by the hypocrisy that springs from them. (To Horace Smith, 29 June 1822, Jones, ii. 442)[24]

However, in several letters to Claire Clairmont written in spring 1822, Shelley recommends passivity:

give up this idle pursuit after shadows, & temper yourself to the season [. . . .] Live from day to day, attend to your health, cultivate literature & liberal ideas to a certain extent, & expect that from time & change which no exertions of your own can give you. (To Claire Clairmont, 24 Mar. 1822, Jones, ii. 400)[25]

Tempering and subduing are easily confused. The self-cultivation Shelley recommends can easily become quietist and resigned. The non-participation it involves will create superciliousness when distance from events is based on elevation above them. Shelley frequently wants (as he says to Lord Byron, quoting his own translation of *Faust*), to create a 'little world within the great world of all'.[26] To remain tempered, however, security such as this needs to be adaptable: responsive 'to the season' though not subdued by circumstances. The nature and difficulty of this watchful position—between acquiescence and exertion, involvement and disdain—is the controlling interest of the poem. Shelley's narrator gradually discovers its precarious balance by sounding less like Faust and more like Dante.[27]

At the beginning of *Purgatorio*, Dante and Virgil emerge from

---

[24] Cf. Orsino in *The Cenci*: 'Should the offender live? | Triumph in his misdeed? [. . .] until thou mayst become | Utterly lost; subdued even to the hue | Of that which thou permittest?' (*PP*, 265).

[25] Claire was trying to get her daughter, Allegra, back from Lord Byron, who would not co-operate. See also Shelley's next letter to Claire: 'The best would probably be to think and act without a plan, and let the world pass' (31 Mar. 1822, Jones, ii. 402). Mary offered comfort of a sort: 'Nothing remains constant, something may happen—things cannot be worse' (20 Mar. 1822, Jones, ii. 398).

[26] To Lord Byron 3 May 1822, Jones, ii. 415. See *PW*, 758 (scene ii, ll. 242–3).

[27] Faust consistently represents an unattainable perfection. See letter to John Gisborne, 18 June 1822: '[I]f the past and the future could be obliterated, the present would content me so well that I could say with Faust to the passing moment, "Remain, thou, thou art so beautiful."' (Jones, ii. 435–6). Faust's contentment is felt and felt to be conditional on what cannot be, the obliteration of past and future. Moreover, Shelley knew that Faust would be damned when he said ' "Verweile doch! du bist so schön" ' (*Faust*, l. 1700.) See also 'To Jane. The Invitation', ll. 41–6, *PP*, 444.

Hell and find themselves within sight of the sea as the sun is rising.[28] This restores them to a familiar world and immediately places them in time. They see first the night sky of the southern hemisphere, something unknown to medieval Europe:

> Dolce color d'oriental zaffiro,
>   che s'accoglieva nel sereno aspetto
>   del mezzo, puro insino al primo giro
> alli occhi miei ricominciò diletto,
>   tosto ch'io usci' fuor dell'aura morta
>   che m'avea contristati li occhi e il petto.
>   (*Purgatorio*, i. 13–18, Sapegno, ii. 4)

(The sweet colour of the oriental sapphire that gathered in the serene aspect of the air, as far as the first circle, gave pleasure back to my eyes as soon as I passed beyond the dead air that had afflicted my eyes and heart.)

At the canto's end, Virgil takes Dante down to the sea-shore and washes his face in the dew. He wipes clean Dante's 'guance lacrimose' ('tear-stained cheeks', l. 127, p. 12)—at once to clear his vision and reveal his face. This is at the command of Cato, who says it would not do if Dante could not see properly when he met even the first of heaven's angels.[29] The bathing of his face, 'alli occhi miei ricominciò diletto'; it gives back pleasure just as the sight of a sapphire sky had done. In both, clear-sightedness seems to be made possible by release from suffering. Dante's

---

[28] See also *Inferno*, xx. 48–51, marked by Shelley in his copy, 'lo Carrarese che di sotto alberga, | ebbe tra' bianchi marmi la spelonca | per sua dimora onde a guardar le stelle | e 'l mar non li era veduta tronca' ('[Aruns, where] the Carrarese farmed below, had among the white marbles a cave to live in, from which his view was uninterrupted of the stars and the sea', Sapegno, i. 224; see Peck, *Shelley: Life & Work*, ii. 359). Carrara, in the hills above Lerici, offers the view, looking westwards, of Shelley's opening. Cf. Weinberg, *Shelley's Italian Experience*, 202–5.

[29] 'ché non si converría, l'occhio sorpriso | d'alcuna nebbia, andar dinanzi al primo | ministro, ch'è di quei di paradiso' (ibid., ll. 97–9, p. 10: 'because it would be unsuitable, with your eyesight hindered by any clouding, to go before the first minister who is one of those from Paradise'). Cato's use of 'primo' echoes 'insino al primo giro', l. 15, where the word is ambiguous, meaning either the lowest or highest of the heavenly spheres, the Moon or the Primum Mobile (see l. 15 n., p. 4). Cato's 'primo ministro' may be either the least or the highest. In 'primo', then, Dante begins to suggest the presence of God in all his ministers and among all the saved. Each saved soul whom Dante meets partakes in God; the first of them is united with the 'First Cause'. They are symbols of God, as is brought out by an ambiguity the moment Dante escapes from Hell.

restored eyesight shows him first, however, not ministers of heaven but the passage of time. By the end of the canto, the dew is already 'fighting' the dawn.[30]

The lowest depths of Hell were characterized by an utter rigidity that could be ruptured only by savagery or violence. The damned are submerged in the frozen Lake Cocytus: Dante kicks one of them and insults another; when Ugolino stops talking he immediately bites Ruggieri; all that can be seen of Judas is his legs, wriggling, while Satan chews the rest of his body.[31] The damned lash out in actions that are as convulsive as death-throes, and as compelling. Dante has to resist his fascination in order to get through Hell. When he escapes the lowest region, its pinioned, immobile fury is replaced, naturally, by a sudden sense of sequential movement. Within one canto:

> L'alba vinceva l'ora mattutina
> che fuggía innanzi, sí che di lontano
> conobbi il tremolar della marina.
> > (*Purgatorio*, i. 115–17, Sapegno,
> > ii. 11)

(Dawn was conquering the last hour of night which fled before it, so that from a distance I could make out the trembling of the sea.)[32]

The darkest hour before the dawn has turned to dawn itself, its sapphire blue retreating westward ahead of first light. Dante, after the murk of Hell, is moved to be able to see so far so clearly. The horrors and fear of the ninth circle have been exchanged for a kind of thrilled suspense—a delicate quivering in 'tremolar' that was unthinkable at the end of the *Inferno*.

Shelley, in the *Prologue to Hellas* (1821), describes with wonder and affection 'The fairest of those wandering isles that gem | The

---

[30] 'la rugiada | pugna col sole', ll. 121–2, p. 11.

[31] *Inferno*, xxxii. 78, xxxiii. 76–8, xxxiv. 61–3, Sapegno, i. 356, 366, 376.

[32] Some editors take 'ora' to mean 'wind | breeze' ('aura') and Sinclair translates the passage on that interpretation: 'The dawn was overcoming the morning breeze' (J. D. Sinclair, *The Divine Comedy of Dante Alighieri*, 3 vols. (New York, 1939–46), ii. 25). Cary gives: 'The dawn had chac'd the matin hour of prime' (Cary, ii. 4). Shelley used *La Divina Commedia di Dante Alighieri* [. . .] *tratta da quella che pubblicarono gli Accademici della Crusca l'Anno MCXCV. Col comento del M. R. P. Pompeo Venturi* [. . .], 3 vols. (Venice, 1772). Venturi glosses 'ora' temporally: 'Dall'Alba chiara rimaneva vinto, e fugato verso Occidente l'albore più debole del primo mattino' ('the faintest whiteness of early morning is conquered by the dawn and driven westwards'). (Venturi, *Divina Commedia*, ii. 10.)

sapphire sea of interstellar air' (ll. 18–19, *PW*, 449). But 'sapph-ire' is one of his favourite words; only in the play itself does he suggest the importance to him of *Purgatorio* i: 'Hesperus flies from awakening night' (l. 1038, *PP*, 438).[33] Dante notices Hesperus at the beginning of the canto:

> Lo bel pianeta che d'amar conforta
> faceva tutto rider l'oriente,
> velando i Pesci, ch'erano in sua scorta.
> (*Purgatorio*, i. 19–21, Sapegno, ii. 4)

(The fair planet that provokes love made all the east smile, veiling [the stars of] Pisces, which were in her train.)

While night lasted Shelley could not sleep: 'But I, whom thoughts which must remain untold | Had kept as wakeful as the stars that gem | The cone of night, now they were laid asleep, | Stretched my faint limbs beneath the hoary stem' (*Triumph*, ll. 21–4, p. 136). In Dante, the rising morning star veils in its light the fainter stars of Pisces and, as day dawns, Venus is herself forgotten;[34] similarly, Shelley's stars are 'laid asleep' by the rising sun. The narrator's transparent vision in *The Triumph of Life* occurs when he is nearly 'laid asleep' in a 'strange trance' and it ends with his being led from one vision to another. 'I knew' he says:

> That I had felt the freshness of that dawn
> Bathed in the same cold dew my brow & hair
> And sate as thus upon that slope of lawn
>
> Under the self same bough, & heard as there
> The birds, the fountain & the Ocean hold
> Sweet talk in music through the enamoured air.
> And then a Vision on my brain was rolled.
> (*Triumph*, ll. 31–40, p. 138)

Shelley, who has imitated the stars by watching with them, is now, as it were, laid asleep in body to become a living soul. The world,

---

[33] See also 'Fragments of an Unfinished Drama' (1821–2): 'And lastly light, whose interfusion dawns | In the dark space of interstellar air' (ll. 26–7, *PW*, 483). The physics of light in Shelley's day are discussed in Nora Crook and Derek Guiton, *Shelley's Venomed Melody* (Cambridge, 1986).

[34] Canto ii traces the approach of day as accurately as canto i: see ll. 7–9 and 55–7, Sapegno, ii. 14–15, 18. Dante does not say that Venus has disappeared, or been veiled in her turn as she had earlier veiled Pisces, but the 'morning star' disappears as the day begins.

'Continent, | Isle, Ocean & all things' have 'in succession due' (ll. 15–16, p. 136) taken up the burden of day or, like the stars, fallen asleep. Shelley seems to be released from that sequence when he enters the trance between wakefulness and sleep, yet this escape places him within a different but equally inevitable process: 'And then a Vision on my brain was rolled [. . .]'. Characteristically in *The Triumph of Life*, no explanation is offered for this. Shelley's *déjà vu* gives him, at first, an intimation of immortality, so that he seems to remain protected from a world that is no longer disguised. 'I knew | That I had felt the freshness of that dawn': it is not only that he has been here before but that he has experienced the present moment before. Each new particular is sensed through recognition. Yet the scene's exact correspondence with what he has known already means he can vouch for it, and for himself, at the same time. He knows what he has felt and that he has, indisputably, felt it. He has been given back the memories that his pre-existing, Platonic soul lost at birth. Since, however, his knowledge is not of a distant past but of the present reduplicated, he has been restored to his own experiences. The doubling of his sensations (such that he knows everything already) creates security, since nothing can possibly surprise him, but a form of security that makes possible authentic personal experience.

What is restored is, none the less, added to at once. Shelley is granted, suddenly, the sense that the world exactly corresponds to his experience of it, but this appears to be the pre-condition of another 'vision'. Just to know, in the passive and entire way that Shelley does when he steps aside from the currents of life, enables (and, possibly, forces) him to receive a vision of what he had not known before. The successiveness resembles Dante's astronomy: Shelley's consciousness is, in some sense, enlightened (and, perhaps, illuminating) before it is veiled in the light of a 'vision', yet his mind has to succumb to the greater light in the same way that Pisces is veiled by Venus and Venus, in her turn, by the sun.[35]

This correspondence between Shelley's mode of vision and Dante's goes further than this, however, because *Purgatorio* is a curiously real vision. The mountain of Purgatory lies at the

---

[35] Shelley had always been interested in Venus/Hesperus (the morning and evening stars). See, among other examples, 'The Revolt of Islam', ll. 262, 498–501, 543–5, *PW*, 43, 49–50. The opening of *Purgatorio* emphasizes the veiling of one light by another that is so important to *The Triumph of Life*.

antipodes of Jerusalem, hence in the southern hemisphere, where Dante is surprised by shadows falling on the wrong side and by the sun moving across the northern part of the sky. It may be something of a looking-glass world but its strange facts cannot be dismissed as phantasms or distortions (as was tempting in Hell) because they are phenomena of an equivalent world. Moreover the interruption of visions by further visions happens repeatedly in the second *cantica* of Dante's poem. Like Shelley, Dante adds the miraculous to the surprisingly substantial:

> Quivi mi cinse sí com'altrui piacque:
> oh maraviglia! ché qual elli scelse
> l'umile pianta, cotal si rinacque
> subitamente là onde l'avelse.
> (*Purgatorio*, i. 133–6, Sapegno, ii. 12)

(There he clothed me in the way the other [Cato or God] wanted. Oh, how marvellous! because what the humble plant which he selected had been, exactly that sprouted again suddenly in the place where he had pulled it up.)

This miracle is uncalled for: Dante is already fully prepared by line 133 which feels as formal and decisive as a closing line.[36] What catches his attention stretches the canto into a further three lines of acclaim and surprise. The resolution and self-discipline demanded of him by *Inferno*, seem now to be marvellously less burdensome. Relief and excitement inspire the extension as Dante discovers that the virtues are only a preliminary to the generosity and abundance of miracle. Dante's contented resignation to what another wishes for him immediately produces insight into marvellous things—a miracle, moreover, that proves one's own and its own participation in time.[37]

---

[36] Each canto closes with an additional line, the last tercet being made a quatrain. More often than not, the last line is syntactically independent (*Inferno*, i: 'Allor si mosse, e io li tenni dietro'; xxxiii: 'e quindi uscimme a riveder le stelle'); where the final line is tied closely into the preceding tercet, it is relatively rare for that tercet's opening line to sound independent, as is the case here. Cf. the endings of *Purgatorio*, iv, v, and vii. The last canto of the *Commedia* closes in the same way as *Purgatorio*, i (Sapegno, i. 16, 380, ii. 45, 56, 79–80, iii. 424–5).

[37] See *Purgatorio*, i. 135 n., Sapegno, ii. 12. The isolation of l. 133 strengthens an echo of Ulysses' speech in *Inferno*, xxvi: 'e la prora ire in giú, com'altrui piacque, | infin che 'l mar fu sopra noi richiuso' (ll. 141–2, Sapegno, i. 295: 'and the prow went under, as pleased another, until the sea closed over us'). What was abruptly curtailed now appears able to carry on for ever. Dante closes *Purgatorio* by saying

In canto ii the gradual veiling of the morning star in the dawn makes way for a greater, unbearable light, that of the boat appearing:

> Noi eravam lunghesso mare ancora
>> come gente che pensa a suo cammino,
>> che va col cuore e col corpo dimora.
> Ed ecco qual, sorpreso dal mattino,
>> per li grossi vapor Marte rosseggia
>> giú nel ponente sovra 'l suol marino,
> cotal m'apparve, s'io ancor lo veggia,
>> un lume per lo mar venir sí ratto,
>> che 'l mover suo nessun volar pareggia.
>> (*Purgatorio*, ii. 10–18, Sapegno, ii. 15)

(We were still going along the seashore like people who are thinking about their route, who go forward with their heart and delay with their body. And, there, just as, near morning, through the dull vapours, Mars glows, low down on the horizon, over the ocean floor, so appeared to me—that I might see it again!—a light coming over the sea so quickly that no wing could match its speed.)

Dante and Virgil are lingering, though whether culpably or help-lessly Dante does not make clear. Their pause is interrupted and completed by the boat's appearance: 'Ed ecco' distracts the reader from the question of what Dante and Virgil think they are up to, in the same way that Dante's own attention is redirected. His movement in imagination and desire, as he wonders about the dangers and possibilities of the path he has found, is replaced by a step forward in the narrative. As it turns out, the souls who are brought to the mountain, and are similarly confused, provoke Cato to hurry them on their way. The boat's appearance, then, satisfies Dante's (possibly unconscious) need in an unexpected way. The boat fulfils his thought while making him, for a moment, unable to think. As in *The Triumph of Life*, the narrator's sub-mission to the immediate vision appears to depend on his hav-ing regained his natural (but previously obscured) clearness of

that the bounds of form constrain him to stop. He ends by echoing *Purgatorio*, i: 'Io ritornai dalla santissima onda | rifatto sí come piante novelle | rinovellate di novella fronda, | puro e disposto a salire alle stelle' (ll. 142–5, Sapegno, ii. 370–1; 'I returned from the most holy stream, refashioned, like new plants renewed with new leaves, pure and ready to ascend to the stars'). This outwits decorum by sending us back to the beginning and suggests Dante is now just like the rush that grows unstoppably.

perception. The immediate, overwhelming vision turns out, also, to be one more in an indefinitely long series. Moreover, the simplicity and abruptness of 'ecco', like 'oh maraviglia', give the impression of a sudden actual discovery. Dante's Purgatory is, he claims, no enraptured vision (with the conventional authority that entails) but a real world of miracles.

In *Purgatorio* xxviii Dante is restored to the clear perception of Paradise. He has reached the summit of the mountain and so, as Virgil declares, is pure once again. He may wait here until Beatrice comes to meet him. Dante's eagerness to explore takes him so far into the forest which clothes the mountain-top that he is lost in it: 'non potea rivedere ond'io mi' ntrassi; | ed ecco piú andar mi tolse un rio' (*Purgatorio*, xxviii. 24–5, Sapegno, ii. 307: 'I could not see again the place where I had entered; and, look, a stream stopped me from going any further'). The stream baffles him, and is at once the beginning of his further progress:

> Coi piè ristretti e con li occhi passai
> di là dal fiumicello, per mirare
> la gran variazion di freschi mai;
> e là m'apparve, sí com'elli appare
> subitamente cosa che disvia
> per maraviglia tutto altro pensare,
> una donna soletta che si gía
> cantando e scegliendo fior da fiore
> ond'era pinta tutta la sua via.
> (*Purgatorio*, xxviii. 34–42, Sapegno,
> ii. 307–8)

(With my feet I held back and with my eyes I crossed the stream from there, in order to gaze on the great variety of fresh May flowers, and in that place appeared to me, in the same way that a thing suddenly appears which drives away with wonder every other thought, a solitary woman, who went singing and picking flowers from the flowers with which her whole path was painted.)

Dante's earlier 'Ed ecco' is intimate with his readership, where 'e là m'apparve' bears more imposing witness. Canto i of *Purgatorio* ended in the tremendous excitement of 'oh maraviglia!'; here Dante's wonder is set back into the subordinate clause ('sí com' elli [. . .]'). His distance and self-awareness seem to possess the composure of a historian or psychologist even as he describes the loss of all other awareness in the surprise and joy of what suddenly appears. By delaying the subject of 'apparve' until after the end of the tercet, Dante gives 'una donna soletta' the tremendous resolving power over a spectator that he has just described. His attention, like his tercets, are suddenly taken up by the woman who appears, yet on this occasion such a conquest is familiar. His lack of surprise makes him attend more completely to the woman herself, and yet preserve a cool independence in the midst of his excitement. He seems at once devoted and composed. The unclouded gaze (that Cato had demanded in canto i and Virgil proclaimed for Dante at the end of canto xxvii) enables him to sustain himself despite his clear perception of overwhelming visions. Indeed, true clarity and true selfhood seem to be interdependent.

Dante's vision of a woman overturns his thoughts and fulfils his hopes as the angel-boat had done earlier. The 'cosa che disvia' sets him back on his 'via' as much as following its own. His collectedness while this is happening indicates, moreover, that his nature participates in what overwhelms him. Dante's mind is at ease with the new vision that commands his attention, because he is now more perfectly similar to Venus: the planet that seems to vanish but remains hidden in the light of day. His serenity is not so much passionless as the sign that his passions are in accord with what happens: he is both properly responsive to whatever he experiences and fully expecting the unpredictable.

This fusion of assurance and vulnerability epitomizes what Shelley admired in Dante. Because Dante's privileged knowledge did not prevent, but made possible, the intensity of his response to events, Shelley's admiration informs both his portrayal of vision and his presentation of feeling. He translates *Purgatorio* xxviii with great skill:

> I moved not with my feet, but amid the glooms
> I peirced [*sic*] with my charmed sight contemplating
> The mighty multitude of fresh May blooms
>
> And then appeared to me—even like a thing
> Which suddenly for blank astonishment
> Dissolves all other thought,
>
> A solitary woman, & she went
> Singing and gathering flower after flower
> With which her way was painted and besprent.[38]

---

[38] Text from Jean de Palacio, 'Shelley Traducteur de Dante: Le Chant XXVIII du Purgatoire', *Revue de littérature comparée*, 36 (1962), 574.

When Medwin published this he corrected Shelley's loss of the rhyme-scheme at 'Dissolves all other thought' by putting instead 'Charms every sense, and makes all thought take wing'.[39] This shallow-minded ecstasy replaces Shelley's impression of thought being concentrated in what is seen. 'Dissolves all other thought' combines what is apparently opposed: the self-loss and rapture of 'dissolves all thought' is qualified by consideration and attentiveness because the woman has become his only thought. This vision dominates him by drawing all his attention, not by charming and liberating it (as Medwin's version suggests), nor by destroying his mind.

If such a Dantean perspective does inform the ambitions of *The Triumph of Life*, it must bear especially on Rousseau's meeting with the 'shape all light'—a passage in which Shelley combines the dissolution of thought and the veiling of planets in light. The shape resembles Dante's rising sun. Her feet 'blot | The thoughts of him who gazed on them':

> As Day upon the threshold of the east
> >   Treads out the lamps of night, until the breath
> 'Of darkness reillumines even the least
> >   Of heaven's living eyes—like day she came
> Making the night a dream
> (*Triumph*, ll. 352, 383–4, 389–93, pp. 184, 188, 190)

When Rousseau drinks from the cup she offers him, his mind is once again wiped clean when another 'Vision on his brain is rolled'. The woman herself disappears:

> >   the fair shape waned in the coming light
> As veil by veil the silent splendour drops
> >   From Lucifer, amid the chrysolite
> 'Of sunrise ere it strike the mountain tops—
> >   And as the presence of that fairest planet
> Although unseen is felt by one who hopes
> >   'That his day's path may end as he began it
> In that star's smile
> • • • • • • • •

<hr>

[39] See *PW*, 729 and headnote p. 727.

'So knew I in that light's severe excess
The presence of that shape which on the stream
Moved, as I moved along the wilderness
(Ibid., ll. 411–19, 424–6, pp. 191, 193)

The next in a series of visions either erases what came before or
makes it gradually fade. The new will 'Burst [. . .] on my sight' like
a wave on sand (ibid., ll. 405–11, pp. 190, 192) or 'veil by veil'
diminish the brightness of the last. In either case, something survives:
the shape can still be felt, the thoughts are hidden in the new light
but not destroyed. Just as a planet survives being hidden in light,
the mind is swamped but not eradicated by the visions it experi-
ences. The clarity of perception that seemed the prerequisite of
vision continues within the visions, whether latently or as a memory.

The drink Rousseau is offered appears (to him at least) to offer
full insight into his origins and, therefore, his nature. Yet his
drinking it apparently robs him of comprehension: his mind is
reduced to a *tabula rasa* where visions are subsequently inscribed.
This disappointment has been taken to prove the deceitfulness,
even the diabolism, of the 'shape all light', or to prove that Rousseau
has been misled by his ambition for understanding. His origins
are, certainly, not revealed objectively or entire, but the vision that
follows offers some insight. Rousseau's experience, in this incident,
follows the pattern of Dante's discoveries in the *Purgatorio*, and
not only in its astronomy and the timing of its verse. After being
immersed in Lethe (*Purgatorio*, xxxi. 91–9, Sapegno, ii. 346),
Dante witnesses the destruction of the Church's triumphal car
(ibid. xxxii. 109–60, Sapegno, ii. 357–60).[40] The Earthly Paradise
is violated by the world's historical evil when Dante has had all
his memories of sin erased. The corruption of the Church appears,
moreover, as a corollary of Dante's own sins (in deserting the
memory of Beatrice for other women). What happens to the car
takes all Dante's attention and shows him something of himself
that, if presented more directly, he could not have withstood.[41]

[40] The dominance of the Earthly Paradise cantos over the later sections of *The
Triumph of Life* encourage one to think them the only Dantean source. *Purgatorio*
i is itself recollected by the opening of *Purgatorio*, xxviii (where at dawn Dante
enters a new world); astronomy is not mentioned in the latter canto, in part
because successiveness is forgotten.

[41] Orsino in *The Cenci* suggests that Shelley perceived this quality in Dante's
encounter: 'even I, | Since Beatrice unveiled me to myself, | And made me shrink
from what I cannot shun, | Shew a poor figure to my own esteem, | To which I
grow half reconciled' (*PP*, 260).

Rousseau's 'new vision, and its cold bright car' are as astonishing as Dante's, and equally disturbing; in both works, however, seeing the truth is made dangerous not impossible.

None the less in these lines Rousseau's thoughts are 'trampled', where Dante's (in Shelley's translation) *dissolve*. The violence of the extinction he suffers appears to deny any continuance of identity, and hence any connection between past and future. Shelley's poem, on this reading, counters Dante's interlinked visions with successive moments of total erasure. Rousseau is extinguished by each vision as it occurs and (depending on how one takes this) the poem, in consequence, either cannot impose a structure on its sequence of visions or successfully avoids doing so. 'Trampling' is compared, however, to the sun's extinction of the stars, that are hidden but not destroyed, until 'the breath | Of darkness reillumines even the least | Of heaven's living eyes'.[42] The mind that is in abeyance, yet not consumed, survives within the visions so that (as in Dante), each new vision may extend the self that is lost in viewing it.

All the same, 'trampling' is more violent. Rousseau's longing for complete understanding is more painfully disappointed than Dante's because he suffers the desire more wilfully, and because he cannot acquire the serenity that governs the *Commedia*: 'the rhyme | Of him whom from the lowest depths of Hell | Through every Paradise & through all glory | Love led serene' (*Triumph*, ll. 471–4, pp. 198, 200). Similarly, Rousseau's 'shape' only 'glimmers' through the everyday; her obscure presence lends Rousseau's waking world no more than a trace of heavenly reality. After the 'trampling' he regains a sadly diminished version of Dante's fullness. This suggests either Rousseau's peculiar inadequacy or that Shelley is presenting himself as a belated reader of the *Commedia*.

If we blame Rousseau, the poem is arguing for the inadequacy of his sensibility. His self-loss in vision becomes equivalent to his self-destructive involvement in the world, and prevents his perceiving the truth within the world. Rousseau's self-criticism can, however, be read as Shelleyan irony. It may be that his apparently self-destructive involvement is actually a step towards attaining a proper engagement with 'Life', in the same way that the trampling of his mind necessarily precedes a visionary reawakening. His ignorance

---

[42] The *OED* gives *Queen Mab* (1813), vii. 180 as the first use of 'reillumine'; see *PP*, 56. Its unfamiliarity in the 1820s would have emphasized the drawn-out process of its four syllables, by contrast with the available alternative, 'relumes'.

of that purpose leads him, mistakenly, to despair. However, if the ironies were as clear as such an explanation requires, Shelley and his readers would be confident about Rousseau's destiny. His sorrows would be resolved in advance as part of a process. Instead, the ambiguity surrounding Rousseau's self-assessment persists: *The Triumph of Life* finds fault with his ambitions and his despair yet makes no sure claim to have surpassed him. (Neither does the poem turn its accusation unequivocally against itself.) Instead, the poem continues in pursuit of what might prove unattainable while trying to govern that pursuit so that it avoids becoming self-destructive.

The Dantean astronomy of the poem corresponds, therefore, as I hope to show, to both its understanding of visionary experience and its relation to other poets. The poem is led by Rousseau (towards an ideal he has not reached and the poem may or may not reach itself). It 'follows his example' without being confined to his achievements and (of course) without any certainty of not being confined to them. Rousseau in turn is (as the allusions suggest) following Dante who is himself being led by Love. Rousseau is, perhaps, to be blamed for not continuing the unceasing pursuit of the vision of Love that Dante (more passively) attained and that Shelley now takes up. Shelley seems to criticize the confidence with which Rousseau embraced his hopes, seeing in that naïvety the source of his despairing view of Life's oppressive destructiveness. From Shelley's position, however, going on is the means of gaining Dante's enviable serenity because, as much as the full vision of truth can never be possessed, Dante's achievement may be sought after and never, with certainty, reproduced. His achievement was itself the product of a continual movement which Shelley in his day repeats. The relation to Rousseau and Dante which Shelley presents in the poem (and through them his relation to literary tradition in general) tries, therefore, to establish that he is continuing a historical process. That attempt demands his avoidance of opposite extremes: he must neither turn his supposed solidarity with the great into a reason for complacency or a consolation in despair ('How long will you be at rest?') nor must he give up visionary ambitions in favour of political engagement ('As I lay asleep in Italy'). These concerns govern Shelley's adoptions from Dante.

The Italian poet's perfect serenity might appear to place him within the radiance of Eternity, inaccessible and enviable, but to accept the finality of his achievement destroys both it and its successors. The alternative for Shelley to belated regret does not lie in the parodic rejection of Dante, since that would negatively confirm the authority it denies. Rather, his approach to the *Commedia* exemplifies 'A Defence of Poetry':

A great Poem is a fountain forever overflowing with the waters of wisdom and delight; and after one person and one age has exhausted all of its divine effluence which their peculiar relations enable them to share, another and yet another succeeds, and new relations are ever developed, the source of an unforeseen and an unconceived delight.   (*PP*, 500)

The *Commedia* has, like Dante, a perpetual existence through being perpetually revived. Shelley's development of new relations from the poem will prevent it from becoming speciously authoritative and dead, while holding back his lust for transcendent surety and peace. His behaviour and the *Commedia*'s both accord with the nature of great poetry. Dante was 'the Lucifer of that starry flock which in the thirteenth century shone forth from republican Italy' (*PP*, 499). Lucifer, 'the star of the morning', epitomizes poetry: the 'most unfailing herald, companion, and follower of the awakening of a great people to work a beneficial change in opinion or institution' (*PP*, 508).[43] By being all three, 'a herald, companion, and follower' Dante (like a planet) remains within the cycles of nature he oversees. Shelley's extension of the *Commedia* in *The Triumph of Life* seeks to continue the succession of visions and poems. His aim is to become, like Dante, another morning star.

For that reason, the poem qualifies its envy for those who escape the processes of time as much as it laments the fate of those, like Rousseau, who succumb to 'Life'. Socrates and Christ are praised for being unable to compromise:

> [they] could not tame
> Their spirits to the Conqueror, but as soon
> As they had touched the world with living flame
>
> Fled back like eagles to their native noon [. . . .]
>   (*Triumph*, ll. 128–31, p. 152)

---

[43] '[T]he starry flock' emphasizes the stellar rather than Satanic aspects of Lucifer but, for Shelley, the two are not in conflict. Poets offer the tempered resistance to oppression visible in *Prometheus Unbound* and *Paradise Lost*. Cf. Giuseppe Baretti, *A Dissertation Upon the Italian Poetry* (London, 1753), 29: 'but *Dante* appeared, and like a Morning-Sun, almost dispersed the Mists that hovered for so many Ages over the *Parnassean* Mountain'.

Such praise is repeated in *Prologue to Hellas* (*PW*, 452) and is similar also to Byron's celebration of the poetic spirit in *The Prophecy of Dante*:

> Yes, and it must be;
> For, form'd of far too penetrable stuff,
> These birds of Paradise but long to flee
>   Back to their native mansion, soon they find
>   Earth's mist with their pure pinions not agree,
> And die or are degraded; for the mind
>   Succumbs to long infection, and despair,
>   And vulture passions flying close behind [. . . .]
>   (*Prophecy*, iii. 167–74, McGann, iv. 232)[44]

The difference between Byron's and Shelley's *terza rima* is interesting here. As Donald Reiman's edition shows, Shelley's *terza rima* separated each tercet and, at the same time, his layout indented alternate lines. Byron was more conventional in indenting the second and third lines of each tercet. In part, Shelley's arrangement highlights the interconnectedness implicit in the rhyme-scheme. A sequence 'aba bcb cdc' would either indent or justify the two 'a' and the three 'c' rhymes. Dante in the *Commedia* would indent 'ba', 'cb' and 'dc', using the layout to accentuate separate tercets. In Shelley's verse, as a result, each 'aba' stanza flows more readily into the next: the first line of the following stanza completes the rhymes and suggests the pattern of indenting in an 'abab' quatrain. On the other hand, the pulse of Shelley's indentation gains a momentum of its own, that sweeps across the gaps between stanzas without relying on a rhyme-scheme.

This patterning of the lines in *The Triumph of Life* contributes to its neutrality and impartial receptivity to events as will be clearer from relineating the lines about Socrates and Christ. Suppose they read:

> All but the sacred few who could not tame
>   Their spirits to the Conqueror, but as soon
>   As they had touched the world with living flame

---

[44] Charles Robinson sees this similarity as an allusion intended by Shelley 'to announce [. . .] that Byron was the main cause of his purgatorial torments'. This is too restrictive. Robinson is convincing about Shelley's recognition in 1822 that envy of Byron's success was unavoidable, and that writing poetry implied an involvement in the world of 'blood and gold'. See Robinson, *Byron & Shelley*, 228–9.

> Fled back like eagles to their native noon,
>   Or those who put aside the diadem

This is fractionally more heroic and judgemental. The subordinate clause ('as soon | As they') delays and prepares for the main clause, that sounds the more authoritative because its resumption coincides with the new tercet. Shelley's original arrangement moves his reader rapidly across the gaps it creates so that, in this instance, 'the sacred few' who 'Fled back like eagles' seem to do so of their own accord, without needing his prompting or praise. It is more simply a fact that 'as soon | As they had touched the world' they escaped it.[45]

By studying fluidity Shelley is looking, in this case, partly to imitate the speed with which Socrates and Christ return to their native noon but, more generally, to make his poetry as immediately and naturally responsive as they are. They leave 'as soon as' they touch, without delay or self-doubt or a process of conscious thought. Their judgement naturally corresponds with their true nature, which is also their best interests. In aiming to emulate that untroubled responsiveness and natural judgement, Shelley is aware that it belongs to his own native noon. The intense receptiveness he brings to *The Triumph of Life* seems both to practise and postpone the fulfilment of this ideal, while wrestling with the thought that the two may (but may not) coincide.

The poem's nuances of style frequently, therefore, focus on the possibility and dangers of observing events impassively and yet feelingly. Rousseau, by the end, seems able to view political disaster with equanimity: 'the old anatomies' may 'reassume the delegated power' and degrade all around but Rousseau is unmoved:

> 'And others like discoloured flakes of snow
>   On fairest bosoms & the sunniest hair
> Fell, and were melted by the youthful glow
>
>   'Which they extinguished; for like tears, they were
> A veil to those from whose faint lids they rained
>   In drops of sorrow.—I became aware
>
> 'Of whence those forms proceeded which thus stained
>   The track in which we moved'
>   (*Triumph*, ll. 511–18, pp. 204, 206)

[45] Cf. the effect of Shelley's lineation at e.g. *Triumph*, ll. 301–4, 532–5, pp. 176, 208, 210.

By contrast with Rousseau's previous discoveries ('So knew I in that light's severe excess' or 'I arose & for a space | The scene of woods & water seemed [. . .]') the wording 'I became aware' suggests that the realization dawns on him in the process of observing. But it is curiously blank and abrupt. Rousseau's new awareness sounds remote, stiff, and mutedly triumphant: the track in which he moves remains secondary by comparison with his knowledge of origins.

These lines draw on Dante's *Inferno*, cantos xiv–xv and vi particularly. Capaneo and Brunetto Latini are burnt by snowflakes of fire: 'Sovra tutto 'l sabbion, d'un cader lento, | piovean di foco dilatate falde, | come di neve in alpe sanza vento.' (*Inferno*, xiv. 28–30, Sapegno, i. 156: 'Over all the sand, gently falling, rained down broad flakes of fire, like those of snow in the mountains without wind.') These burn Latini's face so that it is scarcely recognizable: '[io] ficca' li occhi per lo cotto aspetto, | sí che 'l viso abbruciato non difese | la conoscenza sua al mio intelletto' (ibid. xv. 26–8, p. 168, '[I] fixed my eyes on his baked features, so that his blackened face did not prevent my mind from recognizing him'). Although Shelley seems to have had this encounter in mind when he narrates the meeting with Rousseau (*Triumph*, ll. 182 ff., p. 160), the 'discoloured flakes of snow' recall more precisely canto vi: 'Grandine grossa, acqua tinta e neve | per l'aere tenebroso si riversa' (*Inferno*, vi. 10–11, Sapegno, i. 67: 'Enormous hail, dirty water and snow | fell down through the gloomy air').[46] Moreover, these miserable conditions in canto vi effectively extinguish 'the youthful glow' of love that had partially and movingly survived in Paolo and Francesca (canto v). Through Rousseau, Shelley is condensing into these lines one aspect of Dante's narrative in cantos v and vi.[47] Youth, with its ardour and love, is eroded by the

---

[46] Shelley marks each of these passages in his copy. See Peck, *Shelley: Life & Work*, ii. 357, 358. For a longer discussion of Latini, see above pp. 27–30, 135. Rousseau's likeness to 'an old root which grew | To strange distortion out of the hill side' (*Triumph*, ll. 182–3, p. 160) suggests an allusion to Dante's 'Wood of the Suicides' in *Inferno* xiii and to Pier della Vigna (whose shade is imprisoned in a tree). See l. 37: 'Uomini fummo, e or siam fatti sterpi' (Sapegno, i. 145: 'We were men, and are now made into trees'). Latini, however, is the most striking example of Dante coming to recognize one of the damned as Shelley comes to recognize Rousseau: 'that [. . .] which methought [. . .] was but' (*Triumph*, ll. 185–6, p. 160).

[47] Cf. Keats's mixing of elements from cantos v and vi in his 'As Hermes once took to his feathers light'. See above p. 158. See also Shelley's manuscript: ll. 472–3 ('him whom from the lowest depths of Hell | Through every Paradise') at one stage read: '*How from the highest Heaven unto the hoary | Abyss, of whirling rain*' (*Triumph*, 201).

afflictions it defeats. The end result is mediocrity and a weary disappointment closer to canto vi than to Dante's awe-struck grief in canto xv. Although, for example, 'Which they extinguished' pounces on the hopes of the previous line, the lineation does not allow it to be pointedly disillusioning or arch. It succeeds more evenly and resignedly because 'Fell' has made such a dramatic pause just before: what follows has the understated importance of an afterthought.

Such resignation and self-restraint is in danger of becoming thoroughly despondent. In other words, by making the extinction of youth appear an inevitable consequence, rather than an artful observation, Rousseau may have subdued himself to the element that surrounds him. He resists that by saying the afflictions are destructive in so far as they resemble tears. His awareness of the truth is made possible by his refusing to be veiled by 'drops of sorrow'. Yet the loftiness in his manner seems far from youthful or glowing. He is, at once, critical of those 'whose faint lids' succumb to such feelings and drawn to the pathos in 'drops of sorrow'.

The *Inferno* repeatedly warns against the delusions of sympathy: when, for instance, Dante and Virgil first see those punished for divination, whose heads are twisted backwards so that their tears run down their backs, Dante cries himself.

> Certo io piangea, poggiato a un de' rocchi
> del duro scoglio, sí che la mia scorta
> mi disse: 'Ancor se' tu delli altri sciocchi?
> Qui vive la pietà quand'è ben morta'
> (*Inferno*, xx. 25–8, Sapegno, i. 222–3)

(Certainly I cried, leaning against one of the rocks in that craggy ridge, so that my guide said to me: 'Are you still like the other fools? Here pity lives when it is properly dead')

Dante finds it impossible to extinguish pity completely, and when he does so most successfully, hostility rather than indifference takes its place. Though Virgil is himself occasionally compassionate against his better judgement,[48] the relation between Rousseau and Shelley's narrator follows Dante's and Virgil's example most closely on the question of sympathy. Rousseau is neither condemned nor held up as an ideal; like Dante's Virgil he is admirable

---

[48] See e.g. *Inferno*, iii. 43–4, and iv. 19–21, Sapegno, i. 33, 42.

and to be surpassed. For Shelley's narrator to acquire a truer relation to 'Life' than Rousseau's involves him in pursuing Rousseau's experience, in the same way that reaching the ideal means going on along the wilderness. Therefore when Rousseau boasts of an indifference that reveals its inner contradiction, Shelley's narrator registers grief, yet without sounding overwhelmed by it.[49]

On being shown Napoleon, he says:

> I felt my cheek
> Alter to see the great form pass away
> Whose grasp had left the giant world so weak
>
> That every pigmy kicked it as it lay—
> And much I grieved
> (*Triumph*, ll. 224–8, p. 166)

The depth of feeling is convincing because he sounds startled by it. The line-ending between 'cheek' and 'Alter' creates an enquiring pause, which registers the certainty and considers the surprise of his own feeling. It expresses an unimpassioned and entire sympathy that can barely be sustained. Reflecting on this disappointment tempts Shelley to repudiate all concern:

> and for despair
> I half disdained mine eye's desire to fill
> With the spent vision of the times that were
> (Ibid., ll. 231–3)

The self-awareness he brings to his grief breaks down into self-division, an argument with his own desire that repeats in miniature Rousseau's self-disgust. Possibly a more complete disdain, like Christ's or Socrates', would be the ideal: had he 'forborne' or been given 'purer nutriment', Rousseau says, 'this disguise | [would not have] Stained that within which still disdains to wear it' (ibid., ll. 189, 202, 204–5, pp. 160, 162). Rousseau's opposition is defiant to the last but achieves nothing; disdain confirms subjection so much that the word itself seems the product of what it opposes, the 'disguise [that] Stained'. The narrator's 'half disdained' is judged by this passage to be less heroic and quite as useless as Rousseau's tenacity in defeat. He is made at once to look at something further:

---

[49] Shelley marks *Inferno*, xx. 25–30 and writes 'Smithfield' in the margin, rejecting (I think) the indifference Virgil recommends (Peck, *Shelley: Life & Work*, ii. 359).

> I half disdained mine eye's desire to fill
>
> With the spent vision of the times that were
>> And scarce have ceased to be . . . 'Dost thou behold,'
> Said then my guide, 'those spoilers spoiled'
>> (Ibid., ll. 232–5, p. 166)

Virgil frequently tells Dante to 'behold' the damned soul, monster, or angel that disconcerts him or disrupts his train of thought (perhaps to complete it later).[50] As in Purgatorio ii and elsewhere Dante's private musings suggest a separation from his circumstances which events overturn. Rousseau, similarly, disturbs the narrator's introspection by insisting that he confront a succession of upsetting appearances. To remain willing to look directly at the catastrophes that prompt disdain is apparently what 'Life' asks of Shelley's narrator. Such directness demands that he does not withdraw dismissively or disdainfully but still be 'Struck to the heart by this sad pageantry' (ibid., l. 176, p. 158). As in 'I felt my cheek | Alter', self-observation continues in this phrase amidst the most intense feeling, and is opposed to the self-love or self-protectiveness that would rather despair and 'Let them pass' (ibid., l. 243, p. 168). Shelley's style in these moments of the poem practises what Rousseau so passionately envies, coming between Rousseau's 'I | Have suffered what I wrote, or viler pain!' and the equanimity Rousseau ascribes to 'the great bards of old who inly quelled | The passions which they sung, as by their strain | May well be known' (ibid., ll. 278–9, 274–6, p. 172).

When Rousseau says 'Dost thou behold [. . .]', he interrupts Shelley's narrator with a simple instruction that turns into a moral point. Voltaire and the others are all destroyed by their submission to 'Life'; Rousseau, by contrast, was 'overcome | By [his] own heart alone'.[51] Quite what should be inferred from that difference is not clear, but Rousseau intends his interlocutor to receive instruction. The incident differs in this respect from what it prefigures—the moment when Rousseau begins the story of his life. 'Mine eyes are sick' the narrator says, 'of this perpetual flow | Of people, & my heart of one sad thought.— | Speak.' (ibid., ll.

---

[50] See e.g. the continuation of Virgil's speech in canto xx (esp. ll. 31, 40 ff.) and the opening of canto xvii (Sapegno, i. 223–4, 188–9). See the discussion of canto x, above pp. 32–6.

[51] See A. C. Bradley's discussion of the syntactical ambiguities of these lines, 'Notes', 450–2.

298–300, p. 176). In answer to this request, Rousseau gives the narrator the narrative that may offer, but cannot provide, a justification of Rousseau's earlier remarks. The narrator seems, moreover, to have followed the direction to 'behold' because he now asks Rousseau just to 'Speak'. 'Mine eyes are sick' is as quietly emphatic as 'Struck to the heart', and the narrator's more feeling despair leads, on this occasion, beyond either disdain or vindication to the plea for more: another opportunity to 'behold' that may help explain.

So, as much as Dante is led by love, Shelley's narrator needs to follow Rousseau. His willingness to listen should create a form of involvement that prevents him from being either a spectator or the victim of his actions. The narrator asks for no more than speech, and Rousseau now disavows the ability to answer fundamental questions:

> Why this should be my mind can compass not;
>   'Whither the conqueror hurries me still less.
> But follow thou, & from spectator turn
>   Actor or victim in this wretchedness,
> And what thou wouldst be taught I then may learn
>   From thee.—Now listen . . .[']
>   (Ibid. ll. 303–8, pp. 176, 178)

By listening, Shelley will be following the story of Rousseau's life—both repeating it and finding sense in it. The first person's natural (as well as formally conventional) desire to know may possibly transform him from innocent to precocious guide, making teacher dependent on pupil. His attentiveness will be a kind of participation, and by 'following', in this double sense, Shelley's narrator may give understanding where he sought knowledge.

The lines recall and imply the rebuke which Shelley's 'Second Citizen' makes in *Charles the First*:

>   Canst thou discern
> The signs of seasons, yet perceive no hint
> Of change in that stage-scene in which thou art
> Not a spectator but an actor?
>   (scene i, ll. 33–6, *PW*, 489)

To observe how the seasons are changing is certainly an achievement. The Youth is criticized here for not bringing similar discernment to the changes and strife of specifically human experience. By not doing so, he is ignoring his own agency, using the cycles of the natural world as a diversion and a retreat from the processes in which, according to the Second Citizen, he is unavoidably involved. '[I]n which thou art' pre-empts the division it insists on between spectating and acting, such that remaining a spectator appears equivalent to pretending you are not there. The Citizen's insistence about this is contrasted with the Youth's enthusiasm about everything in the procession that both of them are watching. In the play, Shelley presents the two characters' opposite points of view in such equipoise that it declares his own perfect impartiality. *The Triumph of Life* qualifies these positions, restraining youthful self-confidence and world-weary resignation. Similarly, Shelley's style modifies his own position, recognizing the desires hidden within his pretensions to objectivity, and seeking to portray the experience of grief without succumbing to despair.

In the *North American Review* of 1819, John Chipman Gray noted that 'Through this [*Purgatorio*] the poet proceeds, and is no longer a spectator, as in the Inferno, but an actor in the scenes he describes'.[52] Following Rousseau makes an actor of Shelley's narrator even though he is only listening. And the pursuit may perhaps lead him from an infernal towards a purgatorial realm. At the beginning of *Purgatorio* Dante is prompted to recall Ulysses' journey (narrated in *Inferno* xxvi) because Ulysses saw, but could not reach, the mountain of Purgatory where Dante has just arrived. Rousseau (more pitifully than Ulysses) urges Shelley to go further than him:

> 'If thirst of knowledge doth not thus abate,
> Follow it even to the night, but I
> Am weary[']
>
> (ll. 194–6, p. 162)[53]

His words recall Ulysses' 'orazion picciola' to his fellow-travellers:

---

[52] John Chipman Gray, [untitled review of *La Divina Commedia*], *North American Review*, 8 (1819), 322–47 quoted from *Dante in America: The First Two Centuries*, ed. A. Bartlett Giamatti (Binghampton, NY, 1983), 9.

[53] See *Inferno*, xxvi. 120, 124, 106.

Considerate la vostra semenza:
fatti non foste a viver come bruti,
ma per seguir virtute e canoscenza
(*Inferno*, xxvi. 118–20, Sapegno,
i. 294)

(Reflect on your origins: you were not made to live like beasts but to follow virtue and knowledge)

Ulysses rouses his friends to a final effort against the impulses of old age: ' "Io e' compagni eravam vecchi e tardi" ' (' "I and my companions were old and tired" '), but he urges them to travel further westward beyond Gibraltar, towards the unpeopled world 'di retro al sol' ('behind the sun').[54] What Ulysses' determination can overcome, Rousseau is defeated by. At this point (though not so clearly later on), made petulant and self-pitying by exhaustion, he hands on responsibility to the younger generation. But any criticism of this inability to repeat Ulysses' heroic resolution is immediately disarmed:

Am weary' . . . Then like one who with the weight

Of his own words is staggered, wearily

He paused

(*Triumph*, ll. 196–8, p. 162)[55]

He seems to realize the truth of what was perhaps originally a self-dramatizing excuse. The narrator observes this shock of self-recognition, and his use of 'wearily' compassionately restores authority to Rousseau's description of himself.

Rousseau's disintegrating speech is a further modification of Dante's Ulysses, who is similarly troubled before he starts to speak. He and Diomede are imprisoned together within a twin flame. When Virgil addresses him he cannot answer at once:

Lo maggior corno della fiamma antica
cominciò a crollarsi mormorando
pur come quella cui vento affatica
(*Inferno*, xxvi. 85–7, Sapegno, i. 291)

(The larger horn of the ancient flame began to shake, murmuring just as if it was being beaten by the wind)

---

[54] Ibid., ll. 106, 117, p. 294. See also l. 91 n., pp. 292–3.

[55] The effect is comparable with that discussed in *The Fall of Hyperion*: 'some old man of the earth | Bewailing earthly loss', ll. 440–1, p. 489. See above p. 143.

Ulysses conquers this bodily stammer so that his speech when it comes has already defeated the paralysing self-consciousness that overwhelms Rousseau. Such heroic resilience may be admirable, and even enviable, but Shelley seems interested in contrasting it with inevitable modern failings. The contrast does not simply bemoan the degeneracy of the modern world, it establishes a form of compassionate attention that is able, despite the afflictions of our mortal day, to leave the 'thirst of knowledge' unabated.[56]

Ulysses' presence in *The Triumph of Life* is an example of heroism that cannot be followed, as is confirmed by Rousseau's description of Plato:

> 'All that is mortal of great Plato there
> Expiates the joy & woe his master knew not;
>   That star that ruled his doom was far too fair—
> 'And Life, where long that flower of Heaven grew not,
>   Conquered the heart by love which gold or pain
> Or age or sloth or slavery could subdue not[']
>   (*Triumph*, ll. 254–9, p. 170)

Plato's master is Socrates: one of those who swiftly discarded earthly concerns and so never experienced the 'joy & woe' of 'love'. Dante's Ulysses is another contrast to Plato but at the opposite extreme to Socrates. Despite his long life and many ties to human society, he remained 'unconquered' by any affection:

> né dolcezza di figlio, né la pièta
>   del vecchio padre, né 'l debito amore
>   lo qual dovea Penelopé far lieta,
> vincer potero dentro a me l'ardore
>   (*Inferno*, xxvi. 94–7, Sapegno, i. 293)

(neither fondness for my son, nor respect for my aged father, nor the debt of love that ought to have made Penelope joyful, could conquer in me the desire)

---

[56] Ulysses is bound to Diomede in a parody of the companionship he supposedly enjoyed with his crew and by contrast with the friendship between Virgil and Dante. In this respect he forms part of the sequence in *Inferno* from Paolo and Francesca to Ugolino and Ruggieri. Also, interestingly, Virgil rather than Dante speaks to him, which is unusual and necessary, Virgil says, because as a Greek Ulysses might despise an Italian speaker. Ulysses' disdain reveals Virgil's helpfulness in the same way that Rousseau's collapse prompts Shelley's sympathy. Cf. *Inferno*, viii. 118–23 (where Virgil is at a loss) and xix. 124–33 (where he carries Dante) (Sapegno, i. 96, 219).

Plato was similarly unsubdued by the world's corrupting influences and yet was conquered by love. Within the *Commedia* Ulysses' dismissal of 'dolcezza' and 'amore' is, of course, an implicit reason for his being damned. The speech is fearful because Ulysses seems so indifferent to, and consequently defiant of, its ironies. Such indifference strikes one as superhuman in its dedication to knowledge, and then as inhuman—partly because Ulysses seems able to evoke within his definitive assessment a tone of bitter self-recrimination while demonstrating that, in fact, he has no regrets about losing Penelope or Telemachus.[57] Understandable remorse is subsumed, like everything else, by his 'ardore'.

By mentioning 'All that is mortal' of Plato, Rousseau recalls his description of himself: ' "Corruption would not now thus much inherit | Of what was once Rousseau" ' (*Triumph*, ll. 203–4, p. 162). Their conquest by love condemns them to a form of vulnerability that Socrates and Ulysses easily avoid. The poem draws together its two lesser heroes, Plato and Rousseau, as examples of weakness that need to be followed. It may be that the narrator's attention to Rousseau's story will reveal to him the damaging consequences of the 'conquest' by love; of Rousseau's and Plato's being 'subdued' rather than 'tempered' by their experience. That depends, however, on the narrator's own attention being tempered and affectionate. And being tempered implies that the narrator's ardour for truth must continue to embrace all of human life, instead of dismissing most of it as Ulysses had done.[58]

The Triumph of Life, then, is arguing that ideal love will comprehend without being overwhelmed by the world of suffering. In doing so, it counters Petrarch's *Trionfi*, particularly the 'Triumphus Mortis', whose consolation lay in a world of love beyond the world. Shelley is frequently close to Petrarch in his wording and imagery, but rewrites the *Trionfi* in the light of *Purgatorio*.[59] Death

---

[57] Cf. Julian in *Julian and Maddalo*: 'If I had been an unconnected man | I, from this moment, should have formed some plan | Never to leave sweet Venice' (*PP*, 126). See also T. S. Eliot, *The Sacred Wood: Essays on Poetry and Criticism* (London, 1920; 7th edn., London, 1950), 31.

[58] This account of Plato squares with 'A Defence of Poetry': 'Love, which found a worthy poet in Plato alone of all the ancients' (*PP*, 497).

[59] Alan Weinberg points out many verbal similarities (see Weinberg, *Shelley's Italian Experience*, 206–7, 211, 215–18, 227–8) but adds 'this oblique reference to Dante [*Triumph*, ll. 471–2] is the most definite instance of a broader and more positive framework within which the triumphal pageant should be viewed' (p.

in the first half of the 'Triumphus Mortis' assures Laura that ' "è pur il migliore | fuggir vecchiezza e' suoi molti fastidi" ' (' "it is simply better to flee from old age and its many vexations" '). In the second part, Laura returns from the dead and assures the poet that life is death: ' "Viva son io e tu se' morto ancora" ' (' "I am alive and you are still dead" '). None the less, she has cared for him ever since she died. Her apparent cruelties were all to the good in moderating his passion. The love between them can cross from one realm to the other and, as Petrarch himself claims at the close, it has already lifted him out of the changing world:

> 'Questo no,' rispos'io 'perché la rota
> terza del ciel m'alzava a tanto amore,
> ovunque fusse, stabile ed immota!'

('Oh no,' I answered, 'for the third sphere of Heaven raised me to such a form of love that, wherever you were, it was constant and immovable!')[60]

Laura's appearance in the second half is exclusively supportive and consoling. Through speaking to her the poet is confirmed in the worth of his immutable attachment. In comparison with Dante, the result is at once more touching and more cosy.[61]

Rousseau's vision, like Shelley's narrator's, distinctively prevents the secure assessment of the past by wiping it out. This may be

---

239). Charles Robinson observes the sequentiality of the *Trionfi*: 'the "Sun" of Time in Petrarch's *The Triumph of Time* had obscured the "star" of Fame which ruled *The Triumph of Fame*' (Robinson, *Byron and Shelley*, 223). He does not consider the Dantean qualities latent in such successiveness.

[60] 'Triumphus Mortis', i. 65–6, ii. 22, 172–4, Francesco Petrarca, *Rime—Trionfi e Poesie Latine*, ed. F. Neri, G. Martellotti, E. Bianchi, and N. Sapegno (Milan and Naples, 1951), 519, 524, 530. In the only translation published in the period, Henry Boyd gives these passages as follows: 'If the long toils of slow consuming age | You wish to shun, and leave the earthly stage | with unreluctant feet'; ' "Oh! mine is life indeed!" with matchless grace | She said; "but you are bound in Death's embrace" '; ' "O no!" I cried, "the rolling spheres above | That kindled first the nascent spark to love, | Whatever clime your heav'nly presence own'd, | Had led me there by sacred instinct bound." ' (*The Triumphs of Petrarch: Translated into English Verse [. . . .]* (London, 1807), 122, 133, 144). The translations reflect Boyd's understanding of 'The design of all these Poems [which] is evidently to direct the mind from degrading pursuits, to such objects as become a rational and immortal being' (ibid., p. xlvi).

[61] Shelley noticed this essential difference in perspective between Dante and Petrarch by marking in his copy the unfamiliar *Inferno*, xxi. 85–93. In the lines marked, Dante is required to come out of his relatively secure hiding-place and join the procession of devils who will guide him (until the end of xxii). Cf. xii. 85–90, also marked (Sapegno, i. 237, 136; Peck, *Shelley: Life & Work*, ii. 358, 359).

one further step towards the perception of the eternal. By contrast, Petrarch's vision of Laura explains the past and makes it partake in the eternal realm. Because it views the consolations of love more sceptically, *The Triumph of Life* considers the third circle of Heaven, the sphere of Venus, in a more specifically Dantean way. The third circle is the last of the heavenly spheres that is touched by the shadow of earth:

> Da questo cielo, in cui l'ombra s'appunta
> che 'l vostro mondo face, pria ch'altr'alma
> del triunfo di Cristo fu assunta.
> (*Paradiso*, ix. 118–20, Sapegno, iii. 119–20)

(By this Heaven, in which the shadow that is made by your world reaches a point, she [Rahab] was raised up before any other soul in the triumph of Christ.)

According to Dante's Ptolemaic astronomy, the shadow cast by the earth reaches the Moon, Mercury, and lastly Venus, but extends no farther. Its cone 's'appunta'—it reaches a point, is focused, and finished in the sphere of love.[62] This astronomy characterizes the third sphere of Heaven as always on the brink of going beyond the shadow of earth, and yet remaining within it. Love may be for Shelley what lifts us outside the limits of our selves and our 'mortal day', but in *The Triumph of Life* it does so while continually drawing us back into the shadow of the world. We may be condemned to create a little world within the great world of all, yet for Shelley Petrarch is misled by taking that construction for the truth.

In this respect, Petrarch's form of vision and form of love both resemble 'the dark creeds which cover with eclipse | Their pathway from the cradle to the tomb' whom Shelley attacks in his 'Hate-song' ('To the [Lord Chancellor]', ll. 39–40, *Poems*, 561). In *The Triumph of Life*, 'Gregory & John and men divine' have occluded Heaven in the same way:

> [they] rose like shadows between Man & god
> Till that eclipse, still hanging under Heaven,
> Was worshipped by the world o'er which they strode
>
> For the true Sun it quenched.
> (*Triumph*, ll. 288, 289–92, pp. 174, 176)

---

[62] See ibid., l. 118 n., pp. 119–20.

In the final demise of the chariot, Rousseau reports that 'some made a cradle of the ermined capes | "Of kingly mantles" ' (ll. 495–6, p. 202).[63] Such capes match the skies they obscure, covering successiveness in a false permanence, and creating a circle which encloses each individual in a motionless, invulnerable solipsism. Shelley is arguing therefore that the chariot's triumphal processions require and produce the same self-captivity as creates the dominance of blood and gold. The twin anarchies of Church and State are, however, analogous to Petrarch's clinging reliance on transcendent love. The mode of vision that both entail will prevent the progress through experience that Dante was granted: a 'triumph' that in Shelley's view could overcome life only by remaining continually vulnerable to it, by still rejecting the consolations of hope, and by living from 'day to day'. Dante's theological astronomy is placed in the service of Shelley's poetics of vision: where the 'triunfo di Cristo' lifts Rahab into glory and still keeps her within the shadow of earth, Shelley's writing continues to claim a visionary perspective and authority, both of which now depend upon Shelley's remaining in (and being ready to transform) the world that goes from 'day to day'.

When Rousseau meets the 'shape all light', he speaks to her ' "as one between desire and shame | Suspended" ' (*Triumph*, ll. 394–5, p. 190). He is, for a moment, like the souls of the great poets in Limbo in *Inferno* iv, who say ' "sanza speme vivemo in disio" ' (' "without hope we live in desire" ').[64] Dante is moved by realizing 'che gente di molte valore | conobbi che in quel limbo eran sospesi' ('that I knew people of great worth who were suspended in this limbo'). Moses, Abraham, and the other patriarchs had been rescued by Christ in the Harrowing of Hell, rather as in

---

[63] The 'leaden cowls' of 'To the [Lord Chancellor]' suggest an echo (that may inform both poems) of *Inferno* xxiii where Dante portrays the hypocrites wearing monastic hoods: 'Di fuor dorate son [. . .] ma dentro tutte piombo' (ll. 64–5, Sapegno, i. 256). It is also in this canto that Dante sees Caiaphas crucified on the ground and trodden on by each monk as he passes. The memory of this may have suggested Shelley's 'giant world so weak | That every pigmy kicked it as it lay' (*Triumph*, ll. 226–7, p. 166).

[64] Shelley marked ll. 40–2 in his copy and *Inferno*, ii. 52–7 where Virgil says, 'Io era tra color che son sospesi, | e donna mi chiamò beata e bella' (Sapegno, i. 22). The lady is Beatrice, asking Virgil's assistance in Dante's salvation. The meeting prefigures the Earthly Paradise and confirms the likeness between Virgil and Rousseau. See also *Purgatorio*, iii. 40–5, Sapegno, ii. 27.

Shelley's poem Socrates and Christ have escaped the world.[65] *The Triumph of Life* resembles this because it works in desire without hope and in hope freed from desire. It argues that to be suspended rather than saved is inevitable and, possibly, a sign of human advancement. Dante's Christian teaching is not opposed so much as developed in order that, perhaps, it may now be surpassed.

In 'A Defence of Poetry' Shelley claimed that Dante could not himself have believed the *Commedia*'s theology.[66] In *The Triumph of Life* such a separation of beauties and meaning, with its confident assumption of human progress, is replaced by an enquiry into what truth Dante's doctrines may be found to contain. The poem seeks to herald, accompany, and follow a progress that, although inevitable, cannot appear so from inside time. To see beyond the self-enclosing and self-confirming circles of Hell means to see into and, at the same time, take part in the process of eternity. The perception of the eternal is never completed and never unquestionable; the process of perceiving asks you, in fact, to imitate what you are becoming and adopt the position of a planet. The planets rotate on their own axes and circle another centre; they are suspended in their circuit, like Virgil and Rousseau, while continuing a movement through time. This position, between desire and shame, time and eternity, equanimity and despair, is where Shelley places himself when he writes *The Triumph of Life*.[67]

---

[65] *Inferno*, iv. 42, 44–5, Sapegno, i. 44. Shelley's affiliation with the 'sospesi' is supported by Dante's list of saved souls, 'd'Abel suo figlio e quella di Noè, | di Moisè legista e obediente; | Abraàm patriarca e Davíd re, | Israèl con lo padre e co'suoi nati' (ibid., ll. 56–9, p. 45). See 'Voltaire, | Frederic, & Kant, Catherine, & Leopold, | Chained hoary anarch, demagogue & sage' (*Triumph*, ll. 235–7, p. 166; and see ll. 283–8, p. 174). Cf., however, Petrarch's 'Ivi eran quei che fur detti felici, | pontefici, regnanti, imperadori: | or sono ignudi, miseri e mendici' ('Triumphus Mortis', i. 79–81, Petrarca, *Rime*, 519–20: 'There were those who were thought happy, pontiffs, rulers, emperors: now they are naked, miserable and indigent').

[66] 'The distorted notions of invisible things which Dante and his rival Milton have idealized, are merely the mask and the mantle in which these great poets walk through eternity enveloped and disguised. It is a difficult question to determine how far they were conscious of the distinction which must have subsisted in their minds between their own creeds and that of the people' (*PP*, 498). Cf. Jones, i. 51, 66, ii. 260, 412.

[67] Cf. 'The world-worn Dante grasp'd his song', 'The Palace of Art', l. 135, *The Poems of Tennyson*, ed. C. Ricks, 3 vols. (2nd edn., Harlow, 1987), i. 447.

6

Byron Turning to Stone

Byron defended *Don Juan* as *'life'*, as *'the thing'*, 'the sublime of *that there* sort of writing' (26 Oct. 1819, *LJ*, vi. 232). In *'that there'*, Byron prefers ungrammatical dialect for its concentration on actual fact, and he epitomizes *Don Juan'*s consistent tactic of lowering the tone to reach *'life'*. The poem's candour about actuality is designed to save it from cant, pre-eminently the moralized poetry of Byron's contemporaries. But this frankness that reaches the truths avoided by conventional pieties operates, Byron claims, within the proper sphere of 'human powers'. As he wrote to Murray, 'you have so many "*divine*" poems, is it nothing to have written a *Human* one?'[1] To seek the 'divine' makes for dull poetry, not only in the servile outpourings of a Southey, but in the greatest poets:

Religion does not make a part of my subject—it is something beyond human powers and has failed in all human hands except Milton's and Dante's—and even Dante's powers are involved in his delineation of human passions—though in supernatural circumstances.[2]

Byron's reading of the *Commedia* bears a clear resemblance to A. W. Schlegel's, Hunt's, or Hazlitt's: he dislikes Dante's theological scheme and even the doctrine of torture itself (in this he is closest to Leigh Hunt);[3] he praises the poem for its portrayal of gentleness amidst unheard of, immoral punishments. Though, in Byron's view, Dante produces the theology efficiently enough, his 'powers are

---

[1] 6 Apr. 1819, *LJ*, vi. 105. See ibid.: 'You sha'n't make *Canticles* of my Cantos.'

[2] 'Letter to John Murray Esqre' (1821), Byron, *The Complete Miscellaneous Prose*, ed. A. Nicholson (Oxford, 1991), 143. Cf. Byron to Augusta Leigh, 17 May 1819, *LJ*, vi. 129: 'Dante is more humane in his "Hell" for he places his unfortunate lovers [. . .] in company—and though they suffer—it is at least together.'

[3] See Leigh Hunt, 'Critical Notice of Dante's Life and Genius' (1846): 'It might have been thought of Dante, if he had not taken a part in the cruelty, that he detailed the horrors of his hell out of a wish to disgust the world with its frightful notions of God.' (Beatrice Corrigan, *Italian Poets and English Critics [. . .]* (Patterns of Literary Criticism, 7, London, 1969), 218).

involved' only in the discovery of 'human passions' where they can barely survive—in Hell—and where you would least expect them—a religious epic. So, for Byron, Dante's 'gentleness' outwits his chosen genre. By escaping the conventions of epic, Dante both lends his doctrines a humanity which Byron thought they could not possibly possess, and offers a corollary for Byron's aims in writing *Don Juan*: another epic that defies expectation and discovers 'human passions' within forms of stony-heartedness comparable to Ugolino's.[4]

Byron's response to the *Commedia*, as revealed by *Don Juan*, is different from Hunt's or Schlegel's because he refuses to isolate the *Commedia*'s 'gentleness'. This is not the consequence of his accepting, or half-accepting, Dante's overarching scheme, whose judgements on the damned restrain his and his readers' desire for unqualified compassion. Byron focuses instead on the imperfections of both the damned and the saved in the *Commedia*. In Dante, such imperfections betray what stands open to judgement; in Byron, they suggest a form of sympathy that remains candid and resists the desire to ennoble feelings of sympathy into the recognition of virtue. Dante's descriptions reveal, therefore, perhaps against his will, a 'humanity' in the damned that Byron continually asks his readers to acknowledge in themselves.

While this high valuation of the human interest in Dante occurs frequently in the period, Byron seems to have adopted his formulation of it from Friedrich Schlegel, whose lectures he read in January 1821. Yet the form of tenderness Byron praises in the *Commedia* differs from Friedrich Schlegel's as much as *Don Juan* avoids the archness and quietism of Romantic irony.[5] Dante's 'singular poem', Friedrich Schlegel states:

---

[4] See 'Detached Thoughts', no. 96: 'and *when* the *World is at an end*—what moral or warning purpose *can* eternal tortures answer? [. . . .] I cannot help thinking that the *menace* of Hell makes as many devils as the severe penal codes of inhuman humanity make villains' (*LJ*, ix. 45–6); and *Manfred*, III. iv. 123–4: 'Must crimes be punish'd but by other crimes, | And greater criminals?' (McGann, iv. 101). On Ugolino and stony-heartedness, see below.

[5] In this I am opposing a conventional judgement: see Stuart M. Sperry, 'Toward a Definition of Romantic Irony in English Literature', *Romantic and Modern: Revaluations of Literary Tradition*, ed. G. Bornstein (Pittsburgh, 1977), 3–28; Anne K. Mellor, *English Romantic Irony* (Cambridge, Mass., and London, 1980), 12–16; and, by contrast, Peter Szondi, 'Friedrich Schlegel and Romantic Irony with some Remarks on Tieck's Comedies', in id., *On Textual Understanding and Other*

is rich beyond all other example in its representation of human life. [...] he has depicted, with equally strong and masterly touches of horror, tenderness, and enthusiasm, every situation in which the human spirit can be placed, beginning with the deepest gloom and hell and despair.[6]

Dante's universality is seen here as poised and indifferent; as able to invest any condition of experience with the life of his protean imagination. His mastery is proved by the equality of his descriptions whatever their subject. For Byron, Dante lacks the power to circumscribe everything (since religious experience eludes him) and he is *involved* in his delineation of human passions' (my emphasis). Elsewhere he is merely repeating obediently the required doctrinal position; only in the feelings of the damned does his poem come to life. Such a distinction between levels of commitment to the work, while so reminiscent of A. W. Schlegel, implies in Byron's reading an involvement that Friedrich Schlegel precludes.

This disagreement about Dante's relation to the poem becomes a conflict when Friedrich Schlegel attacks the *Commedia*: the work has 'strong and masterly touches [...] of tenderness' but, in Schlegel's view, it lacks 'gentle feelings'. Byron's response is indignant:

He says also that Dante's chief defect is a want, in a word, of gentle feelings. Of gentle feelings! and Francesca of Rimini—and the father's feelings in Ugolino—and Beatrice—and 'La Pia!' Why, there is gentleness in Dante beyond all gentleness, when he is tender. It is true that, treating of the Christian Hades, or Hell, there is not much scope or site for gentleness—but who *but* Dante could have introduced any 'gentleness' at all into *Hell*? Is there any in Milton's? No—and Dante's Heaven is all love, and glory, and majesty. ('Ravenna Journal', 29 Jan. 1821, *LJ*, viii. 39–40)

Essays (Manchester, 1986), 57–73. Cf. Peter L. Thorslev, jun., 'Byron and Bayle: Biblical Skepticism and Romantic Irony', *Byron, The Bible, and Religion [...]*, ed. Wolf Z. Hirst (Newark, NJ, London, and Toronto, 1991), 71: 'neither Byron nor Bayle are truly Romantic Ironists [....] Neither of them was willing to deny history, and both retain certain unconditional and "unironized" moral commitments'; and Bernd Fischer, 'Irony Ironized: Heinrich von Kleist's Narrative Stance and Friedrich Schlegel's Theory of Irony', *European Romantic Review*, 1 (1990), 59–74.

[6] Friedrich Schlegel, *Lectures on the History of Literature, Ancient and Modern*, trans. J. G. Lockhart, 2 vols. (Edinburgh, 1818), ii. 13. See *Toynbee*, ii. 277.

Friedrich Schlegel made the accusation on political and theological grounds. Dante's 'Ghibelline harshness' is, he says, the product of expecting 'the whole salvation of mankind from dominion founded on worldly principles'. Dante's loyalties lay with those who sought to rule by absolute force and who, consequently, denied 'the power of that unseen influence, which is however sure to make its existence to be felt on every occasion'. This denial of unseen, providential influences forms the basis of tyrannical ambitions and, in Schlegel's argument, creates the harshness of the *Commedia*. His analysis recapitulates in a medieval context a familiar conservative reaction to the French Revolution, arguing that impiety leads to tyranny. The Ghibelline *philosophes* foster a version of the Terror.

Friedrich Schlegel's reading of Dante assumes that placing no trust in an unknown providence allows you to pursue ambitions for power without the constraint of any sanction. The same error produces Dante's harshness and the Revolution's horrors. For Schlegel, therefore, 'gentleness' is an aspect of a person's willingness to submit to the unseen. *Don Juan* repeatedly attacks those who put themselves in the hands of fate, arguing that this is usually both self-deceiving (fate is nearly always what we want) and enfeebled (fate is the name for forces we dare not resist). The presence of such remarkable gentleness in Dante proves to Byron that the quality does not depend upon a submissive acquiescence to the supposedly inevitable. To argue that gentleness does depend on a sensitive trust in 'unseen influences' restricts it to the delicate and superstitious. It makes 'gentle feelings' the exclusive domain of the conservative and orthodox. *Don Juan*'s project is to assault this and cognate assumptions because it seeks to rescue 'gentleness' and 'humanity' from the ironist's passivity and the conservative's presumption. In doing so, Byron's poem analyses and adapts the peculiar gentleness that Dante manifests in his treatment of the shades—Ugolino particularly.

Thomas Medwin reports Byron and Shelley disagreeing about Ugolino's cannibalism. Byron 'interpreted the last words, "Più che dolor potè il digiunò" to mean (an interpretation in which Shelley by no means agreed with him) that Ugolino actually did feed on his children after their death'.[7] Shelley's disagreement is evident in

---

[7] Medwin, *Life of Shelley*, ii. 21–2; repr. Toynbee, ii. 387–8. Medwin's Italian is slightly inaccurate.

his and Medwin's translation, where the last line reads 'Famine of grief can get the mastery'. Hunger killed Ugolino (where grief had not) and prevented his continuing to grieve. The translation argues that even the most heartfelt grief requires sustenance. Understanding the line in this way makes it surprising, to say the least, that Ugolino, when he stops speaking, immediately begins devouring Ruggieri's brains, and odd that he can appear so grief-stricken when his grief has supposedly been overpowered. For Shelley, Ugolino's speech may recall the human feelings he has since lost in the bestial violence of Hell, but he is speaking of things he must, categorically, no longer be able to experience.

Shelley's sympathy for Ugolino protects him from the suggestion of cannibalism; it secures the nobility of Ugolino's resistance to hunger, inasmuch as it directs the sympathetic reader to an admirable figure. If, as Byron thought, Ugolino had eaten his children then the compassion he attracts becomes separate from his heroism. Dante's reader is asked to notice the weakness of the figure who was reduced to cannibalism and who now uses ambiguity to defend himself against a confession he cannot avoid. Moreover, as Byron observed, the eating of his children is made the prelude to his attack on Ruggieri. Medwin continues, 'Lord Byron thought [his interpretation] was clearly borne out by the nature of the retribution of his tormentor, as well as the offer of the children to make themselves a sacrifice for their father.'[8] Byron's reading enables the damned soul to be seen as continuing the behaviour of the living person. If pathos and heroism are divided, human and infernal worlds are more closely joined, so that the grief (which Shelley suggests has been replaced by merciless violence) now persists within it, just as, in prison, Ugolino had been both a cannibal and a feeling person.

Shelley's view also allows Ugolino's attack on Ruggieri to seem an allegory of treachery: the betrayers who destroyed each other by ignoring the bonds of trust on which social life depends, now show the end of that betrayal, the oppressed feeding on the oppressor.[9] This implication is part of Dante's point: treachery is the worst of sins because it denies the trust between persons (and between God and his creation) that allows society to be a relation between

---

[8] Ibid. ii. 22; Toynbee, ii. 378.
[9] See Shelley's 'The Tower of Famine', PW, 623–4.

persons and not the preying of one beast on another. Having destroyed that trust, Ugolino and Ruggieri inevitably fall back into the anarchy and inhumanity cannibalism represents. If, however, Ugolino has already turned into a cannibal in prison, the allegorical sense of his later action has to hold its own against the psychology of vengeance. Remembering what he did to his children he attacks Ruggieri, doing something worse while aiming to expunge, and so repair, the past. (Ugolino's cannibalism in Hell is worse because Ruggieri remains, somehow, sentient and because Ugolino eats his brains: both his offal and his seat of consciousness.) The logicality of what he does endows the sin of treachery with a recognizable history. Dante's reader is able not only to perceive the nature of treachery but follow its advance from crime to crime, and its gradual consumption of Ugolino's powers as he consumes Ruggieri's.

Neither Ugolino's actions nor Dante's descriptions seem particularly to exemplify or encourage 'gentleness'. The 'gentleness' of Ugolino's paternal feelings would be far easier to accept if he did not eat his children. Byron's distinctive achievement, when reading Dante and writing *Don Juan*, is to find both the feeling and its extinction, and to see that their combination creates a new definition: a 'gentleness in Dante beyond all gentleness, when he is tender'. Ugolino says he does not weep while his sons do:

> 'Ben se' crudel, se tu già non ti duoli
>   pensando ciò che 'l mio cor s'annunziava;
>   e se non piangi, di che pianger suoli?
> Già eran desti, e l'ora s'appressava
>   che 'l cibo ne solea essere addotto,
>   e per suo sogno ciascun dubitava;
> e io senti' chiavar l'uscio di sotto
>   all'orribile torre; ond'io guardai
>   nel viso a' mie' figliuoi sanza far motto.
> Io non piangea, sí dentro impetrai:
>   piangevan elli; e Anselmuccio mio
>   disse: "Tu guardi sí, padre! che hai?"
> Perciò non lacrimai né rispuos'io
>   tutto quel giorno né la notte appresso,
>   infin che l'altro sol nel mondo uscío.'
>   (*Inferno*, xxxiii. 43–54, Sapegno, i. 365)

('You are certainly cruel if you do not mourn now, thinking about what my heart foretold; and if you do not weep, what will you ever weep at?

They were awake already, and the time was approaching when our food
was usually brought to us, and each was afraid because of his dreams;
and I heard the door down below of the horrible tower being locked; at
this I looked into the faces of my sons without saying a word. I did not
weep, I was inwardly so turned to stone: they wept; and my little Anselm
said, "You stare so, father! what is it?" At this, I neither cried nor gave
an answer all that day and the following night, until another sun rose on
the world.')

Ugolino has just recounted the dream in which he foresaw the
death he now describes. Dante, he says, would be cruel indeed if
he was left unmoved by thinking about what Ugolino's heart had
revealed in advance: the prophecy itself and the inwardness it
betrays. Ugolino's children have bad dreams too ('e per suo sogno
ciascun dubitava') but Ugolino alone holds a dialogue within him-
self: 'ciò che 'l mio cor s'annunziava'. His heart announces to itself
what is to come. Ugolino cannot experience the innocent fear that
his sons feel, because he has been made conscious that he knows
in his heart what will happen. The 'thinking' he demands of Dante
appears a repetition of his own coming to realize that the dream
was something true and not just a terrible nightmare. On the other
hand, his realization had compelled silence 'in front of the chil-
dren', while he challenges Dante not to weep. He demands from
Dante the alert sympathy which recognizes how much knowledge
and a sense of responsibility restrict the capacity to feel. Such a
recognition must, however, provoke compassion that is more con-
sidered than (and yet equal to) the instinctual sympathy that his
sons possess.

Ugolino's imperious demand for sympathy is spoken in ignor-
ance, we feel, of Francesca's 'Nessun maggior dolor [. . .]' and, at
the same time, stands in parallel to it.[10] As earlier in the *Inferno*,

---

[10] Francesca is mentioned in the letter quoted above; Byron translated her speeches
from *Inferno*, v. 97–142 in Mar. 1820 (see McGann, iv. 280–5; *LJ*, vii. 58). In Jan.
1821, after completing *Don Juan* v (on 27 Nov. 1820), Byron planned to write,
'life and circumstances permitting', four tragedies: 'Sardanapalus, already begun,
Cain, a metaphysical subject, something in the style of Manfred, but in five *acts*,
perhaps, with the chorus; Francesca of Rimini, in five acts; and I am not sure that
I would not try Tiberius' ('Ravenna Journal', 28 Jan. 1821, *LJ*, viii. 36–7).
Sardanapalus was finished in May 1821; *Cain: A Mystery*, though it ran to only
three acts, was completed by Sept. 1821; but *The Two Foscari* (June 1821) seems
to have replaced the projected plays on Francesca and Tiberius. Byron returned to
Don Juan in Jan. 1822. (See McGann, v. 694, 715.) See also Frederick L. Beaty,
'Byron and the Story of Francesca da Rimini', *PMLA*, 75 (1960), 395–401.

Dante is being asked for an absolute commitment of his attention and feelings which he must neither accept nor reject but transform. His 'thinking', while it follows Ugolino's thoughts, must travel beyond his understanding. The more considered sympathy which Ugolino claims from his observer must keep in mind the limits of his knowledge. When, therefore, Ugolino became stony-hearted ('dentro impetrai') he endured the isolation that knowledge creates, an isolation Dante's compassion must, he argues, comprehend and overcome.[11] Dante's comprehension, however, as the *Commedia* asserts overall, creates a form of sympathy that remains as silently unresponsive as Ugolino himself. His pity is most complete when it identifies itself with Ugolino's necessary silence—silence, in Dante's case, in the face of his own inevitable separation from all the damned. Anselmuccio's question '"che hai?"' is what Ugolino would ask Dante, if he knew, and what his own question earlier, '"e se non pianger, di che pianger suoli?"' unwittingly implies.

The scene possesses such tenderness, then, because resistance to and acknowledgement of human feeling occur in observer and protagonist alike. Ugolino did not weep, he says; they, his sons, did. The chiasmic construction ('"Io non piangea [. . .] piangevan elli"') makes their tears a substitute for his and their weeping a further instance of division between them. Ugolino's envy and admiration of his children's behaviour reappears when his son's question, '"che hai?"', rhymes with 'impetrai' and 'guardai', and then, internally, with 'lacrimai'. The first person past tense of these verbs echoes the second person present. Ugolino can echo but not imitate his children's conduct; Anselmuccio's question sounds like his own voice and contradicts it. Ugolino's sons do not need to appear later in the *Commedia*, in *Purgatorio,* or *Paradiso,* for us to realize they are saved.[12] Their innocence of Ugolino's guilt

---

[11] Byron had echoed this line in 'The Prisoner of Chillon' (1816): 'I had no thought, no feeling—none— | Among the stones I stood a stone, | And was scarce conscious what I wist, | As shrubless crags within the mist' (ll. 235–8, McGann, iv. 11). I discuss this further below. Dante makes Ugolino a reminder of his own *rime petrose* (Foster and Boyde, nos. 77–80; see esp. no. 77, ll. 71–2, and no. 79, ll. 33–6). On the relation between the *rime petrose* and Ugolino, see Robert M. Durling and Ronald L. Martinez, *Time and the Crystal: Studies in Dante's* Rime Petrose (Berkeley, Calif., Los Angeles, and Oxford, 1990), 217–23.

[12] Cf. Dante's meeting with Cavalcante, who fears for his son, Guido, in *Inferno,* x. Dante extends families across the *cantiche*: Buonconte da Montefeltro (*Purgatorio,* v) is the son of Guido da Montefeltro (*Inferno,* xxviii); Piccarda Donati (*Paradiso,* iii) is the sister of Forese Donati (*Purgatorio,* xxiii).

divides father and son, although it manifests itself first in a search for unity. In the same way, their words cannot avoid creating the separation they seek to overcome. How their words fit into Ugolino's speech exemplifies and creates Dante's distanced tenderness for his protagonist.

Ugolino's rigidity insists on his resistance: 'io senti [. . .] ond'io guardai [. . . .] Io non piangea [. . . .] né rispuos'io'. The tragic pathos that attaches to his heroism includes, without being reduced by, an awareness of his egotism. Part of his plight is to be so heroic. Similarly, the rhyme on 'mio', 'io' and 'uscío' discovers, without gloating over, the traces of his pride. Ugolino's self surfaces from his self-imposed impassiveness and, by indicating the strength of his will, proves how powerful the feelings are that have been suppressed. Moreover, the self that outlines Ugolino's apparent self-extinction reveals that his humanity has not been made as 'stony' as he might like. This quality in Dante's verse is designed to make it appear that Ugolino's heart is about to break: 'mio' (in 'Anselmuccio mio | disse'), and 'io' (in 'né rispuos'io | tutto quel giorno'), are both phrases on the brink of admitting the love Ugolino is condemned to repress. Because this danger is seen from a distance, however, Ugolino also appears more vulnerable to than ennobled by the affections he cannot command. Dante's feelings are the more tender here because his detachment recognizes Ugolino's weaknesses.

The other figure in the *Commedia* that Byron particularly praises, apart from Paolo and Francesca, is la Pia in *Purgatorio* v. She speaks six lines only, at the canto's end:

> 'Deh, quando tu sarai tornato al mondo,
>   e riposato della lunga via,'
>   seguitò il terzo spirito al secondo,
> 'ricorditi di me che son la Pia:
>   Siena mi fe'; disfecemi Maremma:
>   salsi colui che 'nnanellata pria
>   disposando m'avea con la sua gemma.'
>   (*Purgatorio*, v. 130–6, Sapegno, ii. 55–6)

('Ah, when you have returned to the world and rested from your long journey,' the third spirit added after the second, 'remember me who am la Pia: Siena made me, my undoing was Maremma: this he knows who led me to the altar and married me with his jewel.')

La Pia was less well known in the period than the other characters Byron mentions,[13] though the pathos she evokes seems much more available and attractive to a nineteenth-century audience than the feelings surrounding Ugolino. La Pia is an innocent victim whose murder (unlike Francesca's) has not made her resentful.[14] Clearing her name involves no recriminations, only an appeal to the truth. La Pia modestly asks to be remembered and emphasizes that there is no hurry. She is the first (and, I think, the only one) of Dante's shades who acknowledges that Dante, after his long journey, may need some time to recover before he begins to recall and pray for those he has met. Yet it is a mistake to see la Pia as an emblem of maiden modesty or transcendent forgiveness. Her husband, whoever he may be, knows who he is. Her words, when Dante repeats them, will accuse him, albeit privately and without dragging his name through the dirt. Similarly, her famous condensation of a life into five words—'Siena mi fe'; disfecemi Maremma'—is an assertion of resignation. The reader may feel more forcefully through her brevity the regret that her own purity of feeling has left behind. In doing so, however, s/he will still recognize the absence in her of self-pity.

Byron's praise for Dante's gentleness does not, then, simply recognize the force of contrast (between the *Commedia*'s usual severity and its glimpses of feeling). Ugolino's speech also displays Dante's unwillingness to separate sources of pathos either from ordinary weakness or the nastiness that should arouse disgust. Byron's reading of the poem perceives, furthermore, the self-detachment that enables la Pia to express truly 'gentle feelings'. Her 'gentleness' is aristocratic because it originates in a form of modesty that is refined and unsubmissive; and her aphoristic account of her earthly life commands the experience: not shrugging it off, but certainly aware of its brutal simplicity.[15] La Pia articulates the form of attention that Ugolino envies and Dante learns

---

[13] *Purgatorio* v attracted far less attention than *Purgatorio* vi and the famous opening of canto viii. See Toynbee, ii. 292, 327, 356, 366, 419 (for references to *Purgatorio* vi) and Toynbee, ii. 234, 274, 379, 400 (for references to *Purgatorio* viii). See also *Don Juan*, iii. 108, McGann, v. 199.

[14] See *Inferno*, v. 106–7, spoken by Francesca: 'Amor condusse noi ad una morte: | Caina attende chi a vita ci spense' ('Love led us to a single death: Caina awaits him who took us from life') (Sapegno, i. 62.)

[15] Byron uses the Ugolino episode on several occasions in *Don Juan* (see below). La Pia's speech is recalled in ix. 10, ll. 7–8, in a passage addressed to Wellington: 'You *did great* things; but not being *great* in mind, | Have left *undone* the

to practise, and she attracts the intelligent sympathy which she gives, both to herself and the world she has left. The *Commedia* possesses such peculiar gentleness because (like la Pia), it views detachedly, and with a sharp sense of other possible forms of behaviour, what it none the less attends to with compassion.

Dante's powers are 'involved' at these moments because they are not relinquished in a passive acceptance of divine judgement. His portrayal of Ugolino registers the conflict between Ugolino's damnation and his fatherly love without arguing that God is therefore unjust. By not siding for or against Ugolino, Dante creates an apparently dispassionate 'gentleness' that Byron began to emulate in *Don Juan*. This fair-minded interest in Ugolino's experience substantiates, moreover, Byron's claim that Dante was 'the poet of liberty'. The mode of Dante's attention to the damned continues, that is to say, his resistance to political and religious despotism. Dante's attentiveness epitomizes the candour that was needed in Byron's day to defy the all-conquering tyranny of cant.

The Prophecy of Dante (1819) shows how fully Byron had accepted the Risorgimento image of Dante. Byron has Dante, in an afterlife, bemoan the corruption and political disintegration of Italy since he died, and plead for unity as the means by which the Italians will recover greatness.[16] *Don Juan*, however, suggests that Byron (possibly as a result of his disappointment with the Carbonari) adopted the undeluded clarity of the *Commedia* in order to further his own poetic and political ambitions.[17] Dante's

---

greatest—and mankind.' (McGann, v. 411). Byron's perception of the comic possibilities of la Pia's line, and his use of them in excoriating a corrupt leader, suggest his intuition of the hostility contained by la Pia's 'gentleness'. *Don Juan*, I argue, adopts and modifies la Pia's fusion of defiant modesty and sensible compassion.

[16] *The Prophecy of Dante* (1819); see canto ii. ll. 136 ff.: 'Oh! my own beauteous land! so long laid low [. . .] What is there wanting then to set thee free, | And show thy beauty in its fullest light? | To make thy Alps impassable; and we, | Her sons, may do this with *one* deed—Unite!' (McGann, iv. 226). See Malcolm Kelsall, *Byron's Politics* (Brighton, 1987), 117: 'The call to the Italians to unite was merely the poetry of politics.' Stuart Curran has kindly drawn my attention to a translation into Italian of *The Prophecy of Dante*, written by Lorenzo da Ponte and published in New York in 1822: *La Profezia di Dante di Lord Byron. Tradotta in Terza Rima da L. Da Ponte, seconda edizione con note ed aggiunte di varie poesie originali* (Nuova-Jorca, 1822).

[17] See Angelo Righetti, 'Letteratura e Vita nelle lettere pisane di Byron', *Paradise of Exiles: Shelley and Byron in Pisa*, ed. Mario Curreli & Anthony L. Johnson (Salzburg and Pisa, 1988), 125–6; see also Byron to Hoppner, 31 May 1821, *LJ*, viii. 130: 'Continue it!—Alas! what could Dante himself *now* prophesy about Italy?'.

exemplary patriotism is no longer invoked as an inspiration, but its mode of attention and poetic technique are adapted for Byron's critique of contemporary Europe. The comedy and ethics of Byron's masterpiece are based in part, therefore, on an idea of 'gentleness' he drew from Dante.[18] In consequence, the poem's perspective frequently discovers 'human feelings amidst' hellish 'circumstances'. Like the *Commedia*, *Don Juan* employs a mode of distanced and sceptical tenderness existing alongside unrestrained invective. Byron's poem, characteristically, also stays 'amidst' the circumstances it describes and disdains—circumstances so appalling, that were they not verified they would be judged supernatural.[19]

The prisoner in Byron's 'The Prisoner of Chillon' turns into another Ugolino: his confession 'Among the stones I stood a stone' echoes *Inferno*, xxxiii. 49: 'Io non piangea, sí dentro impetrai' (Sapegno, i. 365: 'I did not weep, I was inwardly so turned to stone').[20] In the England of *Don Juan*'s English cantos, turning to stone is an occupational hazard.

> But all was gentle and aristocratic
>   In this our party; polish'd, smooth and cold,
> As Phidian forms cut out of marble Attic
> (*Don Juan*, xiii. 110, ll. 1-3, McGann, v. 557)

'Society is smooth'd to that excess, | That manners hardly differ more than dress'; it is 'now one polish'd horde', characterless and

---

[18] On the influence of other Italian writers on *Don Juan*, see Peter Vassallo, *Byron: The Italian Literary Influence* (Basingstoke, 1984). John Hookham Frere's *The Monks and the Giants [...]* (1817-18) ed. R. D. Waller (London, 1926), the mock-heroic poetry of Casti and of Pulci, all contributed profoundly to *Don Juan*. For reasons of space, I am unable to discuss their influence in detail. Byron's translation of the first canto of Pulci's *Morgante Maggiore*, however, shows him already moving towards the form of attention which is so evident in Dante and which distinguishes Byron's mock-heroic from Pulci's or Frere's. Particularly in stanzas 38 and 54 of the translation, Byron transforms into curious facts what Pulci presents as ironies. See McGann, iv. 262, 267-8, and Luigi Pulci, *Morgante*, ed. Franca Ageno (Milan and Naples, 1956), 16, 21. Like the translation 'Francesca da Rimini', Byron's version of *Morgante Maggiore* was written in the period between his composition of cantos iv and v of *Don Juan*.

[19] Byron portrays England in *Don Juan* as a kind of Hell; see i. 200, l. 6, 'A panorama view of hell's in training'; and i. 207, ll. 7-8, 'Besides, in canto twelfth, I mean to show | The very place where wicked people go.' This is one promise Byron keeps (McGann, v. 73, 75).

[20] See 'The Prisoner of Chillon', l. 236 n., McGann, iv. 450, 453. Cf. John Galt, *The Entail or the Lairds of Grippy* (1822), ed. Ian A. Gordon (Oxford, 1970), 4.

dull where 'gentlemen in stays' are 'stiff as stones'.[21] Its unadven-
turous, choking conventionality (though unfelt by most of its
members) defines 'gentle' according to class (one down from
'aristocratic') and as a species of deference. Don Juan adopts the
'suavity' and 'docility' he needs to get on as a diplomat, and he
has, perhaps inevitably, acquired the 'tougher rind' which enables
him to resist sexual temptation and endure dullness. Lady Adeline
is always self-possessed because possessed of 'That calm Patrician
polish in the address' but in the Hell of England she and Don Juan
are endangered because they are imperfectly cold.[22] Don Juan's heart
is certainly less susceptible than earlier and less innocent; Lady
Adeline's marble perfection suits her to her 'Cool, and quite Eng-
lish' husband and to the mansion where 'Steel Barons', 'Judges in
very formidable ermine' and 'Generals [. . .] of the old | And iron
time' adorn the walls. Just as in her gallery 'sweetly spread a
landscape of Lorraine' 'to soothe your vision', Adeline is 'not
indifferent'. In her very centre, Byron says, as in a frozen bottle of
champagne, 'past all price, | About a liquid glassful will remain;
| And this is stronger than the strongest grape.' Similarly, the
reliable Lady Pinchbeck believes that Don Juan, beneath his docil-
ity and polish, is 'a good heart at bottom'.[23]

Because the English cantos are unfinished, the relation between
Lady Adeline and Don Juan remains undeveloped. Byron hints
quite heavily that they will form a liaison more serious and, to
her, more ruinous than Juan's affair with Lady Fitz-Fulke. Because
Adeline's smoothness conceals an intensity of feeling unfulfilled
by her marriage ('Serene, and noble,—conjugal, but cold'), love
for Juan would at once destroy her reputation and prove her
(surprising) worth.[24] The passion would perhaps free her from,
and certainly be punished by, the society to which she has so far
conformed. In a sense, none the less, her capacity for feeling is
already punishment enough since insentience, as Byron happily
admits, makes dullness relatively easy to bear. Without proclaim-
ing that passionate love offers liberation from the world, the story

[21] Ibid. xiii. 94, ll. 7–8; 95, l. 7; 110, l. 8, McGann, 552, 557.
[22] Ibid. xii. 81, l. 6; xiii. 22, ll. 2–3; 34, l. 2, pp. 519, 531, 534.
[23] Ibid. xiii. 14, l. 4; 68, l. 1; 69, l. 1; 70, ll. 1–2; 72, l. 1; 71, l. 1; 36, l. 1; 37,
ll. 5–7; xii. 49, l. 2, pp. 529, 544–6, 535, 509.
[24] Ibid. xiv. 86, l. 8, p. 583. See Byron on 'grande passion', 'a very serious thing
indeed', ibid. xii. 77–8, p. 518.

Byron sketches out seems intended to prove that England's passionless stoniness is hellish: Adeline's love would show feeling surviving amidst polished manners, as Ugolino's feelings emerge from the coldness of Caina; and her later disgrace would argue that English society tries to reduce all its members to the same condition, degrading the exceptional character in the same way that Dante's Hell corrupts Ugolino.[25]

The cold polish of England, that prepares but (due to circumstances beyond Byron's control) does not fully develop the glimpses of passion surviving amidst stoniness, presents a complementary opposite to the siege of Ismail. In serene retirement as in war, indifference appears to be a prerequisite of survival, yet Byron's heroes and heroines manage to survive without it. When battle reduces the other soldiers to automata of violence, Don Juan rescues from a 'yet warm group | Of murdered women' the young girl, Leila, orphaned by the Christian army. Leila 'opened her large eyes, | And gazed on Juan with a wild surprise'.[26] From now on she will accompany him to Russia and England, refusing to be converted from Islam to Christianity and viewing the wonders of Christian Europe with insouciant curiosity. At Canterbury, Leila 'gazed, | And asked why such a structure had been raised'. The steady, straight gaze corresponds to Leila's preservation of a collected, observant equanimity amidst changed circumstances. She possesses, Byron says, 'that gentle, serious character, | As rare in living beings as a fossil | Man, 'midst thy mouldy Mammoths, "grand Cuvier!"'. Her kind of gentleness is innate and undeferential; considerate because not easily impressed. Like Cuvier's pre-Adamites (whom Byron refers to repeatedly in *Cain: A Mystery* as well as in *Don Juan*), Leila puts the modern Lilliputian world in its proper perspective.[27] Her companionship with Don Juan

---

[25] 'It is not clear the Adeline and Juan | Will fall; but if they do, 'twill be their ruin', ibid. xiv. 99, ll. 7–8, p. 587. Byron is allowing the existence of sincere feelings (Adeline's 'liquid glassful' of champagne), but thinking in the English cantos about their endurance of ordinary life where, earlier in *Don Juan*, he had placed sincerity and urbanity poles apart. See Haidée's death (iv. 63–73) while carrying 'within | A second principle of life' (iv. 70, ll. 1–2) and Aurora's competent urbanity (xv. 78, McGann, v. 225, 611).

[26] Ibid. viii. 91, ll. 2–3; 95, ll. 7–8, pp. 392, 394.

[27] See McGann, vi. 229–30; and 'To Thomas Moore', 19 Sept. 1821, *LJ*, viii. 216. In her coolness Leila foreshadows Aurora, 'the quiet way | With which Aurora on those baubles look'd, | Which charm most people in their earlier day', *Don Juan*, xv. 53, ll. 1–3, McGann, v. 604.

suggests there is preserved in him a purity of feeling and percep-
tion otherwise endangered by his involvement in the corrupt world.
The same is true of Byron himself whose 'wild Muse [. . .] don't
forget', he says, this 'pure and living pearl'. While she represents
the qualities that give Juan his 'good heart' (and Adeline her 'hidden
nectar in a cold presence'), she also gives Byron's satire a principle
of human worth.[28]

She can do so because she practises naturally the involved and
sceptical gaze that Byron employs. Juan rescues her and:

> Just at this instant, while their eyes were fixed
>   Upon each other, with dilated glance,
> In Juan's look, pain, pleasure, hope, fear, mixed
>   With joy to save, and dread of some mischance
> Unto his protégée; while hers, transfixed
>   With infant tears, glared as from a trance,
> A pure, transparent, pale, yet radiant face,
> Like to a lighted alabaster vase;—
>
> Up came John Johnson
>   (*Don Juan*, viii. 96, 97, l. 1, McGann, v. 394)

Their meeting is a reminder of Juan's and Haidée's first kiss in
canto ii: 'They heard the wave's splash, and the wind so low, |
And saw each other's dark eyes darting light | Into each other'.
Byron's knowing depiction of romantic love restrains its own
cynicism in the same way that Juan resists the cold-heartedness
required by war. The steps in love's progress follow an entirely
predictable sequence within a conventional setting, but Byron pre-
vents knowledge from creating indifference by dwelling momen-
tarily on their mutual exchange. 'Into each other' develops the
point more than is strictly necessary, interrupting Byron's anatomy
of courtship with the kind of pause the lovers experience them-
selves. The moments of their happiness lose none of their famil-
iarity to an experienced audience (like Zoe or Byron himself) but
familiarity does not breed contempt. Their love for each other
enjoys no independence from the sceptical observation of the world
and yet possesses a momentary sanctity that 'gentle' observation
must acknowledge. To gaze and wonder why, as Leila does, accepts
the facts of the matter without being resigned to them. Indeed, the

[28] *Don Juan*, x. 74, ll. 7–8, 52, ll. 2–4, 51, ll. 6–8, xiii. 38, l. 3, McGann, v.
459, 452, 536.

presence of any attitude—world-weary disbelief in the worth of such feelings, self-pitying nostalgia for their rapture, or resignation to their transitoriness—will prevent the incident from being openly seen. Byron's continual self-interruption in his portrayal of Juan and Haidée aims to discredit any of the simple explanations, whose confidence is polished and unfeeling, however impassioned they may appear.

John Johnson's interruption has a similar effect of leaving unqualified the depth of encounter between Juan and Leila. The fact that this meeting is trespassed on by mundane events proves it neither worthless nor immeasurably poignant. In fact Johnson's appearance only realizes the dangers Juan remained anxious about while he gazed at Leila. In his 'pain, pleasure, hope, fear, mixed | With joy [. . .] and dread', Juan becomes involved in the person he has rescued, not by a loss of interest in all worldly things, but through a more interested engagement with them on Leila's behalf. This interest proves effective: Juan is 'immoveable' until Johnson has guaranteed Leila's safe-keeping and only then goes on to sack Ismail. In Juan's relatively cheerful willingness to carry on the battle, Byron refuses to glamorize either his action or its place in the carnage of war. Juan, Byron says later, '*naturally* loved what he protected': of course, vanity and self-congratulation increased his fondness for her.[29] The battle that Juan returned to was continuing, furthermore, regardless of one humane action, and should not be justified as the arena of heroic compassion:

> If here and there some transient trait of pity
>   Was shown, and some more noble heart broke through
> Its bloody bond, and saved perhaps some pretty
>   Child, or an aged, helpless man or two—
> What's this in one annihilated city,
>   Where thousand loves, and ties, and duties grow?
>   (*Don Juan*, viii. 124, ll. 1–6, McGann, v. 402)

Byron then turns on the 'Cockneys of London' who rejoice in the patriotic celebration of martial glory while willingly ignorant of its actual horrors. Their taste would much have preferred a sentimental version of the rescue (along the lines of Byron's earlier *The Siege of Corinth*) in which Juan and Leila immediately fell in love or managed to escape. Such a story would protect them from the

[29] *Don Juan*, viii. 102, l. 1, p. 395, x 57, l. 4, p. 454.

nastiness of war, servicing the sentimentality that submits to the necessity of the violence it laments. Juan would gaze at Leila, suddenly as unencumbered by natural anxieties as the people who idealize him.

By resisting this impulse to glorify war (which survives in him as well as his audience), Byron limits heroism's nature and effects without denying its existence. His concern for the victims nobody rescued repeats Juan's sense of the danger that continues to threaten Leila and himself. Writer and protagonist display a surprising tenderness which is produced by their healthy respect for the destructive power of war, and argues that gentleness becomes factitious when it disguises an unpleasant truth. Leila is viewed with similar sympathy. Her purity endures within a consciousness traumatized by war. The fact that her look is 'transfixed | With infant terrors' (neither tearful nor angelically serene), does not discount the purity and radiance it might, plausibly, have exaggerated. In the same way, Johnson can insinuate that Juan rescued her because she was attractive, without Byron suggesting that this devalues the action. 'Naturally' some 'pretty | Child' will be saved before an ugly one. In the bustle of war only the striking will catch the eye. Yet this, again, is not to free Juan from all suspicion of base motives but to acknowledge the element of impurity in any admirable action.

Byron's descriptions reflect this by rescuing the pure and noble feelings that exist in such unpromising surroundings; by identifying goodness without fear or favour while staying as aware of virtue's limitations as Byron is aware of his own. Avoiding cant obliges Byron to define his key terms (such as 'courage' and 'humanity') more honestly than other poets do. The process of redefinition will defeat itself, however, if it tries to escape ordinary usage. Byron practises 'humanity' in his writing by seeing his own project as a continued interchange with other ways of talking. The true meaning of 'courage' exists, like Leila in battle, embedded within a multitude of false senses which the truthful ones can neither wish away nor rise above.

'Humanity' is pre-eminently vulnerable to cant meanings. Juan is rewarded for saving Leila:

> This special honour was conferred, because
> He had behaved with courage and humanity;—

> Which *last*, men like, when they have time to pause
> From their ferocities produced by vanity.
> (*Don Juan*, viii. 140, ll. 1–4, McGann, v. 407)

To claim that Juan's compassion characterizes humankind conveniently ignores the 'vanity' and (Byron's next rhyme), the 'insanity' of men. Such forgetfulness is the prerogative sought by the powers that be, who adopt Juan's natural action for political advantage. Their reports, which Byron parodies for a moment here, will glibly state that 'He had behaved with courage and humanity', implicitly claiming the ability to recognize, and the desire to encourage, such behaviour. Yet 'men like' this quality: they know it when they see it. Byron sounds confident that 'humanity' cannot simply be glossed as 'the conduct that makes for good propaganda'. The common man's perception is unreliable none the less, however true it may be, because in the heat of battle ordinary soldiers are caught up in 'ferocities'. The human perception of 'humanity' is constrained by contingencies though forgetful of their influence. To perceive that quality in the human understanding of humanity, to give it credit but no authority, is to respond to the contingencies of our state as Juan does: with intelligence and compassion.

Byron accepts, for instance, that men often do not 'have time to pause'. Their thoughtlessness is imposed on them, but Byron counters this exoneration with the observation that men are imposed on by 'vanity': a quality obvious in a tyrant like Catherine the Great but shared to a lesser extent by her servants. If we are allowed for a moment to ennoble ourselves by ascribing 'humanity' to Juan's actions, Byron's rhyme insists that 'vanity' and 'insanity' are equally universal. He assesses human motives with a coolness that is unflamboyant and shocking; his sang-froid advertises itself, however, less than it concentrates attention on the rules of thumb that emerge from the case.

Similarly in the rest of the stanza Byron claims no credit for the indignation he still feels:

> [Juan's] little captive gained him some applause
> For saving her amidst the wild insanity
> Of Carnage,—and I think he was more glad in her
> Safety, than his new order of St. Vladimir.
> (*Don Juan*, viii. 140, ll. 5–8, McGann, v. 407)

Byron's 'wild insanity' reverts to the high rhetoric of gazettes (whose descriptions of horrors sensationalize and consequently glorify them), in order that he can more forcefully disclose their basis in 'Carnage'.[30] The same polemical irony does not infect so powerfully the moderate applause Juan receives: the line's clichés stand back slightly from the newspaper jargon they recall, allowing the suspicion that the praise had to be talked up to surface in the following lines. The cool, and English, imperturbability of 'some applause' may be a more just assessment than its pretensions expect. If so Byron's hostility to war becomes less strident. It has to jostle with Juan's lack of concern for honours and the other soldiers' possible lack of interest. For a moment, Byron allows the indignation he shows elsewhere to appear as something of a private hobbyhorse which others, who after all were there, would not necessarily have welcomed. The soldiers' resilience does not disprove or render absurd Byron's protest, but it helps ensure that epic events do not degenerate into a prompt for moralizing. Just as his weighting of phrases keeps alert to the mixture of 'pain, pleasure, hope, fear' that Juan feels when most struck by Leila, Byron observes how others would view the events he describes, even when he is himself most critical or indignant. Instead of ironically suspending all judgement in the face of infinite possibilities, Byron's self-awareness sees his exertion of a personal and limited judgement to be influenced by the circumstances he describes.

Immediately after the rescue Juan and Johnson have to confront one of the last defenders of Ismail, a Sultan with five sons who will not give quarter. Each of the sons dies, the eldest last, leaving their father, like Ugolino, to die himself. Byron makes this climax to the war cantos recall the shipwreck section of canto ii where, famously, the crew eat Juan's tutor, Pedrillo, and two fathers watch their sons expire. The sequence of incidents in canto ii also recalls Ugolino, whose cannibalism is cited as a precedent in stanza 83. The differences in emphasis between cantos ii and viii suggest that Byron discovered as he went along the alert scepticism that redefines gentleness and humanity.

The Sultan in canto viii explicitly lacks heroic stature:

---

[30] The capital letter of 'Carnage' may be a direct attack on Wordsworth's loyal praise of Jehovah, God of Battles, in his notorious 'Ode: 1815', ll. 105–7: 'Almighty God [. . .] Carnage is thy daughter'. See *Wordsworth*, iii. 155.

Am I
Describing Priam's, Peleus', or Jove's son?
Neither,—but a good, plain, old, temperate man,
Who fought with his five children in the van.

To *take* him was the point.

(*Don Juan*, viii. 105, ll. 5–8; 106, l. 1,
McGann, v. 396–7)

This description appears at first reading to be a straightforward deflation of epic exaggeration, which finds heroism residing in unspectacular people, not in the worthies of legend. But Byron's line of characterization, 'good, plain, old, temperate man', is thumpingly inelegant. The packed epithets make the narrator sound over-eager to describe him, because the string of nearly synonymous adjectives has apparently been forced into a faint semblance of metrical regularity by the speaker's insistence. This inelegance is deliberate: Byron's wish to deny the Sultan's greatness refuses to glorify his ordinariness, because the narrator sounds so restless when he recounts the simple virtues of an honest man. The eagerness of the description both insists on the normalcy of plain courage and acknowledges its ordinariness by refusing to dwell on it.

In what follows, however, the narrator's momentary earnestness disappears in the simplicity and lucidity with which the Sultan's actions are described, 'Who fought with his five children in the van'. The opening of the next stanza achieves a further shift in tone by replacing the narrator's earnest enthusiasm with the pragmatic mind-set of a soldier: 'To *take* him was the point'. The comedy created by these shifts in tone comforts Byron's reader with the recognition that behaviour in battle turns out to be neither superhuman nor demonic. The Sultan's courage is unthinking and obedient to his sense of duty: 'Who fought with his five children in the van' sounds like the epitaph he would give himself. And, on the other hand, his opponents consider nothing other than the practical necessity of overcoming him in order to secure the town.

Such comfort as this perception offers, however, would disappear if one idealized sense of 'human' were sealed off from nature. Certainly the Sultan's uncompromising and undemonstrative loyalty to Ismail and Islam illuminates the brutality of the ambitions that initiated the siege. His heroism, moreover, wins

respect from his attackers who, 'When they behold the brave
oppressed with odds, | Are touched with a desire to shield and
save'.[31] Juan and Johnson try all they can to persuade him to give
up an unequal struggle but:

> He hewed away, like doctors of theology
> When they dispute with sceptics; and with curses
> Struck at his friends, as babies beat their nurses
> (Ibid. 108, ll. 6–8, p. 397)

Here, as elsewhere in the poem, Byron drops in a conventional
satirical point—that scholars of Christ's religion of love turn as
violent in debate as soldiers have to be in battle. At the same time,
Byron is still interested by the stout single-mindedness of the
Sultan's violence; its determined and almost carefree vigour that
gains in panache what it loses in common sense. The Sultan's
religious conviction, like attachment to one's place of birth or
code of honour, boldly defies the needs and instincts which generally
govern the unglamorous process of war. It produces in the Sultan
a temper tantrum that may not be moral exactly (as Auden sug-
gests some gods' tantrums are) but appears at once impressive and
ridiculous.[32] In Byron's second simile, this rejection of good sense
becomes not the preserve of eminent doctors alone but predict-
able, if not explicable, to anyone who has watched 'babies beat
their nurses'. The comparison does not further belittle the 'doctors
of theology' (though their disputes are probably quite babyish) so
much as it qualifies the elegance of Byron's satire. The satirical
point still holds, but its poise is forgotten when Byron and his
readers perceive that the Sultan's fury is actually (and disturbingly)
a quite normal occurrence. The narrator's earlier susceptibility to
moral indignation made his judgement appear as impassioned,
and even as foolish, as the Sultan's. This loss of satirical authority
extends to the final comparison so that its possible dismissiveness
is itself open to criticism.

---

[31] *Don Juan*, viii. 106, ll. 2–3, McGann, v. 397. The incident repeats the Chris-
tians' encounter with the Seraskier (ibid. 79–81, p. 389).
[32] 'Unable | To conceive a god whose temper-tantrums are moral', W. H. Auden,
'In Praise of Limestone', ll. 26–7, *Collected Shorter Poems: 1927–1957* (London,
1966), 239.

The Sultan is, moreover, not just a harmless old buffer:

> Nay, he had wounded, though but slightly, both
> Juan and Johnson; whereupon they fell,
> The first with sighs, the second with an oath,
> Upon his angry Sultanship, pell-mell
> (Ibid. 109, ll. 1–4, pp. 397–8)

These slight wounds confirm, as convention demands, Juan's and Johnson's excellence as soldiers. But they are also annoying. As much as the Sultan flies into a rage, the 'Russian pathos grew less tender, | As being a virtue, like terrestrial patience, | Apt to wear out on trifling provocations'.[33] Juan and Johnson could not afford to take any further risks and they were provoked more than Juan's sighs might suggest. Byron continues here to treat the opposing sides as equals. By saying 'his angry Sultanship', Byron treats him like a 'little madam', whose foolishness makes him laughable until he is set upon by superior numbers. The 'pell-mell' attack is equally short of dignity and grandeur. Yet the postponement and brevity of 'pell-mell' enable the violence to surface that Byron's comic formulations pretend to discount. The impartiality of his account is grounded in a willingness coolly to imply the experience that indifference would ridicule, probably by implication. The underlying narrative, that could contend satirically with the comic formulation Byron gives, curiously co-exists with it. That balance of forces in the writing expresses the 'intertwisting' of pettiness and absurdity with courage and humanity that Byron believes to be as true of battle as of the rest of human affairs.[34]

Consequently the Sultan's death acquires intense, because momentary and commonplace, pathos. When all his sons have died, he is again offered the chance to surrender, but ignores it:

> He did not heed
> Their pause nor sighs: his heart was out of joint,
> And shook (till now unshaken) like a reed,
> As he looked down upon his children gone,
> And felt—though done with life—he was alone.

---

[33] *Don Juan*, viii. 107, ll. 6–8, McGann, v. 397.

[34] See ibid. xiv. 59, ll. 1–4, p. 576: "'Tis sad to hack into the roots of things, | They are so much intertwisted with the earth: | So that the branch a goodly verdure flings, | I reck not if an acorn gave it birth'.

But 'twas a transient tremor;—with a spring
Upon the Russian steel his breast he flung
As carelessly as hurls the moth her wing
Against the light wherein she dies:
(Ibid. 117, ll. 4–8; 188 ll. 1–4, p. 400)

He borders on romantic grandeur when he stands, at the end of
the stanza, isolated and beyond life.[35] But the perception, which
Byron's Manfred would have enjoyed no end, terrifies him. By
mentioning his fear first, Byron redirects the stanza's final line so
that the reader's pleasure in sublime experience is unsettled by the
memory that, in actual fact, finding oneself alone and about to die
produces a horror that is simple and incalculable. The two paren-
theses contribute to this movement: '(till now unshaken)' could be
arch, but the uncertainty surrounding its tone invites the reader to
decide whether archness is appropriate. Consequently, the phrase
is open to a serious reading which credits the Sultan with excep-
tional courage. The parenthetical phrase suggests poised candour,
whose neutrality of tone seems studied and, therefore, potentially
dispassionate. In '—though done with life—' Byron then creates a
hastier interruption. The dashes, instead of brackets, draw atten-
tion less to the controlling power of the speaker than to the progress
of his feelings. The narrator's customary distance is momentarily
renounced and replaced by a frank involvement in portraying the
Sultan's mind. The reader cannot pump these lines for their pathos
but is arrested by their ability to reach feelings whose peculiarity
cannot be polished.

Canto ii's manner approaches these effects without achieving
the same intensity of interrupted feelings. Byron's tone moves
between sentiment and deflation with more ease, rarely allow-
ing the 'style, graphical and technical' that he sought, to govern
so entirely the course of his writing.[36] Pedrillo's last wish, 'to be
bled to death' meant 'You hardly could perceive when he was
dead'. Like those of Haidée in canto iv and the sons later in canto
ii, Pedrillo's death-scene gains poignancy from its stillness and
delay.

---

[35] Cf. *Hyperion*, i. 90, *Keats*, 332.
[36] To Thomas Moore, 27 Aug. 1822, *LJ*, ix. 198. On this quality in Byron's
style and its relation to his reading of Dante, see Philip W. Martin, *Byron: A Poet
before his Public* (Cambridge, 1982), 203–5.

> He died as born, a Catholic in faith,
>   Like most in the belief in which they're bred,
> And first a little crucifix he kiss'd,
> And then held out his jugular and wrist.
>   (*Don Juan*, ii. 76, ll. 5–8, McGann, v. 112)

It seems pedantic to quibble about how Pedrillo could have 'held out' his jugular vein, but the uncertainty of the phrase shows how determined Byron was to make the rhyme of 'kiss'd' and 'wrist'. The parallel lines of the stanza's closing couplet first complete the loving detail Byron lavishes on Pedrillo's religion and then ridicule its consequences. The same obedience to upbringing that makes him die devoutly prevents him from offering any resistance. Where in canto viii Byron's attack on religion is made and then self-consciously set aside, in this stanza satire remains a remote implication largely suppressed by the collectedness Byron's wit declares. The factual specificity of Byron's 'jugular and wrist' contrasts so markedly with Pedrillo's devotion (and the surgeon's inevitable demand for a fee) that it leaves no doubt about the power of instincts (whether hunger, greed, or cradle Catholicism) to erode principle, compassion and resistance. Byron's comic effects argue the same case with each of the following stanzas' clinching couplets, whose variations on the same theme enforce the impression of dazzling ingenuity.[37]

In the deaths of the two sons (stanzas 87–90), which echo Dante's Ugolino so clearly, Byron admires without qualification the stoicism that underlies his own amusement. The stronger child dies first:

> His nearest messmate told his sire, who threw
>   One glance on him, and said, 'Heaven's will be done!
> I can do nothing,' and he saw him thrown
> Into the deep without a tear or groan.
>   (*Don Juan*, ii. 87, ll. 5–8, McGann, v. 116)

The second father, who watches the 'weaklier child, | Of a soft cheek, and aspect delicate' linger some time before death, grows more attached as the unavoidable conclusion looms. 'Little' the child says:

---

[37] See *Don Juan*, ii. 78, ll. 7–8: '[Juan hardly could] Even in the extremity of their disaster, | Dine with them on his pastor and his master'; and 81, ll. 6–8: 'that which chiefly proved his saving clause, | Was a small present made to him at Cadiz, | By general subscription of the ladies.' (McGann, v. 113–14).

And now and then he smiled,
As if to win a part from off the weight
He saw increasing on his father's heart,
With the deep deadly thought, that they must part.
                (Ibid. 88, ll. 1–2, 5–8, p. 116)

The internal rhymes and half-rhymes—'a part', 'heart', 'part'; 'weight', 'thought'—accentuate pathos by lifting the language above comedy. As a result the bathos of 'deep deadly thought' sounds unconscious. The memory of Ugolino seems to have prompted Byron to introduce a moment of tenderness into the pain of star- vation by repeating Dante's narrative. By contrast with canto viii, however, the pathos lies less 'amidst' than beyond the rest of the story, and remains quite separate from the comedy of circumstances.

These stanzas' loss of conflicting perspectives makes them notably unfunny and gives the impression of a set-piece whose elegance remains uninvolved with the objects of its apparent compassion. They defend Byron against the accusation of being relentlessly cynical, but only at the same time as he displays his control over the habitual manner of the poem. The brilliance of his *tour de force* restricts any comedy in the incident to lofty amusement. The blatant heightening of effect (both in the sequence of the deaths and the sudden simplicity of feeling) dares the reader to stand away from the pathos Byron achieves so well, and to adopt the same compo- sure he assumes. Characteristically, and perhaps deliberately, Byron approaches the human absurdities canto viii depicts, and the form of compassion he practises there, in this earlier incident's closing lines, when he describes the physical effects of shock. The second father watches his son's dead body borne away by the waves:

Then he himself sunk down all dumb and shivering,
And gave no signs of life, save his limbs quivering.
                (*Don Juan*, ii. 90, ll. 7–8, McGann, v. 117)[38]

When Byron mentions (in 'save his limbs quivering'), the fact that this swoon was not conventionally perfect, his triple rhyme points

[38] Cf. 'And then eternal darkness sunk | Through all the palpitating trunk; | Nought of life left, save a quivering | Where his limbs were slightly shivering', *The Siege of Corinth*, ll. 836–9, McGann, iii. 349, The earlier poem's view of military courage makes the distinctiveness of *Don Juan*, vii–viii more apparent. See *The Siege of Corinth*, ll. 736–63, 776–801, McGann, iii. 346–8.

up the indignity. A reader might prefer either the fainting away of the romantic heroine or a screamingly funny parody of that cliché, but Byron avoids both extremes equally well. The triple rhyme prevents Byron or his reader from participating in the father's experience, but his wording avoids turning him into a figure of fun. Byron moves from the jaunty redundancy of 'all dumb and shivering' (which places the father in a ballad) to the diagnostic observation and cautious self-qualification of the following line. The transition rebukes the first line's cheeriness, but the completeness of Byron's rhymes, plus the internal rhyme (of 'gave' and 'save') and the smooth alliterative links (between 'signs of life' and 'save his limbs'), alert the reader to the predictability of such a rebuke. (Detective fiction often includes a forensic scientist or pathologist who points out, with similar calculated understatement, the errors that an untutored eye will inevitably make.) Byron's ironizing of the implied rebuke prevents his reader from becoming too earnest about it: resolute plainness appears another rhetorical ploy whose claim to accuracy must be doubted. The double movement of the lines will not, therefore, endorse either of the postures that are sketched in by the couplet. None the less Byron's apparent afterthought, 'save his limbs quivering', is imposing. The ironic posture (that rises above any descriptive attitude, whether it be breezy or chastely attentive) is not exactly corrected by Byron's inclusion of disturbing, unexplained physical particulars. Rather, the ironic stance seems put in perspective by it. All Byron's generous expenditure of entertainment, ingenuity, and wit leads up to this unpleasant but arresting image of a quivering body (though with what degree of forethought his manner successfully disguises). Byron then lets the image go by. Stanza 91 begins: 'Now overhead a rainbow'. His casualness and his rapid continuation of the story do not diminish the momentary but intense impression of a bodily experience that is visible but inscrutable. Byron's delightful, wicked triumphs over all kinds of cant avoid becoming cant-ridden and boring themselves because, as here, he occasionally uses them to represent things no one can be confident about.

Byron's plain speech about the Sultan's last moments ('And felt—though done with life—he was alone'), gives credence to natural fears in such a way that recognizing the common humanity of such feelings does not appropriate them. The Sultan's loss of heart establishes the limits of courage and its nature: a willed resistance to fears it cannot remove. Courage wavers when the Sultan loses the family (and the city) that give him status and self-respect. His reaction to losing these sources of attachment reveals, behind the mask of ferocity that war demands, the same sympathies that lie hidden in Juan and Adeline. Similarly, and curiously, Leila, whose 'taciturn Asiatic disposition [. . .] saw all Western things with small surprise', illustrates the power of self-possession, while she bears the marks of her attachments.[39] The Sultan's sudden vulnerability lends him an integrity that Leila grows to symbolize in the remaining cantos: an integrity that depends in her case on the memory of being wounded.

Juan rescues her from the heap of murdered women where she had tried to gain safety:

> And she was chill as they, and on her face
> A slender streak of blood announced how near
> Her fate had been to that of all her race;
> For the same blow that laid her Mother here,
> Had scarred her brow, and left its crimson trace
> As the last link with all that she held dear
> (*Don Juan*, viii. 95, ll. 1–6, McGann, v. 393)[40]

In a similar way, in *Purgatorio* iii, Dante's Manfred is striking because scarred:

> Io mi volsi ver lui e guardail fiso:
> biondo era e bello e di gentile aspetto,
> ma l'un de' cigli un colpo avea diviso
> (*Purgatorio*, iii. 106–8, Sapegno, ii. 31)

(I turned towards him and looked closely: he was fair-haired, beautiful, and noble-looking but a blow had severed one of his eyebrows)

Manfred finishes the story of his death, repentance, and disturbed grave by asking Dante to tell his daughter, Costanza, the truth:

---

[39] *Don Juan*, xii. 27, ll. 2–3, McGann, v. 503.

[40] Byron's focusing on a 'streak' of blood is consistent with his interest, throughout the war cantos, in what joins together bodies of men: Johnson '(like Galvanism upon the dead) | Acted upon the living as on wire, | And led them back into the heaviest fire'; 'those who were left alive [. . .] could form a line and fight again' (*Don Juan*, viii. 41, ll. 6–8; 47, ll. 4–5; McGann, v. 377, 379). Byron's view of Johnson's invigorating courage runs parallel, in my view, to developments in the understanding of human physiology—in particular, of the nervous system's role in connecting mind and body.

Vedi oggimai se tu mi puoi far lieto
revelando alla mia buona Costanza
come m'hai visto, e anche esto divieto;
ché qui per quei di là molto s'avanza.
(Ibid. ll. 142–5, p. 34)

(See, now, whether you can make me joyful by revealing to my good
Costanza how I was when you met me and, in addition, this prohibition;
because much is achieved here by those down there.)

Dante's saved repeatedly ask to be remembered to their loved
ones, whose prayers can shorten the time they spend either in
Purgatory itself or, in Manfred's case, in waiting to be allowed
entry. Manfred, however, also grasps, with characteristic forceful-
ness, the opportunity to clear his name and the good name of his
family. This is now represented by Costanza and descends from
another Costanza, Manfred's grandmother. As a bastard son,
Manfred might feel some compunction about naming his father,
but his implicit exclusion from one lineage enables him to be
placed in the female line: the line that runs, moreover, from
'Constance' to 'Constance'.

Manfred's determined claim to constancy resists the power of
the Church to destroy his wholeness by dismembering his corpse.
But he has also to deny the apparent opportunism of his last-
minute repentance. In this respect his wound is analogous to his
illegitimacy; both are flaws that can be seen as establishing greater
integrity. The Bishop of Cosenza, slavishly following the Pope's
orders, had, Manfred says, removed his dead body from the papal
states. This desecration scattered him to the winds: 'Or le bagna
la pioggia e move il vento' (ibid., l. 130, p. 33: 'now the rain washes
them [my bones] and the wind drives them'). On earth, he has no
memorial and his body no resting-place; but his spiritual body,
that casts no shadow, somehow, and surprisingly, carries the traces
of his lost body, establishing a continuity with his living self. The
scar argues that his act of repentance (which might appear to an
outsider to have contradicted the materialist and atheist principles
that governed Manfred's life) kept him, at the last, true to his true
self. Moreover, the corporeality of his 'shade' defeats the efforts
of political intrigue. His body survives in the afterlife despite its
destruction on earth and as if to emphasize the powerlessness of
man to put asunder what God has taken to Himself. In Manfred's
speech, the bishop's name, 'Cosenza' (l. 125), falls roughly half-

way between 'Costanza' (l. 113) and 'Costanza' (l. 143): the obe-
dient bishop appears as an interloper into Manfred's family line
and sets an example of the worldly inconstancy that suffers the
loss of integrity it seeks to inflict.

This reading of Dante's canto emphasizes what would have
interested Byron.[41] Though there is no external evidence, apart
from the name, to connect *Manfred*, Byron's play of 1817, with
Purgatorio iii, the canto and the drama share the same concerns.[42]
In *Manfred* Byron presents his hero's refusal to be swayed, either
by threats of damnation or promises of salvation, as the source
and guarantee of his isolated worth. For that play, repentance is
another form of the apostasy and time-serving that infects 'this
double-dealing and false-speaking time of selfish Spoilers' (as
Byron writes in his Preface to *Don Juan* cantos vi, vii, and viii).[43]
In the later poem, however, the integrity that is consistently and
passionately opposed to Southey's and others' duplicity exists in
and through the human inconsistency Byron's Manfred rises far
above.[44] When Leila is rescued, Byron recalls the scar on Dante's
Manfred: the purity Leila possesses, in the other worlds of Christian
Europe, endows her with an unworldliness that this 'last link with
all she had held dear' qualifies and redefines. She remains con-
nected and evidently vulnerable to the world she looks at dis-
interestedly, and this quality links her, furthermore, to Byron's
ambitions for the poem. Like Lady Adeline and, in the English
cantos at least, Don Juan, Leila is adaptable to and uncorrupted
by the polish of the courts. She sees through the self-importance
and self-deception of English life with more confidence because of
a continuing attachment to the Islamic world she has left behind.

[41] In being denied a place of burial, Manfred resembles Byron's Dante; see *The
Prophecy of Dante*, i. 77–84, McGann iv. 218. See Freccero, *Dante: The Poetics
of Conversion*, ed. Rachel Jacoff (Cambridge, Mass., 1984), 195–208, for a more
wide-ranging analysis of Manfred's wounds.

[42] Dante's Manfred dies like Byron's hero, 'unshrived—untended' and 'contuma-
cious'; both figures are 'obstinately resisting [the] authority' of the Church. Byron's
is heretical, Dante's excommunicate. See 'Act III, original version' (McGann, iv.
471), and *OED*, 'contumacious', definition 1.

[43] McGann, v. 297.

[44] See *Don Juan*, 'Dedication', 1–11; xi. 36, 56; McGann, v. 3–6, 476, 482.
Manfred attacks with equal conviction the demons who would condemn him and
the Abbot who would save him, saying to the first, 'Thou never shalt possess me,
that I know: | What I have done is done'; and to the second, 'then wonder not that
I | Am what I am, but that I ever was' (McGann, iv. 101, 93).

Her exile, like Byron's in Italy, creates a dispassionate view of England—though not by creating objectivity so much as self-awareness about where her loyalties lie. Her presence in Russia and England keeps in mind the attachment to home which prompts Byron's apparently disdainful (but evidently loyal) satire on England: 'that spot of earth | Which holds what *might have been* the noblest nation'.[45]

Byron wrote canto viii of *Don Juan* in autumn 1822; later in Cephalonia, he followed Juan's example:

I have obtained the release of about thirty Turkish prisoners—and have adopted one little girl of about nine years old—her name is Hato or Hatagée—her family were nearly all destroyed in the troubles (To Tom Moore, 4 Mar. 1824, *LJ*, xi. 25)

But as well as a precedent for his later generosity Leila also provided a last link with Byron's daughter Allegra, who died in April 1822 at 5 years old. Byron had planned Juan's rescue of a girl before Allegra died but, according to Medwin, had intended Juan and Leila to fall in love. The change of plan and (presumably) a change in Leila's age followed Allegra's death.[46] She becomes for Byron what the scar was for her: a link with the past that survives a continuing encounter with the world. In Byron's writing of *Don Juan*, therefore, it is natural for him to remember the requests made by Dante's saved in Purgatory;

> Nepote ho di là c'ha nome Alagia,
>   buona da sé, pur che la nostra casa
>   non faccia lei per essemplo malvagia;
> e questa sola di là m'è rimasa.
>   (*Purgatorio*, xix. 142–5, Sapegno,
>   ii. 214)

---

[45] *Don Juan*, x. 66, ll. 1–2, McGann, v. 456. Byron's 'mixed regret and veneration' for England proves Philip Martin half right: 'Byron is evidently moved, even perplexed, by the passage of events in his day, but he never degenerates into sentimentality, finding instead the independently conceived voice of cynical detachment' (Martin, *Poet before his Public*, 193). '[C]ynical detachment' would make the poem boring and, probably, sentimental. I am arguing for a more sceptical detachment, that is, sceptical about its own detachment.

[46] For the dating of cantos vi–viii see McGann, v. 714–18; see also Thomas Medwin, *Medwin's Conversations of Lord Byron*, ed. Ernest J. Lovell (Princeton, NJ, 1966), 164–5.

(I have a niece down there whose name is Alagia, good in herself, if, that is, our family has not corrupted her by its example; and she is all that remains to me down there.)

Byron never mentions these words, spoken by Pope Hadrian V, which (like Manfred's speech in canto iii and la Pia's in canto v), finish his speech and the canto that includes them. 'Alagia' is, however, temptingly close to 'Allegra', and 'the last link with all she had held dear' could plausibly have been prompted by 'e questa sola di là m'è rimasa'. More importantly, though, the Pope's affection neither exaggerates her virtues nor imagines her to be as invulnerable before death as he is after. She is, certainly, 'buona da sé'—the possessor of a goodness the Pope recognizes with accomplished confidence. Yet she may have been corrupted by the world: in particular, by the other members of her family. While not idealizing her, the Pope equally avoids sentimentalizing his own affection: she is all that remains to him, so she has a particular responsibility to pray for his soul. His affection looks steadily at her nature (and its possible defilement) without getting distracted by nostalgia. His interest is notably dispassionate, even cool, yet the pressures of his present business (to be purged from sin) seem to have purified his memory. His desire to be remembered to her remains honest about their separation, and about the different risks and pains attendant on their different states. Though concerned for his niece, the Pope clings to her no more than he clings to the world. Byron's *Don Juan* adopts a perspective similar to the Pope's. In the poem he anatomizes Restoration Europe and, in particular, English stupidity, while remaining as dispassionately involved as Pope Hadrian. Byron's disdain is qualified by nothing except a recognition of attachment, and his comedy remains 'determined to see—as one should see everything once—with attention': watching without regard (for propriety or power or discretion) and yet without disregard.[47]

[47] To John Murray, 30 May 1817, *LJ*, v. 229.

Bibliography

Place of publication is London unless otherwise stated.

ABRAMS, M. H., *The Mirror and the Lamp: Romantic Theory and the Critical Tradition* (New York, 1953).

—— (ed.), *English Romantic Poets: Modern Essays in Criticism* (London, Oxford, and New York, 1960).

ADAIR, PATRICIA M., *The Waking Dream: A Study of Coleridge's Poetry* (1967).

AKENSIDE, MARK, *The Pleasures of Imagination* (5th edn., 1796).

ALFORD, HENRY, *Life, Journals and Letters*, ed. by his widow (3rd edn., 1874).

ALLEN, GLEN O., 'The Fall of Endymion: A Study in Keats's Intellectual Growth', *K–SJ*, 6 (1957), 37–57.

ALLOTT, KENNETH, 'Bloom on "The Triumph of Life"', *Essays in Criticism*, 10 (1960), 222–8.

ALLOTT, MIRIAM (ed.), *Essays on Shelley* (Liverpool, 1982).

ALPERS, PAUL J., *The Poetry of* The Faerie Queene (Princeton, NJ, 1967).

ALTICK, RICHARD D., *Paintings from Books: Art and Literature in Britain, 1760–1900* (Columbus, Oh., 1985).

ANDREWS, KEITH, *The Nazarenes* (Oxford, 1964).

APPLEYARD, J. A., *Coleridge's Philosophy of Literature: The Development of a Concept of Poetry, 1791–1819* (Cambridge, Mass., 1965).

ARMOUR, PETER, *The Door of Purgatory: A Study of Multiple Symbolism in Dante's* Purgatorio (Oxford, 1983).

—— *Dante's Griffin and the History of the World: A Study of the Earthly Paradise (Purgatorio, cantos xxix–xxxiii)* (Oxford, 1989).

ARMSTRONG, A. H., 'Platonic *Eros* and Christian *Agape*', *The Downside Review*, 79 (1961), 105–21.

ARMSTRONG, ISOBEL, *Language as Living Form in Nineteenth-Century Poetry* (Brighton, 1982).

ARTHOS, JOHN, *Dante, Michelangelo and Milton* (1963).

ASHTON, ROSEMARY, *The German Idea: Four English Writers and the Reception of German Thought 1800–1860* (Cambridge, 1980).

ASKE, MARTIN, *Keats and Hellenism: An Essay* (Cambridge, 1985).

AUBRY, MAURICE, 'Dantes Rhetorische Stilistik', *Studi Danteschi*, 51 (1978), 1–58.

AUDEN, W. H., *Collected Shorter Poems: 1927–1957* (1966).

AUERBACH, E., *Mimesis: The Representation of Reality in Western Literature*, trans. Willard Trask (Princeton, NJ, 1953).

AUERBACH, E., *Scenes from the Drama of European Literature: Six Essays* (New York, 1959).

—— *Dante, Poet of the Secular World*, trans. R. Manheim (Chicago, 1961).

—— 'Entdeckung Dantes in der Romantik', in id. *Gesammelte Aufsätze zur romanischen Philologie* (Berne and Munich, 1967), 176–83.

AVALLE, D'ARCO SILVIO, *Ai luoghi di delizia pieni—saggi sulla lirica italiana del XIII secolo* (Milan and Naples, 1977).

BAILLIE, JOHN, *The Belief in Progress* (London, Glasgow, Toronto, 1950).

BAINE, RODNEY M., 'Blake's Dante in a Different Light', *Dante Studies*, 105 (1987), 113–36.

BAKER, CARLOS, *Shelley's Major Poetry: The Fabric of a Vision* (Princeton, NJ, 1948).

—— *The Echoing Green: Romanticism, Modernism, and the Phenomena of Transference in Poetry* (Princeton, NJ, 1984).

BALL, PATRICIA M., 'Sincerity: The Rise and Fall of a Critical Term', *Modern Language Review*, 59 (1964), 1–11.

BARBI, M., *Problemi di Critica Dantesca* (Florence, 1934).

—— 'Razionalismo e Misticismo in Dante', *Studi Danteschi*, 17 (1933), 5–44, and 21 (1937), 5–91.

BARETTI, GIUSEPPE, *Prefazioni e Polemiche*, ed. Luigi Piccioni (2nd edn., Bari, 1933).

—— *A Dissertation Upon the Italian Poetry* (1753).

BARNARD, JOHN, 'Keats's Tactile Vision: "Ode to Psyche" and the Early Poetry', *Keats–Shelley Memorial Bulletin*, 6 (1983), 1–24.

—— *John Keats* (Cambridge, 1987).

BAROLINI, TEODOLINDA, *Dante's Poets: Textuality and Truth in the Comedy* (Princeton, NJ, 1984).

—— 'Re-presenting what God presented: The Arachnean Art of Dante's Terrace of Pride', *Dante Studies*, 105 (1987), 43–62.

BARRELL, JOHN, *The Idea of Landscape and the Sense of Place, 1730– 1840: An Approach to the Poetry of John Clare* (Cambridge, 1972).

—— *English Literature in History: An Equal, Wide Survey* (1983).

—— *The Political Theory of Painting from Reynolds to Hazlitt: 'The Body of the Public'* (New Haven, Conn., and London, 1986).

BARTH, J. ROBERT, SJ, 'Symbol as Sacrament in Coleridge's Thought', *Studies in Romanticism*, 11 (1972), 320–31.

—— *The Symbolic Imagination: Coleridge and the Romantic Tradition* (Princeton, NJ, 1977).

BARTH, KARL, *The Theology of Schleiermacher: Lectures at Göttingen, Winter Semester of 1923–24*, ed. Dietrich Ritschl, trans. G. W. Bromiley (Edinburgh, 1982).

BATE, JONATHAN, *Shakespeare and the English Romantic Imagination* (Oxford, 1986).

BATE, W. JACKSON, *The Stylistic Development of Keats* (New York and London, 1945).

—— *John Keats* (Cambridge, Mass., 1963).

—— *The Burden of the Past and the English Poet* (1970).

BATESON, F. W., *Wordsworth: A Re-interpretation* (London and Toronto, 1954).

BAXTER, ANDREW, *An Enquiry into the Nature of the Human Soul*, 2 vols. (1745).

BAYLEY, J., *The Uses of Division: Unity and Disharmony in Literature* (1976).

BEATTIE, JAMES, *The Minstrel; or, The Progress of Genius* (1771).

—— *Dissertations Moral and Critical* (Edinburgh, 1783).

BEATY, F. L., 'Byron and the Story of Francesca da Rimini', *PMLA*, 75 (1960), 395–401.

BECKFORD, WILLIAM, *Vathek*, ed. Roger Lonsdale (World's Classics edn., Oxford, 1970).

BEER, JOHN, *Coleridge the Visionary* (1959).

—— *Coleridge's Poetic Intelligence* (1977).

—— 'Influence and Independence in Blake', in *Interpreting Blake*, ed. Michael Phillips (Cambridge, 1978), 196–261.

BELL, ARTHUR H., ' "The Depth of Things": Keats and Human Space', *K–SJ*, 23 (1974), 77–94.

BELLAMY, RICHARD (ed.), *Victorian Liberalism: Nineteenth-century Political Thought and Practice* (London and New York, 1990).

BERES, DAVID, 'A Dream, a Vision, and a Poem: A Psycho-Analytic Study of the Origins of the Ancient Mariner', *The International Journal of Psycho-Analysis*, 32 (1951), 97–116.

BERGIN, THOMAS G., 'Dante Translations', *The Yale Review*, 60 (1970–1), 614–17.

BIAGINI, ENZA, 'Le prime due stanze della canzone 71', *Paragone*, 296 (1974), 24–37.

BINDMAN, DAVID, *Blake as an Artist* (Oxford, 1977).

BLAKE, WILLIAM, *Illustrations to The Divine Comedy of Dante* (New York, 1968).

—— *The Complete Poetry and Prose*, ed. David. V. Erdman (rev. edn., New York, 1982).

—— *The Complete Poems*, ed. W. H. Stevenson (2nd edn., London and New York, 1989).

BLAKEMORE, STEVEN, *Burke and the Fall of Language: The French Revolution as Linguistic Event* (Hanover, New Haven, Conn., and London, 1988).

BLASUCCI, L., 'L'Esperienza delle "Petrose" e il linguaggio della "Divina Commedia" ', *Belfagor*, 12 (1957), 403–31.

BLOOM, HAROLD, *Shelley's Mythmaking* (1959).

—— *The Ringers in the Tower: Studies in Romantic Tradition* (Chicago, 1971).

—— *The Visionary Company: A Reading of English Poetry* (2nd, rev. edn., Ithaca, NY, and London, 1971).

—— *The Anxiety of Influence: A Theory of Poetry* (New York, 1973).

—— *A Map of Misreading* (New York, 1975).

—— *Poetry and Repression: Revisionism from Blake to Stevens* (New Haven and London, 1976).

—— *Agon: Towards a Theory of Revisionism* (New York, 1982).

—— PAUL DE MAN, JACQUES DERRIDA, GEOFFREY H. HARTMAN, and J. HILLIS MILLER, *Deconstruction and Criticism* (London and Henley, 1979).

BLOOMFIELD, MORTON W. (ed.), *Allegory, Myth, and Symbol* (Harvard English Studies, 9, Cambridge, Mass., 1981).

BLUNT, ANTHONY, *The Art of William Blake* (1959).

BONADEO, ALFREDO, *L'Italia e gl'italiani nell'immaginazione romantica inglese: Lord Byron—John Ruskin—D. H. Lawrence* (Naples, 1984).

BOND, D. F. (ed.), *Spectator*, 5 vols. (Oxford, 1965).

BONE, J. DRUMMOND, 'On "Influence" and on Byron's and Shelley's Use of *Terza Rima* in 1819', *Keats–Shelley Memorial Bulletin*, 4 (1981), 38–45.

BORNSTEIN, GEORGE, (ed.), *Romantic and Modern: Revaluations of Literary Tradition* (Pittsburgh, 1977).

—— *Poetic Remaking: The Art of Browning, Yeats, and Pound* (University Park and London, 1988).

BOULGER, JAMES D., 'Coleridge: The Marginalia, Myth-making and the Later Poetry', *Studies in Romanticism*, 11 (1972), 304–19.

BOYD, HENRY, *A Translation of the Inferno of Dante Alighieri, in English Verse*, 2 vols. (Dublin, 1785).

—— *The Divina Commedia of Dante Alighieri consisting of Inferno— Purgatorio—and Paradiso*, 3 vols. (1802).

—— *The Triumphs of Petrarch: Translated into English Verse, with an Introduction and Notes* (1807).

BOYDE, P., *Dante's Style in his Lyric Poetry* (Cambridge, 1971).

—— 'Perception and the Percipient', *Italian Studies*, 35 (1980), 19–24.

—— *Dante Philomythes and Philosopher: Man in the Cosmos* (Cambridge, 1981).

BRADLEY, A. C., 'Notes on Shelley's "Triumph of Life"', *Modern Language Review*, 9 (1914), 441–56.

BRAND, C. P., *Italy and the English Romantics: The Italianate Fashion in Early Nineteenth-Century England* (Cambridge, 1957).

—— 'Dante and the English Poets', in *The Mind of Dante*, ed. U. Limentani (Cambridge, 1965), 163–200.

—— 'Dante and the Middle Ages in Neo-Classical and Romantic Criticism', *Modern Language Review*, 81 (1986), 327–36.

BRETT, R. L., *Reason & Imagination: A Study of Form and Meaning in Four Poems* (Oxford, 1960), 78–107.

BRINKLEY, ROBERT, and DENEEN, MICHAEL, 'Towards an Indexical Criticism: on Coleridge, de Man and the Materiality of the Sign', in *Revolution and English Romanticism: Politics and Rhetoric*, ed. K. Hanley and R. Selden (Hemel Hempstead and New York, 1990), 277–302.

BRISMAN, LESLIE, *Milton's Poetry of Choice and its Romantic Heirs* (Ithaca, NY, 1973).

—— 'Coleridge and the Supernatural', *Studies in Romanticism*, 21 (Summer 1982), 123–59.

BROMWICH, DAVID, *Hazlitt: The Mind of a Critic* (New York and Oxford, 1983).

BROWER, REUBEN A. (ed.), *On Translation* (Harvard Studies in Comparative Literature, 23, Cambridge, Mass., 1959).

—— *Alexander Pope: The Poetry of Allusion* (Oxford, 1959).

BROWN, FRANK BURCH, *Transfiguration: Poetic Metaphor and the Languages of Religious Belief* (Chapel Hill and London, 1983).

BROWN, MARSHALL, 'The Urbane Sublime', *ELH*, 45 (1978), 236–54.

BROWNLEE, KEVIN, ' "Dante and Narcissus": Purg. xxx 76–99', *Dante Studies*, 96 (1978), 201–5.

—— 'Dante's Poetics of Transfiguration: The Case of Ovid', *Literature and Belief*, 5 (1985), 13–29.

BRYSON, NORMAN, *Tradition and Desire: From David to Delacroix* (Cambridge Studies in French, Cambridge, 1984).

BURKE, EDMUND, *A Philosophical Enquiry into the Origins of our Ideas of the Sublime and the Beautiful* (1757), ed. James T. Boulton (2nd, rev. edn., Oxford, 1987).

BUSH, DOUGLAS, *Mythology and the Romantic Tradition in English Poetry* (Cambridge, Mass., 1937).

BUTLER, MARILYN, *Romantics, Rebels and Reactionaries: English Literature and its Background 1760–1830* (Oxford, New York, Toronto, and Melbourne, 1981).

BUXTON, JOHN, 'A Second Supplement to Toynbee's Dante in English Literature', *Italian Studies*, 27 (1972), 40–3.

BYRON, GEORGE GORDON, LORD, *Byron's Letters and Journals*, ed. Leslie A. Marchand, 12 vols. (1973–81).

—— *The Complete Poetical Works*, ed. Jerome J. McGann, 7 vols. (Oxford, 1980–93).

—— *Don Juan, 'Cantos VI–VII Manuscript'. A Facsimile of the Original Draft Manuscripts in the British Library*, ed. A. Nicholson (The

Manuscripts of the Younger Romantics: Lord Byron: Volume V, New York and London, 1989).

BYRON, GEORGE GORDON, LORD, *The Complete Miscellaneous Prose*, ed. A. Nicholson (Oxford, 1991).

CAESAR, MICHAEL (ed.), *Dante: The Critical Heritage 1314(?)–1870* (London and New York, 1989).

CALDWELL, JAMES RALSTON, *John Keats' Fancy: The Effect on Keats of the Psychology of his Day* (Ithaca, NY, 1945).

CANNON-BROOKES, PETER (ed.), *The Painted Word: British History Painting: 1750–1830* (Woodbridge, Suffolk, and Rochester, NY, 1991).

CARNICELLI, D. D., *Lord Morley's Tryumphes of Fraunces Petrarke: The First English Translation of the* Trionfi (Cambridge, Mass., 1971).

CARY, HENRY, *Memoir of the Rev. Henry Francis Cary, M.A., translator of Dante. With his Literary Journal and Letters*, 2 vols. (1847).

CARY, HENRY FRANCIS, *The Inferno of Dante: with a translation in English blank verse*, 2 vols. (1805–6).

—— (trans.), *The Vision; or, Hell, Purgatory, and Paradise of Dante Alighieri*, 3 vols. (1814).

—— *The Vision [. . .]* (2nd, rev. edn., 1819).

—— *The Vision [. . .]* (3rd edn., 1844).

—— *The Early French Poets* (1846).

—— *Lives of the English Poets from Johnson to Kirk White: Designed as a Continuation of Johnson's Lives* (1846).

CASSELL, ANTHONY A., *Dante's Fearful Art of Justice* (Toronto, 1984).

CATUREGLI, ANNA FOCHI, 'Shelley Interprete di Dante e Guido Cavalcanti', *Italianistica*, 14 (1985), 47–56.

CERVIGNI, DINO S., *Dante's Poetry of Dreams* (Florence, 1986).

CHADWICK, WILLIAM OWEN, *The Secularisation of the European Mind in the Nineteenth Century* (Cambridge, 1975).

—— *From Bossuet to Newman* (2nd edn., Cambridge, 1987).

CHARITY, A. C., *Events and Their Afterlife: The Dialectics of Christian Typology in the Bible and Dante* (Cambridge, 1966).

CHATTERJEE, BHABATOSH, *John Keats: His Mind and Work* (New Delhi, 1971).

CHIAMPI, JAMES T., *Shadowy Prefaces: Conversion and Writing in the Divine Comedy* (Ravenna, 1981).

CHIRILLI, EMILIA, 'La contemplazione della morte in *Vita Nuova*, XXXIII e *Triumphus Mortis*, I', *L'Alighieri*, 24: 1 (1983), 16–37.

CHRIST, CAROL T., *The Finer Optic: The Aesthetic of Particularity in Victorian Poetry* (New Haven, Conn., 1975).

CHRISTENSEN, JEROME, 'The Symbol's Errant Allegory: Coleridge and his Critics', *ELH*, 45 (1978), 640–59.

—— *Coleridge's Blessed Machine of Language* (Ithaca, NY, and London, 1981).

CHURCH, F. C., 'A Translation of *De Monarchia*', in R. W. Church, *Dante: An Essay* (1878), 175–308.

COHEN, MURRAY, *Sensible Words: Linguistic Practice in England, 1640–1785* (Baltimore, Md., and London, 1977).

COHN, JAN and MILES, THOMAS H., 'The Sublime: In Alchemy, Aesthetics and Psychoanalysis', *Modern Philology*, 74 (1976–7), 289–304.

COLEMAN, DEIRDRE, *Coleridge and* The Friend *(1809–10)* (Oxford, 1988).

COLERIDGE, S. T., *Poems* (1796).

—— *Specimens of the Table Talk of the Late Samuel Taylor Coleridge*, ed. H. N. Coleridge, 2 vols. (1835).

—— *Biographia Literaria*, ed. J. Shawcross, 2 vols. (Oxford, 1907).

—— *Poetical Works*, ed. E. H. Coleridge, 2 vols. (Oxford, 1912).

—— *Coleridge's Miscellaneous Criticism*, ed. T. M. Raysor (Cambridge, Mass., 1937).

—— *Philosophical Lectures*, ed. Kathleen Coburn (1949).

—— *Collected Letters*, ed. E. L. Griggs, 6 vols. (Oxford, 1956–71).

—— *Notebooks*, ed. K. Coburn, in progress (London, New York, and Princeton, NJ, 1957–).

—— *Collected Works*, gen. ed. Kathleen Coburn, in progress (London and Princeton, NJ, 1969–).

—— *On the Constitution of the Church and State*, ed. John Barrell (1970).

—— *Coleridge's Verse: A Selection*, ed. William Empson and David Pirie (1972).

COLISH, MARCIA L., *The Mirror of Language: A Study in the Medieval Theory of Knowledge* (New Haven, Conn., 1968).

COLMER, JOHN, *Coleridge: Critic of Society* (Cambridge, 1959).

CONTINI, G. (ed.), *Poeti del Duecento*, 2 vols. (Milan and Naples, 1960).

—— 'Dante come personaggio-poeta della *Commedia*', *Varianti e altra linguistica* (Turin, 1970), 335–61.

—— *Un'idea di Dante* (Turin, 1976).

CORRIGAN, BEATRICE (ed.), *Italian Poets and English Critics, 1755–1859: A Collection of Critical Essays* (Patterns of Literary Criticism, 7, 1969).

—— 'Foscolo's articles on Dante in the *Edinburgh Review*: A Study in Collaboration', *Collected Essays on Italian Language and Literature presented to Kathleen Speight* (Manchester and New York, 1971).

CORTI, MARIA, *La Felicità Mentale: Nuove Prospettive per Cavalcanti e Dante* (Turin, 1983).

COTTLE, AMOS S., *Icelandic Poetry, or the Edda of Saemund, translated into English Verse* (Bristol, 1797).

COULSON, JOHN, *Newman and the Common Tradition* (Oxford, 1970).

COWPER, WILLIAM, *The Iliad and Odyssey, translated into English Blank Verse*, 2 vols. (1791).

CRONIN, RICHARD, *Shelley's Poetic Thoughts* (1981).

238 BIBLIOGRAPHY

CROOK, NORA, and GUITON, DEREK, *Shelley's Venomed Melody* (Cambridge, 1986).

CUNNINGHAM, G. F., *The Divine Comedy in English: A Critical Bibliography, 1782–1966*, 2 vols. (1965–6).

CURRAN, STUART, *Shelley's Annus Mirabilis: The Maturing of an Epic Vision* (San Marino, Calif., 1975).

CURRELI, MARIO, and JOHNSON, ANTHONY L. (eds.), *Paradise of Exiles: Shelley and Byron in Pisa* (Salzburg and Pisa, 1988).

CURTIUS, E. R., *European Literature and the Latin Middle Ages*, trans. Willard R. Trask (1953).

DANTE ALIGHIERI, *Dante con l'espositioni di Christoforo Landino, et d'Alessandro Vellutello [. . . .] riformato, riueduto & ridotto alla sua vera Lettura, per Francesco Sansovino fiorentino* (Venice, 1578).

—— *La Visione. Poema di Dante Alighieri diuiso in Inferno, Purgatorio, & Paradiso* (Vicenza, 1613).

—— *La Visione [. . .]* (Padua, 1629).

—— *La Divina Commedia di Dante Alighieri [. . .] tratta da quella che pubblicarono gli Accademici della Crusca l'Anno MCXCV. Col comento del M. R. P. Pompeo Venturi della Compagnia di Gesù*, 3 vols. (Venice, 1772).

—— *La Divina Commedia*, 2 vols. (London and Leghorn, 1778).

—— *La Divina Commedia [. . .] Passo passo riscontrata con lunga e scrupolosa diligenza su i testi delle più approvate edizioni, antiche e moderne, e da ogni tipografico neo tersa ed emendata. Da G. B. Boschini*, 3 vols. (1808).

—— *La Divina Commedia di Dante Alighieri illustrata da Ugo Foscolo*, i (1825).

—— *La Divina Commedia [. . .] con comento analitico di Gabriele Rossetti. In sei volumi*, i, ii (1826–7).

—— *La Divina Commedia di Dante Allighieri [sic], illustrata da Ugo Foscolo*, 4 vols. (1842–3).

—— *The Divine Comedy of Dante Alighieri with Translation and Comment*, trans. John D. Sinclair, 3 vols. (New York, 1939–46).

—— *Vita Nuova—Rime*, ed. Freda Chiapelli (Milan, 1965).

—— *Dante's Lyric Poetry*, ed. K. Foster and P. Boyde, 2 vols. (Oxford, 1967).

—— *La Divina Commedia*, ed. Natalino Sapegno, 3 vols. (2nd edn., Florence, 1968).

—— *Il Convivio*, ed. Bruna Cordati (Classici Italiani Commentati, Turin, 1968).

—— *Rime della Maturità e dell'Esilio*, ed. M. Barbi and V. Pernicone (Florence, 1969).

DARWIN, ERASMUS, *The Botanic Garden; A Poem, in Two Parts* (1791) (Scholar Press Facsimile, Menston, 1973).

DAVIE, DONALD, *The Language of Science and the Language of Literature, 1700–1740* (1963).
—— 'Hardy's Virgilian Purples', *Agenda*, 10: 2–3 (spring–summer 1972), 138–56.
DE ALMEIDA, HERMIONE, *Romantic Medicine and John Keats* (New York and Oxford, 1991).
DELL'AQUILA, MICHELE, 'Il canto IX dell'*Inferno*', *Italianistica*, 18 (1989), 291–304.
DE BOLLA, PETER, *Harold Bloom: Towards Historical Rhetorics* (London and New York, 1988).
D'ENTRÈVES, A. P., *Dante as a Political Thinker* (Oxford, 1952).
DE MAN, PAUL, 'The Epistemology of Metaphor', in *On Metaphor*, ed. Sheldon Sacks (Chicago, 1979), 11–28, 191–3.
—— *Blindness and Insight: Essays in the Rhetoric of Contemporary Criticism* (2nd, rev., edn., 1983).
—— *The Rhetoric of Romanticism* (New York, 1984).
DE PALACIO, JEAN, 'Shelley Traducteur de Dante: Le Chant XXVIII du *Purgatoire*', *Revue de littérature comparée*, 36 (1962), 571–8.
DE STAËL, MADAME, *Corinne, or Italy* (1807), trans. Avriel H. Goldberger (New Brunswick and London, 1987).
DE SUA, WILLIAM J., *Dante into English: A Study of the Translation of* The Divine Comedy *in Britain and America* (Chapel Hill, 1964).
DÉDÉYAN, CHARLES, *Dante en Angleterre*, 2 vols. (Paris, 1961–6).
—— *Dante dans le romantisme anglais* (Paris, 1983).
DEKKER, GEORGE, *Coleridge and the Literature of Sensibility* (1978).
DONNE, JOHN, *The Epithalamiums, Anniversaries and Epicedes*, ed. W. Milgate (Oxford, 1978).
DOUGHTY, OSWALD, 'Dante and the English Romantic Poets', *English Miscellany*, 2 (1951), 125–69.
DRONKE, PETER, *Poetic Individuality in the Middle Ages: New Departures in Poetry: 1000–1150* (Oxford, 1970).
—— 'The Procession in Dante's Purgatorio', *Deutsche Dante-Jahrbuch*, 53/4 (1978–9), 18–45.
—— *The Medieval Poet and his World* (Rome, 1984).
—— *Dante and Medieval Latin Traditions* (Cambridge, 1986).
DUFFY, EDWARD, *Rousseau in England: The Context for Shelley's Critique of the Enlightenment* (Berkeley, Calif., Los Angeles, and London, 1979).
DURLING, ROBERT M., and MARTINEZ, RONALD L., *Time and the Crystal: Studies in Dante's* Rime Petrose (Berkeley, Calif., Los Angeles, and Oxford, 1990).
ECONOMOU, GEORGE D., 'The Pastoral Simile of *Inferno* 24 and the Unquiet Heart of the Christian Pilgrim', *Speculum*, 51 (1976), 241–62.
ELIOT, T. S., *The Sacred Wood: Essays on Poetry and Criticism* (1920; 7th edn., 1950).

ELIOT, T. S., *The Sacred Wood: Selected Essays* (3rd enlarged edn., 1951).
—— *Collected Poems 1909–1962* (1963).
—— *To Criticize the Critic* (1965).
ELLIS, STEVE, *Dante and English Poetry: Shelley to T. S. Eliot* (Cambridge, 1983).
ENDE, STUART A., *Keats and the Sublime* (New Haven, Conn., 1976).
ENGELL, JAMES, *The Creative Imagination: Enlightenment to Romanticism* (Cambridge, Mass., and London, 1981).
ERDMAN, DAVID V., *Blake, Prophet Against Empire: A Poet's Interpretation of the History of His Own Times* (Princeton, NJ, 1969).
EUSTON, RALPH W., jun., *The Literary Theories of A. W. Schlegel* (The Hague, 1972).
EVEREST, KELVIN (ed.), *Shelley Revalued: Essays from the Gregynog Conference* (Leicester, 1983).
EVERT, WALTER H., *Aesthetic and Myth in the Poetry of Keats* (Princeton, NJ, 1965).
FAIRCHILD, HOXIE, *Religious Trends in English Poetry*, 6 vols. (New York, 1939–68).
FALLANI, G., *L'esperienza teologica di Dante* (Lecce, 1976).
FERGUSON, FRANCES, *Solitude and the Sublime: Romanticism and the Aesthetics of Individuation* (New York and London, 1992).
FERGUSSON, FRANCIS, *Dante's Drama of the Mind: A Modern Reading of the* Purgatorio (Princeton, NJ, 1951).
—— (ed.), 'The Dante Number', *Kenyon Review*, 14: 2 (spring 1952).
—— *Trope and Allegory: Themes Common to Dante and Shakespeare* (Athens, Ga., 1977).
FERRANTE, JOAN M., *The Political Vision of the* Divine Comedy (Princeton, NJ, 1984).
FIELDING, HENRY, *The Complete Works of Henry Fielding*, ed. W. E. Henley, 16 vols. (repr. New York, 1967).
—— *A Journey from this World to the Next*, with an introduction by Claude Rawson (1973).
FINCH, G. J., 'Wordsworth, Keats and "the language of the sense" ', *Ariel: A Review of International English Literature*, 11 (1980), 23–36.
FINNEY, C. L., *The Evolution of Keats's Poetry*, 2 vols. (Cambridge, Mass., 1936).
FISCHER, BERND, 'Irony Ironized: Heinrich von Kleist's Narrative Stance and Friedrich Schlegel's Theory of Irony', *European Romantic Review*, 1 (1990), 59–74.
FITZGERALD, EDWARD, *The Letters*, ed. A. M. and A. B. Terhune (Princeton, NJ, 1980).
FLAXMAN, JOHN, *Compositions by John Flaxman, Sculptor, R.A., from the Divine Poem of Dante Alighieri* (1807).

—— *Flaxman e Dante*, ed. Corrado Gizzi (Milan, 1986).

FLETCHER, ANGUS, *Allegory: The Theory of a Symbolic Mode* (Ithaca, NY, 1964).

FLICK, ADRIAN, 'Dante in English Romanticism: Aspects of English Critics', Translators' and Creative Artists' response to the *Commedia* (1782–1822) as it helps to define their Aims and Achievements' (unpublished Ph.D dissertation, University of Cambridge, 1977).

—— 'Dante and the Romantics', *Labrys*, 4 (1979), 59–79.

FOGLE, R. H., 'Dante and Shelley's *Adonais*', *Bucknell Review*, 15 (1967), 11–21.

FOLLIOT, KATHERINE, *Shelley's Italian Sunset* (Richmond, Surrey, 1979).

FOSCOLO, UGO, *Ultime Lettere di Jacopo Ortis* (Milan, 1802).

—— *The Letters of Ortis to Lorenzo* (2nd edn., 1818).

—— 'Biagnoli's Edition of the Divina Commedia—Cary's Vision of Dante', *Edinburgh Review*, 29 (Feb. 1818), 454 ff.

—— 'Cancellari's Observations concerning the Question of the Originality of the Poem of Dante', *Edinburgh Review*, 30 (Sept. 1818), 317 ff.

—— *Essays on Petrarch* (1823).

FOSTER, K., 'Dante's Canzone "Tre Donne . . ." ', *Italian Studies*, 9 (1954), 56–68.

—— *The Two Dantes and Other Studies* (1977).

—— and BOYDE, P. (eds.), *Cambridge Readings in Dante's* Comedy (Cambridge, 1981).

FRECCERO, JOHN (ed.), *Dante: A Collection of Critical Essays* (Englewood Cliffs, NJ, 1965).

—— *Dante: The Poetics of Conversion*, ed. Rachel Jacoff (Cambridge, Mass., 1984).

—— 'Virgil, Sweet Father', in *Dante among the Moderns*, ed. Stuart Y. McDougal (1985), 3–10.

FRERE, JOHN HOOKHAM [pub. under pseud. of William and Robert Whistlecraft], *Prospectus and Specimen of an Intended National Work [. . .] Intended to Comprise the Most Interesting Particulars Relating to King Arthur and His Round Table*, 2 vols. (1817–18).

—— *The Monks and the Giants (Prospectus and Specimen of an Intended National Work [. . . .])*, ed. R. D. Waller (1926).

FREUD, SIGMUND, *The Standard Edition of the Complete Psychological Works*, gen. ed. James Strachey, 24 vols. (1953–74).

FRIEDRICH, WERNER P., *Dante's Fame Abroad: 1350–1850* (Rome, 1950).

FRUMAN, NORMAN, *Coleridge: The Damaged Archangel* (New York, 1971).

FUCHS, CLARA-CHARLOTTE, 'Dante in der deutschen Romantik (die Gebrüder Schlegel, Schelling, Bouterwek, Hegel, Solger)', *Deutsches Dante-Jahrbuch*, 15 (1933), 61–131.

FULFORD, TIMOTHY, *Coleridge's Figurative Language* (Basingstoke, 1991).

FULLER, DAVID, 'Blake and Dante', *Art History*, 11 (1988), 349–73.

FUSELI, HENRY, *Remarks on the Writing and Conduct of J. J. Rousseau* (1767).

—— [review of Richard Payne Knight, 'Landscape'], *Analytical Review*, 19 (May–Aug. 1794), 174–80.

—— *The Life and Writings of Henry Fuseli, Esq. M.A.R.A.*, ed. John Knowles, 3 vols. (1831).

FÜSSLI, JOHANN HEINRICH, *Sämtliche Gedichte*, ed. M. Bircher and K. S. Guthke (Zurich, 1973).

—— *Füssli e Dante*, ed. Corrado Gizzi (Milan, 1985).

GALT, JOHN, *The Entail or the Lairds of Grippy*, ed. Ian A. Gordon (Oxford, 1970).

GARDNER, HELEN, *The Composition of Four Quartets* (London and Boston, 1978).

GIAMATTI, A. BARTLETT, *Dante in America: The First Two Centuries* (Binghampton, NY, 1983).

GIANNANTONIO, P., 'Giammbattista Vico, precursore del dantismo moderno', *L'Alighieri*, 10 (1969), 52–61.

GILCHRIST, ALEXANDER, *Life of William Blake*, 2 vols. (1880).

GILSON, E., *Dante the Philosopher*, trans. David Moore (1948).

—— *History of Christian Philosophy in the Middle Ages* (1955).

GINGUENÉ, PIERRE-LOUIS, *Histoire littéraire d'Italie*, 9 vols. (Paris, 1811–19).

GINSBERG, MORRIS, *The Idea of Progress: A Revaluation* (1953).

GITTINGS, ROBERT, *John Keats: The Living Year, 21 Sept. 1818 to 21 Sept. 1819* (1954).

—— *The Mask of Keats: A Study of Problems* (London, Melbourne, and Toronto, 1956).

—— *John Keats* (1968).

GLADSTONE, W. E., *The State and Its Relations with the Church* (4th edn., rev. 1838).

GOETHE, J. W., *Sämtliche Werke nach Epochen seines Schaffens*, ed. Karl Richter, H. G. Göpfert, N. Miller, and G. Sander, in progress (Munich, 1985–).

GOSLEE, NANCY MOORE, *Uriel's Eye: Miltonic Stationing and Statuary in Blake, Keats, and Shelley* (University, Ala., 1985).

GRAY, THOMAS, *The Poems of Thomas Gray, William Collins, and Oliver Goldsmith*, ed. Roger Lonsdale (1969).

GRAYSON, CECIL (ed.), *The World of Dante: Essays on Dante and his Times* (Oxford, 1980).

GREEN, F. C., *Rousseau and the Idea of Progress* (Oxford, 1950).

GREENE, THOMAS M., *The Light in Troy: Imitation and Discovery in Renaissance Poetry* (New Haven, Conn., and London, 1982).

GRIFFIN, DUSTIN, *Regaining Paradise: Milton and the Eighteenth Century* (Cambridge, 1986).

GUILLÉN, CLAUDIO, *Literature as System* (Princeton, NJ, 1973).

HAGSTRUM, JEAN, *The Sister Arts: the Tradition of Literary Pictorialism and English Poetry from Dryden to Gray* (Chicago, 1958).

—— *William Blake—Poet and Painter: An Introduction to the Illuminated Verse* (Chicago and London, 1964).

—— *Sex and Sensibility: Ideal and Erotic Love from Milton to Mozart* (Chicago and London, 1980).

HALLAM, HENRY, *A View of the State of Europe during the Middle Ages*, 2 vols. (1818).

HALLEY, A. R., 'The Influence of Dante on Nineteenth-century English Poets' (unpublished doctoral dissertation, Harvard University, 1922).

HAMILTON, PAUL, *Coleridge's Poetics* (Oxford, 1983).

HARDING, ANTHONY, *Coleridge and the Idea of Love: Aspects of Relationship in Coleridge's Thought and Writing* (Cambridge, 1974).

HARRIS, JOCELYN, *Jane Austen's Art of Memory* (Cambridge, 1989).

HART, HENRY, 'Ghostly Colloquies: Seamus Heaney's "Station Island"', *Irish University Review*, 18 (1988), 233–50.

HARTLEY, DAVID, *Observations on Man, His Frame, His Duty, and His Expectations*, 2 vols. [bound together] (1749, repr. New York, 1971).

HARVEY, DAVID A., *The Origins of the Liberal Party and Liberal Imperialism: The Career of Charles Buller, 1806–1848* (New York and London, 1987).

HASSAN, IHAB B., 'The Problem of Influence in Literary History: Notes Towards a Definition', *Journal of Aesthetic and Art History*, 14 (1955), 66–76.

HAVEN, RICHARD, 'Coleridge, Hartley, and the Mystics', *Journal of the History of Ideas*, 20 (1959), 477–94.

HAYLEY, WILLIAM, *An Essay on Epic Poetry; in five epistles to the Revd. Mr Mason. With Notes* (1782).

HAYTER, ALETHEA, *Opium and the Romantic Imagination: Addiction and Creativity in De Quincey, Coleridge, Baudelaire and Others* (rev. edn., 1988).

HAZLITT, WILLIAM, *The Complete Works*, ed. P. P. Howe, 21 vols. (London and Toronto, 1930–4).

HEANEY, SEAMUS, 'Envies and Identifications: Dante and the Modern Poet', *Irish University Review*, 15 (1985), 7 ff.

Hell Opened to Christians; or, Considerations on the Infernal Pains, for Every Day in the Week, Illustrated by Plates Emblematic of the Infernal Agonies (1807).

HERTZ, NEIL, *The End of the Line: Essays on Psychoanalysis and the Sublime* (New York, 1985).

HERZMAN, RONALD B., 'Cannibalism and Communion in *Inferno* XXXIII', *Dante Studies*, 98 (1980), 53–78.

HILL, GEOFFREY, *The Mystery of the Charity of Charles Péguy* (1983).

HILLES, FREDERICK W., and BLOOM, HAROLD (eds.), *From Sensibility to Romanticism: Essays Presented to Frederick A. Pottle* (New York, 1965).

HILTON, BOYD, *The Age of Atonement: The Influence of Evangelicalism on Social and Economic Thought 1785–1865* (Oxford, 1988).

HINCK, W. (ed.), *Sturm und Drang: ein literaturwissenschaftliches Studienbuch* (Kronberg, 1978).

HIRST, WOLF Z. (ed.), *Byron, The Bible, and Religion: Essays from the Twelfth International Byron Seminar* (Newark, NJ, London, and Toronto, 1991).

HOAGWOOD, TERENCE A., *Prophecy and the Philosophy of Mind: Traditions of Blake and Shelley* (University, Ala., 1985).

HODGSON, JOHN A., 'The World's Mysterious Doom: Shelley's *The Triumph of Life*', *ELH*, 42 (1975), 595–622.

HOGLE, JERROLD E., *Shelley's Process: Radical Transference and the Development of his Major Works* (New York and Oxford, 1988).

HOLLANDER, JOHN, *The Figure of Echo: A Mode of Allusion in Milton and After* (Berkeley, Calif., and Los Angeles, 1981).

HOLLANDER, ROBERT, *Allegory in Dante's* Commedia (Princeton, NJ, 1969).

—— *Il Virgilio dantesco: tragedia nella* Commedia (Florence, 1983).

HOLSBERRY, JOHN E., 'Hawthorne's "The Haunted Mind", and the Psychology of Dreams, Coleridge and Keats', *Texas Studies in Literature and Language*, 21 (1979), 307–31.

HONOUR, HUGH, *Neo-Classicism* (Style and Civilization Series, Harmondsworth, 1969).

—— *Romanticism* (Style and Civilization Series, Harmondsworth, 1979).

HORNE, P., and WOODHOUSE, J. R., 'Gabriele Rossetti and Charles Lyell: New Light on an Old Friendship', *Italian Studies*, 38 (1983), 70–86.

HOUGH, GRAHAM, *Selected Essays* (Cambridge, 1978).

HOUSE, HUMPHRY, *Coleridge: The Clark Lectures, 1951–2* (1953).

HOWARD, NATHANIEL, *The Inferno of Dante Alighieri, Translated into English Blank Verse* (1807).

HUGHES, JOHN, *An Essay on Allegorical Poetry* (1715).

HUME, JOSEPH, *Inferno: A Translation* (1812).

HUNT, BISHOP C., jun., 'Coleridge and the Endeavour of Philosophy', *PMLA*, 91 (1976), 829–39.

HUNT, LEIGH, *The Feast of the Poets* (1814).

—— *Stories from the Italian Poets. With the Lives of the Writers* (1846).

—— *The Poetical Works*, ed. H. S. Milford (Oxford, 1923).

IRWIN, DAVID, *English Neoclassical Art: Studies in Inspiration and Taste* (1966).

JACK, IAN, *Keats and the Mirror of Art* (Oxford, 1967).

JACK, R. D. S., *The Italian Influence on Scottish Literature* (Edinburgh, 1972).

JACKSON, J. R. DE J., *Poetry of the Romantic Period* (The Routledge History of English Poetry, iv, London, Boston, and Henley, 1980).

JACOFF, RACHEL (ed.), *The Cambridge Companion to Dante* (Cambridge, 1993).

JAMES, D. G., 'Keats and King Lear', *Shakespeare Survey*, 13 (1960), 58–68.

JARVIS, ROBIN, *Wordsworth, Milton and the Theory of Poetic Relations* (Basingstoke and London, 1991).

JASPER, DAVID, *Coleridge as Poet and Religious Thinker: Inspiration and Revelation* (Basingstoke and London, 1985).

JAY, GREGORY S., *T. S. Eliot and the Poetics of Literary History* (Baton Rouge and London, 1983).

JOHNSON, SAMUEL, *A Dictionary of the English Language* (1755, repr. Oxford, 1978).

JOHNSTON, ARTHUR, *Enchanted Ground: The Study of Medieval Romance in the Eighteenth Century* (1964).

JONES, JAMES LAND, *Adam's Dream: Mythic Consciousness in Keats and Yeats* (Athens, Ga., 1975).

JONES, JOHN, *John Keats's Dream of Truth* (1969).

KAMES, LORD, *Elements of Criticism*, 2 vols. (Edinburgh, 1788).

KEACH, WILLIAM, *Shelley's Style* (New York and London, 1984).

KEATS, JOHN, *The Letters 1814–1821*, ed. H. E. Rollins, 2 vols. (Cambridge, Mass., 1958).

—— *The Poems*, ed. Miriam Allott (2nd impression, 1972).

—— *The Complete Poems*, ed. John Barnard (2nd edn., Harmondsworth, 1977).

—— *The Poems*, ed. Jack Stillinger (Cambridge, Mass., 1978).

KELSALL, MALCOLM, *Byron's Politics* (Brighton, 1987).

KESSLER, EDWARD, *Coleridge's Metaphors of Being* (Princeton, NJ, 1979).

KING, R. W., *The Translator of Dante: The Life [. . .] of Henry Francis Cary (1772–1844)* (1925).

KIPPERMAN, MARK, 'Fichtean Irony and Some Principles of Romantic Quest', *Studies in Romanticism*, 23 (1984), 223–36.

KIRKPATRICK, R., *Dante's* Paradiso *and the Limits of Modern Criticism* (Cambridge, 1978).

—— *Dante's* Inferno: *Difficulty and Dead Poetry* (Cambridge, 1987).

KITSON, PETER J., and CORNS, THOMAS N. (eds.), *Coleridge and the Armoury of the Human Mind: Essays on his Prose Writings* (1991).

KLONSKY, MILTON, *Blake's Dante: The Complete Illustrations to the Divine Comedy* (1980).

KNAPP, STEPHEN, *Personification and the Sublime: Milton to Coleridge* (Cambridge, Mass., 1985).

KNIGHT, G. WILSON, *The Starlit Dome: Studies in the Poetry of Vision* (Oxford, 1941).

KOCH, JUNE Q., 'Politics in Keats's Poetry', *JEGP*, 71 (1971), 491–501.

KÖHLER, REINHOLD, *Dante's Göttliche Komödie und ihre deutsche Uebersetzungen* (Weimar, 1865).

KORSHIN, PAUL J., 'The Development of Abstracted Typology in England, 1650–1820', in *Literary Uses of Typology from the Late Middle Ages to the Present*, ed. Earl Miner (Princeton, NJ, 1977), 147–203.

KROEBER, KARL, *The Artifice of Reality: Poetic Style in Wordsworth, Foscolo, Keats, and Leopardi* (Madison and Milwaukee, 1964).

—— and WALLING, WILLIAM (eds.), *Images of Romanticism: Verbal and Visual Affinities* (New Haven, Conn., 1978).

KUHNS, OSCAR, *Dante and the English Poets* (New York, 1904).

LA PIANA, ANGELINA, *Dante's American Pilgrimage* (New Haven, Conn., 1948).

LAMB, CHARLES AND MARY, *Works*, ed. E. V. Lucas, 7 vols. (London and New York, 1903–5).

LANDOR, WALTER SAVAGE, *Landor as Critic*, ed. Charles L. Proudfit (Routledge Critics, London and Henley, 1979).

LANSING, RICHARD, *From Image to Idea: A Study of the Simile in Dante's Commedia* (Ravenna, 1977).

LEASK, NIGEL, *The Politics of Imagination in Coleridge's Critical Thought* (Language, Discourse, Society Series, 1988).

—— *British Romantic Writers and the East: Anxieties of Empire* (Cambridge, 1993).

LEAVIS, F. R., *Revaluation: Tradition and Development in English Poetry* (1936; repr. Harmondsworth, 1972).

LEFEVERE, ANDRÉ, *Translating Literature: The German Tradition From Luther to Rosenzweig* (Assen and Amsterdam, 1977).

LEIGHTON, ANGELA, *Shelley and the Sublime: An Interpretation of the Major Poems* (Cambridge, 1985).

LEO, ULRICH, 'The Unfinished *Convivio* and Dante's Re-reading of the Aeneid', *Medieval Studies*, 12 (1951), 41–64.

LEVINAS, EMMANUEL, 'Transcendence and Evil', *Collected Philosophical Papers*, trans. Alphonso Lingis (Dordrecht, Boston, and Lancaster, 1987), 175–86.

LITTLE, JUDY, *Keats as a Narrative Poet: A Test of Invention* (Lincoln, 1975).

LOCKE, JOHN, *An Essay Concerning Human Understanding*, ed. Peter H. Nidditch (Oxford, 1975).

LOEWENSTEIN, JOSEPH, *Responsive Readings: Versions of Echo in Pastoral, Epic, and the Jonsonian Masque* (New Haven, Conn., and London, 1984).

LONGFELLOW, HENRY WADSWORTH, *The Divine Comedy of Dante Alighieri*, 3 vols. (1867).

LONSDALE, ROGER, 'Gray and "Allusion": The Poet as Debtor', in *Studies in the Eighteenth Century*, 4, ed. R. F. Brissenden and J. C. Eade (Canberra, 1979), 31–55.

LOWES, JOHN LIVINGSTON, 'The Pure Serene', *Times Literary Supplement* (12 Oct. 1933), 691.

—— 'La Belle Dame Sans Merci', *Times Literary Supplement* (3 May 1934), 322.

—— 'Hyperion and the *Purgatorio*', *Times Literary Supplement* (11 Jan. 1936), 35.

—— 'Moneta's Temple', *PMLA*, 51 (1936), 1098–113.

—— *The Road to Xanadu: A Study in the Ways of the Imagination* (2nd, rev., edn., 1951).

LYELL, CHARLES, *The Canzoniere of Dante Alighieri, including the Poems of the Vita Nuova and Convito* (1835).

—— *The Poems of the Vita Nuova and Convito of Dante Alighieri* (1842).

MCFARLAND, THOMAS, *Coleridge and the Pantheist Tradition* (Oxford, 1969).

MCGANN, JEROME J., *Fiery Dust: Byron's Poetic Development* (Chicago, 1968).

—— *The Romantic Ideology: A Critical Investigation* (Chicago and London, 1983).

—— *The Beauty of Inflections: Literary Investigations in Historical Method and Theory* (Oxford, 1985).

MACINTYRE, ALASDAIR, *After Virtue: A Study in Moral Theory* (1981).

MALLIN, ERIC S., 'The False Simile in Dante's *Commedia*', *Dante Studies*, 102 (1984), 15–36.

MANDELSTAM, OSIP, 'Conversation about Dante', *The Collected Critical Prose and Letters*, ed. Jane Gray Harris (1991), 397–451.

MANNING, PETER J., *Byron and His Fictions* (Detroit, 1978).

—— *Reading Romantics: Texts and Contexts* (New York, 1990).

MANWARING, ELIZABETH WHEELER, *Italian Landscape in Eighteenth Century England: A Study Chiefly of the Influence of Claude Lorrain and Salvator Rosa on English Taste 1700–1800* (New York, 1925).

MARCHETTI, GIOVANNI, 'Nuova interpretazione della prima e principale allegoria del poema di Dante', *La Divina Commedia* [. . . .], 3 vols. (Bologna, 1819–21), i. 17–44.

MARKS, E. R., *Coleridge on the Language of Verse* (Princeton, NJ, 1981).

MARSHALL, DAVID, *The Surprising Effects of Sympathy: Marivaux, Diderot, Rousseau, and Mary Shelley* (Chicago and London, 1988).

MARSHALL, WILLIAM H., *Byron, Shelley, Hunt, and 'The Liberal'* (Philadelphia, 1960).

MARTIN, PHILIP W., *Byron: A Poet before his Public* (Cambridge, 1982).

MASON, EUDO C., *The Mind of Henry Fuseli: Selections from his Writings with an Introductory Study* (1951).

MATTHEWS, G. M., 'On Shelley's "The Triumph of Life"', *Studia Neophilologica*, 34 (1962), 104–34.

—— (ed.), *Keats: The Critical Heritage* (1971).

MAZZEO, J. A., *Medieval Cultural Tradition in Dante's* Comedy (Ithaca, NY, and London, 1960).

MAZZOTTA, GIUSEPPE, 'The *Canzoniere* and the Language of Self', *Studies in Philology*, 75 (1978), 271–96.

—— *Dante, Poet of the Desert: History and Allegory in the Divine Comedy* (Princeton, NJ, 1979).

MEDWIN, THOMAS, *The Life of Percy Bysshe Shelley*, 2 vols. (1847).

—— *Medwin's Conversations of Lord Byron*, ed. Ernest J. Lovell (Princeton, NJ, 1966).

MELLOR, ANNE K., *English Romantic Irony* (Cambridge, Mass., and London, 1980).

MERCURI, R., 'Conosco i segni de l'antica fiamma', *Cultura Neolatina*, 31 (1971), 237–93.

MIALL, DAVID S., 'The Meaning of Dreams: Coleridge's Ambivalence', *Studies in Romanticism*, 21 (1982), 57–71.

MICKLE, WILLIAM, *The Lusiad; or, The Discovery of India. An Epic Poem. Translated from the Original Portuguese* (Oxford, 1776).

MILEUR, JEAN-PIERRE, *Vision and Revision: Coleridge's Art of Immanence* (Berkeley, Calif., Los Angeles, and London, 1982).

MILTON, JOHN, *Paradise Lost. A New Edition*, 2 vols. (Edinburgh, 1807).

—— *Paradise Lost*, ed. Alastair Fowler (6th impression, 1981).

MINEO, N., *Profetismo e Apocalittica in Dante* (Catania, 1968).

MODIANO, RAIMONDA, 'Coleridge's Views on Touch and Other Senses', *Bulletin of Research in the Humanities*, 1 (1978), 28–41.

—— *Coleridge and the Concept of Nature* (London and Basingstoke, 1985).

MONK, SAMUEL H., *The Sublime: A Study of Critical Theories in Eighteenth-Century England* (1935, repr. Ann Arbor, Mich., 1960).

MONSMAN, GERALD, *Confessions of a Prosaic Dreamer: Charles Lamb's Art of Autobiography* (Duke, NC, 1984).

MONTANARI, FAUSTO, *Studi sul Canzoniere del Petrarca* (Rome, 1958).

MONTGOMERY, ROBERT L., *The Reader's Eye: Studies in Didactic Literary Theory from Dante to Tasso* (Berkeley, Calif., and Los Angeles, 1979).

MONTUCCI, ANTONIO, *Italian Extracts; Being an Extensive Selection From the Best Classic & Modern Italian Authors [. . .]* (2nd. edn., 1818).

MOORE, EDWARD, *Studies in Dante: First Series* (Oxford, 1896).

—— *Studies in Dante: Second Series* (Oxford, 1899).

MOORE, THOMAS, *Life, Letters and Journals of Lord Byron [. . .]* (1860).

MORGAN, ALISON, *Dante and the Medieval Other World* (Cambridge, 1990).

MORGAN, LADY [Sydney], *Italy*, 2 vols. [bound together] (1821).

MUIR, KENNETH (ed.), *John Keats: A Reassessment* (Liverpool, 1969).

MULLAN, JOHN, *Sentiment and Sociability: The Language of Feeling in the Eighteenth Century* (Oxford, 1988).

MUNSTER, ARNOLD, *Über Goethes Verhältnis zu Dante* (Frankfurt, 1990).

MURRY, JOHN MIDDLETON, *Keats and Shakespeare: A Study of Keats's Poetic Life from 1816 to 1820* (1924).

—— *Keats*, REVISED AND ENLARGED (4th edn., 1955).

MUSSETTER, SALLY, ' "Ritornare al suo principio": Dante and the sin of Brunetto Latini', *Philological Quarterly*, 63 (1984), 431–48.

NABHOLTZ, JOHN R., *'My Reader My Fellow Labourer' : A Study of English Romantic Prose* (Columbia, Mi., 1986).

NARDI, BRUNO, *Dal Convivio alla Commedia* (Florence, 1960).

—— *Saggi e noti di critica dantesca* (Milan, 1966).

—— 'Il mito d'Eden', *Saggi di Filosofia Dantesca* (2nd edn., Florence, 1967), 311–40.

NEWLYN, LUCY, *Coleridge, Wordsworth, and the Language of Allusion* (Oxford English Monographs, Oxford, 1986).

NICOLSON, MARJORIE HOPE, *Mountain Gloom and Mountain Glory: The Development of the Aesthetics of the Infinite* (Ithaca and London, 1959).

NOLAN, BARBARA, *The Gothic Visionary Perspective* (Princeton, NJ, 1977).

NOVAK, MAXIMILLIAN (ed.), *English Literature in the Age of Disguise* (Berkeley, Calif., Los Angeles, and London, 1977).

NUTTALL, A. D., *Overheard by God: Fiction and Prayer in Herbert, Milton, Dante and St John* (London and New York, 1980).

O'NEILL, MICHAEL, *The Human Mind's Imaginings: Conflict and Achievement in Shelley's Poetry* (Oxford, 1989).

O'NEILL, TOM, *Of Virgin Muses and Love: A Study of Foscolo's Dei Sepolcri* (Dublin, 1981).

—— 'Foscolo and Dante', in *Dante Comparisons: Comparative Studies of Dante and: Montale, Foscolo, Tasso, Chaucer, Petrarch, Propertius and Catullus*, ed. Eric Haywood and Barry Jones (Dublin, 1985), 109–35.

ORDIWAY, FRANK B., 'In the Earth's Shadow: The Theological Virtues Marred', *Dante Studies*, 100 (1982), 77–92.

ORSINI, GIAN N. G., *Coleridge and German Idealism: A Study in the History of Philosophy with Unpublished Materials from Coleridge's Manuscripts* (Carbondale, Ill., 1969).

OSOLS-WEHDEN, IRMGARD, 'Dante im Tempel der deutschen Kunst: Eine Betrachtung zur Dante-Rezeption in der frühromantischen Dichtung', *Deutsches Dante-Jahrbuch*, 66 (1991), 25–42.

OSTERMANN, T., *Dante in Deutschland* (Heidelberg, 1929).

OWEN, WILFRED, *The complete poems and fragments*, ed. Jon Stallworthy, 2 vols. (1983).

PAGE, ALEX, 'Faculty Psychology and Metaphor in Eighteenth-Century Criticism', *Modern Philology*, 66 (1968–9), 237–47.

—— 'The Origin of Language and Eighteenth-Century English Criticism', *JEGP*, 71 (1972), 12–21.

PARKER, PATRICIA, 'Dante and the Dramatic Monologue', *Stanford Literature Review*, 2 (1985), 165–83.

PARSONS, WILLIAM, 'The Story of Francesca from the Fifth Canto of Dante's Inferno: A Free Translation' [Poems by Mrs Piozzi, B. Greatheed, R. Merry, W. Parsons, and others], *The Florence Miscellany* (Florence, 1785), 116–22.

PARTRIDGE, ERIC, *The Three Wartons: A Choice of their Verse* (1927).

PEACOCK, THOMAS LOVE, *The Novels*, ed. D. Garnett, 2 vols. (1963).

—— *Nightmare Abbey, Crotchet Castle*, ed. Raymond Wright (Harmondsworth, 1969).

PECK, W. E., *Shelley: His Life and Work*, 2 vols. (1927).

PEIRONE, LUIGI, *Autonomia e diacronia linguistica nella lirica di Dante* (Genoa, 1987).

PETRARCA, FRANCESCO, *Rime—Trionfi e Poesie Latine*, ed. F. Neri, G. Martellotti, E. Bianchi, and N. Sapegno (Milan and Naples, 1951).

PITE, RALPH, 'The Watching Narrator in *Isabella*', *Essays in Criticism*, 40 (1990), 287–302.

—— 'Brackets and *Authority* (my emphasis)', *English*, 41 (1992), 175–88.

PITTOCK, JOAN, *The Ascendancy of Taste* (1973).

PITWOOD, MICHAEL, *Dante and the French Romantics* (Geneva, 1985).

PLUMPTRE, E. H., *The Commedia and Canzoniere of Dante Alighieri*, 2 vols. (1886–7).

POCOCK, J. G. A., *Virtue, Commerce, and History: Essays on Political Thought and History, Chiefly in the Eighteenth Century* (Cambridge 1985).

POLLOK, ROBERT, *The Course of Time: A Poem, in Ten Books*, 2 vols. [bound together] (Edinburgh and London, 1827).

POPE, ALEXANDER, *The Twickenham Edition of the Poems*, gen. ed. John Butt, 11 vols. (1939–69).

PRAZ, MARIO, *The Flaming Heart: Essays on Crashaw, Machiavelli, and Other Studies in the Relations between Italian and English Literature from Chaucer to T. S. Eliot* (1958).

—— 'Dante in England', *Forum for Modern Language Studies*, 1 (1965), 99–116.

PRESSLY, NANCY L., *The Fuseli Circle in Rome: Early Romantic Art of the 1770s* (New Haven, Conn., 1979).

PRIEST, PAUL, 'Dante and the Song of Songs', *Dante Studies*, 49 (1972), 78–113.

PRIMEAU, RONALD (ed.), *Influx: Essays on Literary Influence* (Port Washington, NY, and London, 1977).

PRINCE, F. T., *The Italian Element in Milton's Verse* (Oxford, 1954).

PULCI, LUIGI, *Morgante*, ed. Franca Ageno (Milan and Naples, 1956).

PURCELL, SALLY, *Dante: Literature in the Vernacular (De Vulgari Eloquentia)* (Manchester, 1981).

RABEN, JOSEPH, 'Milton's Influence on Shelley's Translation of Dante's "Matilda Gathering Flowers" ', *Review of English Studies*, NS, 14 (1963), 142–156.

RADCLIFFE, ANN, *The Italian; or, the Confessional of the Black Penitents* (1797).

READE, JOHN EDMUND, *Italy: A Poem, In Six Parts: With Historical and Classical Notes* (London, 1838).

REARDON, BERNARD M. G., *Religion in the Age of Romanticism: Studies in Early Nineteenth-Century Thought* (Cambridge, 1985).

REDPATH, THEODORE, *The Young Romantics and Critical Opinion, 1807–1824: Poetry of Byron, Shelley, and Keats as Seen by their Contemporary Critics* (1973).

REEVES, MARJORIE, and GOULD, WARWICK, *Joachim of Fiore and the Myth of the Eternal Evangel in the Nineteenth Century* (Oxford, 1987).

REID, RICHARD, 'Determined Cones of Shadow', *Helix*, 13–14 (1983), 109–16.

REIMAN, DONALD H., *Shelley's* The Triumph of Life: *A Critical Study, Based on a Text Newly Edited [. . . .]* (Urbana, Ill., 1965).

RENUCCI, P., *Dante juge et disciple du monde gréco-romain* (Paris, 1954).

RICKS, CHRISTOPHER, *Keats and Embarrassment* (Oxford, 1974).

—— 'Allusion: The Poet as Heir', in *Studies in the Eighteenth Century*, 3, ed. R. F. Brissenden and J. C. Eade (Canberra, 1976), 209–40.

—— 'Tennyson Inheriting the Earth', in *Studies in Tennyson*, ed. Hallam Tennyson (London and Basingstoke, 1981), 66–104.

—— 'Benignant Influence', *Yale Review*, 72 (1982–3), 439–45.

—— *The Force of Poetry* (Oxford, 1984).

RICOEUR, PAUL, *The Conflict of Interpretations: Essays in Hermeneutics*, ed. Don Ihde (Evanston, 1974).

—— 'The Metaphorical Process as Cognition, Imagination, and Feeling', *Critical Inquiry*, 5 (1978–9), 143–59.

RIDLEY, M. R., *Keats' Craftsmanship: A Study in Poetic Development* (Oxford, 1933).

RIEDE, DAVID G., *Oracles and Hierophants: Constructions of Romantic Authority* (Ithaca, NY, and London, 1991).

ROBINSON, CHARLES E., *Byron and Shelley: The Snake and the Eagle Wreathed in Fight* (Baltimore, 1976).

ROBINSON, PETER, *Overdrawn Account* (1980).

—— *In the Circumstances: About Poems and Poets* (Oxford, 1992).

ROE, ALBERT S., *Blake's Illustrations to the Divine Comedy* (Princeton, NJ, 1953).

ROE, NICHOLAS, 'Keats's Lisping Sedition', *Essays in Criticism*, 42 (1992), 36–55.

ROGERS, CHARLES, *The Inferno of Dante Translated* (1782).

ROGERS, NEVILLE, *Shelley at Work: A Critical Inquiry* (2nd edn., Oxford, 1967).

ROGERS, SAMUEL, *Italy: A Poem* (1823).

ROLLINS, H. E. (ed.), *The Keats Circle [. . .]*, 2 vols. (2nd edn., Cambridge, Mass., 1965).

RONTE, D., *Die Nazarener und Dante* (Leipzig, 1970).

ROSCOE, WILLIAM, *The Life of Lorenzo de Medici, called the Magnificent* (Liverpool, 1795).

ROSENBERG, J., 'Keats and Milton: The Paradox of Rejection', *K–SJ*, 6 (1957), 87–95.

ROSENBLUM, ROBERT, *Transformations in Late Eighteenth Century Art* (2nd printing, Princeton, NJ, 1969).

ROSSETTI, GABRIELE, *Sullo spirito antipapale che produsse la Riforma, e sulla segreta influenza che'esercitò nella letteratura d'Europa* (1832).

—— *Disquisitions on the Antipapal Spirit which produced the Reformation*, trans. Miss Caroline Ward (1834).

ROSSETTI, W. M., *The Comedy of Dante Allighieri* [sic]: *Part I—The Hell* (1865).

ROSSINGTON, MICHAEL, ' "The Voice which is Contagion to the World": The Bacchic in Shelley', *Beyond Romanticism: New Approaches to Texts and Contexts 1780–1832*, ed. Stephen Copley and John Whale (London and New York, 1992), 101–17.

ROWELL, GEOFFREY, *Hell and the Victorians: A Study of Nineteenth-century Theological Controversies Concerning Eternal Punishment and the Future Life* (Oxford, 1974).

RUTHVEN, K. K., 'Keats's *Dea Moneta*', *Studies in Romanticism*, 15 (1976), 445–59.

RZEPKA, CHARLES J., *The Self as Mind: Vision and Identity in Wordsworth, Coleridge and Keats* (Cambridge, Mass., and London, 1986).

SALE, ROGER, *Literary Inheritance* (Amherst, 1984).

SALY, J. V., 'Keats's Answer to Dante: *The Fall of Hyperion*', *K–SJ*, 14 (1965), 65–79.

—— *Dante and the English Romantics* [doctoral dissertation, Columbia University, 1959] (High Wycombe, 1972).

SAMUEL, IRENE, *Dante and Milton: The Commedia and Paradise Lost* (Ithaca, NY, 1966).

SANDERSON, DAVID R., 'Coleridge's Political "Sermons": Discursive Language and the Voice of God', *Modern Philology*, 70 (1973), 319–30.

SCARTAZZINI, G. A., *Dante in Germania* (Milan, 1883).

SCHELLING, FRIEDRICH, *Werke*, ed. Manfred Schröter, 6 vols. (Munich, 1927, repr. 1958).

SCHIFF, GERT, *Johann Heinrich Füssli: 1741–1825*, 2 vols. (Zurich and Munich, 1973).

SCHLEGEL, A. W., 'Ueber Zeichnungen zur Gedichten und J. Flaxman's Umrisse', *Athanaeum*, 2 [1799], 193–246.

—— *Sämtliche Werke*, ed. Eduard Böcking, 12 vols. (Leipzig, 1846–7).

SCHLEGEL, FRIEDRICH, *Lectures on the History of Literature, Ancient and Modern*, trans. J. G. Lockhart, 2 vols. (Edinburgh, 1818).

SCHNAPP, JEFFREY T., *The Transfiguration of History at the Center of Dante's Paradise* (Princeton, NJ, 1986).

SCHNEIDER, ELISABETH, *Coleridge, Opium and 'Kubla Khan'* (Chicago, 1953).

SCHRICKX, W., 'Coleridge and the Cambridge Platonists', *Review of English Literature*, 7 (1966), 71–91.

SCHULZE, EARL, 'The Dantean Quest of *Epipsychidion*', *Studies in Romanticism*, 21 (1982), 191–216.

—— 'Allegory against Allegory: *The Triumph of Life*', *Studies in Romanticism*, 27 (1988), 31–62.

SCORRANO, LUIGI, *Modi ed esempi di dantismo novecentesco* (Lecce, 1976).

SELLS, A. LYTTON, *The Italian Influence in English Poetry* (Bloomington, Ia., 1955).

SHAFFER, E. S., *'Kubla Khan' and the Fall of Jerusalem: The Mythological School in Biblical Criticism and Secular Literature, 1770–1880* (Cambridge, 1975).

SHARP, RONALD A., *Keats, Skepticism and the Religion of Beauty* (Athens, Ga., 1979).

SHAWCROSS, JOHN T. (ed.), *Milton 1732–1801: The Critical Heritage*, (London and Boston, 1972).

SHEEHAN, DONALD, 'A Reading of Dante's *Rime Petrose*', *Italica*, 44 (1967), 144–62.

SHELLEY, MARY, *The Letters of Mary Wollstonecraft Shelley*, ed. Betty T. Bennett, 3 vols. (Baltimore, 1980–8).

—— *The Mary Shelley Reader*, ed. Betty T. Bennett and Charles E. Robinson (New York, 1990).

SHELLEY, PERCY BYSSHE, *The Letters of Percy Bysshe Shelley*, ed. F. L. Jones, 2 vols. (Oxford, 1964).

—— *Poetical Works*, ed. Thomas Hutchinson, corrected by G. M. Matthews (Oxford and New York, 1970).

—— *Shelley's Poetry and Prose*, ed. Donald H. Reiman and Sharon B. Powers (New York and London, 1977).

—— *The Poems of Shelley*, ed. G. M. Matthews and Kelvin Everest, 3 vols. [projected] (London and New York, 1989–).

SHERWIN, P., 'Dying into Life: Keats's Struggle with Milton in *Hyperion*', *PMLA*, 93 (1978), 383–95.

SHILSTONE, FREDERICK W., *Byron and the Myth of Tradition* (Lincoln, Nebr., and London, 1988).

SHOAF, R. A., *Dante, Chaucer and the Currency of the Word: Money Images, and Reference in Late Medieval Poetry* (Norman, Okla., 1983).

—— 'The Crisis of Convention in Cocitus: Allegory and History', in *Allegoresis: the Craft of Allegory in Medieval Literature*, ed. J. Stephen Russell (New York, 1988), 157–69.

SHORT, CLARICE, 'The Composition of Hunt's *The Story of Rimini*', *K–SJ*, 21–2 (1972–3), 207–18.

SIDNEY, MARY, *The Triumph of Death and Other Unpublished and Uncollected Poems*, ed. G. F. Waller (Salzburg Studies in English Literature, Salzburg, 1977).

SINGLETON, C. S., *Studies in Dante, 1: Commedia: Elements of Structure* (Cambridge, Mass., 1954).

—— *Studies in Dante, 2: Journey to Beatrice* (Cambridge, Mass., 1958).

—— (ed.), *Interpretation: Theory and Practice* (Baltimore, 1969).

SISMONDI, JEAN CHARLES LEONARD SIMONDE DE, *De la littérature du Midi de l'Europe*, 4 vols. (Paris, 1813).

SLOMAN, JUDITH, *Dryden: The Poetics of Translation* (Toronto, Buffalo, and London, 1985).

SLOTE, BERNICE, *Keats and the Dramatic Principle* (Lincoln, Nebr., 1958).

SMITH, ADAM, *The Theory of Moral Sentiments*, ed. D. D. Raphael and A. L. Macfie (Oxford, 1976).

SMITH, A. J., *The Metaphysics of Love: Studies in Renaissance Love Poetry from Dante to Milton* (Cambridge, 1985).

SOUTHEY, ROBERT, *The Poetical Works, collected by himself*, 10 vols. (1837–8).

SOWELL, MADISON U. (ed.), *Dante and Ovid: Essays in Intertextuality* (Binghampton, NY, 1991).

SPACKS, P. M., *The Poetry of Vision: Five Eighteenth-Century Poets* (Cambridge, Mass., 1967).

SPERRY, STUART M., 'Keats, Milton and *The Fall of Hyperion*', *PMLA*, 77 (1962).

—— *Keats the Poet* (Princeton NJ, 1973).

SPRINGER, CAROLYN, *The Marble Wilderness: Ruins and Representation in Italian Romanticism, 1775–1850* (Cambridge, 1987).

SPURGEON, CAROLINE M., *Keats's Shakespeare: A Descriptive Study* (Oxford, 1928, repr. 1966).

STAWELL, E. MELIAN, 'Shelley's "Triumph of Life" ', *Essays and Studies by Members of the English Association*, 5 (1914), 104–31.

STEINER, T. R., *English Translation Theory, 1650–1800*, Approaches to Translation Studies, 2 (Assen and Amsterdam, 1975).

STEWART, GARRETT, '*Lamia* and the Language of Metamorphosis', *Studies in Romanticism*, 15 (1976), 15–41.

STILLINGER, JACK, *The Hoodwinking of Madeline and other Essays on Keats's Poetry* (1971).

STYAN, J. L., *The Dark Comedy* (Cambridge, 1968).

SWIATECKA, M. JADWIGA, OP, *The Idea of the Symbol: Some Nineteenth-Century Comparisons with Coleridge* (Cambridge, 1980).

SYMMONS, SARAH, 'John Flaxman and Francisco Goya: Infernos Transcribed', *Burlington Magazine*, 113 (1971), 508–12.

—— 'French Copies after Flaxman's Outlines', *Burlington Magazine*, 115 (1973), 591–9.

SZONDI, PETER, *On Textual Understanding and Other Essays* (Manchester, 1986).

TAAFE, JOHN, *A Comment on the Divine Comedy of Dante Alighieri*, vol. i [no more published] (1822).

TANNENBAUM, LESLIE, 'Lord Byron in the Wilderness: Biblical Tradition in Byron's *Cain* and Blake's *The Ghost of Abel*', *Modern Philology*, 72 (1974–5), 350–64.

TAYLOR, ANYA, 'Superhuman Silence: Language in *Hyperion*', *Studies in English Literature, 1500–1900*, 19 (1979), 673–87.

TAYLOR, BEVERLY, 'Byron's Use of Dante in The Prophecy of Dante', *K–SJ*, 28 (1979), 102–19.

TAYLOR, MARK C. (ed.), *Deconstruction in Context: Literature and Philosophy* (Chicago, 1986).

TENNYSON, ALFRED, LORD, *The Poems*, ed. C. Ricks, 3 vols. (2nd edn., Harlow, 1987).

THOMAS, REVD JOHN WESLEY, *The Trilogy, or Dante's Three Visions. Translated into English, in the Metre and Triple rhyme of the Original*, 3 vols. (1859, 1862, 1866).

THOMPSON, ANDREW, 'George Eliot, Dante, and Moral Choice in *Felix Holt, the Radical*', *Modern Language Review*, 86 (1991), 553–66.

THOMPSON, DAVID, *Dante's Epic Journeys* (Baltimore, 1974).

THOMPSON, E. P., 'Disenchantment of Default? A Lay Sermon', in *Power and Consciousness*, ed. Conor Cruise O'Brien and W. D. Vanech (1969), 149–81.

THOMSON, JAMES, *The Seasons*, ed. James Sambrook (Oxford, 1981).

THORPE, CLARENCE D., 'Review of *The Mask of Keats*', *K–SJ*, 6 (1957), 116.

TINKLER-VILLANI, V., *Visions of Dante in English Poetry: Translators of the* Commedia *from Jonathan Richardson to William Blake* (Amsterdam, 1989).

TOMELLI, L., *Dante e la poesia dell' ineffabile* (Florence, 1934).

TOSCANO, TOBIA, *La tragedia degli ipocriti e altre lettere dantesche* (Naples, 1988).

TOYNBEE, PAGET, *Dante in English Literature from Chaucer to Cary (c.1380–1844)*, 2 vols. (1909).

—— 'The Earliest English Illustrators of Dante', *Quarterly Review*, 211 (1909), 395–417.

TOYNBEE, PAGET, *Britain's Tribute to Dante in Literature and Art: A Chronological Record of 540 Years (c.1380–1920)* (1921).

—— *Dante in English Art: A Chronological Record of Representations by English Artists (Painters, Sculptors, Draughtsmen, Engravers) of subjects from the Works of Dante, or connected with Dante (c.1745–1919)* (Cambridge, Mass., 1921).

TRAVI, ERNESTO, 'Il Paradiso in terra della Chiesa militante', *L'Alighieri*, 22: 2 (1981), 31–45.

TRICKETT, RACHEL, 'Henry Vaughan and the Poetry of Vision', in *Essays and Studies*, ed. Anne Barton (1981), 88–104.

TUCKER, SUSIE I., *Enthusiasm: A Study in Semantic Change* (Cambridge, 1972).

TUVESON, E. L., *The Imagination as a Means of Grace: Locke and the Aesthetics of Romanticism* (Berkeley, Calif., and Los Angeles, 1960).

TWITCHELL, JAMES, B., *Romantic Horizons: Aspects of the Sublime in English Poetry and Painting, 1770–1850* (Columbia, Mi., 1983).

VALLONE, ALDO, *Profili e problemi del dantismo otto–novecentesco* (Naples, 1985).

VASSALLO, PETER, *Byron: The Italian Literary Influence* (Basingstoke, 1984).

VENDLER, HELEN, 'Stevens and Keats' "To Autumn"', in *Wallace Stevens: A Celebration*, ed., Frank Doggett and Roger Buttel (Princeton, NJ, 1980), 171–95.

—— *The Odes of Keats* (Cambridge, Mass., and London, 1983).

VICKERS, NANCY, 'Seeing is Believing: Gregory, Trajan, and Dante's Art', *Dante Studies*, 101 (1983), 67–85.

VINCENT, E. R. P., *Gabriele Rossetti in England* (Oxford Studies in Modern Languages and Literature, Oxford, 1936).

—— *Byron, Hobhouse and Foscolo: New Documents in the History of a Collaboration* (Cambridge, 1949).

VOGLER, THOMAS A., *Preludes to Vision: The Epic Venture in Blake, Wordsworth, Keats and Hart Crane* (Berkeley, Calif., Los Angeles, and London, 1971).

VON JAN, EDUARD, 'Dante in der Französischen Romantik', *Deutsches Dante-Jahrbuch*, 33 (1954), 5–21.

—— 'Dante als Prophet bei Byron (Prophecy of Dante, 1820)', *Deutsches Dante-Jahrbuch*, 36 (1958), 1–12.

WADDINGTON, RAYMOND B., 'The Death of Adam: Vision and Voice in Books XI and XII of *Paradise Lost*', *Modern Philology*, 70 (1972–3), 9–21.

WALKER, D. P., *The Decline of Hell* (1964).

WALLACE, C. M., *The Design of Biographia Literaria* (1983).

WALLER, MARGUERITE, 'Poetic Influence in Hollywood: *Rebel without a Cause* and *Star Wars*', *Diacritics*, 10: 3 (Sept. 1980), 57–66.

—— *Petrarch's Poetics and Literary History* (Amherst, 1980).

WARNER, JANET A., *Blake and the Language of Art* (Kingston, Montreal, and Gloucester, 1984).

WARTON, THOMAS, *The History of English Poetry, from the Close of the Eleventh to the Commencement of the Eighteenth Century*, 3 vols. (1774, 1778, 1781).

WASSERMAN, EARL, *The Finer Tone: Keats's Major Poems* (Baltimore, 1953).

—— *Shelley: A Critical Reading* (Baltimore and London, 1971).

WATKINS, DANIEL P., *Keats's Poetry and the Politics of the Imagination* (London and Toronto, 1989).

WEBB, EDWIN, ' "Reality's dark dream": Coleridge's Language of Consciousness', *Critical Quarterly*, 25 (1983), 25–43.

WEBB, TIMOTHY, *The Violet in the Crucible: Shelley and Translation* (Oxford, 1976).

—— *Shelley: A Voice Not Understood* (Manchester, 1977).

—— *English Romantic Hellenism 1700–1824* (Manchester and New York, 1982).

WEIL, SIMONE, *First and Last Notebooks*, trans. Richard Rees (1970).

WEINBERG, ALAN M., *Shelley's Italian Experience* (London and Basingstoke, 1991).

WEISKEL, THOMAS, *The Romantic Sublime: Studies in the Structure and Psychology of Transcendence* (Baltimore and London, 1976).

WEST, PAUL, *Byron and the Spoiler's Art* (New York, 1960).

WHALLEY, GEORGE, 'The Bristol Library Borrowings of Southey and Coleridge, 1793–8', *Library*, 5th series, 4 (1949), 114–31.

WHEELER, KATHLEEN M., *Sources, Processes and Methods in Coleridge's Biographia Literaria* (Cambridge, 1980).

—— *The Creative Mind in Coleridge's Poetry* (1981).

—— (ed.), *German Aesthetic and Literary Criticism: The Romantic Ironists and Goethe* (Cambridge, 1984).

WHEELER, MICHAEL, *The Art of Allusion in Victorian Fiction* (Basingstoke, 1979).

—— *Death and the Future Life in Victorian Literature and Theology* (Cambridge, 1990).

WHITE, R. S., *Keats as a Reader of Shakespeare* (1987).

WHITMAN, JOHN, *Allegory: The Dynamics of an Ancient and Medieval Style* (Oxford, 1987).

WICKER, BRIAN, 'The Disputed lines in *The Fall of Hyperion*', *Essays in Criticism*, 7 (1957), 28–41.

WILLEY, BASIL, *The Eighteenth-Century Background: Studies in the Idea of Nature in the Thought of the Period* (1940).

WILLIAMS, MEG HARRIS, *Inspiration in Milton and Keats* (London and Basingstoke, 1982).

WILLIAMS, RAYMOND, *Culture and Society, 1780–1850* (1958).

WILSON, DOUGLAS BROWNLOW, 'Two Modes of Apprehending Nature: A Gloss on the Coleridgean Symbol', *PMLA*, 87 (1972), 42–52.

WILSON, F. P., 'A Supplement to P. Toynbee's *Dante in English Literature*', *Italian Studies*, 3 (1948), 50–64.

WIMSATT, W. K., 'Imitation as Freedom: 1717–1798', in id., *Day of the Leopards: Essays in Defense of Poems* (New Haven, Conn., and London, 1976), 117–39.

WITTKOWER, R., 'Imitation, Eclecticism and Genius', *Aspects of the Eighteenth Century*, ed. E. Wasserman (Baltimore, 1965), 143–61.

WITTREICH, J. A., jun. (ed.), *The Romantics on Milton: Formal Essays and Critical Asides* (Cleveland, Oh., 1970).

WOLFSON, SUSAN J., *The Questioning Presence: Wordsworth, Keats and the Interrogative Mode in Romantic Poetry* (Ithaca, NY, and London, 1986).

WOODHOUSELEE, ALEXANDER FRASER TYTLER, LORD, *Essay on the Principles of Translation* (2nd rev. edn., 1797).

WOODINGS, R. B. (ed.), *Shelley: Modern Judgements* (1968).

WOODMAN, ROSS, *The Apocalyptic Vision in the Poetry of Shelley* (Toronto, 1964).

WOOLF, STUART, *A History of Italy 1700–1860: The Social Constraints of Political Change* (London and New York, 1979).

WORDSWORTH, WILLIAM, *Concerning the relations of Great Britain, Spain, and Portugal, to each other, and to the common enemy, at this crisis; and specifically as affected by the Convention of Cintra* (1809).

—— *The Excursion, being a portion of the Recluse, a poem* (1814).

—— *The Poetical Works*, ed. E. de Selincourt and Helen Darbishire, 5 vols. (Oxford, 1940–9).

—— *The Prose Works*, ed. W. J. B. Owen and J. W. Smyser, 3 vols. (Oxford, 1974).

—— The Prelude, *1795, 1805, 1850*, ed. Jonathan Wordsworth, M. H. Abrams, and Stephen Gill (New York, 1979).

YATES, F. A., 'Transformations of Dante's Ugolino', *Journal of the Warburg and Courtauld Institutes*, 14 (1951), 94–8.

Index